Understanding China

Series Editors

Emmie Yang
Business, Economics China, Springer-Verlag Asia
Beijing, China

Niels Peter Thomas
Heidelberg, Germany

For further volumes:
http://www.springer.com/series/11772

Xianzhi Zhang

Enterprise Management Control Systems in China

Springer

Xianzhi Zhang
School of Accounting
Dongbei University of Finance and Economics
Dalian, China

ISSN 2196-3134 ISSN 2196-3142 (electronic)
ISBN 978-3-642-54714-0 ISBN 978-3-642-54715-7 (eBook)
DOI 10.1007/978-3-642-54715-7
Springer Heidelberg New York Dordrecht London

Library of Congress Control Number: 2014939012

Printed on acid-free paper

Springer is part of Springer Science+Business Media (www.springer.com)

Preface

Along with the process of China's 30-year economic system reform and opening to the outside world, Chinese traditional enterprise system which was generated under the traditional planned economic structure has developed and transformed into the modern enterprise system under the socialist market economic structure. The modern enterprise system has clearly established ownership, well-defined power and responsibility, separation of enterprise from administration and scientific management. With such a system, China's enterprise management control is getting more and more attention and development. In this process, the advanced control theory and methods of western developed countries have a very good reference and promoting effect on the system construction and the academic research of China's enterprise management control. However, the external and internal environments of China's enterprise management control are different from those of western developed countries. Therefore, China's scholars and practitioners, working on enterprise management control theory, have long been exploring to adapt to the enterprise environment management control system in China. An enterprise management control system with Chinese characteristics is under continuous development and improvement.

In order to introduce the status of China's enterprise management control for foreign scholars and entrepreneurs who are focusing on China's economic development and the development of enterprise management, we write this book *Enterprise Management Control Systems in China* and publish its English version oversea, so as to help scholars with the international comparative study on enterprise management and help foreign entrepreneurs with managing Chinese invested enterprises.

Compared with similar foreign works, this book has distinctive Chinese features. Especially the four major modes of management control system, which are based on China's specific environment, have significant value both in theory and application.

First of all, based on China's own control environment, this book summarizes the developing process of Chinese economic structure reform and the enterprise management control, and establishes the systems of management control theory and method adaptive for Chinese characteristic.

Secondly, the book not only classifies management control scientifically, but also defines the relationship among management control, accounting control and audit control. It puts forward the idea of how to coordinate management control, accounting control and audit control, and establishes the position of the management control in the internal control.

Thirdly, it scientifically defines the 10 key elements of management control, which is a further innovation and improvement of three-element, four-element and five-element view of internal control. This is really important for comprehending the connotation of the management control accurately and developing the management control theory.

Finally, the viewpoint that different management control modes and methods should be taken according to different circumstances is put forward in this book. It establishes four kinds of management control system modes: the rule-based control system, budgetary control system, evaluation control system and incentive control system; it also scientifically and systematically demonstrates the characteristics, targets, advantages, disadvantages and application scopes of each mode.

Meanwhile, the publishing of *Enterprise Management Control Systems in China* in English is conducive to make the world come to know the development process and achievement of China's enterprise management control since China's reform and opening up; it is beneficial to the international academic community to learn Chinese scholars' theoretical achievements on enterprise management control; it is also helpful to introduce the theory and practice of enterprise management control with Chinese characteristics.

Dalian, China Prof. Dr. Xianzhi Zhang

Acknowledgments

Enterprise Management Control Systems in China is the achievement of my long-term efforts and all my members of "Development Innovation Team" working on innovation and application of management control theory with Chinese characteristics and "Research Office of Corporate Finance and Management Control". At this very moment of the book publication, I would like to gratefully acknowledge the following relevant institutions and individuals that have made great contributions to the composition, translation and publication of this book.

I would like to extend my gratitudes to:

Prof. Guohua Chi, Prof. Yan Chen, Dr. Wengang Sun, Dr. Xiuye Zhang and Dr. Xiaodong Zhang for their writing and revision of Chinese original;

Dr. Yuanyuan Liu, Prof. Yan Chen, Prof. Yanli Chen, Dr. Lingbing Liu, Dr. Yunjiang Geng, Dr. Yuan Qi, Dr. Xiaodong Zhang, Prof. Guohua Chi and Dr. Shuibin Gu for their contributions as leading translators in charge of different parts of the book;

Dr. Yanqiu Cheng, Dr. Fajing Cui, Ph.D. candidates Yanhong Hu, Ling Yan, Ying Cui, Xingfei Jia, Jia Hao, Fang Zhou and Chao Yan, and master candidates Jiayu Zhang, Rui Wang, Mingxing Dong, Zhuo Sun, Yao Yao, Wei Zou and Jingjing Guo for their contributions as first draft translators;

Prof. Yan Chen, Prof. Liyan Chen, Dr. Lingbing Liu, Dr. Yunjiang Geng, Dr. Yuan Qi and Dr. Xiaodong Zhang for their contributions as translation subeditors;

Foreign Ph.D. candidates, including but not limited to Erasmus Fabian Kipesha, Gwahula Raphael, Jameel Ahmad Mulani, Sultan Skinder Mirza, Ansar Majeed and Amjad Iqbal for their proofreading;

Associate Professor Yuanyuan Liu for her contribution to the translation and publication as a coordinator.

My special appreciation also goes to:

Professor Utz Schäffer from German WHU–Otto Beisheim School of Management, who supported and provided help for publication of the book in Springer-Verlag;

Professor Chia-Ying Ma from Soochow University and Professor Yuanlue Fu from Xiamen University for their comments and appraisals;

Springer-Verlag and Mrs. Emmie Yang for their supports and contributions to publication;

The Dalian Evaluation committee for publishing Academic Works Sponsored. The published book is sponsored by the Dalian Evaluation Committee for Publishing Academic Works Financed.

I would like to express my appreciation to Accounting Department of the Ministry of Finance, Accounting Society of China, Education Department of Liaoning Province, Finance Department of Liaoning Province, and The Science and Research Office, School of Accounting and Sino-German Management Control Research Center of Dongbei University of Finance and Economics. I am grateful to all business groups and their principals for their warm help on research and case studies; and I am thankful to all the writers of my references.

Dalian Prof. Dr. Xianzhi Zhang
31 Nov 2013

Contents

Part II Study on Evolution of West Management Control Theory

List of Figures

List of Tables

Part I
Study on Development of Enterprise Management Control in China

Chapter 1
Reform of Chinese Economy and Management Control in Enterprises

1.1 Planned Economy and Enterprises[1]

When the Communist Party of China came to power in 1949, the fundamental long-range goals of its leaders were to transform China into a modern and powerful socialist nation. In economic terms these objectives meant industrialization, improvement of living standards, narrowing of income differences, and production of modern military equipment. As the years passed, the leaders were still stick to these goals. But the economic policies formulated to achieve them were dramatically altered on several occasions in response to major changes in the economy, internal politics and international political and economic developments.

An important distinction emerged between leaders who felt that the socialist goals of income equalization and heightened political consciousness should take priority over material progress and those who believed that industrialization and general economic modernization were prerequisites for the attainment of a successful socialist order. Both the economic policies and their underlying economic models remained relatively stable, which might differ from the predecessors. Thus the form of the economic model and the policies that were expressed at any given point in Chinese history reflected both the current policy emphasis and a structural foundation built up during the earlier periods.

1.1.1 Recovery from War, 1949–1952

The main objective of the government for the 1949–1952 periods was simply to restore the economy to normal working order. The administration moved quickly to repair transportation and communication links and revive the flow of economic activity. The banking system was nationalized and centralized under the People's

---

[1] Economic history of China [1].

X. Zhang, *Enterprise Management Control Systems in China*, Understanding China,
DOI 10.1007/978-3-642-54715-7_1, © Springer-Verlag Berlin Heidelberg 2014

Bank of China. To bring inflation under control by 1951, the government unified the monetary system; tightened credit, restricted government budgets at all levels and put them under central control, and guaranteed the value of the currency. Commerce was stimulated and partially regulated by the establishment of state trading companies (commercial departments), which competed with private traders in purchasing goods from producers and selling them to consumers or enterprises. Transformation of ownership in industry proceeded slowly. About a third of the country's enterprises had been under state control when the Guomindang government was in power (1927–1949), as was much of the modernized transportation sector. The Communist Party of China immediately made these units state-owned enterprises upon taking power in 1949. The remaining privately owned enterprises were gradually brought under government control except 17 % of industrial units were still completely outside the state system in 1952.

1.1.2 First Five-Year Plan, 1953–1957

Having restored a viable economic base, the leadership was prepared to embark on an intensive program of industrial growth and socialization. For this purpose the administration adopted the Soviet economic model, based on state ownership in the modern sector, large collective units in agriculture, and centralized economic planning. The Soviet approach to economic development was manifested in the First Five-Year Plan (1953–1957). As in the Soviet economy, the main objective was a high rate of economic growth, with primary emphasis on industrial development at the expense of agriculture and particular concentration on heavy industry and capital-intensive technology. Soviet planners helped their Chinese counterparts formulate the plan. Large numbers of Soviet engineers, technicians, and scientists assisted in developing and installation of new heavy industrial facilities, including many entire plants and pieces of equipment purchased from the Soviet Union. Government control over industry was increased during this period by applying financial pressure and inducements to convince owners of private, modern firms to sell them to the state or convert them into joint public-private enterprises under state control. By 1956 approximately 67.5 % of all modern industrial enterprises were state owned and 32.5 % were under joint public-private ownership. No privately owned firms remained. During the same period, the handicraft industries were organized into cooperatives, which accounted for 91.7 % of all handicraft workers by 1956.

In terms of economic growth the First Five-Year Plan was quite successful, especially in those areas emphasized by the Soviet-style development strategy. A solid foundation was created in heavy industry. Key industries, including iron and steel manufacturing, coal mining, cement production, electricity generation, and machine building were greatly expanded and were put on a firm, modern technological footing. Thousands of industrial and mining enterprises were constructed, including 156 major facilities. Industrial production increased at an average annual rate of 19 % between 1952 and 1957, and national income grew at a rate of 9 % a year.

1.1.3 Great Leap Forward, 1958–1960

Before the end of the First Five-Year Plan, the growing imbalance between industrial and agricultural growth, dissatisfaction with inefficiency, and lack of flexibility in the decision-making process convinced the nation's leaders that the highly centralized, industry-based Soviet model was not appropriate for China. In 1957 the government adopted measures to shift a great deal of the authority for economic decision making to the provincial-level, county, and local administrations. In 1958 the Second Five-Year Plan (1958–1962), which was intended to continue the policies of the first plan, was abandoned. In its place the leadership adopted an approach that relied on spontaneous heroic efforts of the entire population to produce a dramatic "great leap" in production for all sectors of the economy at once. Further reorganization of agriculture was regarded as the key to the endeavor to leap suddenly to a higher stage of productivity. A fundamental problem was the lack of sufficient capital to invest heavily in both industry and agriculture at the same time. To overcome this problem, the leadership decided to attempt to create capital in the agricultural sector by building vast irrigation and water control works employing huge teams of farmers whose labor was not being fully utilized. Surplus rural labor was also employed to support the industrial sector by setting up thousands of small-scale, low-technology, "backyard" industrial projects in farm units, which would produce machinery required for agricultural development and components for urban industries. Mobilization of surplus rural labor and further improvements in agricultural efficiency were to be accomplished by a "leap" to the final stage of agricultural collectivization and the formation of people's communes.

During the Great Leap Forward, the industrial sector also was expected to discover and use slack labor and productive capacity to increase output beyond the levels previously considered feasible. Political zeal was to be the motivating force and to "put politics in command" enterprising party branches took over the direction of many factories. In addition, central planning was relegated to a minor role in favor of spontaneous, politically inspired production decisions from individual units.

The result of the Great Leap Forward was a severe economic crisis. In 1958 industrial output did in fact "leap" by 55 %. Mines and factories continued to expand output through 1960, partly by overworking personnel and machines but largely because many new plants constructed during the First Five-Year Plan went into full production in these years. Thereafter, however, the excessive strain on equipment and workers, the effects of the agricultural crisis, the lack of economic coordination, and, in the 1960s, the withdrawal of Soviet assistance caused industrial output to plummet by 38 % in 1961 and by a further 16 % in 1962.

1.1.4 Readjustment and Recovery: "Agriculture First," 1961–1965

Faced with economic collapse in the early 1960s, the government sharply revised the immediate goals of the economy and devised a new set of economic policies to replace those of the Great Leap Forward. Top priority was given to restoring agricultural output and expanding it at a rate that would meet the needs of the growing population. Planning and economic coordination were to be revived in a less centralized form than before the Great Leap Forward, so as to restore order and efficient allocation of resources to the economy. The rate of investment was to be reduced and investment priorities reversed, with agriculture receiving first consideration, light industry second, and heavy industry third.

In a further departure from the emphasis on heavy industrial development that persisted during the Great Leap Forward, the government undertook to mobilize the nation's resources to bring about technological advancement in agriculture. Organizational changes in agriculture mainly involved decentralization of production decision making and income distribution within the commune structure. The role of the central commune administration was greatly reduced, although it remained the link between local government and agricultural producers and was important in carrying out activities that were too large in scale for the production brigades. Production teams were designated the basic accounting units and were responsible for making nearly all decisions concerning production and the distribution of income to their members. Private plots, which had disappeared on some communes during the Great Leap Forward, were officially restored to farm families.

In industry, a few key enterprises were returned to central state control, but control over most enterprises remained in the hands of provincial-level and local governments. This decentralization had taken place in 1957 and 1958 and was reaffirmed and strengthened in the 1961–1965 period. Planning rather than politics once again guided production decisions and material rewards rather than revolutionary enthusiasm became the leading incentive for production. Major imports of advanced foreign machinery which had come to an abrupt halt with the withdrawal of Soviet assistance starting in 1960, were initiated with Japan and Western Europe countries.

During the 1961–1965 readjustment and recovery period, economic stability was restored, and by 1966 production in both agriculture and industry surpassed the peak levels of the Great Leap Forward period. Between 1961 and 1966, industrial output was increased at an average annual rate of 10.6 %, largely by reviving plants that had operated below capacity after the economic collapse in 1961. Another important source of growth in this period was the spread of rural, small-scale industries, particularly coal mines, hydroelectric plants, chemical fertilizer plants, and agricultural machinery plants. The economic model that emerged in this period combined elements of the highly centralized, industrially oriented, Soviet-style system of the First Five-Year Plan with aspects of the decentralization of ownership and decision making that characterized the Great Leap Forward and with the strong emphasis on agricultural development and balanced growth of the "agriculture first" policy. Important changes in economic policy occurred in later years, but the basic system of ownership, decision-making structure, and development strategy that was forged in the early 1960s was not significantly altered until the reform period of the 1980s.

1.1.5 Cultural Revolution Decade, 1966–1978

The Cultural Revolution, unlike the Great Leap Forward, was primarily a political upheaval and did not produce major changes in official economic policies or the basic economic model.

The effect was a 14-percent decline in industrial production in 1967. A degree of order was restored by the army in late 1967 and 1968, and the industrial sector returned to a fairly high rate of growth in 1969. To revive efficiency in industry, Communist Party of China committees were returned to positions of leadership over the revolutionary committees, and a campaign was carried out to return skilled and highly educated personnel to the jobs from which they had been displaced during the Cultural Revolution.

After the fall of the Gang of Four, the leadership reaffirmed the modernization program. They also set forth a battery of new policies for the purpose of accomplishing the Four Modernizations.

The new policies strengthened the authority of managers and economic decision makers at the expense of party officials, stressed material incentives for workers, and called for expansion of the research and education systems.

This new policy initiative was capped at the Fifth National People's Congress in February and March 1978, when the leadership presented the draft of an ambitious 10-year plan for the 1976–1985 periods. The plan called for high rates of growth in both industry and agriculture and included 120 construction projects that would require massive and expensive imports of foreign technology.

Between 1976 and 1978, the economy quickly recovered from the stagnation of the Cultural Revolution. Industrial output jumped by 14 % in 1977 and by 13 % in 1978.

1.1.6 Period of Readjustment, 1979–1981

The first few years of the reform program were designated the "period of readjustment," during which key imbalances in the economy were to be corrected and a foundation was to be laid for a well-planned modernization drive.

The major goals of the readjustment process were to expand exports rapidly; overcome key deficiencies in transportation, communications, coal, iron, steel, building materials, and electric power; and redress the imbalance between light and heavy industry by increasing the growth rate of light industry and reducing investment in heavy industry.

The central policies of the reform program were introduced experimentally during the readjustment period. The most successful reform policy, the contract responsibility system of production in agriculture, was suggested by the government in 1979 as a way for poor rural units in mountainous or arid areas to increase their incomes. The responsibility system allowed individual farm families to work a piece of land for profit in return for delivering a set amount of produce to the collective at a given price. This arrangement created strong incentives for farmers to reduce production costs and increase productivity. Soon after its introduction the responsibility system it was adopted by numerous farm units in all sorts of areas.

In the industry, the main policy innovations increased the autonomy of enterprise managers, reduced emphasis on planned quotas, allowed enterprises to produce goods outside the plan for sale on the market and permitted enterprises to experiment with the use of bonuses to reward higher productivity. The government also tested a fundamental change in financial procedures with a limited number of state-owned units: rather than remitting all of their profits to the state, as was normally done. These enterprises were allowed to pay a tax on their profits and retain the balance for reinvestment and distribution to workers as bonuses.

The government also actively encouraged the establishment of collectively owned and operated industrial and service enterprises as a means of soaking up some of the unemployment among young people and at the same time helping to increase supplies of light industrial products. Individual enterprise (true capitalism) was also allowed, after having virtually disappeared during the Cultural Revolution, and independent cobblers, tailors, tinkers, and vendors once again became common sights in the cities. Foreign-trade procedures were greatly eased, allowing individual enterprises and administrative departments outside the Ministry of Foreign Trade (which became the Ministry of Foreign Economic Relations and Trade in 1984) to engage in direct negotiations with foreign firms. A wide range of cooperation, trading, and credit arrangements with foreign firms were legalized so that China could enter the mainstream of international trade.

1.2 Courses of Economic Reform in China[2]

Economic reforms began after Deng Xiaoping and his reformist allies ousted the Gang of Four Maoist faction. By the time Deng took power, there was widespread support among the elite for economic reforms. As the defector leader, Deng's policies faced opposition from party conservatives but were extremely successful in increasing the country's wealth.

1.2.1 From Planned Economy to Planned Commodity Economy

1.2.1.1 From 1978 to 1984

Reforms were implemented in urban industry to increase productivity. A dual price system was introduced, in which state-owned industries were allowed to sell any production above the plan quota, and commodities were sold at both plan and

[2] Chinese economic reform [2].

market prices, allowing citizens to avoid the shortages of the Maoist era. Private businesses were allowed to operate for the first time since the Communist takeover, and they gradually began to make up a greater percentage of industrial output. Price flexibility was also increased, expanding the service sector.

1.2.1.2 From 1984 to 1992

During this period, Deng Xiaoping's policies continued beyond the initial reforms. Controls on private businesses and government intervention continued to decrease, and there was small-scale privatization of state enterprises which had become unviable. A notable development was the decentralization of state control, leaving local provincial leaders to experiment with ways to increase economic growth and privatize the state sector. Township and village enterprises, firms nominally owned by local governments but effectively private, began to gain market share at the expense of the state sector. However, Deng stood by his reforms and in 1992, he affirmed the need to continue reforms in his southern tour. He also reopened the Shanghai Stock Exchange closed by Mao 40 years earlier.

Although the economy grew quickly during this period, economic troubles in the inefficient state sector increased. Heavy losses had to be made up by state revenues and acted as a drain upon the economy. Privatizations began to accelerate after 1992, and the private sector surpassed the state sector in share of GDP for the first time in the mid-1990s. Chinese government slowly expanded recognition of the private economy, first as a "complement" to the state sector (1988) and then as an "important component" (1999) of the socialist market economy.

1.2.2 From Planned Commodity Economy to Socialist Market Economy

1.2.2.1 From 1992 to 2002

In the 1990s, Deng allowed radical reforms to be carried out. Despite Deng's death in 1997, reforms continued under his handpicked successors, who were ardent reformers. In 1997 and 1998, large-scale privatization occurred, in which all state enterprises, except a few large monopolies, were liquidated and their assets sold to private investors. From 2001, the number of state-owned enterprises decreased by 48 %. During the same period, the leaders also reduced tariffs, trade barriers and regulations, reformed the banking system, dismantled much of the Mao-era social welfare system, forced the People's Liberation Army to divest itself of military-run businesses, reduced inflation, and joined the World Trade Organization. These moves invoked discontent among some groups, especially the laid off workers of state enterprises that had been privatized.

1.2.2.2 From 2002 to Present

Following the Chinese Communist Party's Third Plenum, held in October 2003, Chinese legislators unveiled several proposed amendments to the state constitution. One of the most significant was a proposal to provide protection for private property rights. The Fifth Plenum in October 2005 approved the 11th Five-Year Economic Program (2006–2010) aimed at building a "socialist harmonious society" through more balanced wealth distribution and improved education, medical care, and social security. On March 2006, the National People's Congress approved the 11th Five-Year Program. The plan called for a relatively conservative 45 % increase in GDP and a 20 % reduction in energy intensity (energy consumption per unit of GDP) by 2010.

China launched its Economic Stimulus Plan to specifically deal with the Global financial crisis of 2008–2009. It has primarily focused on increasing affordable housing, easing credit restrictions for mortgage and SMEs, lower taxes such as those on real estate sales and commodities, pumping more public investment into infrastructure development, such as the rail network, roads and ports. By the end of 2009 it appeared that the Chinese economy was showing signs of recovery. At the 2009 Economic Work Conference in December 'managing inflation expectations' was added to the list of economic objectives, suggesting a strong economic upturn and a desire to take steps to manage it.

By 2010 it was evident to outside observers that China was poised to move from export dependency to the development of an internal market. Wages were rapidly rising in all areas of the country and Chinese leaders were calling for an increased standard of living.

China's GDP grew 10.0 % in 2003, 10.1 %, in 2004, and even faster 10.4 % in 2005 despite attempts by the government to cool the economy. In 2010, China's GDP was valued at $5.87 trillion, surpassed Japan's $5.47 trillion, and became the world's second largest economy after the U.S. China could become the world's largest economy (by nominal GDP) sometime as early as 2020.

1.3 Courses of Enterprises Reform in China[3]

After the founding of the P.R. China in 1949, the government nationalized almost the entire industrial economy by taking over the previous state owned companies, subsidiaries of foreign firms as well as private companies. Two categories of ownership were created along the Soviet model: ownership by the state and ownership by the people, often called collective ownership.

Under the former planned economy, the State owned enterprises (SOEs) had little discretion over their business operations. Production, purchase, sales and even the wage rates were all decided and allocated by the government. Moreover, SOEs had

[3] Stella Nie [3].

multi-functions at that time. On one hand, they were supposed to reach production targets and generate profits, on the other hand, they should act as policy executors who had to provide job opportunities and undertake social welfare functions for their body of employees. With this burden of multiple and sometimes conflicting tasks, the economic performance of the state-owned sector was extremely poor. Many SOEs just survived on the government's protection and subsidies, e.g. cheap raw materials and low interest loans from the state banks, among which a large percentage became non-performing eventually.

1.3.1 Reform of State-Owned Enterprises (SOEs)[4]

Since 1978, the state started to change from pure planned economy to a planned economy with the market as a supplement, planned commodity economy and social market economy. At the same time, the managerial and operational system of SOEs had improved. Specifically, the reform of SOEs could be divided into three phases, namely initial stage, comprehensive reform stage and the establishment of modern enterprises stage.

1.3.1.1 Initial Stage of SOE Reform (1978.12–1984.9)

The initial stage of SOE reform was experienced from December 1978 to September 1984. It mainly focused on the reform of concentrated planned economic management system through the expansion of operational autonomy and the delegation of financial rights to enhance the vitality of enterprises.

In July 1979, State Council enacted the five documents concerning operational autonomy, profit retention, taxes on fixed assets, an increase in the rate of depreciation and improvement of depreciation method, and full credit on liquid assets. State Council also requested the local departments to select pilot enterprises for the implementation of the five documents. Public transportation industry has been chosen as pilot for economic responsibility system from 1981 to 1982. Since 1983, the returning of profit started to be replaced by taxes, which led to the coexistence of taxes and the returning of profit. Change from profit returned to taxes was further implemented in 1984. In 1985, the government decided to implement "changes from appropriation of capitals to bank loan", which means the sources of funds were transformed from the free appropriation of capitals from government financial plan into commercial loans from the banks. This implementation intended to enhance economic responsibilities of enterprises and to promote the awareness of economic account in the investment and the use of funds.

Although the above actions improved the incentive mechanism in the micro aspect, the prevailing planned mechanism still distorted the pricing system and

[4] Xianzhi Zhang [4], Justin Lin and Peilin Liu [5], Shengming Yang [6], Fuyong Tang and Ye Lu [7].

the "dual track" phenomenon of pricing still populated. Therefore, it was hard to make the objective assessment of the real performance of enterprises. Besides, due to the lack of accounting system and audit system, inequality such as different tax rates for similar companies and "power retention" was very common. "Power retention" is that the power delegated to companies from central government was retained by local government. Compared with non-SOE, the autonomy of SOE was still inadequate.

In general, the strategies in this period did not increase the enterprise vitality and the government revenues. Although power was released from central government to enterprises, part of it was still retained by local government. Enterprises gained some power, but phenomenon like management and employees take advantage of the state still existed due to the information asymmetry and absence of related supervision and regulation. Under this circumstance, the government took the separation of ownership from operation into consideration to give enterprises more autonomy. As investors, government enjoyed shareholders' rights as well as shareholders' obligations. But it could not happen overnight as it had to experience periods of contracting, cooperation, property reform, etc.

1.3.1.2 Comprehensive Reform Period (1984.10–1991.12)

In this stage, the guideline of reforms was both the separation of government and enterprises and the separation of ownership and management. Change enterprises into autonomous and self-financing economic entities to establish a system of responsibility. The variety of responsibility system includes the manager responsibility system in state-owned enterprises; the contractual responsibility system for the majority of state-owned enterprises; operation leasing among some small state-owned enterprises; and privatization reform in a few enterprises.

In October 1984, the party's Third Plenary Session of the Twelfth Central Committee set up the goal of state-owned enterprise reform, that is to enable enterprises to become a relatively independent economic entity, to become autonomous, self-financing producers and operators of social commodities, to enable themselves improvement and development, and to become the corporation with certain rights and obligations. In December 1986, the State Council's Provisions on strengthening enterprise reform and enhancing the vitality of enterprises proposed to carry out various reforms on management responsibility system to give the managers full autonomy, after which the contractual management responsibility system were widespread among large and medium-sized enterprises.

During this period, the implementation of contractual management responsibility system was a suboptimal choice due to inefficient economic system, the distorted pricing mechanism and weak supervision mechanism. However, in order to increase the vitality of enterprises and government income, good policies were needed to ensure the implementation of the contract system. Contracts were signed after "one to one negotiation" between enterprises and authorities. During such negotiations, the state-owned enterprises had the information advantages so that they could strive for more favorable conditions in their bargains. Additionally, two other problems occurred during the implement of the contract. One is the short-term behavior, in which the remuneration of managers was only based on the performance during the contract period. Managers utilized resources predatorily to complete their tasks. The other problem was that managers were only responsible for profits, not for losses.

Considering these problems, the state began to implement the joint-stock reform in some pilot enterprises. On April 1984, the State Commission for Economic Restructuring decided to take the privatization system by issuing shares as pilots for collective enterprises in city and small state-owned enterprises. In 1991, there were 3,220 pilot joint-stock enterprises in all.

1.3.1.3 Establishment of Modern Enterprise System (Since 1992)

Since Deng Xiaoping's southern tour speech in 1992, the enterprises reforms in China were transformed from policy adjustment to system innovation. In November 1993, the third plenary session of the fourteenth central committee passed some policy reforms concerning the establishment of the socialist market economic system. The policy clearly pointed out the reform of state-owned enterprises was to establish a modern enterprise system with clear property rights, clear powers and responsibilities, and the separation of government functions from enterprise management. "The People's Republic of China Company Law" was promulgated in February 1993, and taken into effect on July 1, 1994. Since that time, the establishment of "modern enterprise system" has been the focus of reform of Chinese state-owned enterprises, especially for those large and medium-sized state-owned enterprises. At the end of 2003, among the national 4,223 state-owned large and medium-sized enterprises, 2,514 firms, nearly 60 % had become diversified holding corporations through various forms of restructuring.

In the process of establishing modern enterprise system, the state began to adjust the layout of state-owned enterprises. In March 1996, the eighth session of the National People's Congress approved the Ninth Five Year plan and the long-term goals for 2010 of the People's Republic of China National Economic and social development. It puts forward new ideas for the reform of state-owned enterprises. In addition to continuance of pushing forward the modern enterprise system, it also puts forward reform ideas to invigorate large enterprises while relaxing control over small ones. It focused on the improvement of the whole economy and the implementation of the strategic reorganization of state-owned enterprises. According to situations of different firms, different forms of restructuring such as combination, merger, stock cooperative system, leasing, contracting and the sale, were used to speed up the reform of small state-owned enterprises.

For small and medium-sized state-owned enterprises, especially for the small state-owned enterprises, it is undoubtedly correct. For small and medium-sized state-owned enterprises, the intensity level of capital is low, the strategic and social policy burden is small, and direct supervision of the owners is relatively easy. However, for large and medium-sized state-owned enterprises, the problems from a contract system were not solved by the modern enterprise system either. The effectiveness of modern corporate governance structure depends on a market system with fully competitive products, elements, managers, and stocks. Such market system was weak in China and the policy burdens still existed. Therefore, the soft budget constraint was still difficult to be eradicated.

Southeast Asian financial crisis which broke out in 1997 brought new attention to the risk of the Chinese financial system. High debt rate restricted the survival and development of enterprises and the high debt ratio of state-owned enterprises and low solvency exacerbates financial risks of the Chinese banking system. For these reasons, the "debt-equity swap" reform was implemented. Though the balance sheets of state-owned enterprise and banks were improved by technical operations rapidly, the success of the SOE reform also depended on the improvement of the competitive ability and elimination of bad debt, which required the elimination of all kinds of political burden of SOEs.

During this period, the government took a series of revolting measures to improve the operational environment for enterprises, such as

1. Establishment and improvement of capital market and establishment of Shanghai and Shenzhen Securities Exchange.
2. Downsizing of government, reduced industry regulation agency and reduced intervention of government to enterprises.
3. Established and improved incentive mechanism and constraint mechanism of entrepreneurs, trial with annual salary system and implementation of supervision panel system and designated accountant system.
4. Established state-owned assets management system where central government and local government are treated as investors to enjoy the shareholders' rights and obligations.
5. Established property-rights market system and evaluated state-owned assets properly.

1.3.2 Development of Private Enterprises in China[5]

Chinese economic reform provides previous historical opportunities for the private enterprises to recover and develop. During this period, private enterprises became stronger and played more and more important role in promoting economic development and social employment. The development of private enterprises can be divided into three periods.

---

[5] Xiaoguang Wang [8].

1.3.2.1 From Recovery to Confirm Status (1978–1989)

The Third Plenary Session of the Eleventh CCCPC marked the beginning of the transformation of Chinese society with self-employed and private businesses starting recovering and developing. In 1981, the State Council pointed out that under the fundamental premise of the dominance of socialist public ownership, a variety of economic forms and a variety of management way coexist is a strategic decision for a long time. In 1982, China constitution stipulates obviously that urban and the rural laborer individual economy within the scope of the law is a complement to the socialist public ownership. And the state protects the lawful rights and interests of the individual economy. In this way, the status of individual economy was confirmed and individual economy become the supplement to the socialist public ownership. The private enterprises were developing rapidly. The thirteenth national party congress pointed out the necessity to develop an economy with different types of ownership, especially emphasized the importance of the development of the private economy which was the necessary and beneficial supplement of public-owned economy. In the Constitutional amendment which was promulgated in 1988, the state permitted the private economy to exist and develop within the limits prescribed by law. Private economy was a complement to the socialist public-owned economy. The state protected the lawful rights and interests of the private economy and provided guidance, supervision and management to the private economy. From then on, the status of private economy was confirmed.

In this period, planned economy was the dominant economic system and the macro economy was labeled as shortage economy which means that all the products and materials are in shortage. Slight market-oriented reform brought remarkable economic effect. The improvement of the private enterprises' status stimulated fast development of private enterprises. The private enterprises made use of the state-owned enterprises to accumulate assets by means of contract operation, leasing management and transform operation mechanism. The limited expansion of private enterprises which was caused by means of increasing capital investment made a lot of private enterprises to have a considerable scale. The expansion of private enterprises was a rational impulse which was under the induction of market economy. Since political environment was not clear at that time, the impulse was depressed and the expansion of private enterprises was limited. Private economy was still in the development and accumulation phase.

1.3.2.2 From the Twists and Turns to Development

In 1989, the nature of private enterprises was a controversial issue which made private economy to be doubted and the development of private enterprises was in great trouble. From 1989 to 1992, the development of private economy was in twists and turns, a lot of private enterprises were forced to be voluntary conveyance to government (or collective), some private enterprises had to affiliate in government departments, or take the form of cooperation with state-owned enterprises. In 1992, after

Deng Xiaoping made his southern tour, the 14th Congress of the Communist Party of China brought forward the strategic goal for building socialism market economy, and further affirmed the necessity of the private economy. In the meantime, the 14th Congress of the Communist Party of China points out that the ownership structure should insist on including state-owned economy and collective economy with public ownership as the main body, the individual economy, private economy and foreign economy as supplements. A variety of economic elements developed freely for a long time, and various forms of joint venture also showed up in different sectors. In 1993, 8th National People's Congress (NPC) session at a time passed a constitutional amendment in which the state practices of socialist market economy were confirmed. From then on, China gradually established and perfected the system of socialist market economy and the development of private economy got more favorable macroeconomic conditions.

The development of private enterprises entered the new stage after Deng Xiaoping made his southern tour in 1992. In this period, the private economy was a beneficial supplement of public economy, and private enterprises had become an active force in market economy. The development of economy entered an accelerated new period. There was a strong demand for various merchandises which brought new opportunities for private enterprises. Private enterprises developed into diversification and the diversity and richness of private economy was presented. Private enterprises' organizational level and management level was gradually improved, and a number of private enterprises with assets of tens of millions, even hundreds of millions were grown up. Some conglomerate of private enterprises began to form. The rapid development of private enterprises and the positive role in which the private enterprises played was confirmed by all walks of life. Although there were still some constraints in spite of the land, financing, taxation, but private enterprises had started to enjoy more and more relaxed policy environment and market environment.

1.3.2.3 From All-Round Development to Standardized Development (Since 1997)

In 1997, the 15th National Party Congress pointed out that individual private and other non-public sectors of the economy should continue to be encouraged, guided, and ensure the healthy development of them. This is essential to meet people's diversified needs, increase employment, and promote the development of national economy. In 1999, Nine National People's Congress second conference passed a constitutional amendment in which the status of non-public economy was confirmed. Individual economy, private economy and other non-public sectors of the economy which is within the scope of the law were important parts of socialist market economy. 16th NPC and 17th NPC pointed out that the government should unswervingly encourage, support and guide non-public economic development, which had a significant role in the development of the private economy. Especially in 2005, the publication of "the state council support to encourage and guide private and other non-public sectors of the economic development of the several opinions" (36 Guidelines on non-public economy sector) made law, policy and market environment of private enterprises continuously be improved, and private economy had obtained a bigger development.

During this period, the private economy had become an important part in the national economy. Private enterprises were playing more and more important role in promoting the economic development and decreasing unemployment rate. Especially since the twenty-first century, with both breadth and depth of reform and opening-up, the market economy has become the dominant economic system in the national economy. The competition between the enterprises becomes increasingly comprehensive competition and fierce. Private enterprises evolved into the stage of standardized development. Specialization and diversification are endowed with new meaning. In this period, more and larger scale private enterprises started to take the organization form of share-holding system, which make private enterprises from the realm private enterprises into joint-stock enterprises, such development comprised of a new forms and characteristics.

1.4 Development of Management Control in China

1.4.1 Courses of Management Control in China

According to the reform of China economy, the development of management control theory has experienced three stages. These are planned economy, Planned Commodity Economy and Socialist Market Economy in sequence. Management control in each stage enjoys different features.

1.4.1.1 Planned Economy and Management Control

Stage one (before 1978) is the period of enterprises' management control under a planned economy. During this period, China mainly borrowed the planned economy system from the former Soviet Union as the method of resource allocation, strove to grope cost accounting and cost management methods in the planning economy within theoretical and practical scopes, and paid attention to cost and management accounting. All decisions about production, distribution and consumption were made by government planning agencies. Hence, enterprises only played the role of a producing module. Under this circumstance, enterprises' management control solely ensured the completion of the production task. Its functions were mainly production control, value management, monitoring of object productivity or technique efficiency. The type of corporate management control was regulation control, which meant that the enterprises could operate only by the regulatory rules and therefore limited the ability of managers and staff. Thus, the management control theory in this period consisted mainly of cost accounting and regulation control.

Management control in this stage was based on operation of products. Operation of products is closely linked to the production-oriented enterprises. The production-oriented enterprises are only responsible for the production, without consideration of the supply, sales, financing, and investment etc. Strictly speaking, production-oriented enterprises are not real business but a production workshop. The goal of production-oriented enterprise is to complete production assignments, reduce cost of production. Therefore, the basic feature of production-oriented enterprise is to produce qualified products with certain labor and materials on time, under the guidance of the state plan.

1.4.1.2 Planned Commodity Economy and Management Control

In stage two (1978–1993) the enterprises' management control was in a planned commodity economy. In 1978, China proposed to reform the economy system towards a mixed one. Enterprises were socialist commodity producers and responsible for their own management decisions.

At that time the management control thought experienced the first understanding of managerial accounting beyond cost management. From 1978 to the end of 1993, the objective of China's economic reform was to establish a planned commodity economy and to solve many problems left behind by the planned economy. Enterprises began to emphasize on managing their business according to the laws and the management control evolved to the form of process controlling. Finally, from October 1984 to the end of 1993, the separation of government and enterprises as well as the separation of ownership and management was completed. The objective of enterprises' management control afterwards was not only revenues and profits, but also the profits contrasted with assets occupancy. Hence, company directors took more responsibilities on return on assets (ROA) and the content of management control extended to investment and asset control. Accordingly, the method of enterprises' management control began to diversify.

Management control in this stage was based on the operation of commodity and operation of assets. Operation of Commodity is connected to the production-market-oriented enterprises. Production-market-oriented business focuses on the operation and marketing of products and its responsibilities include supply production and marketing as well as investment and financing. Chain of supply production, market and profitability of products are the focus of production-market-oriented enterprises. The feature of operation of commodity is that market-oriented business manages activities of supply production and marketing to satisfy the demand of society by producing with labor and materials. There are differences and similarities between operation of commodity and operation of production. First operation of production is the most important part of operation of commodity; operation of commodity is the extension of operation of production. Second, operation of products focuses on the physical form of products rather than the price of inputs and outputs, while operation of commodity take the price of inputs and outputs into consideration. Third the goal of operation of commodity is more comprehensive than operation of products. To fulfill the goal of operation of commodity, business is required to not only to manage the production process and improve the efficiency but also focus on the chain of supply production and market, and value-based management to improve the profitability of commodity.

Operation of assets is connected to the asset-oriented enterprises. Asset-oriented enterprises take the assets as inputs and focus on the allocation restructure and utilization of assets. Under the context of operation of assets, operation of production and operation of commodity are all based on operation of assets. The goal of operation of assets is the growth of assets and value-added or maximization of profitability for assets employed. Therefore the basic feature of operation of assets is rational allocation and utilization of assets and obtains as much proceeds as possible with certain assets.

1.4.1.3 Socialist Market Economy

In stage three (1993 to today) the enterprise management control has been in a socialist market economy. Enterprises continue to complete the economy responsibility system, while academia tries to introduce theories and methods of western management control. Since the end of 1993, reforms have transformed China towards a system innovation, stepping into a new stage of establishing socialist market economy. In a similar vein, enterprise reforms have established a modern enterprise system with clear ownership structures, well-defined rights and responsibilities.

Hence, sophisticated management control theories and methods are increasingly required. With the growing responsiveness of enterprises to market forces, some enterprises have created many responsibility accounting models by summarizing their own practical experience and utilizing western management control theories and approaches. As a market economy entity, enterprises began to fully carry out managerial functions such as planning, decision-making, budgeting, controlling and pay emphasis on pursuing economic benefits. The target of management control advanced from the pursuit of simple profits and the maximization of profits under certain assets to the maximization of profits under certain capital – namely the basic target of capital appreciation. The functions of enterprise management control extended further into capital control, capital structure control, capital cost control and capital profit control. Consequently, the system developed from a closed one into an open one.

Management control in this stage is based on the operation of capitals. Operation of capitals is connected to the capital-oriented enterprises. Capital-oriented enterprises focus on operation and management on the value-added. Return on capital is the core of management's mission. The operation of assets commodity and products are all subject to operation of capitals. The goal of capital-oriented enterprises is value-added or maximization of profitability for capital employed. So the operation of capital is based on the capital employed and improves efficiency of capitals by optimizing the allocation of resources. Through operating activities such as merger and acquisition and restructure, operation of capital creates capital gains as much as possible with given capitals.

1.4.2 *Features of Management Control in SOEs*

Due to the ownership of SOEs, the subject of management control plays an even more important role than in other enterprises. The subject of management control has been shifting from government to top management. The reform of SOEs made evaluation the key method in management control.

1.4.2.1 Subject of Management Control in SOEs[6]

Before 1978, there was no management control in SOEs due to the planned economy. From 1978 to 1984, the government began to separate the ownership from operation but there were still social functions and political interventions in SOEs. In Jan 1988, the state council decided to isolate the rights of operating SOEs from administrative function and macro-economy function of government by setting up National Bureau of the Administrative of State-Owned Assets. However, the SOEs were still intervened by the government directly who acted as the managers of SOEs and there was no clear line between the function of macro-economy and administration of state-owned-assets. The new administrative bureau could not improve the management control in SOEs.

During the restructuring of state council in 1998, National Bureau of the Administrative of State-Owned Assets was integrated into the Ministry of Finance. In March 2003, the State-owned Assets Supervision and Administration Commission of the State Council (SASAC) was founded. SASAC was found through integrating the responsibilities of guiding SOE's reform and management from the former State Economic and Trade Commission (SETC), the responsibilities of former CPC Enterprise Work Commission, responsibilities of related state-owned asset management of the Ministry of Finance, and certain responsibilities of the Ministry of Labor and Social Security. The mission of SASAC includes: administration of managers in the enterprises funded by SASAC; decision-making on vital projects; administration of state-owned assets. Later, SASAC helped in the foundation of local administrative agencies at province level. By 2004, the framework of SASAC system had been set up. SASAC is not allowed to intervene in the operation to preserve the autonomy of SOEs except for the protection of shareholders' interests.

[6]China State-owned assets management system reform entering new stage [9].

1.4.2.2 Methods of Management Control in SOEs

Budgetary Control

The traditional budget system was consistent with the function of government in the planned economy. Ownership of SOEs was the major economic function of government. And revenues and expenses in public finance were mixed with those in SOEs. The only goal of control is the total amount of revenues and expenses. The role of shareholders in SOEs was replaced by administrators from government. As the result, the management control of operational state-owned assets was distorted.

The history of state-owned capital budget is divided into four stages, namely constructive budget, state-owned assets budget, state-owned capital budget, operational budgeted system of SOE.

(1) Constructive budget

In 1988, Ministry of Finance submitted a proposal of double budget to the State Council. Meanwhile, State Council ordered that from 1992, central budget should be prepared in accordance to namely operating budget and constructive budget. From 1992, central budget and regional budget in some provinces were prepared in the form of operating budget and constructive budget.

(2) Budget of State-owned Assets

In 1993, it was suggested that double budget system should be improved and regulated through the establishment of public budgets and operating budget of state-owned assets, social security budget system and other budgets as needed. It was the very first time that operating budget of state-owned assets was put forward and constructive budget was shifted to operating budget of state-owned assets. The Budget Law approved in 1994 stated that "central and local government budget should be made in the form of double budget". Budget Law was implemented in 1995 and double budget confirmed its legitimate position.

(3) Budget of State-owned Capital

With the restructure of central government in 1998, National Bureau of the Administrative of State-Owned Assets was integrated into the Ministry of Finance. It focused on "the improvement of budget system, enhancing of budget constraints, establishment of public budget step by step, and establishment of state-owned capital budget and social security budget system". Meanwhile, "operating budget of state-owned assets" was transformed into "Budget of state-owned capital".

In 2002, administration of state-owned assets was changed to serve as investors on behalf of state and provinces which focus on both the consistency of rights obligations and responsibilities and the combination of responsibilities on assets human resources as well as operations.

(4) Operating Budget of State-owned Capitals

In April 2003, SASAC was founded. The responsibilities of SASAC are clearly defined as budgetary control of supervised SOEs and when the conditions are ready,

SASAC is required to compile operating budget of supervised SOEs. In 2003, it was suggested again that operating budgets system of state-owned capitals should be established as well as the evaluation system of SOEs. At the same time, the operating budget system of state-owned capitals was formalized.

Since 2004, SASAC in Beijing and Shanghai initially launched the local State-owned capital operating budget system. In 2004, Premier Wen Jiabao once again claimed: "improve laws and regulations and implementation measures related to SASAC quickly. Study and establish operating budget system of state-owned capital and performance evaluation system of SOEs. And further implement the state-owned asset operating responsibility."

Early in November 2006, the State Council Executive Meeting studied the problem of state-owned capital adjustment and clearly pointed out the need to accelerate the establishment of operating budget system of state-owned capital and to arrange overall use of profits from state-owned capital.

1.4.2.3 Courses of Performance Evaluation

The courses of performance of evaluation are divided into three stages since the reform which started in 1978.

(1) Performance Evaluation Based on Contractual Responsibility System

Since the start of reform, the operational mechanism has been seen as the key problem of SOEs. In order to eliminate the constraints from planned economy, operational system that was related to contractual responsibilities showed up.

The contractual responsibility system was invented in the rural reform and later became a transient institution for SOEs. From the perspective of performance evaluation, contractual responsibility systems focus on the relation between the compensation of contractors who used to be managers and the performance of the enterprises. It was the first time that personal incentives were connected to performance evaluation. Contractual responsibilities were the major parts of performance evaluation. If the contractors tried to get bonus, they had to clarify the responsibilities in the contract which were the criteria for the performance evaluation. The contractual responsibilities were profit-oriented. When the contract was signed, the emphasis was profit rather than volume of production which was the focus in planned economy. Due to the inherent incentive, contractual responsibilities system was extended inside the enterprises which connect personal income with disaggregated responsibilities.

However, as the contractual responsibility system became popular, the dark side began to dominate. Because the term of the contract was short and the indicators used in the evaluation were not objectively assessed, the short-term behavior increased significantly and the conflicts of interest were serious.

(2) Performance Evaluation Based on Modern Enterprises and Management of State-owned Capitals (1992–2003)

In 1995, "Evaluation system of efficiency in enterprises" was officially enacted. It projected a brand-new performance evaluation system including turnover, liquidity, profit and social responsibilities. The system was still viewed as a transient institution with obvious flaws. Too much emphasis on financial ratios failed to lead enterprises into the future, make strategic decisions or control the operation. The subjects of evaluation were not clarified in the system. Value-added could not be measured from the perspective of financial year. When the role played by the government became clear, the system was revised to get more rationale. The concept of investors and state-owned capitals were introduced as the base of the performance system. In 1999, evaluation system was rebuilt on the basis of state-owned capitals, which included three levels of indicators such as basic indicators, corrective indicators and ranking from experts.

(3) Performance Evaluation Based on Modern Property Rights and Role of Investors (2003-)

Modern theory on property right provides both the foundation of performance evaluation for the government and the basis of management control for managers. In this performance evaluation system, the subject is SASAC who serves as the investor of SOEs and the object is the manager of SOEs. The performance was evaluated by financial year as well as service term. The results of the evaluation which includes both outcome and process were connected to incentives. Basic rules of evaluation were presented in this system. The first rule was value-oriented which evaluate the performance of managers by the value-added in state-owned assets, maximization of gains on capitals and sustainable growth. The second rule was relative-performance evaluation which was based on the industry, size and operation. The third rule was the compatibility of evaluation and incentives. The forth rule was balanced-growth which focus on strategic management, innovation, environment protection to enhance core competence and sustainable growth. The content of the evaluation included both financial-year-based operating performances which focus on profits and return on equity and term-based operating performance which focuses on value-added from state-owned capitals and average growth rate for the last 3 years. EVA was also introduced to underline the importance of value-added.

1.4.3 Features of Management Control in Chinese Private Enterprise

As the development of Chinese private enterprises history, from the early 1980s to the late 1990s, private enterprises mainly experienced four typical development model- “Sunan model”, “Wenzhou model”, “Pearl River Delta model ”and“ Zhongguancun model”.

Sunan model is generally referred to the development of township enterprises in collective ownership radiated by Suzhou, Wuxi, Changzhou and other big and medium-sized cities with strong economic development in Sunan region (the south of JiangSu Province). With the completion of ‘restructuring’ of township enterprises in Sunan region, which was started in 1996, Sunan model reached its end and was replaced by private enterprises based on limited liability.

Wenzhou model is generally referred to the development of individual and private enterprises based on household industries in Wenzhou, Zhejiang. In the new century, private enterprises in Wenzhou showed the trend of enterprise cluster.

The Pearl River Delta model is generally referred to the development of export-oriented enterprise in the Pearl River Delta region, which was based on process and export and investment in Hong Kong, Macao and foreign enterprises in order to promote regional economic development. This model still enjoys thrives.

Zhongguancun model is mainly originated in Beijing Zhongguancun area. It refers to the development of private technology enterprises which are based on research institutes and universities or intellectual elite entrepreneurial business. In the early days, high-tech private enterprises in Zhongguancun were often affiliated to some government agencies and research institutes, or run by the government. But after several years, no matter how the enterprises were financed, by commercial loans or start-up fund from the parent government agencies, the property rights were unrecognizable and the ownership of assets could not be figured out. Restructuring became the only solution for private enterprises established early. In the late 1990s, some innovative high-tech enterprises were founded, with clear property rights and strong innovation and became an important group among private enterprises.

Because of the short history of private enterprises in China and drastically changing economic environment, the management control in private enterprises shows salient features compared to others. Family ties are vital in enterprises. Professionals are not so popular in management. And expansion becomes the top priority in many firms.

1.4.3.1 Family Control Oriented Model

Most private enterprises are controlled by families. Family-controlled can be defined as family members are both owners and managers at the same time. Consanguinity, phylogeny and geology together guarantee the success of the operation. As compared to formal organizations, family-controlled business is a loose, unstable and informal type of organization. It utilizes informal rules and policies to manage the enterprise, with a strong personal attitude on the management/owner's preference. Family management constraints the enterprise's development and discourages professionals whom possesses management talents and techniques from joining the enterprise. As enterprises go diversely and internationally, control by family can be an apparent obstacle. On the one hand, family management cannot reproduce corresponsive mechanisms to deal with contemporary challenges. Family management also prefers to elect the management from the inner circle and exclude outsiders, even if these outsiders are more talented and compatible.

Family-controlled enterprises usually don't separate rights of ownership from rights of management, in other words, family wealth is tangled with enterprise assets. This leads to chaos in the financial system. From the perspective of capitals, family-controlled enterprises highly rely on private capitals, which can be interpreted as making profits from your own money. Ownership is sealed within the private capitals, mainly depending on owners' reinvestment and accumulated profits. Cumulative profits are limited, and public financing and investing activities are restricted by the current financing mechanism, so family-controlled enterprises are hard to develop.

1.4.3.2 Lack of Professional Managers

The biggest constraint in private enterprise is that families and friends possess a higher priority than outsiders when it comes to the election of management. This invisible criterion can be found in every level of positions. Descendants are usually the first option as candidates for most entrepreneurs. The first generation of Chinese entrepreneurs is usually considered as the beneficiary of a specific period. If a company intends to continuously develop, the management should carve out a new path, a path that is completely different from their founders'. However, the second generation is usually criticized as "lack of perseverance and sense of crisis", which becomes another obstacle to private enterprises. Most Chinese private enterprises are evolved from family-owned, and built by several family members, not somebody solely. If family members are trained by the market and equipped with management skill-sets, it will be completely reasonable to have the family manage it. Professional managers used to be the constraint to private enterprise. If such constraint can be broken by a stronger family management, private enterprises would thrive with no doubt, and make a bigger contribution to our economy.

1.4.3.3 Focus on Expansion Instead of Risk Control

Private enterprises grow rapidly in China, with some of them developing into multiple industries within only few years of operations. High growth becomes the top priority on the list in many private enterprises. However, pursuing growth blindly exposes the lack of risk control. Some companies were incapable of dealing with crisis or emergencies, and to go bankrupt soon.

References

1. Economic history of China from Wikipedia website: http://en.wikipedia.org/wiki/Economic_history_of_China_ (1949–present)
2. Chinese economic reform from Wikipedia website: http://en.wikipedia.org/wiki/Chinese_economic_reform
3. Stella Nie (2005) Short history of reforms concerning Chinese state owned enterprises, Shanghai Flash, Consulate General of Switzerland in Shanghai Commercial Section website: http://www.sinoptic.ch/shanghaiflash/texts/pdf/200502_Shanghai.Flash.pdf
4. Xianzhi Zhang (2001) Management, supervision and operation of state – owned assets, 1st edn. China Financial & Economic Publishing House, Beijing

5. Justin Lin, Peilin Liu (2000) Reform of Chinese SOEs in prospect and retrospect, CCER working paper no.C2000006
6. Shengming Yang (2004) Process of China's reform on economic system, Hong Kong Commercial Daily, August 25th to September 17th
7. Fuyong Tang, Ye Lu (2004) Feeling the stones across the river: ten years of reform of SOEs in China, China Economic Times, October 26th
8. Xiaoguang Wang (2008) Study on competence of large private enterprise. Phd dissertation, Jilin University
9. China state-owned assets management system reform entering new stage from SASAC website: http://www.sasac.gov.cn/n2963340/n2964727/n2974401/2976097.html

Chapter 2
Demand of Management Control in Chinese Enterprises

2.1 Theory on Demand of Management Control

2.1.1 Internal Control Theory and Management Control

Both management control theory and its practice are driven by the demand of management control. However, the development of internal control shows that external stakeholders' demand dominates the improvement of internal control inside enterprises. This is also the same in China that the external regulators such as Ministry of Finance, Securities and Regulatory Committee, State-owned Assets Supervision and Administration Commission are in charge of the Internal Control Standards Committee and the formulation of Guidance on Internal Control for Enterprises. The external demand of internal control which is also known as "required to control" fits in the mission of regulation.

The subject of control is supposed to be enterprises rather than external regulators. No matter how complete guidance or standards are, the guidance and standards set by external regulators are not effective unless enterprises are willing to control to accomplish their goals, which is also known as "willing to control". From the perspective of "willing to control", there are some basic rules that should be noted.

First, the subjects of "willing to control" are shareholders, directors, management and employees, that is all the members inside enterprises. The ultimate goal of control is to fulfill the goal of the enterprise which includes strategic goal and operational goal. The key elements to ensure the accomplishment of the goals, is to improve "efficiency and effectiveness" during the process of control. Second, the improvement of "efficiency and effectiveness" is based on relevance of decision-making and effectiveness of control where quality of accounting information plays an important role. So accounting information with high quality is not only the requirement from external control of enterprises, but also the control goal of improvement in "efficiency and effectiveness". Effectiveness of operation could not be achieved without relevant accounting information. Third, goal of "required to control" is connected to goal "willing to control". The accomplishment of

X. Zhang, *Enterprise Management Control Systems in China*, Understanding China,
DOI 10.1007/978-3-642-54715-7_2, © Springer-Verlag Berlin Heidelberg 2014

"efficiency and effectiveness" is based on compliance with law and codes as well as honesty and protection of stakeholders. From this perspective, "required to control" from outside is the foundation and presumption of "willing to control" from inside.

2.1.2 Management Theory and Management Control

Controlling is an important role of managers, which has caught attention from management scientists and enterprises long time age. Accordingly, in the twentieth century, Fayol, Henri [1] presented five managerial functions for successful leadership, namely planning, organizing, directing, coordinating and controlling.[1] In modern times, Koontz Harold [2] revisited the functions and specified them as planning, organizing, leading, personnel and controlling. Taking these two scholars as example, it is obvious that controlling plays a basic role in the realization of managerial targets.[2]

From the point of corporate management, controlling seems to be a key element assuring the realization of targets. Thus managers use figures and evaluations to adjust plans as well as actions in order to get results which are close to the desired ones. Controlling which thereby includes business coordination and communication in order to achieve long-term corporate goals is meant to be the operating guideline for all business units.

2.1.3 Management Accounting Theory and Management Control

Management accounting is also known as internal report accounting. The basic of internal report is to provide fundamental information for operating decision making and comprehensive control. From the inside demand of operation and management, the relevance of accounting information requires that accounting department and other departments provide decision-making related information, as well as various useful information for control evaluation and communication. With the help of accounting information on prediction, decision-making, planning and control, the decision-making, management control and operational control will be more scientific and operational, which improves the performance and fulfill the goal of enterprises. So management accounting and management control are closely connected and mutually affected. The theory and methodology of management control promote the development of management accounting.

First, the evolution of the type of management control promotes the development of management accounting. Contemporary management control extends from strategic management control to activity management control. These extensions also provide

[1] Henri [1].

[2] Koontz et al. [2].

future directions of management accounting. Based on the traditional accounting for decision making and control, strategic management accounting, activity management accounting developed rapidly.

Second, procedures of management control promote the development of management accounting. The information provided by management accounting are crucial for the procedures of management control which include the disaggregation of strategic goal, standard setting for control, internal control report, evaluation of performance and incentive of managers. In order to satisfy the information demand by management control, management accounting must innovate and improve the types and contents of internal accounting report. The development of management accounting theory is induced by the extension of quality and quantity of information on demand.

Third, the innovation of management control methods promotes the development of management accounting. As the development of modern management science, methods of management control are kept improved and innovated. The emerging methods of management control provide assurance and support for the development of management accounting and promote the development in the methods system of management accounting.

2.2 Demand of Management Control in Practice

2.2.1 Enforcement of Guidance on Internal Control

The demand of articulation of Guidance or Standards on internal control is from external regulators and investors, which targets at the formulation of internal control to ensure the compliance with laws and codes and reliability of the process of accounting information production. The goal is to ensure the reliability of accounting information and disclosure. Under this context, accounting control is the core of internal control.

With the development of practice, the features of internal control are changing. "Internal control is implemented by directors, supervisors, managers and employees to fulfill the goal of control." The goal of internal control is to ensure the compliance with laws and codes, the safety of assets and reliability of financial reports in order to improve the efficiency of operation. According to the goals, internal control can be divided into three layers. The first layer is to ensure the compliance with laws and codes, which is also called enactment control. The second layer is the reliability of financial reports, which is called accounting control. The third layer is the safety of assets, improvement in efficiency and effectiveness of operation and the accomplishment of strategy, which is also known as management control.

The three layers are in different hierarchies of internal control systems. The first layer is presumption. If the enactment control fails, there will be no accounting control and management control. The second layer is foundation. Accounting control is the foundation of operating decision and management control as well as external regulation and investment decision. The third layer is orientation.

Management control improves the efficiency and effectiveness to accomplish strategic goal which is the ultimate goal of control. Management control is in the top hierarchy in internal control. It is rational that the emphasis of internal control shift from accounting control to management control according to the shift from "required to control" to "willing to control".

2.2.2 *External Regulator and Management Control*

Among the regulators in China, Accounting Department in Ministry of Finance, China Securities Regulatory Commission and Chinese Institute of Certified Public Accountants are all very concerned about management control. The standard system set up by Accounting Department in Ministry of Finance is divided into four parts: "Basic Standard for Enterprise Internal Control", "Implementation Guidelines for Enterprise Internal Control", "Guidelines for Assessment of Enterprise Internal Control" and "Guidelines for Audit of Enterprise Internal Control". The demand on management control focus on "control of risk" and "value creation" among regulators.

2.2.2.1 Demand for the Control of Risk

In the context of regulation, the regulators who are concerned about management control are mainly the regulators of security markets. Those regulators are responsible for the efficiency of market mechanism as well as the avoidance of financial frauds. The top priority of regulators is to provide assurance for the reliability and relevance of information. They also need to pay attentions to the events that could destroy the efficiency of markets. Frauds are the main reasons for the decrease of information quality, which make the control of risk as the core of demand. Besides, regulators usually don't get access to the daily operation of enterprises. The main source of information is the disclosure by enterprises. Control of risk can improve the compliance with standards and the information provided to the regulators, which also help regulators define responsibilities to avoid lawsuit.

2.2.2.2 Value Creation

Most enterprises are still immature due to the developing stage of market economy in China. Structure of organizations and behaviors of management have not reached the standard level especially for private enterprises. The lack of management control will lead to unexpected distress for enterprises. Normally distresses are related to the increase of risk and the decrease of values for enterprises. When the drop of value becomes systemic, the market system will face the probability of failure. So the regulators require the enterprises use value-based management control. The ultimate goal of management control is to create more values for the investors. If all the investors' interests are protected by value creation, the market would thrive and the regulators would fulfill their goals.

2.2.3 *Stakeholders and Management Control*

The demand on management control from debt holders is different from managers and investors. Debt holders provide loan to enterprises voluntarily, on the other hand, debt holders are very concerned about the probability of default or bankruptcy of enterprises. Generally speaking, banks and other debt holders require not only the repayment of principals but also the interests. However the interest earned are related to the risk taken by debt holders. The longer the loans are, the higher the risks are. So the demand on management control from debt holders focuses on both the efficiency of cash loaned and the compliance with debt contract. The efficiency of cash loaned is connected to the accomplishment of strategic goals. And the compliance with contracts is the bottom line for management control. The demand from debt holders agrees with the basic feature of management control.

Customers and suppliers are also connected to the demand of management control. To protect their own interests, customers and suppliers need to know the process of management control inside the enterprises. Customers buy products from the enterprise. Suppliers provide raw materials for the enterprises. From a broader view, both customers and suppliers are the extension of the enterprise. The management control of the enterprises will affect their process of production as well as financial conditions. So they will choose enterprises with good management control as business partners.

2.2.4 *Managers and Management Control*

Management control is the process that managers try to influence others inside the organization to accomplish the strategic goal. The goal of management control is to choose the right strategy and put it into practice, which will lead to the delivery of organization target. Management control includes: (1) strategic control or control or control by corporate governance; (2) operational control or control by management; (3) activity management or control by employee. Effectiveness is the core goals of strategy operation or activity, which is efficiency and effects. Efficiency is calculated as the output divided by input. Both efficiency of technology and efficiency of economy are in sub-categories belong to efficiency. Efficiency of technology is often calculated as the output divided by inputs in physical terms while efficiency of economy is calculated in term of values. Efficiency of technology is the foundation of efficiency of economy which is the key to maximization of values. Efficiency of economy leads to economic profits, creates value and produce economic effects. Management control is to accomplish the goal of enterprises by control of strategic operational and other activities.

2.3 Investors Demand for Management Control

In China, the subjects of management control are managers or regulators, and the method of management control is standard research. The purpose of management control is to answer the question of "does Investors need management control or not", "which kinds of management control investors need."

2.3.1 Differences Between Different Types of Management Control

According to the existing literature, internal accounting control and internal management control have four aspects of differences: control objectives and style, relationship with the company environment, design structure and control means (dominant means of control, control methods and internal auditing). Differences of two types of management control are shown in Table 2.1.

2.3.2 Questionnaire Design and Sample Selection

In this study, the investor preferences for different types of management control were obtained through questionnaires.

2.3.2.1 Questionnaire Design

In this study, Likert scale with five-point was used. "1" represents "strongly disagree", "5" represents "strongly agree". The questionnaire includes 22 survey questions covering different types of management control differences (shown in Appendix). Survey questions were adopted from O'Reilly-Allen [6] and Hermanson [7] studies. Before the survey, a small scale pilot study was carried out in order to determine whether the questionnaire was expressed clearly and was understood by the respondents.

2.3.2.2 Sample Selection

In this study, the respondents included the investors or potential investors such as "part-time MBA students," "Graduates" and "employees". The respondents represented all investors in China. Sample selection focused on ensuring good representation of the entire population of Chinese investors. During the pre-investigation process, it was found out that the investigation effect is not ideal in the securities business department. It was also found out that the respondents of the questionnaire did not take it seriously. Most respondents were not cooperative, did not accept investigation and answered the questionnaire wrongly or inappropriately which invalidated the questionnaires.

Table 2.1 Differences between internal accounting control and management control

		Internal accounting control	Management control
Control objectives and style	Control objectives	Ensure the security and integrity of assets; provide true and reliable accounting information [3].	Efficiency and effectiveness of operations control is the fundamental objectives of management control [12].
	Control style	Conservative, defensive style	Radical, aggressive style.
Relationship with the company environment		Less impact by environment, a single optimal management control model trends [4].	More impact by environment, according to environmental characteristics, each enterprise select one of model from four different management control mode (system control, budget control, evaluation, control and Motivation control) [12].
Design structure		The business cycle method used to establish the management control system. the business cycle model is used to analyze the common drawbacks, proposed management control points, design management control text [5].	According to Enterprise Strategy and the characteristics of Enterprise to construct management control system.
Control means	Dominant means of control	Emphasize accounting as the primary control methods and means, the accounting control (including financial control) as the dominant means of management control [3].	Any means adapt to the specific circumstances and strategy can be as the dominant means of control.
	Control methods [12]	The object of the management control includes variety of accounting elements. Assets, costs and other factors are widespread concern in the management control.	Include not only formal specific control methods, including some informal control methods (such as corporate culture and values).

The reasons lies in the respondents of the questionnaire, as most of them did not take it seriously and the questionnaire was too professional. At the same time, when choosing the samples, the country conditions and culture were taken into account; civil investigation is generally difficult to obtain information in China, especially in the case where the respondents and investigators are unfamiliar to each other. To overcome these difficulties, the study used the encounter survey method, which selects individuals who are easily accessible for the survey sample. The respondents of the questionnaire cannot fully representative all the investors in China. However, this study is an exploratory study. The samples are typical in this study, can show a tendency of the development of the management control.

In this study, a total of 326 questionnaires were distributed to the respondents, among them, 300 questionnaires were returned which represents 92.02 % response rate. Among the returned questionnaires 249 questionnaires were valid and 51 questionnaires were invalid. Gender distribution in this survey included 109 female respondents which accounting for 43.78 % and 140 male respondents which accounting for 56.24 %. The results on education and knowledge background show that most of the respondents have good background on finance and accounting knowledge. Among the total respondents included in the analysis 87.15 % had learned finance and accounting and 12.85 % respondents did not have any background in finance and accounting. The results also show that 63.86 % respondents have ability to understand annual reports of listed companies while 36.14 % respondents are not able to understand the annual reports and financial information. In investment strategy, 65.06 % respondents chose the "long-term investment" and 34.94 % respondents chose the "short-term speculative".

2.3.2.3 The Reliability Analysis of the Questionnaire

To ensure the reliability and accuracy of the conclusions, we first conducted the survey questionnaire reliability analysis, the results are as follows:

Reliability Results

Number of items in scale: 22

Number of valid cases: 249
Number of cases with missing data: 0
Missing data were deleted: casewise

SUMMARY STATISTICS FOR SCALE

Mean: 76.2329	Sum: 18,982.0000
Standard Deviation: 7.5280	Variance: 56.6713
Skewness: −.26457	Kurtosis: −.1099
Minimum: 43.0000	Maximum: 106.0000
Cronbach's alpha: .6731	Standardized alpha: .6853

In calculating the reliability, the questions raised from the opposite direction were taken score adjustments.

Table 2.2 Demand on management control of investors

Part one	Mean	Std. Dev.	N	Std. Err	t-value	df	p	Attitude
Question 1	4.333	0.874	249	0.055	24.080	248	0.000	Agree
Question 2	4.000	0.950	249	0.060	16.604	248	0.000	Agree
Question 3	3.968	0.884	249	0.056	17.280	248	0.000	Agree
Question 4	2.116	1.088	249	0.069	−12.813	248	0.000	Oppose
Question 5	1.888	1.072	249	0.068	−16.379	248	0.000	Oppose

The reliability test results show a Cronbach's alpha of 0.6731 and a Standardized alpha is 0.6583. A Cronbach's alpha value of 67.31 % is considered to be a good confidence interval. Therefore, the survey questionnaire is scientific. Also, the study conclusion is reliable.

2.3.3 Empirical Results and Correlation Analysis

In order to determine the attitude of investors to management control, bilateral t-test under the conditions of 5 % is used through STAT.

2.3.3.1 Investor Demand for Management Control

This was a pre-procedure used to determine whether investors have demands for management control or not. The other four parts are indicates the investors' preference to different types of management control. If investor is against a particular type of management control, it is likely to be due to the fact that investor think such management control does not have any effect.

This section includes five questions (question 1–5) which inspects the role of management control (questions 1–3), the impact of management control to investment decisions (Question 4) and the impact of management control to the company (Question 5). From the results shown in Table 2.2, the investigators have shown a tendency, and have a relatively strong demand on management control.

2.3.3.2 Investors' Demand on Objectives and Styles on Management Control

This section includes five questions (questions 6–10) which inspect three aspects; the investor's investment objective (Question 6), management control objectives (questions 7–9) as well as management control styles (Question 10). The section also compares the two types of management control.

The results in Table 2.3 show that most of the respondents agreed on the presence of two different types of management control objectives (questions 7 and 8). On the other hand, respondents have not shown any preference to the management control

Table 2.3 Demand on the goal and style of management control

Part two	Mean	Std. Dev.	N	Std. Err	t-value	df	p	Attitude
Question 6	3.859	0.972	249	0.062	13.951	248	0.000	Agree
Question 7	3.855	0.989	249	0.063	13.642	248	0.000	Agree
Question 8	4.169	0.790	249	0.050	23.333	248	0.000	Agree
Question 9	3.855	0.973	249	0.062	13.873	248	0.000	Agree
Question 10	2.936	1.087	249	0.069	−0.933	248	0.352	Neutral

style. Furthermore, in order to determine the investors demand for management control objectives, questions 7 and 8 were compared. The comparison results are presented in Table 2.4. The results show that respondents pay more attention on improvement of operational efficiency.

According to investment objective and capital market information, Investors showed a strong preference on internal management control objectives.

1. **The investor's investment objective.** The purpose of investment is to obtain a normal investment income and the excess return. In order for Investor to obtain normal return two conditions must be met: first, the management of listed companies should be efficient and second, listed companies should develop a reasonable dividend policy. These two conditions depend on a good management control of the listed companies as the core management controls. Management control that adapts to corporate strategy can improve the performance of enterprises; only effective internal management controls can ensure that investor's interests in listed companies are not compromised. Therefore, management control can ensure investors receive regular investment income. If Investors want to obtain excess returns are mainly dependent on the analysis of financial reports. According to Beaver [8], the financial statements are mainly used to find undervalued stocks on the market for investment to obtain excess returns on investment. But the premise of obtaining excess returns is the normal operation of the capital market; the phenomenon of the stock price is overvalued or undervalued can be corrected by the market. The reality is that the capital market operates inefficiently in China and the quality of financial statements of listed companies is low. Moreover, the poor quality of financial statements of listed companies is not a simple internal act, but a social phenomenon subject to various aspects of social factors. Therefore, even if listed companies establish a sound accounting control type of management control, it may not be able to meet the needs of investors. China's capital market conditions determine the investor's investment tendency. According to Question 6, respondents agree that their best hope is to invest in companies with high operating efficiency. Thus, Respondents pay more attention to improve operational efficiency than to provide true accounting information.
2. **Capital market information disclosure does not meet investor demand**. China's capital market is still in its infancy, and the rules and regulations are not perfect. Capital markets are basically dominated by accounting information, and these accounting information are basically historical information. There is a big

Table 2.4 Differences of demand on the goal of management control

	Question 7	Question 8	t-value	df	p	Valid N	Valid N	Question 7	Question 8	F-ratio	p
	Mean	Mean						Std. Dev.	Std. Dev.		
Question 7 vs. Question 8	3.855	4.169	−3.903	496	0.000	249	249	0.989	0.790	1.567	0.000

information gap between the information provided by the capital market and the information required by investors for decision making. The information provided by capital market cannot fully guarantee the investors demand to make investment decisions (Wu Liansheng [9]; Lu Zhengfei and Liu Guijin [10]). Thus, even to establish a perfect internal accounting control, its role is limited to providing real legitimate historical accounting information. To be able to carry out scientific and correct investment decisions in order to obtain investment returns, investors will inevitably produce internal management and control preferences. This type of management control established on the basis of the company's strategy is able to explain the company's future development trends and circumstances. If we can be assured that this type of management control play a role in the company's production and management, it can greatly ease the adverse impact on investors.

Respondents showed no preference in the style of management control. This may be due to the respondent's limitations to the strategy recognition. At present, company strategic awareness is generally low in China. Many companies did not even establish their own Strategic plan. Therefore, even if the investor has an initial Strategy idea, the strategy content, such as Strategy classification, etc., were not available. In the research on management control trends, using strategies related terms (such as "defensive" and "offensive") is inevitable. Therefore, we hypothesized that the respondents did not show bias in the answer to question 10.

2.3.3.3 Investors' Demand on the Relationship of Management Control and Company Environment

This section includes three questions (questions 11–13). This section includes the relationship of management control and corporate environment. From the results of Table 2.5, we found that the respondent's attitude maintain a consistent with internal management controls.

Investor's choice of internal management control mode is mainly due to China's capital market particularity. In present stage, the environment is more complex in the survival and development process, Listing Corporation should consider the various problems in the process of business operation of in the process and the complex social political environment. Theoretical transition abroad also confirmed this point. In the initial stage of management control, many company used the single management control model. Those single management control model includes all various factors, such as political environment. With economic development, economic and social have a huge change and companies' environment has changed dramatically. The original single model is not suited to the new environment. Then the diversification models of management control are set up. Similarly, China is in a transformation period, the companies are surrounded by uncertainty; investors therefore need a specific management control model which is adapted to the company environment. In determining the management control model, the company's strategy and the specific circumstances plays a decisive role.

Table 2.5 The investors demand of management control and corporate environments

Part three	Mean	Std. Dev.	N	Std. Err	t-value	df	p	Attitude
Question 11	2.651	1.005	249	0.064	–5.485	248	0.000	Oppose
Question 12	2.618	1.094	249	0.069	–5.504	248	0.000	Oppose
Question 13	4.052	0.763	249	0.048	21.765	248	0.000	Agree

Table 2.6 The investors demand of management control and design structure

Part four	Mean	Std. Dev.	N	Std. Err	t-value	df	p	Attitude
questions 14	2.671	1.061	249	0.067	–4.899	248	0.000	Oppose
questions 15	3.590	0.824	249	0.052	11.312	248	0.000	Agree
questions 16	3.659	0.880	249	0.056	11.812	248	0.000	Agree
questions 17	3.811	0.912	249	0.058	14.041	248	0.000	Agree

2.3.3.4 Investors Demand for Management Control Design Structure

This section includes four questions (questions 14–17). This section includes two aspects; the management control design ideas (questions 14–15) and management control design focus (issue 16–17). From the results in Table 2.6, we can see that respondents have shown a tendency to demand for the two types of management control design ideas.

From the results in Table 2.6, we can also see that respondents have shown a tendency to demand for the two types of management control design process. In order to further determine the investors' management controls focus of the design process, we compared Question 16 and Question 17. As seen in Table 2.7, at 10 % significance level, the score of question 17 was greater than question 16. So in the designing process of management control, investors pay more attention to accounting elements.

According to the limitations of respondents to corporate strategy and the dominant position of accounting in the company, investors showed strong demand for internal accounting controls in the structure design stage of management control. As a response to question 10, the respondents did not show the clear attitude. Respondents only have a preliminary understanding of corporate strategy. They recognize that company's strategy is important to the management control design, but how to implement and convert it into a workable management control system is above investors' capacity. Meanwhile, as long as accounting is an important method of management control, investors naturally has a strong knowledge on the accounting. At the same time, China has experienced a long period of planned economy, supervision and control has always been the center of accounting work. So the accounting controls have received considerable attention in China. In the past decades during the planned economy period, businesses were ancillary units of government department, whose main task was to complete scheduled assigned by the government. Also, this schedule is assigned based on accounting data. Accounting play an important role in the enterprise management, it is a primary means of

Table 2.7 Investors demand in the design process

	Question 16 Mean	Question 17 Mean	t-value	df	p	Valid N	Valid N	Question 16 Std. Dev.	Question 17 Std. Dev.	F-ratio	p
Question 16 vs. Question 17	3.659	3.811	−1.901	496	0.058	249	249	0.880	0.912	1.074	0.576

Table 2.8 Demand on investors to management control

Part five	Mean	Std. Dev.	N	Std. Err	t-value	df	p	Attitude
Question 18	3.707	1.062	249	0.067	10.504	248	0.000	Agree
Question 19	3.438	0.896	249	0.057	7.706	248	0.000	Agree
Question 20	3.912	0.808	249	0.051	17.796	248	0.000	Agree
Question 21	3.177	1.157	249	0.073	2.409	248	0.017	Agree
Question 22	3.968	0.827	249	0.052	18.461	248	0.000	Agree

government to control the enterprise. After the reforms, accounting also plays an important role in the development of enterprises. Thus, investors thought that the cycle of accounting method is important to the company's management control and Investors are likely to keep the consistency of management control and strategy through the accounting cycle design of management control. In addition, investors have some impact to internal accounting controls design.

2.3.3.5 Investor Demand for Management Control Method

This part includes five questions (questions 18–22). This part comprises of two aspects, the choice of control method (Question 18), and the relationship between the different methods (Questions 19–22). Table 2.8 shows that, respondents prefer to choose internal management control methods. However, in the relationship between the different methods, respondents prefer to choose the internal accounting controls.

An internal accounting control method is widespread concern by investors. It may be due to the following reasons:

1. Accounting plays a dominant position in the enterprise, so the accounting control is very important in people's minds. At present, China's enterprise management level is still relatively low. Since the reform and opening up, companies learn from the advanced theory and experience abroad, but the management level of most company is still low. In the current management models, accounting control also played an important role, so investors has always pay more attention to the accounting and accounting management.
2. "Accounting Law" provides a legal basis for accounting. China is in the process of legalization, investors' awareness of the law is increasing, and the attention of the relevant laws is growing. "Accounting Law", clearly stated, "All units shall establish, build the whole system of internal accounting controls of the unit," which provides the basis for the accounting control in the law. The laws promote the implementation of accounting control. Before the "accounting law" was promulgated, the media has advertised the "accounting law" many times. So investors has a clear understanding on the role of the "accounting law" .thus, investors believe that the accounting control method is an effective means of control, and can be protected by law.

2.3.4 Conclusions and Recommendations

From the above analysis, we can draw some basic conclusions. Investors have a relatively strong demand on management control, and Investors will consider the impact of management control to their investment. Therefore it is important for listed companies establish and improve management control.

For listed companies to establish what type of internal management controls, investors showed a clear hierarchy. From the second and fifth parts of the questionnaire, we can clearly see this level of performance. For management control objectives (Part II) and management control development model (Part III), investors thought that internal management control is a good management tool to achieve the company's strategy. Design ideas on management control (Part IV), investors showed a preference for the method of internal management control or internal accounting controls. In the control method for management control (Part V), investors showed a preference for the method of accounting controls.

Investor demand for management control, according to the line from direction to operational, from the internal management control to internal accounting control. According to the answer of Questionnaire, investors have strong demand on establishing internal management control, but in the management control practice, investors rely on internal accounting control method.

With the development of capital market and management control, the management control based on internal management control will be established. Only in this way, investors' demand on management control can be met fundamentally. However, the conditions of establishing a perfect internal management control system do not exist. Especially, the existing control method cannot meet the demand of management control. Therefore, a complex type of management control should be built. In other words, the complex type of management control is a forward-looking and practical management control, can meet investors' demand.

The control objectives of Management control should be consistent with the internal management control objectives. The control objectives of Management control are committed to improving the company's operating efficiency and promote the realization of corporate strategy. Control mode selection should also be consistent with the internal management control, according to the company's strategy and the environment. The design of Management control is similar to the design of internal management control or internal accounting control. The method of Management control method is similar to the method of internal accounting control.

In addition to limitations of the questionnaire survey, the questionnaire samples also had some impact for this study. Since samples were not a random sample, so the conclusions will have some impact to range of application. In terms of content and object, there is no in-depth comparative study on design ideas and control methods for management control. Different control design ideas and control methods will be subject to various factors. But in this study we have not considered those factors. In this study, the relationships of different types of management control methods are ignored. Therefore, these aspects are future research directions.

Appendix

Survey questions designed of Management control demand of listed companies' investor

Question 1. Management Control System is an important part of listed company operating mechanism.

Question 2. Effective management control of listed companies can reduce the risk of fraud on investors.

Question 3. Effective management control of listed companies can improve operating efficiency and improve company performance.

Question 4. The merits of the company's management control will not affect your investment decisions.

Question 5. Lack of management control of listed companies will not affect the survival and development.

Question 6. When investing, most want to invest in companies with high operating efficiency.

Question 7. To ensure safety of the assets, provide true and reliable accounting information is the main objective of management control.

Question 8. Management control goal is not just a simple troubleshooting, but should focus on improving operating efficiencies.

Question 9. Management control objectives should be consistent with the company's strategic goals.

Question 10. Management control is a defensive mechanism; just to prevent damage occurred.

Question 11. Management control mode is not affected by certain internal and external factors which produce a variety of modes.

Question 12. One management control mode for the vast majority of the company exists.

Question 13. Management control's mode should be depending on the type of the company's strategy and the company's specific circumstances.

Question 14. If not based on company's strategy to design, management control is also able to play a role in normal.

Question 15 management control designed according to the Company's accounting business can be a good play.

Question 16. The core of the management control is related to the corporate strategy.

Question 17. Management control design process needs to focus on accounting factors (assets, liabilities, costs, etc.).

Question 18. Management control can used formal control (regulation), can also used informal control (corporate culture, values).

Question 19. Accounting work and accounting work is the most important quality control management control methods.

Question 20. Compared with other means of control, internal auditing should receive special attention in management control.

Question 21. As long to complete management control objectives, the specific control methods adopted, the use of several control methods are not important.

Question 22. The main control method depends on the company's strategy and their own characteristics.

References

1. Fayol H (1930) General and industrial administration. International Management Institute, Geneva
2. Koontz H, O'Donnell C, Weirich H (1980) Management. McGraw-Hill Kogakusha Ltd, New York
3. Yan Dawu, Yang Youhong (2001) Tentative on the construction of internal control framework. Account Res 2:9–14
4. Spicer BH, Balle V (1983) Management accounting and control systems and the economics of internal organization. Account Organ Soc 8:73–96
5. Zhu Rongen (2001) Some views on establishing and improving internal control system in China. Account Res 1:24–31
6. O'Reilly-Allen M, McMullen D (2002) Internal control reporting and users' perceptions of financial statement reliability. Am Bus Rev 20:100–108
7. Hermanson HM (2000) An analysis of the demand for reporting on internal control. Account Horiz 14:325–342
8. Beaver WH, Xue Yunkui (1999) Financial reporting: an accounting revolution. DUFE Press, Dalian
9. Wu Liansheng (2000) A survey and an analysis of investors' demands for listed companies' accounting information. Econ Res J 4:41–48
10. Lu Zhengfei, Liu Guijin (2002) An exploration on China private investors' information demand and decision-variable choice. Econ Res 4:36–43
11. Giovanni B, Bedeian AG (1974) A conspectus of management control theory: 1900–1972. Acad Manage J 17(2):292–305
12. Zhang Xianzhi (2003) Management control systems based on management procedures [J]. Finance & Acc 25(11):65–79

Chapter 3
Enterprise Management Control Systems

3.1 Control and Types of Control

3.1.1 The Connotation of Control

Control is that the controller keeps activities or people in track and prevents them from moving randomly or beyond the scope, making them follow the controller's intention. Thus, there are four components of control: the subject, the object, the objective and the process. The subject of control is the controller; the object of control refers to the controlled activities or people; control objective is the intention of controller and control process is the control activities. Control can be regarded as the synonyms of correction, influence, manipulation and adjustment, but it cannot be interpreted as the same.

Control can be classified as external control and internal control from the perspective of control subject. External control is that the controllers are outsider of the organization (or enterprises), that is, the subject and object come from different organizations, e.g. controls from government sector, financial control, taxation control, government audit control and etc. External control also includes the control from intermediary agencies and the audit by CPA.

Internal control is that the controller comes from inside the organization, or the subject and the object are in the same organization. Therefore, internal control is defined by 1992 COSO Report as follows:

Internal control is a process, effected by an entity's board of directors, management, and other personnel, to provide reasonable assurance about the achievement of the entity's objectives with regard to reliability of reporting, effectiveness and efficiency of operations and compliance with applicable laws and regulations.

X. Zhang, *Enterprise Management Control Systems in China*, Understanding China,
DOI 10.1007/978-3-642-54715-7_3,

COSO stated the enterprise risk management integrated framework in 2004 based on internal control framework:

> Enterprise risk management is a process, effected by an entity's board of directors, management and other personnel, applied in strategy setting and across the enterprise, designed to identify potential events that may affect the entity and manage risks to be within its risk appetite, to provide reasonable assurance regarding the achievement of entity's objectives.

According to the descriptions above, both internal control and enterprise risk management are process, effected by enterprise, designed to manage risks, and to provide reasonable assurance regarding the achievement of entity objectives. From this meaning, they are essentially enterprise control. The subjects of control are the staffs including the entity's board of directors and management; the objects of control are operating activities at every level of the organization; the objectives of control are the implementation of strategies, the reliability of financial reporting, the effectiveness and efficiency of operations and the compliance with applicable laws and regulations; the process of control is the process provides reasonable assurance with regard to the achievement of the entity's control objectives.

3.1.2 Types of Control by Subject of Control

There are three levels of people in an organization: the board of directors, management and personnels. Thus control can be classified as:

1. Corporate governance control: the major controllers are the board of directors
2. Management control: usually implemented by managers
3. Task control: employees are the main people who implement this kind of control

3.1.2.1 Corporate Governance Control

The primary role of corporate governance control is to establish strategic management control, including the determination of corporate goals, corporate strategy and tactics, responsibility and rights of management, the establishment of corporate supervisory mechanism. From the perspective of internal control, the control from the board of directors is essentially strategic formulation which is the process of deciding on the goals of the organization and the strategies for attaining these goals. Strategies are general and major plans, in which senior managers indicate how organizations should use their resources to meet their objectives. The organization goals encompass both financial and non-financial objectives. In the strategy formulation process, the goals of the organization are usually given, although occasionally strategic thinking can focus on the goals themselves. There are many ways to achieve the objectives of organizations. Different organizations will choose different approaches during strategy formulation.

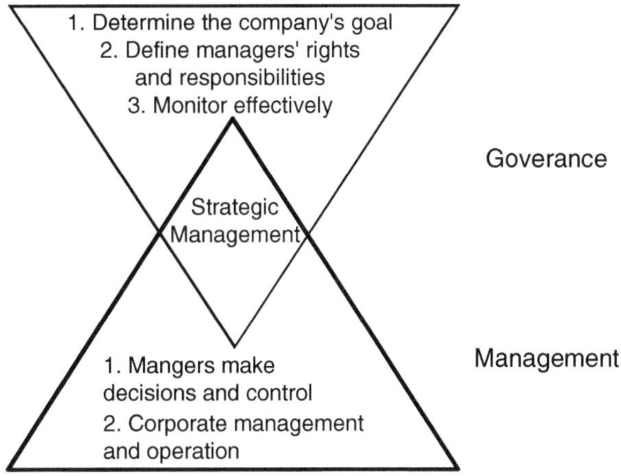

Fig. 3.1 Corporate governance and management control

3.1.2.2 Management Control

Management control is the process conducted mainly by managers. Managers monitor other members of the organization to implement the organization's strategies. The purpose of management control is strategic implementation, which will fulfill the organization's objectives. Management control involves a variety of activities, including planning, coordination, communicating information, evaluating information, deciding what, if any action should be taken, and influencing people to change their behavior.

There are, however, significant differences between strategy formulation and management control:

First, strategy formulation is the selection of new strategy; management control is the implementing of those strategies.

Second, from the standpoint of systems design, strategy formulation is essentially unsystematic and management control is systematic.

Third, analysis of a proposed strategy usually involves relatively few people. By contrast, the management control involves managers and staffs at all levels in the organization.

Forth, strategy formulation only involves several parts of the organization. When some parts of strategies are changed, the rest are unaffected. By contrast, the management control process must involve the whole organization in order to coordinate.

Corporate governance control and management control are connected by strategic management. Such connections are shown in Fig. 3.1 above[1]:

[1] Yang Youhong [1].

3.1.2.3 Task Control

Task control is the process of assuring that specific tasks are carried out effectively and efficiently. The standards which the task control must follow are parts of management control process.

There are, however, significant differences between management control and task control:

First, task control systems are usually seen as scientific, whereas management control can never be reduced to a science. In definition, management control involves the behaviors of managers, which cannot be expressed by equations. There are serious errors if principles developed by management scientists for task control are applied to management control issues.
Second, in management control, managers interact with other managers; in task control, the interaction is between managers and non-managers such as operating process.
Third, the focus of management control is organization unit rather than the specific task assigned which is the focus of task control.
Forth, management control is concerned with the broadly defined activities. Managers should decide what, if any, action should be taken so that the organization will achieve the objectives, while task control requires activities should be complied with standards with little or no judgment.

Strategic formulation, management control and task control are closely connected and they are influenced by and interact with each other. Internal control is an organic synthesis of them.

3.1.3 Control by Objectives

Based on the objective, control can be grouped into four general categories: control of attaining corporate strategic objectives, control of the reliability of financial reporting, control of the effectiveness and efficiency of operations and control of complying with applicable laws and regulations. They are different types of control. The control of the reliability of financial reporting belongs to accounting control. The control of the effectiveness and efficiency of operations is part of management control. The control of complying with applicable laws and regulations belongs to enactments control. The control of accomplishing strategic objectives belongs to strategy control.

3.1.3.1 Accounting Control

The objective of accounting control is the reliability of financial reporting. This objective determines that internal accounting control is actually financial accounting control. First, it focuses on financial reporting which is external reporting rather than the internal reporting. Second, it also emphasizes the reliability of financial reporting instead of the relevance. The reason is that relevance is decided by accounting standards and accounting systems but not internal control. Another view on the objective of internal accounting control is to assure the quality of accounting information. It includes the assurance of the relevance and reliability for both financial accounting and management accounting. Compared to financial accounting, management accounting is more relevant to the effectiveness and efficiency of operations. Financial accounting provides reliable information to outside stockholders. Internal accounting control emphasizes the reliability of financial reporting which is the base of internal control.

3.1.3.2 Management Control

This objective of management control is the effectiveness and efficiency of operations, which includes both the effectiveness and the efficiency of operations. Efficiency is not only the core of economics but also the basic goal of operation. Effectiveness is the core of management as well as the basic goal of administration. Both efficiency and effectiveness are objectives of internal control and plays an important role in the process of internal control.

3.1.3.3 Enactment Control

Compared to accounting control and management control, enactment control has special characteristics. However, it is also connected to accounting and management control. Since both the reliability of financial reporting and the effectiveness and efficiency of operations must be achieved after the compliance with laws and regulations, the enactment control lays fundamental for accounting control and management control.

3.1.3.4 Strategic Control

The objective of strategy control is to accomplish the goals of an enterprise. Strategic control includes strategic analysis, strategic choice and strategic implementation. It set the direction for control in an enterprise. To achieve overall objectives, management control and accounting control follow the guidance from strategy control.

3.1.4 Control Type by Process

An entity or an organization grows by the processes of resources investment, operating management, outputs of outcomes and distribution of benefits. Thus, control can be classified into four types based on different stage of those processes.

3.1.4.1 Resources Investment

An entity or an organization needs both resources-human resources and capital resources to survive and thrive. Control of resources investment focuses on human resources and capital resources. From the angle of finance and accounting, capital resource investment includes capital raising control and capital investment control. The direction, quantity, quality and structure of resource investment determine the effectiveness and effect of the organization's operation.

3.1.4.2 Operating Management

The operating management is the integration of supply, production and sale. In order to get output, an enterprise is required to manage operation after investing resources. It suggests that the enterprise must control sales price, sales revenue and cash inflows as well as costs such as procurement costs, production costs, administration expenses and operating expenses during operating process. Control of operating management ensures the achievement of objective of corporations and influences the efficiency and effectiveness of output.

3.1.4.3 Output of Outcomes

Outcomes cover the effectiveness and efficiency of output. Efficiency is the ratio of output to input, including assets turnover, return on equity, cost profit margin. Effectiveness is determined by output and their objectives, including revenue, profit, and capital gain. Control of output outcomes includes output efficiency control and output effectiveness control, which is a type of output control not process control. The distribution of benefits to managers and employees is influenced and decided by the effectiveness of output control.

3.1.4.4 Distribution of Benefits

Benefit distribution control is distribution of output among stakeholders in a broad sense. Stakeholders include investors, managers, employees, and government. It is usually based on the contributions to total output by stakeholders. Benefit distribution control establishes relationship between benefit distribution and results control, that is, only when stakeholders make contribution to the total output, can they yield profit. In its narrower sense, benefit distribution control is a mechanism in which managers are forced to make greater contributions in order to obtain profits.

These four types of control are mutually connected inclusive which are linked by a cycle of operations. It means that resources investment control is the base of operating management, and output control will be available on the basis of operating management and resources input control. Obviously, benefits allocation control needs to be exerted after the three above.

The hierarchy of these four types of control is shown in Fig. 3.2:

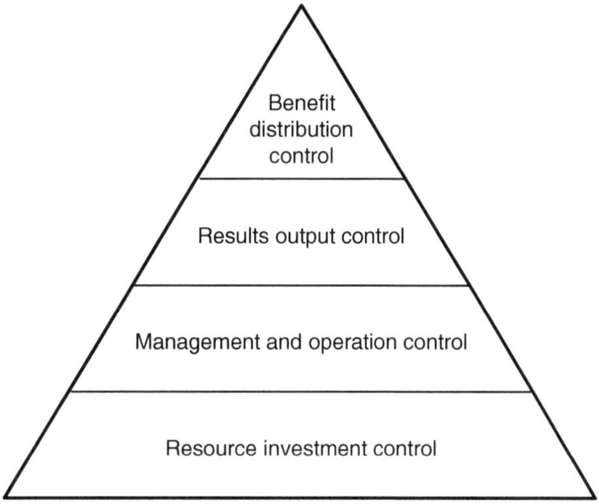

Fig. 3.2 Hierarchy of control types

3.1.5 Control Types by Different Contents

The contents of control are related to the activities of an organization. Fayol divides activities of organization into six categories:

Technical activity: production, research and development
Business activity: purchase, sales and exchange
Financial activity: looking for capital and using capital in the most proper way
Safety activity: safeguarding assets and people
Accounting activity: inventory inspection, the statement of financial position, costs and statistics
Administration activity: planning, organizing, leading, staffing and controlling

Therefore, from the perspective of control contents, internal control can be classified as production and R&D control, procurement and sales control, financial control, assets and human resources control and accounting control with management control underlying all the five types of control.

3.1.5.1 Production and R&D Control

The production plays a significant role in the process of creating value and using value. Amount, variety, quality and costs are closely related to production, and production control is the focus of internal control. In the modern competitive market environment, R&D has significant influence on the quality of production, costs of production, and the variety of productions. Only when enterprises strengthen the R&D control and grasp core technology, they can be survivals and win the development.

3.1.5.2 Procurement and Sales Control

The purchasing and sales are mainly geared to the needs of market, enterprises purchase from supplier and sale to customers. In market economy conditions, purchasing and sales control plays a significant role in the process of achieving internal control objectives, and purchasing and sales control becomes more difficult and complex when the complexity of the market environment strengthens. Purchasing control refers to purchase cost, procurement quality, delivery time and payment time, and so on. Sales control refers to sale price, quantity of sale, selling expenses, payment collection, and etc.

3.1.5.3 Financial Control

Financial activities include financing activities, investing activities and distribution activities. Financial control should enhance the control of these three activities. Because these three controls are closely related to the creation of enterprise value, the core of internal control is financial control. Financing control includes financing volume, capital structure, ownership structure and cost of capital. Investing control is concerned with investment direction, investment structure, investment risks, and assets utilization. Distribution control involves compensation levels, incentive methods and dividend policy.

3.1.5.4 Assets and Human Resources Control

Assets and human are two major resources of enterprises, and the security of assets and human is a basic requirement of internal control. That assets and human resources which are safe and integrated means that resources are reasonable utilized, not being damaged or wasted. Accordingly, assets control refers to the security and integrity of assets control, efficient use of assets control; human resources control refers to human security control, human resource configuration control, labor productivity.

3.1.5.5 Accounting Control

Accounting is an information system, and accounting becomes a universal commercial language. The accounting information affects financial situation, operating results and cash flows of the organization. The objective of accounting control is to ensure the relevance of accounting information by controlling the reliability of accounting information.

There are overlaps between different types of control. The importance of classification standard is different, so there are different levels of control types. To study internal control, focus should be on leading and key types. Since objective is key and dominating factor for control, the types classified by objective should be core of research. Therefore, management control and accounting control are the main categories of control which includes other types of control based on different standards.

3.2 The Connotation and Objectives of Management Control

Management control is a process, effected by internal controllers, to provide reasonable assurance of effective management activities. If the controllers of management control are considered as hierarchy which is mainly consisted of managers and other members of the organization and the effectiveness of management activities is considered as the organization's strategies. Management control is the process by which managers influence other members of the organization to implement the organization's strategies.[2] The objective of management control is the implementation of strategies so that the goals of organization can be achieved. Accordingly the connotation of management can be described as follows.

3.2.1 The Connotation of Management Control from the Point of Functions

From the point of management control functions, the connotation of management control can be divided into extensive meaning, normal meaning and narrow meaning. From the point of extensive meaning, management control is a process established to execute management functions, especially control functions. The connotation of management control refers to strategy control and operational control. Management control is established to coordinate among organizations to ensure the achievement of organizational goals, and management control can be divided into planning, organizing and leadership function.[3] William Newman (1961) regards the connotation of management control as the function of management control. Control is the basis of management control, and management control covers every area of management. In this connotation of management control, management control includes qualitative control and quantitative control, that is, qualitative control and quantitative control are of equal importance.

From the point of normal meaning, management control is a system which consists of standard setting, performance evaluation, and correcting deviation. In this point of view, the core of management control is a strategy implementation control. Accordingly, in this connotation of management control, the characteristic of management control is quantitative control, that is, quantitative control is the core of management control.

---

[2] Anthony [2].

[3] Maciariello and Kirby [3].

From the point of narrow meaning, management control refers to responsibility accounting. The characteristic of management control is a monetary measurement control, that is, monetary measurement is core of management control.

There are three kinds of connotation of management control which is classified by different functions, and each classification has been studied by professional scholars. Management scholars pay more attention on extensive meaning of management control, strategy scholars and financial scholars pay more attention on normal meaning of management control and accounting scholars pay more attention on the narrow meaning of management control. In this book, we employ the normal explanation of management control.

3.2.2 *The Connotation of Management Control from the Point of Management Controllers*

The subjects of management control are managers and other personnel. Management control also can be regarded as a control which is implemented by management to coordinate management activities. The mainstay of management control is managers, and management control can't be implemented successfully without the coordination of other personnel. Besides managers, the subjects of management control include board of directors who are representatives of stockholders and staff who are representatives of personnel. From this point of view, the connotation of management control can be divided into extensive meaning, normal meaning and narrow meaning.

From the point of extensive meaning, management control includes corporate governance control or strategy control which is mainly implemented by board of directors; management control which is mainly implemented by managers; and task control or operation control which is mainly implemented by personnel. The three levels of control give service to organization strategy goals together.

From the point of narrow meaning, management control refers to management control which is mainly implemented by managers, excluding task control or operational control.

From the point of normal meaning, management control is a process which is implemented by managers to affect other personnel to achieve strategic goals. In this point of view, management control mainly refers to control by manager, and involves board of directors' control and personnel control.

In this book, we employ the normal explanation of management control.

3.2.3 *The Objectives and Status of Management Control*

The objective of management control is to implement a strategy so that the organization goals can be achieved. Specifically, the objective of management control is to coordinate organization activities to ensure the achievement of organization goals. Organization goals can be divided into individual goals and goals of different levels.

Organization purpose is the direct and most important mission of the organization, which is established to meet the needs of customers and society. The objective of organization refers to goals which are specific and of short-term. There are a lot of objectives of the organization, which are established to constrain the activities of managers and other personnel. The goals of the organizations are specific long-term aspiration of the organizations, which are established to meet the needs of owners. The relationships among different levels of goals and individual goals are interactive and interplay. The key to achieve organization goals are the effectiveness of organization activities which refers to the efficiency and effectiveness of operation.

3.2.3.1 The Effect of Operations

The effect of operations refers to the output of operations. In the modern enterprise system, the output results which enterprises pursue generally refer to capital appreciation and profit. When it comes to the study of the efficiency of operations, the connotation of value-preserved and value-added of capital and the connotation profit should be clearly defined, and the relationship between them should be clarified.

(1) The connotation of value-preserved and value-added of capital

When it comes to study the connotation of value-preserved and value-added of capital, we should clarify the connotation of capital and the connotation of value-preserved and value-added. Enterprise capital can be divided into financial capital and physical capital.

International accounting standards committee (IASC) defines financial capital as "currency invested or purchasing power invested which are the synonyms for net assets or equity", and physical capital is defined as "operational capacity which is measured by daily production capacity of enterprises". Generally, the connotation of capital refers to financial capital in accounting.

The hinge of value-preserved is value-preserved, as the additional amount besides value-preserved is the value-added. The connotation of value-preserved and value-added is based on capital preservation theory. Capital preservation theory which is closely associated with accounting is the core of the corporate earnings measurement theory. Value-preserved of capital refers to financial capital maintenance and physical capital maintenance. Financial capital maintenance means the capital value which is invested by owners is preserved intact, that is, the final value of capital equals to the initial capital value. Physical capital maintenance means operation capacity which is invested by owners is preserved intact, that is, the final actual operation capacity equals to initial actual operational capacity.

Are capital maintenance and value-preserved totally the same? Capital maintenance and value-preserved are closely related, but there are differences between them. Value-preserved is the basis of capital maintenance. Value-preserved, guaranteeing a normal income of the owners, promoting the increment of capital, and evaluating the performance of operators are objectives of capital maintenance.

When comes to the connotation of value-preserved and value-added. We should consider whether the answer is financial or physical capital value preservation and increase. It's necessary to distinguish these two concepts. Actually, firstly, physical capital value-preserved refers to technological progress, capital structure, product structure, price structure. So it's difficult to accurately measure physical capital. Secondly, the footholds of physical capital value-preserved and financial capital preserved are value preservation, and financial capital value-preserved can totally substitute for physical capital preservation.[4] Thirdly, which is the priority when financial capital preservation value is larger than physical capital value-preserved? The answer is financial capital value-preserved because it can realize financial capital preservation and physical capital preservation at the same time, and the measurement of income is reasonable. Otherwise, it can only realize physical capital preservation, and current earnings contain earnings which are converted from initial ownership equity. Going-concern enterprise will not distribute investment capital for the purpose of physical capital preservation. Then we can come to the conclusion that financial capital preservation and value maintenance and appreciation are more practical than physical capital preservation.

(2) The connotation of profit and the relation of it to value-preserved and value-added of capital

Profit generally is equal to income (or output) minus costs (or investment). The elements of profit include accounting profit and economic profit. And the equations are described as follows:

$$Accounting\ profit = Income - Accounting\ cost$$

$$Economic\ profit = Income - Economic\ cost$$

From the equations above, the relations of accounting cost and economic cost can be described as follows:

$$\begin{aligned} Economic\ profit &= Income - \left(Accounting\ cost + Implicit\ costs\left(or\ Normal\ profit\right)\right) \\ &= \left(Income - Accounting\ cost\right) - Implicit\ costs\left(or\ Normal\ profit\right) \\ &= Accounting\ profit - Implicit\ costs\left(or\ Normal\ profit\right) \end{aligned}$$

[4](1) Financial capital preservation is usually consistent with physical capital preservation when there are no significant changes in price and technology circumstance. (2) General purchasing power of financial capital preservation can realize physical capital preservation when there are only significant changes in price. (3) When there are significant changes in price and technology circumstance, the achievement of financial capital preservation means the achievement of physical capital preservation though financial capital preservation isn't totally equal to physical capital preservation. Technical progress can raise productivity and reduce investment with other things equals.

The accounting theory of capital preservation is the core of the corporate earnings measurement theory. So value-preserved and value-added of capital are closely related to profit, the relation of them can be described as follows without the consideration of changes of the capital, price and profit distribution.

$$Beginning\,capital = Ending\,capital + Profit$$
$$Change\,in\,capital = Beginning\,capital - Ending\,capital = Accounting\,profit$$

When accounting profit = 0, capital maintenance can be described as follows:

$$Value - preserved\,of\,capital = Ending\,capital - Beginning\,capital$$

When accounting profit > 0, and economic profit = 0, capital preservation can be described as follows:

$$Value - preserved\,of\,capital = Ending\,capital - Beginning\,capital \times (1 + Normal\,profit\,rate)$$

When economic profit > 0, and capital appreciation can be described as follows:

$$Value - added\,of\,capital = Ending\,capital - Beginning\,capital \times (1 + Normal\,profit\,rate)$$

The equations above show that profit is the core of value-preserved and value-added of capital, especially economic profit.

3.2.3.2 Operating Efficiency

Operating efficiency refers to the ratio of income to costs. The elements of operating efficiency include economic efficiency and technical efficiency.

(1) The connotation of economic efficiency

Economic efficiency is the ratio of income to costs measured by monetary value, and technical efficiency is the ratio of income to costs under physical measure. The relation of them can be described as follows:

$$Economic\,efficiency = \frac{\sum (Obtained\,volume \times Obtained\,price)}{\sum (Expensed\,volume \times Expensed\,price)}$$

The equation above shows that economic efficiency is a function of technical efficiency and ratio of obtaining price to expensed price. When there is no change in the ratio, the higher the technical efficiency is, the better the economic efficiency is; and the lower the technical efficiency is, the worse the economic efficiency is. When there is no change in technical efficiency, the change of ratio can also significantly influence economic efficiency.

(2) The relationship between economic efficiency and profit

Profit is closely linked to economic efficiency, which can be described both from a perspective of accounting profit and from the perspective of economic profit.

(1) Calculation of accounting profit and economic efficiency

The relation of accounting profit and economic efficiency can be described as follows:

$$\begin{aligned} Accounting\,profit &= Income - Accounting\,cost \\ &= Accounting\,cost \times \left({Income}/{Accounting\,cost} - 1 \right) \end{aligned}$$

Or,

$$\begin{aligned} Accounting\,profit &= Capital \times \left({Accounting\,profit}/{Capital} \right) \\ &= Capital \times Return\,on\,capital \end{aligned}$$

The relationship between accounting profit and economic efficiency shows that when there is profit, there is economic efficiency. And the increase of profit doesn't mean the improvement of economic efficiency. When there is economic efficiency, there is accounting profit, and the improvement of economic efficiency leads to the increase of profit. The conclusion is that profit only determines the existence of economic efficiency. The numerical value of economic efficiency has little relation with profit.

(2) Calculation of economic profit and economic efficiency

The relationship between economic profit and economic efficiency can be described as follows:

$$\begin{aligned} Economic\,profit &= Accounting\,profit - Normal\,profit \\ &= Capital \times \left({Accounting\,profit}/{Capital} - {Normal\,profit}/{Capital} \right) \\ &= Capital \times \left(Return\,on\,capital - Normal\,profit\,rate \right) \end{aligned}$$

The relationship between economic profit and economic efficiency shows that economic profit can be used to evaluate economic efficiency. Economic profit is larger than zero which means economic efficiency is perfect. Economic profit is less than zero which means economic efficiency is unsatisfactory. The Zero economic profit which means economic efficiency achieves a normal level of economic efficiency. And economic profit reflects the integration of economic efficiency and operating effect.

The conclusion is that economic profit is better than accounting profits in reflecting the economic efficiency and economic effect.

3.2.3.3 Capital Operation Efficiency Goals and the Relationship of It to Other Operation Efficiency Goals

The elements of business Operation include capital operation, assets operation, commodity operation, and product management, and the relationships among different kinds are connected.

(1) Capital operation goals and asset operation goals

Profit is direct goals of capital operation and asset operation, but the core goals of capital operation and assets operation are different. When we study the relation between capital operation and assets operation, we should start from economic efficiency which is the core goals of operation. Return on equity is an indicator which reflects the core goals of capital operation. Return on equity (ROE) is the ratio of net income to net assets (or equity). Return on total asset is an indicator which reflects the core goals of assets operation, and return on total asset is the ratio of EBIT to total assets. The relation of capital operation goals and assets operation goals can be reflected by ROE.

$$ROE = \left[\begin{array}{l} Return\,on\,total\,asset + (Return\,on\,total\,asset - Debt\,interest\,rate) \\ \times \dfrac{Total\,liabilities}{Capitalization} \end{array}\right] \times (1 - Income\,tax\,rate)$$

The equation above shows that enterprises who focus on capital operation should pay more attention to the increase of ROE. The managers should make operation of assets effective, and increase return on total asset or ROE. On the other hand, the managers should make operation of capital effective so that the capital structure can be improved.

(2) Assets operation goals and commodity operation goals

Profit is direct goals of assets operation and commodity operation, and the core goals of assets operation and commodity operation are different. Return on total asset is an indicator which reflects the core goals of assets operation. When come to study the relationship between assets operation goals and commodity operation goals, we should clarify the indicator which reflects the core of commodity operation goals. Return on sales is an indicator which reflects commodity operation economic benefits. The elements of return on sales include profit rate on cost and profit margin. The relation of return on total asset and return on sales can reflect the relation of product management goals and commodity operation goals which is described as follow:

$$Return\,on\,total\,asset = Total\,assets\,turnover \times Return\,on\,sales$$

In the equation, return on sales is the ratio of EBIT to sales.

The equation above indicates that enterprises whose goals are capital operation should pay more attention on return on total asset. The managers should make operation of commodity effectively, and increase return on sales or the profitability of commodity. On the other hand, the managers should make allocation of asset and asset reorganization effective so that asset turnover can be raised.

(3) Commodity operation goals and product management goals

Among commodity operation, assets operation and capital operation, the differences of them are indicators of core goals. The direct goals of them are profit. And the differences between product management and commodity operation are core goals. The core goals of product management are production maximization, and the relation of commodity operation goals and product management goals can be described as follows:

$$Sales\,revenue \times Return\,on\,sales = \sum\left[Output \times Selling\,rate \times \left(Price - Cost\right)\right]$$

The left side of the equation indicates that increasing return on sales and increasing the amount of sales are ways to realize profit maximization. The right side of the equation indicates that product management is the basis of commodity operation profit maximization. In the meantime, the balance of production and sales and the price of input and output are important for enterprises.

3.2.3.4 The Status of Management Control

We have defined the connotation of management control and decomposed the objective of management control, which has established the priority of management control in internal control. The conclusion can be described as follow.

Firstly, management control covers every part of management from the perspective of control function. Broadly speaking, internal management control equals to internal control, that is, the areas of internal control belong to management control.

Secondly, management control is the highest level of internal control from the perspective of internal control objective. The efficiency and effect of internal management control are generally in accordance with organization goals, especially with enterprise goals. Other objectives of control, such as task control objective and accounting control objective, are obedient to objective of management control.

Thirdly, management control is more comprehensive than accounting control from the perspective of means of internal control. Internal control is implemented by means of monetary measurement and reporting. And in the implementation of management control, determining standard, evaluating performance and the correction of deviation are process in which non-monetary measurement are employed besides monetary measurement.

3.2.4 The Principles and Requirements of Internal Management Control

In the above, the connotation, objective and status of management control have been clarified, which is the basis of the study of management control. Compared with control in technical area, internal management control is more complex and broader. And there are many uncertain factors in the process of internal management control. The implementation of management control should be in accordance with certain principles and requirements.

3.2.4.1 The Principles of Management Control

There are many principles which are associated with control and internal control. Management control belongs to control, or internal control. And the general principles of control or the general principles of internal control are applicable to management control. In the meantime, management control isn't entirely same with other kinds of control, and the principles of management control are special. The principles of control refer to the immanence of control, and requirements of control refer to the externality of control, which will be described respectively in the following. The principles of management control can be divided into six principles.

(1) The planned principle

The planned principle indicates that management control must reflect the demand of plan and achievement of it. The principle function of management control is planning. The essence of management control is to assure the achievement of organizational planning. So the planned principle is the essence demand of management control. The quality of plan, which includes systematization, comprehensiveness and accuracy, determines the quality of management control.

(2) The appropriate principle

The appropriate principle indicates that management control should coordinate the organization environment. The development of internal management control has inverted from closed type to open type, and control environment is the basis factor of management control. Management control can't be implemented effectively without the consideration of control environment. And the implementation of management control in China should be concerned with the characteristic of China.

(3) The materiality principle

The materiality principle indicates that the implementation of management control should focus on critical points. There are several advantages of materiality principle in the implementation of management control. Firstly, the decomposition and implement of objectives of management control become easier. Secondly, the risk of financial activities and operation activities can be avoided effectively. Thirdly, the implementation of the materiality principle can raise the efficiency of management control, that is, enterprises can implement larger control results with fewer inputs.

(4) The trend control principle

The trend control principle indicates that management control should establish a mechanism to correct deviations which are summarized from the trend of historical materials. Management control should identify potential problems and risk in time according to the situation and trend of control objects, and the organizations can operate effectively in accordance with strategic goals.

(5) The exception control principle

The exception control principle indicates that management control should attach its importance to abnormal events, which is the basic demand of management control. The abnormal events should be defined according to the characteristics of the organization and the requirements of control. The standards of abnormal are different in different circumstances. The judgment standards of exceptions are different according to different demands of control degree. In tight control, more than 2 % of changes are considered as exceptions, while less than 4 % of changes are considered as normal in loose control.

(6) The direct control principle

The direct control principle indicates that management control should improve the quality of management control subjects for prevention and control in advance. The direct control principle emphasizes the importance of control subjects, and emphasizes the training of control subjects in the process of control. The qualified controllers can be observed on the looming problems and can take measures to correct them in time. And indirect control only corrects the problems after it happened. Direct control can overcome the problems which are caused by indirect control. In some cases, direct control and indirect control should be implemented together so that the problems which are not totally corrected by direct control can be corrected by indirect control.

3.2.4.2 The Requirements of Management Control

(1) People orientation of management control

The subjects and objects of management control are people who participate in the process of control. People oriented in the process of management control indicate that people are the most important elements of management control. The elements of management control theory include management art, behavioral science, and human resources. In management control practices, people's subjective initiative should be considered in the aspects of governance structure, organizational structure, leadership and assignment of responsibility.

(2) Objective criterion of management control

The determination of management control standards is an important and difficult link. The utilization of objective criterion is the guarantee of the achievement of organization goals. The objective criterion is the link of organizational goals and the activities of controllers. The determination of objective criterion should consider variety of factors, such as historical level, industrial characteristics, and organization goals.

(3) Cost effectiveness of management control

Human resources, material resources and financial resources must be invested in enterprises in order to achieve management control objective, and the resources which are measured by money are management control cost. Management control requires not only the effectiveness of organization activities but also the effectiveness of management control itself, that is, less investment (or cost) but more outputs (or profit). Cost effectiveness indicates that in the process of management control, enterprises should control management control cost and avoid the situation in which management control cost is larger than outputs.

(4) The flexibility of management control

The flexibility of management control indicates that control objectives, control standards, and control mode should be coordinated with control environment. And the personnel's initiative and creativity can be inspired. The flexibility of management control is a kind of positive flexibility instead of passive flexibility. Positive flexibility refers to management control can coordinate the degree of control according to the changes of environment so that it can raise organization goals. And passive flexibility refers to management control reduce control objectives and standards when the environment changes.

(5) The controllability of management control

The controllability of management control indicates that the subject of management control is in accordance with the object of management control, that is, control subject has the obligation to responsible for the activities of control objects. The organizations should put controllability on an important position in the implementation of institution setting, and goal decomposition so that the entire management control system can operate effectively.

(6) Global conception of management control

Management control is a fully integrated system. The elements, links, contents and hierarchy of management control are correlated with each other. So the overview conception runs through the process of the design of management control and the operation of management control. It's inadvisable to pursue of local goals and interests at the cost of organization goals and interests.

3.3 Relation Between Management Control and Related Fields

3.3.1 *Management Control and Accounting Control*

Accounting control is a series of control methods, measurements and procedures, formulated and implemented by the entity, to improve the quality of accounting information, to protect the safety and integrity of assets, and to ensure the compliance with applicable laws and regulations.

To study the connotation of internal accounting control it should identify the following questions:

Does accounting control refer to financial accounting, managerial accounting, or it encompasses the both? Narrowly speaking, accounting control is financial accounting, but in general it should include both financial and managerial accounting. We define it as financial accounting to study the relation between internal accounting control and internal management control.

Does accounting control refer to the control for accounting activities? Is it the control implemented by accountants? Is it the control exerted by accounting means? Or does it encompass the three? We think accounting control should include the three aspects above.

Based on the above-mentioned problems, we can further define the meaning of accounting controls:

First, accountants are the major people in accounting control of the organization or entity, but the board of directors, the board of supervisors, managers and other personnel are also contained in accounting control. Thus, accounting control must obtain attention and participation of all members.

Second, accounting control concerns about accounting activities in the organization or entity. Accounting activities are a process of recognizing, recording, measuring and reporting on economic activities of an organization or entity. So every activity related to accounting is in the content of accounting control.

Third, the objective of accounting control is to ensure the reliability of accounting information. The relevance of accounting information, especially financial accounting information, is determined by accounting standards and regulations. Furthermore, the reliability of accounting information reflects the implementation of accounting regulations. The reliability of accounting information thereby includes relevance and compliance. As for the safety of assets, it is only an indirect objective of accounting control which is one of direct objectives of management control.

The organization must align management control with accounting control to improve the control of the entity. To coordinate the relation between management control and accounting control, it should start with the following several respects:

3.3.1.1 Control Objectives

According to classification of internal control, management control objectives are the effectiveness and efficiency of operations, whereas accounting control objectives are the reliability of financial reporting. The effectiveness and efficiency of management control, the objective of management control, is often consistent with the goals of the organization especially the goals of the entity. The accounting control objective, the reliability of financial reporting, provides service for ensuring the effectiveness and efficiency of operations. There will be neither the accuracy of decision-making or control nor the effectiveness and efficiency of operations without the reliability of financial reporting. Thus, accounting control objectives and management control objectives can be in the consistency with each other.

3.3.1.2 Control Status

Objectives of accounting control and objectives of management control decide what the status of them. Objective of management control decide that it is the highest level of internal control. Other controls, e.g. task control and accounting control, whose objectives should be subject to management control objectives, must ensure cohering with management control.

3.3.1.3 Control Approaches

The procedures and approaches used in management control system for the achievement of the goals contain: understanding strategic planning; determining control standards; preparing for performance report; evaluating management performance; and undertaking management compensation. As for internal accounting control, the control procedures and approaches include: accounting recognition control; accounting record control; accounting measure control; and accounting reporting control. In order to coordinate management control with accounting control, on the one hand, it is necessary to undertake accounting approaches to ensure the relevance and reliability of management control information in every link of accounting control; on the other hand, it is necessary to ensure that accounting control is in favor of operating efficiency and effectiveness in terms of management control approaches in every link of management control.

3.3.1.4 Control Content

The contents of management control from the view of management activities contain five classes: production and manufacturing control, procurement and sales control, finance control, assets and human resources control and accounting control. Accounting control may reflect the efficiency and effectiveness of production monitoring, marketing, finance and resources utilization by measuring and reporting the relevance and reliability. Based on control process, management control can be grouped into four categories: resources investment control, operating process control, production outcomes control and benefits allocation control. Accounting control can keep monitoring the effectiveness and efficiency of these processes by reviewing the accounting reports in these four processes.

3.3.2 Management Control and Internal Auditing

Recently, a new term "auditing control" has been used in auditing, which is a concept combined with "auditing" and "control" emphasizing the economic essence of auditing. So we can still simply regard it as auditing itself. In a long term, management control did not have certain connections with auditing control. Management control focuses on the effectiveness and efficiency of operations, and external auditing focuses on the truth and fairness of financial materials. However, they got close combination since auditing had developed from transaction-oriented auditing to system-oriented auditing. Auditing control will work by test of control and internal control assessment, whereas management control is just a major component of internal control. Management control also needs auditing control to provide with materials and evidences, such as audit report and management letter, to enhance the effectiveness, efficiency and scientific of control.

Compared to auditing from CPA, internal auditing was tied closely to management control due to its characteristic of being into the entity. Management control and internal auditing were mutually promoted, interdependent and continuously improved in the process of joint development. Internal auditing was gradually fitting into management control and had become a necessary approach or mean of management control. Additionally, management control had propelled internal auditing to develop from financial audit stage to managerial audit stage. The International Organization of Supreme Audit Institutions passed *The Lima Declaration of Guidelines on Auditing Precepts* in 1977, which said in chapter one that "Audit is not an end in itself but an indispensable part of a regulatory system whose aim is to reveal deviations from accepted standards and violations of the principles of legality, efficiency, effectiveness and economy of financial management early enough to make it possible to take corrective action in individual cases, to make those accountable accept responsibility, to obtain compensation, or to take steps to preven--r at least render more difficul--uch breaches."[5] Here, the auditing of "the principles of legality, efficiency, effectiveness and economy", is the application of internal auditing in management control.

The managers of the entity cannot examine or control all operations only by their own as before because of the expansion of business scale, the diversification of operating location and the complexity of operating transactions since the twenty

[5] http://www1.worldbank.org/publicsector/pe/befa05/LimaDeclaration.pdf

centuries. They can only carry out decentralized management and hierarchical control, as well as the restraints and incentives to all levels of managers, by which management control has come out accompanying formally with internal control nearly at the same time. Innate goal congruency of management control and internal auditing make them connect closely and promote together in the process of joint development.

3.3.2.1 Internal Auditing Promoted by Management Control

After the establishment of management control systems, it required the staffs who were relatively independent with analysis capability, particularly those who can analyze the control systems, to review, appraise and report what are the managers' capacities and whether the operating goals can be attained, especially with the application of management tools such as budget systems, EVA, balanced scorecard and benchmarking system. And internal auditors exactly possessed such conditions. Furthermore, internal auditors also have strengths of low costs and familiarity with the entity's actual situations compared with external auditors.

Internal auditing had broken out the extent of traditional financial auditing and deeply got into broader fields of production operations, which resulted in a role of assisting managers to improve operating management and to increase economic benefits. From then, internal auditing had gradually developed from financial auditing to managerial auditing. We can see that management control played a role of direct propelling. Several definitions of internal auditing determined by *the Institute of Internal Auditors* illustrated this evolution process.

In 1947, IIA issued *the Statements of Responsibilities of Internal Auditors* which gave the first authoritative definition that "Internal auditing is an independent appraisal activity within an organization for the review of finance, accounting and other operations as a service to management. It provides protective and constructive service for management to deal with financial and accounting problems, as well as involving problems of operating management at some time."[6] The definition indicated that internal control was an independent profession separated from accounting and still in the stage of financial auditing. But management control was just in its infancy at that time, for which scientific management theory, organizational management theory and control theory had provided basic theories.

In 1955, the book *Management* written by Harold Koontz and Cyril O'Donnell was a symbol of the preliminary establishment of management control systems principled by management control. By 1957, the modified *Statements of Responsibilities of Internal Auditors* had been considerably broadened to define internal control: "Internal auditing is an independent appraisal activity within an organization for the review of finance, accounting and other operations as a service to management. It is a management control which functions by measuring and evaluating the effectiveness of other controls." The definition identified the

---

[6] IIA [4].

direction of the service to management, but still emphasized the relationships it had with finance and accounting. It had taken a big stride, nevertheless, to treat operations and finance or accounting as the same. In addition, in 1958, the announcement of audit procedures NO.29 released by AICPA formally divided internal control into accounting control and management control.

The development period of management control in the 1960s, in which scholars like Anthony and Jerome devoted to developing management control as a course in science. Books and articles of management control boomed to make management control theory grown with the assimilation of systematic theory. In 1971, IIA modified the definition of internal control at the second time: "Internal auditing is an independent appraisal activity within an organization for the review of operations as a service to management. It is a management control which functions by measuring and evaluating the effectiveness of other controls." This modification presented that internal auditors also concerned about every important respect of operating transactions to make internal auditing penetrate all respects of management in the organization. From then, internal auditing had changed from accounting auditing to managerial auditing and it had been combined with management control by mutual promotion. Internal auditing had become a dispensable part of management control.

After the 1980s, with the spring up of enterprise competitive strategy theory, specific objectives of management control turned to strategic execution, which promoted internal auditing from operating transaction development to strategy achievement, bringing out internal auditing to transit from managerial auditing to strategic auditing. For instance, IIA gave the newest definition of internal auditing n 1999: "Internal auditing is an independent, objective assurance and consulting activity designed to add value and improve an organization's operations. It helps a organization accomplish its objectives by bringing a systematic, disciplined approach to evaluate and improve the effectiveness of risk management, control, and governance processes."[7]

It is evident that management control played a considerable role of promoting internal auditing to develop from financial auditing to managerial auditing even strategic auditing. In particular, managerial auditing developed from internal financial auditing was just the one referring management control as center. The Report No. 19 issued by International Institute of Internal Auditors in 1975 stated that "management audit is a future-oriented, independent and systematic appraisal carried out by internal auditors on various levels of management activities, which aims to enhance the organization's profitability and to enhance the accomplishment of other goals through the promotion of a variety of management functions, project goals, society goals and staff development." "The appraisal of management audit comprises appraisal for existence, conformity and appropriateness of management control institution..." Nowadays, management control has become parts of a must

[7] IIA [4].

in International Certificated Internal Auditors,[8] which requires an internal auditor to "be applied to professional changes and challenges caused by the newest management techniques, management control principles, risk management and internal control."[9]

3.3.2.2 Management Control Promoted by Internal Control

In the process of management control promoting internal auditing evolution, internal auditing also promoted the continuous development of management control. As for this, the former President of the Council of IIA, Anthony Ridley, pointed out in his article: "...internal auditing is being conducted worldwide to participate in control and management of various institutions....we have been admitted as a key player of fields in control and corporate management."[10]

Internal auditing promotes the management control mainly through the following aspects:

Above all, internal auditing requires the company to appraise the effectiveness and efficiency of internal control, naturally including examining and evaluating management control. Internal auditing can appraise all procedures for management control, rectifying deviations and correcting errors, to promote the whole management control systems operating effectively, based on its relatively independent standpoint and its understanding of operating circumstances.

Then, internal auditors intend to understand actual situations in operations, to help solve all kinds of problems, by the meeting among every department and every level of management in the entity. Thereby, the internal auditing can play a bridge role between the upper and lower, thereby enhance management control systems and effective management.

Moreover, the effectiveness and efficiency of management control systems are a dynamic process due to the change of operating environment and the development itself. Management control systems should gradually apply to the change and be adjusted at appropriate time. By contrast, internal auditing is a daily management activity differed from external auditing. It can apply to the adjustment of management control systems on time. Therefore, internal auditing has a critical impact on perfecting management control systems.

Internal auditing and management control promoted and complemented mutually in joint development demonstrated by the history of western modern internal auditing development. It is an actual opportunity of promoting internal auditing to achieve the top-down development by aligning internal auditing with management control. We will conduct the discussion of coordination in internal auditing and management control from both theoretical and practical aspects bellow:

---

[8] Quoted from Wang Guangyuan [5].

[9] IIA [4].

[10] Ridley [6].

Theory Convergence Between Internal Auditing and Management Control

(1) Goal convergence

Goals are the start point of behaviors in internal auditing. They are also ideal conditions or statuses of internal auditing activities. The goals of internal auditing should be consistent with the goals of management control because they both give service to overall goals of the entity. According to *Audit provisions on internal audit work* issued in 1995, the second order required that the goals of internal audit at present can reduce to safeguarding assets of the entity, maintaining the compliance of financial revenue and expenditure and the reliability of accounting information. Although the goals are necessary and understandable in the primary stage of the development of internal auditing, they belong to the lower levels of goals in enterprise management, after all. Gaps are between achieving the goals of maximizing enterprise value and the goals of internal auditing. The goals of enterprise internal auditing in our country can be repositioned on "add value and improve an organization's operations". Specifically speaking, it helps managers to improve operating management, to examine whether the transaction activities are consistent with the overall objectives and every specific objectives after division. We need to identify that the goals of internal auditing are only to help managers improve operating management, which are, in essence, suggestive but not administrative or they will influence the independence of internal audit.

(2) Function convergence

The function of internal auditing is the impact that it has on operation in the entity. Nowadays, the major function of internal auditing is still supervision, for instance, the forth order in *Audit provisions on internal audit work* presented that "the function is to provide internal auditing supervision for the finance, financial balance and economic benefits of the units and the subordinate units to independently conduct internal auditing supervision power". This is decided by the development stages of internal auditing in our country, and it is also resulted by the large effect had by government auditing on the production and development of internal auditing, which makes internal auditing function be an extensiveness of government auditing function. However, another vital function of modern internal auditing is the service function, which cannot be demonstrated in our country's organizations. Service function uses modern techniques and approaches of internal auditing to analyze the weakness of production operations and help managers establish and improve the management institutions, to provide consulting activity for the existence and development of the entity in market competence.

The entity can reestablish the situations mainly by management control and subsidiary by internal auditing, aligning control function with internal auditing to make internal audit carry out monitoring function, establishing the realization of service to managers at the same time.

Hereby, the role of internal auditing has been played more widely, which makes the necessity of the existence of internal control acknowledged by managers sincerely.

Practice Convergence Between Internal Auditing and Management Control

(1) Scope of work convergence

After coordinating the goals of internal auditing and management control, internal auditing can be expanded to manage organizational effectiveness, scientific management system, and management processes-effectiveness from accounting information reliable. Internal Auditing objectives can move away from the historical of accounting data, towards the current and future business activities. Specifically speaking, the scope of work of internal audit will be extended to: appraising the entity's organizational structure to ensure its integrity and goal congruency and to effectively utilize all staffs and other resources; appraising the management institutions of planning and controlling to ensure its adequacy and understandability to be used continuously; appraising the techniques of management control, for example, budget control and standard costs, to ensure that all resources are timely and appropriately transmitted to every level of managers for compliance and implementation; appraising performance of all managers and whether the overall goals and the goals divided have been accomplished; appraising the objectives and policies of the organization to judge whether they are consistent with the entity's strategy and can make them accomplish. For all these new internal control working ranges, managers should understand adequately and cooperate positively.

(2) Techniques and approaches convergence

The wider range of internal audit must require internal auditors to be familiar with the institutions and approaches of management control, by which, internal auditors should not only learn to use accounting techniques, but also learn to handle techniques of management control e.g., setting responsibility centers, preparing for budget, selecting transfer pricing, planning for long-term and short-term incentives and even other management control methods developed sooner within our country like EVA, the balanced scorecard, and just in time. In addition, internal auditors need not only to master traditional auditing procedures such as observation, inspection and analytical procedures, but also know other appraisal methods like the management control system diagrams and check sheets. Management control system diagrams is that internal auditors draw ideal control system diagrams about organizational situations, functional structure situations and information communication situations of control system according to the organization's policies, industry reports, government regulations and their knowledge and experiences. Internal auditors then compare these to circumstances actually set up to discover the weakness and analysis the problems and dangers may occur. Check sheets are to investigate a proportion of functions and staffs for obtaining relative analysis evidences by designing numbers of check sheets about relative management problems, then taking the method of questionnaires. From this standpoint, the extensive range of internal auditing raises more and more claims on future internal auditors' knowledge structure.

(3) Organizational convergence

The organizational institutes are the basis of internal auditing. A scientific and effective internal organizational institute plays a critical role of internal auditing. After the fields of internal auditing extended to the effectiveness and efficiency of operating management, internal audit institute has been required to possess higher independence and authority. The establishment of internal auditing institutes has many modes, for instance, some internal institutes set audit committees in the board of directors and keep double relationships by setting audit institutes in administrative systems; some are set in the board of supervision or the board of directors; some are attached to chief accountant or president; some are attached to inspection and monitoring department; some are even attached to financial accounting department. Relatively speaking, the most ideal mode is to set audit committee in the board of directors or to set audit institute in administrative system. For the entity not taking corporate system, it should make internal audit institutes attach to the highest leader in the entity, at least attaching to management function department being audited. Furthermore, it requires that "it should assure engagement are properly supervised" in accordance with NO.230 of the International Standards for the Professional Practice of Internal Auditing issued by IIA, the independence of internal auditing institute also creates conditions for internal auditors being monitored by other departments.

With the development of internal auditing from internal financial auditing to internal managerial auditing and strategic auditing, management control has gradually close relationships with internal auditing. On the one hand, internal managerial auditing and strategic auditing are a necessary component of a perfect internal management control system; on the other hand, management control system can indicate directions and objectives of internal auditing. Therefore, enforcing the coordination of internal auditing and management control is the vital and key point of the internal auditing and management control work in our country at present.

In the process of the development of western internal auditing and management control, management control promotes the evolution of internal auditing, and internal auditing facilitates the continuous perfection of management control. Our internal auditing and management control both encounter rare development opportunities. We believe that it must play a direct and effective role on promoting the transformation of the roles of internal auditing and improving the level of management control by cohering internal auditing and management control.

The coordination of internal auditing and management control should be taken from both theory and practice. Convergence in theory must align the objectives of both internal auditing and management control and must transfer the functions of them. Convergence in practice should be taken from three aspects, organization, techniques and contents. We should link theory with practice at the same time. However, we should identify that regardless of theory and practice is still in the stage of development both in internal auditing and management control. For the research of the convergence both in theory and in practice of internal auditing and management control, we still have far to go.

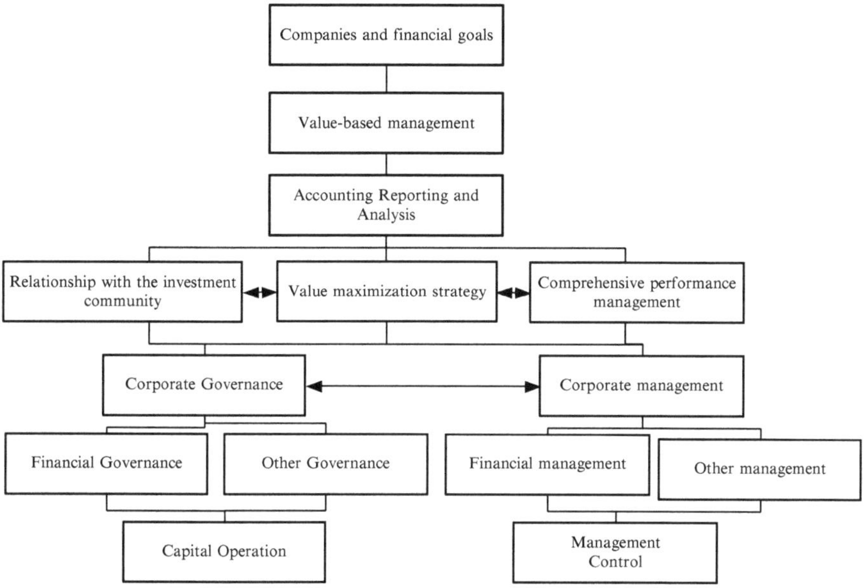

Fig. 3.3 Corporate finance system framework

3.3.3 Management Control and Corporate Finance

Corporate finance is the management of corporate financial activities and financial relationships. That is, coordinating and dealing with relationships with the entity's stakeholders, by managing funs and capital financing of the entity. The ultimate goal is to attain the effectiveness and efficiency of funs and capital financing.

Corporate finance system framework can be expressed as a comprehensive, systematical, integrated theory and application system with: The corporate and financial objectives of capital maintenance; The orientation of value based management; The finance basis of accounting reporting analysis; The finance fields of handling linkages with investment communities, appraising strategy for maximum values and creating values in comprehensive performance management; The wings of finance which are capital operation and management control.

The corporate finance system framework is illustrated in Fig. 3.3.

We can see that operation of capital and management control have been defined as two pillars of corporate finance. On the one hand, corporate finance is capital operation, when it involves study on how to operate capital with the use of economic theories to make capital the most effective utilize. On the other hand, corporate finance is management control when it uses the theory of management to make the operation of capital proceeding in line with the settled objectives by control.

Management control, by which the company can take all kinds of activities, is extensive from the view of control targets and contents. Corporate financial activities and their effectiveness and efficiency must become the mainline and focal point of management control due to the comprehensiveness of its activities and the consistency of effectiveness and efficiency. In particular, VBM (value based management) is the essence of management control under the environment of modern corporate finance in VBM. The purpose of corporate finance is to exert control of the whole directions and processes on the targets of finance or core contents which is capital operation by taking advantage of the means and ideas of management control.

3.3.3.1 Value-Based Strategic Objectives and Decomposition

The goals and objectives of the company must be maximizing shareholder value and the strategic choice will set the orientation of creating shareholder value in VBM system. The decomposition of strategic objectives is conducted in accordance with value-created linkages or value chain intended to assure the accomplishment of the goals of strategy. The company makes sure to align short-term value goal and long-term value goal and to make partial value goal cohere with the whole value goal.

3.3.3.2 Value-Based Management Standards Setting

The determination of control variables and control standards must indicate the value creation links and value goals. For instance, the company can use capital maintenance, economic profits, ROE, ROA and assets turnover which are value variables and efficiency indexes as the most important and crucial index of control. The company can also regard capital maintenance or creation of shareholder value as basic standards. Additionally, the company develops the comprehensive budget system with the orientation of financial budget.

3.3.3.3 Value-Based Management Control Reports

Management control reporting must reflect characteristics of value management which covers financial accounting reporting and managerial accounting reporting with the center of accounting reporting system. Operating transacting reporting, as components of management control reporting systems, reflects budget performance status of every transaction. Alternatively, it is a supplement and instructions of accounting reporting.

3.3.3.4 Performance Evaluation Based on Value Management

The performances of the company are supposed to be demonstrated by creation of shareholder value, with the fundamental standards of whether to consider the evaluation of the creation of shareholder and enterprise value. Evaluation indexes mainly contain value variables, including efficiency indexes and effectiveness indexes.

3.3.3.5 Value-Based Managerial Compensation

In value-based management, the motivation of managers is linked to capital appreciation and value creation. Then, managers' income is linked to capital growth or economic efficiency, so that shareholder value is the proportional increase in managerial compensation.

Then, in the modern corporate system, the management control focus on the management of capital process or value-based management control process. In essence, the management control is the corporate finance.

References

1. Yang Youhong (2011) Internal control framework of enterprise, 1st edn. Zhejiang People's Publishing House, Hangzhou
2. Anthony RN (1998) Management control system, 9th edn. McGraw-Hill, Burr Ridge
3. Maciariello JA, Kirby CJ (1994) Management control systems, 2nd edn. Prentice Hall, Englewood Cliffs
4. IIA website, http://www.theiia.org/
5. Wang Guangyuan (1996) Manage auditing theory. Renmin University of China Press, Beijing, pp 232–233
6. Ridley A (1997) Internal auditing – prospects for the 21st century, Auditing research no. 1

Part II
Study on Evolution of West Management Control Theory

Chapter 4
A Review of West Management Control Research

4.1 Research Purpose and Research Design

The evolution of MCS in the West dates back to 1965 when Robert Anthony from Harvard University published his **book** *Planning and control systems: a framework for analysis,* this marked the beginning of the use of management control systems in West organizations [1]. After that, management control left its footstep in ages, from the mass production of prosperity in the United States in 1960s, to the lean manufacturing and quality management mode which promoted the rise of economy in Japan in 1990s, and to the latest global competition and innovation strategy-oriented. Flamholtz and Randle [2] pointed out that management control is very important for the growth of an organization. The west experience in Management Control Systems tells us that management control is essential in the organization's growth and hence can be used for the development of Chinese economy as well. In the planned economy period, the Chinese government could manage the entire arrangement of control. However, with the evolutions of the economy and changes in the environment, the operation mode of enterprises has completely changed. Enterprises need to apply scientific management control to deal with a series of challenges such as discontinuous, seditious, non-linear and high frequency change and global competition in the twenty-first century. However, the management control research and practice in China is still lagging behind due to the lack of attention from the government, academics and other stakeholders. We run a simple test with the keyword management control in the Chinese CNKI, finding only 24 CSSCI indexed paper, 10 of which is in the Internal Control.[1] In China, the awareness of

[1] In CNKI, the keywords "internal control", the time window for 1970–2010 years were retrieved, and screened by 2010–2011 version of the CSSCI standard for internal control, obtained 417 articles. The same time window, with the keyword "management control" retrieval, 24 articles for management control. The same time window, and then with the keyword "management control" and "internal control" search, access to internal control and management control of 10 references. This paper is not on the management control of all content areas by retrieval.

X. Zhang, *Enterprise Management Control Systems in China*, Understanding China,
DOI 10.1007/978-3-642-54715-7_4, © Springer-Verlag Berlin Heidelberg 2014

internal control is far more popular than management control, but management control is the core of internal control from the perspective of their scope.[2]

Management control is an evolutionary science. In the different times, management control presents its contingency and evolving characteristics, which are the important premise of keeping management control theory effective and scientific in different conditions. There are two kinds of research on the review of management control in the existing western literatures, one is summarized to show the formation and development of management control, and the other is a on a single specific theme. However, little attention is paid to the summary of research theme or content, and even less to discover the evolution of management control researches and research methods.

One basic rule in academic research is developing new research by summarizing the existing ones. We took full use of the west literatures and some excellent review methods to help summarize management control literatures, to sort out topics and methods, to exhibit the evolution of management control. This book can deepen Chinese scholars' understanding of western management control and cause more attention from Chinese scholars on the importance of management control theory, and provide guidance in learning from management control theory and selecting research starting point. We confidently believe that this book is of great significance for the promotion of management control research and for the reference of review study.

4.2 Research Steps and Designs

Scientific review is a senior product of information analysis, which can serve as a guidance and foundation for researchers. In the west, there is a certain experience and development in review research. The most common pattern to carry out a review is as follows: select ten relevant international top journals around 10 years, search in database with a certain topic to collect the related literatures and sort them by the same content, statistic and attribute methods used in the research, and finally rank the authors by the popularity. Although the procedures are relatively complete, it will miss some literatures via search, and the research will be lack of depth. The readers cannot find out what perspectives and what methods are involved in a specific theme and how the research is carried out. Therefore, the review cannot be very useful for the future researchers. We borrowed some idea from Western review and made some improvements, paying close attention to the evolution of management

[2]The internal control from the perspective of control subjects within the organization can be divided into board control, management control and employee control, management control more localized in from the angle of management, pay close attention to the strategy implementation process control perspective, internal control is an important part of 2002(Zhang Xianzhi "establish the enterprise internal management control system framework " in China, young financial cost of annual meeting of academic research innovation award winning paper).

control and trying not to miss any important literature while searching in the database to ensure a more reliable, more scientific and deeper review.

4.2.1 Research Steps

We comprehensively used the review methods by Harrison and McKinnon [3], Poston and Grabski [4], Hesford et al. [5] and Elbashir et al. [6] and make the following improvements. (1) We expanded the sample window period. The above reviews all took a fragment from history. While management control is a dynamic subject, we can present the evolution of management control theory and research from the perspective of the historical development. Therefore, we collect papers right after the first official release of management control system; (2) We paid attention to the authority and comprehension of sample selection. The above references all subjectively chose ten journals to review, which can cause a large number of documents missing, especially the papers in other areas. We located all articles in Class A journal to ensure the comprehensiveness and authority of the study; (3) We enriched research themes. The above references usually involve topics distribution only. We presented not only the evolution themes, but also the contents and perspectives, which emphasize the evolution and depth characteristics of management research; (4) We covered management research methods. The above references just do the statistics of research methods, but we will analyze the research methods according to research topics. By doing so, we can discuss the themes and methods.

4.2.2 Research Design

Because a few important journals were not founded until 1970, and little changes happened in management control theory during 1965–1970, therefore we chose the period of 1971–2010 as the sample time window. In case of missing some important papers, we used the Elsevier, EBSCO, Wiley, JSTOR and Google Scholar to collect papers, we did not involve the textbooks and monographs, which is one limitation of our research, but this limitation can be fixed to some extent by the citations from those textbooks and monographs.[3] To avoid the missing of relevant papers, we used management control, planning and control and control system as keywords to help search. Noting that many international journals do not provide keywords, we additionally made a search in the abstract using these words. Finally, we got 469 papers, excluding book reviews, Call for Papers, Edit Summary and education. The distribution is shown in Fig. 4.1.

[3]These journals came from different database, we didn't offer the correspondence between the journals and the databases and the details of databases, but only listed the databases' names.

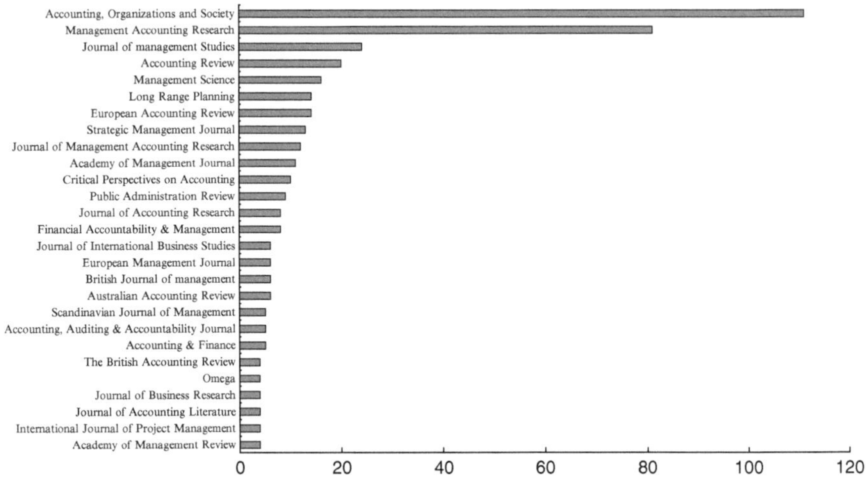

Fig. 4.1 Distribution of the journals that published management control literature

If we collect management control papers according to the definition of Chenhall [7], the number would be unimaginable and the themes will be very distractive.[4] In addition, the International Journals vary in quality, and also representativeness and authority. Therefore, we refine the articles. The criteria are as follows: first, keep only Class A and A+ journals papers[5]; second, keep only the literatures that are directly related to management control . Articles that belong to management control but indirectly related were abandoned, which is another limitation of our research. Ultimately, we got 233 articles. Tables 4.1 and 4.2 give a summary of the distribution of journals and year.

4.3 Themes and Evolution of Management Control Research

In order to properly organize the literature and present the evolution pattern of the research, we classified literature by the themes, and do the statistics by the themes and the year. We summarized the themes and distributed the similar themes to one category. We did not choose all themes but only the important, representative and

[4]Chenhall [7] regarded that Managerial Accounting meant the practice of Budgetary Accounting, Cost Accounting and etc., and that Managerial Accounting System was the system used by Managerial accounting. Management Control System was a broad concept, which involved Managerial Accounting System and other Control system.

[5]We used the latest of international journals rankings of ABDC (Australian Business Deans Council, www.abdc.edu.au) in 2010 as a reference. The ABDC is a national council comprising Deans, Heads and Directors of Australian University business faculties and schools. According to the ABDC, the international journals were classified into A*, A, B and C, and A* or A journals were the highest level and highest authority ones.

Table 4.1 Summary of journals[a]

Level	Journals	Abbr.	Academic subject	First issue	#Issue /year	Volumes covered
A*	Journal of International Business Studies	JIBS	Management	1970	4	2–41
A*	Academy of Management Review	AMR	Management	1976	4	1–35
A*	Journal of Management Studies	JMS	Management	1964	8	8–47
A*	Academy of Management Journal	AMJ	Management	1958	6	14–53
A*	Strategic Management Journal	SMJ	Management	1979	13	1–31
A*	Management Science	MS	Management	1954	12	18–57
A*	Decision Sciences	DS	Management	1970	4	2–41
A*	Administrative Science Quarterly	ASQ	Management	1956	4	16–55
A	Long Range Planning	LRP	Management	1968	6	4–43
A	British Journal of Management	BJM	Management	1990	4	1–21
A	European Journal of Operational Research	EJOR	Management	1977	21	1–207
A	Journal of Business Research	JBR	Management	1973	12	1–63
A	Omega	OM	Management	1973	6	1–38
A	Critical Perspectives on Accounting	CPA	Accounting	1990	8	1–21
A*	The Accounting Review	AR	Management	1926	5–6	46–85
A*	Journal of Accounting Research	JAR	Management	1963	5	9–48
A	Journal of Accounting Literature	JAL	Management	1982	1	1–29
A	Journal of Management Accounting Research	JMAR	Management	1989	1	1–22
A	Management Accounting Research	MAR	Management	1990	4	1–21
A	The European Accounting Review	EAR	Management	1992	4	1–19

(continued)

Table 4.1 (continued)

Level	Journals	Abbr.	Academic subject	First issue	#Issue /year	Volumes covered
A	Financial Accountability & Management	FAM	Management	1985	4	1–26
A	Accounting Horizons	AH	Management	1987	4	1–24
A	British Accounting Review	BAR	Management	1969	4	3–42
A	International Journal of Production Economics	IJPE	Economics	1976	16	1–128
A*	Accounting, Organization and Society	AOS	Multidiscipline	1976	8	1–35
A	Accounting and Finance	AF	Multidiscipline	1960	4–5	12–51
A	Journal of Accounting and Public Policy	JAPP	Multidiscipline	1982	6	1–29
A	Technological Forecasting and Social Change	TFSC	Multidiscipline	1969	9	2–77

Note: The information of journals and the discipline is compiled according to the database
[a]Here, Management Science mainly refers to the Science of Enterprise Management. In order to emphasize the multidisciplines distribution of Management Control and the relationships between the Management Control and the Enterprise Management and the Accounting, and to take a different view of the importance of Accounting Science, Accounting, Management and Multidiscipline are tied listed here. For details, See "Xianzhi Zhang, Research on Domain & Discipline Position of Accounting and Finance, China Financial & Economic Publishing House, 2011"

Table 4.2 The literature distribution during 1971–2010

	Year								
Journal	1971–1975	1976–1980	1981–1985	1986–1990	1991–1995	1996–2000	2001–2005	2006–2010	
JMS	2(22.2)	2(11.1)	1(7.1)	1(5.9)	2(5.4)	2(5.6)	2(4.2)		12(5.2 %)
AMJ	2(22.2)	2(11.1)		2(11.8)	2(5.4)	1(2.8)			9(3.9 %)
LRP	2(22.2)	2(11.1)	2(14.2)	1(5.9)		3(8.3)			10(4.3)
SMJ			1(7.1)		3(8.1)	1(2.8)	1(2.1)		6(2.6 %)
BJM					4(10.8)			1(1.9)	5(2.1 %)
JIBS			3(21.4)		2(5.4)				5(2.1 %)
AR	1(11.1)	2(11.1)					2(4.2)	2(3.7)	7(3.0)
CPA							2(4.2)	3(5.6)	5(2.1 %)
JMAR					3(8.1)	1(2.8)	3(6.3)	3(5.6)	10(4.3 %)
MAR				1(5.9)	5(13.5)	7(19.4)	13(27.1)	23(42.6)	49(21.0 %)
EAR					1(2.7)	2(5.6)	2(4.2)	3(5.6)	8(3.4 %)
FAM			1(7.1)	1(5.9)	1(2.7)	2(5.6)		1(1.9)	6(2.6 %)
AOS		6(33.3)	6(42.9)	10(58.8)	11(29.7)	14(38.9)	14(29.2)	15(27.8)	76(32.6 %)
Others	2(22.2)	4(22.2)		1(5.9)	3(8.1)	3(8.3)	9(18.8)	3(5.6)	25(10.7 %)
Total	9	18	14	17	37	36	48	54	233

Note: The numbers in the brackets are a percent by year

Table 4.3 The theme distributions during 1971–2010

Themes	Year 1971–1975	1976–1980	1981–1985	1986–1990	1991–1995	1996–2000	2001–2005	2006–2010	%
Schools	3	9		2	2	1	4	8	29(12.44)
Theories	1	1	3	2	2		2	5	16(6.87)
Patterns		3	2	1	5	3	11	4	29(12.44)
Environment	1		1	3	11	9	7	6	38(16.31)
MCS and strategy	1		2	4	10	11	9	8	45(19.31)
Procedures	3	2		1	1	1	2	3	13(5.58)
Various MCS		3	6	4	5	10	13	20	61(26.18)
Other					1	1			2(0.86)
Total	9	18	14	17	37	36	48	54	233

summarized ones. From Table 4.3 We can see that management control and strategy, environment, and the different kinds of organization's management control take the dominant position.

4.3.1 *The Evolution of MCS Research*

As we can see from the subjects and types of the journals which published management control literature (Fig. 4.1 and Table 4.1), along with the variation trend of type and number of journals in Table 4.2, management control is a cross-cutting discipline from management, accounting, economics class, as well as other multidiscipline. The diagonal distribution in Table 4.2 shows that management control papers were mainly published in management journals in the early time, while the latter is active in the accounting journals, which reflected the evolution of management control in the disciplines.

The interdisciplinary and evolutionary character of management control are doomed to have multiple schools: In 1960s, standardized mass production model developed budget management into Anthony Accounting Control which is based on the technology of idealism [8]; In 1970s–1980s, Owing to the complexity of production activities and the principal-agent problem, Ouchi [9–11] came up with Result Control, Behavior Control, Clan Control, which is similar to Merchant [12] Results Control, Behavior Control and Personnel/Cultural Control. These two authors constitute a school of management control based on organizational behavior[6]; In 1990s, with the emphasis on strategy and environment, Simons established his interactive control which includes belief systems, boundary systems, diagnostic

[6]Merchant [13] didn't mention the Cultural Control in "Control of Management" (1982, Sloan Management Review), but added it in Merchant [14].

systems and interactive systems (also known as levers of control). Simons argued that management control was not just a strategy execution tool, but also a new strategy formation tool [15]; At the end of last century, Otley set up a "strategy – conduct – performance" framework from the overall control perspective in line with the idea of "what gets measured, gets done", [16]. As we can see in Table 4.3 that the distribution of the literature of management control schools was almost consistent with the time when these schools were raised, and the literature of the management control pattern came right after.

In addition to the evolutions in management control disciplines and schools, the themes of management control research exhibit its even stronger time marching traces.

In the late 1980s, the rise of the Japanese economy triggered a large number of emulation and transplantation of the Japanese management control pattern. This resulted in the intensification of international competition, the shortening of product life cycle which improved the weight of environment and strategies in managing control, making the environment and strategy research focused and emphasized at that time. Especially, the United States attached great importance to the Japanese lean manufacturing, Just in Time and the quality management, as well as the failure in transplanting Japanese management control, which draw many American scholars' attention to the importance of Corporate Strategy, as well as strategy and management control, management control and environment coordination issues. And strategic management and strategic management accounting have also risen in that period.

In the 1990s, Owing to the internationalization, diversity and complexity of the organizational structure, and the rise of the value chain management, many scholars paid close attention to the different organization's management control, such as multinational corporations, the Group, the emerging economies entity, as well as the Joint ventures, particularly the construction of the mode of cooperation across enterprises and the trade-off between control and trust.

In summary, with the elapse of time and changes in the environment, the research theme of management control **evolution**, distinct from each other in different periods, the new themes gradually replaced the old ones.

4.3.2 Content and Perspective of Management Control Research

The statistical analysis can clearly show the structure of content and the popularity of specific themes. While in-depth analysis of the content and perspectives can help present the content from the surface to the center, coarse to fine. And the analysis of researcher's perspective, as well as the procedures to carry out the research will show specific content and the characteristics of specific research ideas at the time.

4.3.2.1 Research on the Fundamental Theory of Management Control

The researches on Management control theory include essence, connotation, functions and their interrelationships. As for the essence and connotation, Dermer and Lucas [17] illustrated the meaning of control from the perspective of criticizing the mechanical control. Flamholtz [18] studied the relationships of accounting, budgeting and control in management control, which was a typical example of research on the interrelationship among concepts. The research on the role of management control try to explore the role of management control from a wider range instead of following the traditional control, for instance, Chenhall and Euske [19] studied the role of management control in organizational innovation and organizational change. Bouillon and Ferrier [20] discussed the role of management control in helping normalize corporate behavior. Dambrin et al. [21] studied the role of management control in supporting the implementation and infiltration of new systems.

4.3.2.2 Research on Management Control Pattern

The researches on management control pattern include the specific construction and design of management control systems. The research on the construction of management control pattern mostly focused on the discussion of the new management control mode and new control method. For instance, Malina and Selto [22] studied the Balance Scorecard based on management control mode. Vosselman [23] raised horizontal management control mode. Abernethy and Lillis [24] came up with external professions involved management control mode. Weaver et al. [25] applied moral control to management control mode. The research on the design of management control system mainly focused on major influencing factors and problems to pay attention to.

4.3.2.3 Research on Management Control Environment

Whether analyzing the driving power of the evolution of the research theme or taking the environment just as a research topic, the environment is a very important factor of management control research(see Table 4.3, accounting for 16.31 % of the total topics). From Table 4.4, we can see that management control environment can be divided into internal environment and external environment. Internal environment mainly involves corporate governance environment, human resources environment, organizational learning environment, cultural environment, manufacturing and technical environment. Corporate Governance Research are mainly from the perspective of the participation in management control of the board, and the perspective of the influence on management control of management behavior, leadership style, company value, stakeholder's value, and etc. Human resource management research mainly investigates how management control systems and human resources management system can be combined with each other. Organizational learning

Table 4.4 Distribution of management control environment research

	Year							
Themes	1971–1975	1976–1980	1981–1985	1986–1990	1991–1995	1996–2000	2001–2005	2006–2010
Internal environment								
Corporate governance				1	3	1		1
Human resource					1	2	2	1
Culture			1	1	5	3	2	1
Manufacturing and technology					1		1	1
Organization learning						1	1	
External environment								
National system					1	2		
Politics and economics	1			1			1	2

research concerns about the relationship between management control and organizational learning, and emphasizes the use of informal management control to enhance organizational learning. Cultural research mainly focuses on the impact of cultural environment on management control; the representative is Chee W. Chow, who respectively studied the impact of culture on management control in the United States, Japan, China, Taiwan, Singapore and so on. Production and technique environmental research focuses on when production and technological environment changes, how does management control adjust. These studies mostly focus on external economic and social environment of management control. For example, Khandwalla [26] studied the effect of market competition on management control. Wickramasing and Hopper [27] discussed the impact of the economic environment on the management control in the different economic development stages (Third World countries). Whitley [28] studied the impact of the national system on management control; Golding [29] studied the impact of customs on management control.

4.3.2.4 Research on Management Control and Strategy

As from Table 4.3, it is evident that the strategy plays an important role in the study of management control, it accounts for 19.31 % of the total. As in Table 4.5, we can see that the study can be divided into general conceptual level and specific strategic level. The research on general concept of strategy was in the mid-1980s, while the specific strategy research appeared after the 1990s. The general level research focused on the interaction between strategy and management control, the impact of management control on strategy, the management control of different types of strategy, and the role of management control in supporting strategic change and the generation of new strategy. Most of the literature was based on Simons' point of view. Specific strategy research includes manufacturing, competition, investment, and research and development strategy. Most of the literature mainly focused on

Table 4.5 Distribution of research on management control and strategy

Themes	Year 1971–1975	1976–1980	1981–1985	1986–1990	1991–1995	1996–2000	2001–2005	2006–2010
General strategy			2	4	4	3	7	3
Specific strategy								
Manufacturing strategy					5	2	1	1
Competition strategy	1							
Investment strategy						2		
R&D strategy					1	4	1	4

manufacturing strategy and R & D strategy. The representative of production strategy is Shirley J. Daniel who published many comparative studies from the perspective of quality management strategy and real-time production strategy between Japan and the United States during the period 1991–1995. A representative figure of the R & D strategy was Davila Antonio, who published many articles of management control on how to support R & D during the period 2000–2009.

4.3.2.5 Research on the Management Control Procedures

Management control procedures usually include planning, budgeting, communicating, performance and incentive, so do the studies. Planning research focuses on how to better adapt controls to control activities, especially the integration of planning and control among the different levels within an organization as well as departments in separate locations; Budgeting research concern how to make budget as an effective means of control, and also involves the trade-off between the budget flexibility and standard control; Research on management control and performance are not much, but the research merely focus on performance are more than enough. The main reason is that it is difficult to isolate the performance of management control system from the other performance; Research on management control and incentive care about how to design and make use of incentives to support the organization's management control. Information system research focus on studying the impact of information system on management control and how can information system perform its management control functions.

4.3.2.6 Research on Different Organization's Management Control

As shown in Table 4.3, different organization's management control is the most popular one (26.18 %), implying the significant importance of its application in practice. There are various classifications of research according to the different nature of organizations. Research from an overall perspective of the organization

Table 4.6 Distribution of different organization's management control

	Year							
Themes	1971–1975	1976–1980	1981–1985	1986–1990	1991–1995	1996–2000	2001–2005	2006–2010
Whole perspective								
Profit organization								
Multinationals company and group		1	2	2		5		2
Joint venture					1		1	1
Service company					2	1	2	
Emerging company						2	1	
Non-profit organization		1	2			1		1
Government		1			1			1
City management				1				
Inter-organization				1		1	6	12
Procedures within organization			2		1		2	1
Different lifecycle stage							1	2

are about the construction and application of management control in profit organizations, mainly refers to multinational corporations, Groups, joint ventures, knowledge-intensive enterprises and new forms of organization (such as flexible enterprise). Besides the research on profit organizations, there are research on non-profit organizations, government departments and urban management as well. Research on links within the organization mainly investigate the management control in the sales department, R&D department, risk management and etc.. Research on enterprise life cycle focus on investigating management control selecting in the start-up period, and the representative is Davila Antonio. Inter-enterprise management control is the most popular topic among the management control research. Most of them were found at the beginning of this century (see Table 4.6) and mainly concerned about management control patterns (such as Caligo and Ditillo [30]) and the trade-offs between control and trust (eg [31]).

4.4 Western Management Control Research Methods and Evolutions

The research topics are important, so are the research methods. So far, there is no uniformity in classifying research methods. We comprehensively borrowed the classifications from Shields [32], Poston and Grabski [4], Hesford et al. [5], Elbashir et al. [6] and Chenhall [33], and divided methods into Archival, Case and Field study, Experimental, Survey, Theoretical analysis, Literature Review and others.[7] Because of the dispute between case study and field study, we follow Shields [32] and present case study and field study together.

4.4.1 Evolution in Management Control Research Methods

According to the statistics in Table 4.7, case and field studies, survey and theoretical analysis are the dominant methods used in management control research, while database-based archival research is barely blank. Zimmerman [34] argued that unlike financial accounting, management accounting research is severely short of databases, which should have included internal and empirical data; therefore it usually turns to survey to meet the empirical requirements of journals. As we can see from Table 4.7 (bold) and Fig. 4.2, theoretical analysis dominated in the previous 20 years (1971–1990), while in the latest 20 years (1991–2010), case study, field study and survey research took the dominant place instead. Early literature makes reviews increase later. One thing should be noticed is that the numbers in Table 4.7 is only general indicative, because a variety of research methods may be used together, and we just picked up only the main one in our classification. Overall, due to the relatively stable environment in early times and serious needs of exploring management control theory, research rely more on theoretical analysis. Later, with the increase in the practical application of management control and the complexity and variability in an organization and the environment which increases the difficulty to set up theoretical assumptions, many problems need more in-depth field study to carry out and discovery, therefore, most studies are inclined to case study, field study and survey.

4.4.2 Management Control Research Methods Analysis

The nature of problems to be solved for different research topics varies, and different reasoning is required, therefore appropriate research methods should differ from each other. When illustrating research methods, research themes should be discussed comparatively, which not only shows how to use these methods but also indicates what kind of methods are often used in certain topics (Table 4.8).

---

[7] The others included simulation and etc.

Table 4.7 Statistics of research methods of management control in 1971–2010

Methods		Year 1971–1975	1976–1980	1981–1985	1986–1990	1991–1995	1996–2000	2001–2005	2006–2010	Total
Empirical	Archival									0
	Case and field	1(11.1)	4(22.2)	2(14.3)	6(35.3)	**11(29.7)**	**10(27.8)**	**23(47.9)**	**29(53.7)**	86
	Survey	2(22.2)	2(11.1)	5(35.7)	4(23.5)	**16(43.2)**	**14(38.9)**	**14(29.2)**	**13(24.1)**	70
	Experimental		1(5.6)		1(5.9)	3(8.1)		1(2.1)		6
	Others		1(5.6)						1(1.9)	2
Normative	Theoretical analysis	**5(55.6)**	**9(50.0)**	**7(50.0)**	**6(35.3)**	4(10.8)	9(25.0)	7(14.6)	7(13.0)	54
	Review	1(11.1)	1(5.6)			3(8.1)	3(8.30)	3(6.3)	4(7.4)	15
	Total	9	18	14	17	37	36	48	54	233

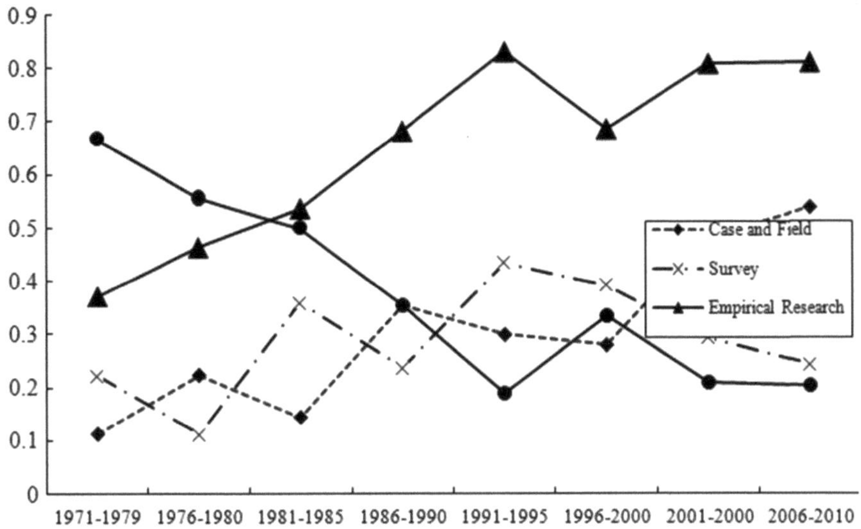

Fig. 4.2 Evolution of research methods of management control in 1971–2010

Table 4.8 Topics and methods

Topic	Year and method						
	Case and field	Survey	Experimental	Theoretical analysis	Review	Other	Total
Schools of MCS	5(17.24)	3(10.34)	1(3.45)	18(62.07)	2(6.90)		29
MCS theory	5(31.25)	2(12.50)		4(25.00)	5(31.25)		16
MCS pattern	10(34.48)	7(24.14)		11(37.93)	1(3.45)		29
MCS environment	15(39.47)	15(39.47)	2(5.26)	4(10.53)	2(5.26)		38
MCS and strategy	14(31.11)	22(48.89)	1(5.22)	6(13.33)	2(4.44)		46
MCS procedure	7(53.85)	4(30.77)		2(15.38)			13
MCS of different organization	30(49.18)	17(27.87)	2(3.28)	9(14.75)	1(1.64)	2(3.28)	61
Others					2(100)		2
Total	86	70	6	54	15	2	233

4.4.2.1 Case Study and Related Topics

Case studies are generally applicable to qualitative research and exploratory research which lacks pre-theoretical basis and data [35]. As shown in Table 4.8, case study is the most widely used in management control studies, mostly used in the environment, strategy, procedures, management control role models, as well as different organizations management control study. Depending on the number and the time of sample used in the case study, we can divide case study into single-case study and multi-case studies, single-period cross-section case study and multi-year longitudinal case study.

Single case contributes to deep exploratory study, [36]. Multi-case studies help to strengthen the commonness and the differences in the case [35]. Typical example of single case was Marginson [37] who studied Telco Ltd Company of a large British communications company during 1994–1996. He analyzed different management control mode including Anthony control mode and Simons control mode; As for the typical multi – case, Van der Meer-Kooistra and Scapens [38] compared NAM with HS to illustrate differences between the within organization and inter-organizational management control mode.

Single cross-section case is case study on a single time point or a short time period. Longitudinal case study normally takes track of the sample for a longer time and is from the perspective of historical development. This method is relatively more popular in management control research. The typical Single cross-section case study was, Efferin and Hopper [39] examined the impact of Chinese culture on management control in a Chinese-funded enterprise in Indonesia over a year. Typical multi-phase case, for instance, Chenhall [7] studied the relationships among trust within the organization, management control and performance in a large-scale aluminum manufacturers CIGGC from 1980 to 1990.

4.4.2.2 Survey and Related Topics

The survey is a method used to systematically and directly collect sample data from a certain population by (self-administered) questionnaires or (structured) interview, and get to know the object and discover the rules by the statistical analysis of data. In Table 4.8, the survey, which is the second most popular after case study, is frequently used in the management control environment, strategy, procedures, as well as different organizations. The methods that can be seen in management control literature mainly include pure questionnaire, pure interviews and their combination, supplemented by partial least squares method, factor analysis and structural equation measurement methods.

Some scholars use questionnaire. For example, Mahama [40] used self-administered questionnaire (with stamped envelope) and partial least squares regression to study the management control in mining enterprises. Some use interviews. For example, Chapman and Kihn [41] used semi-structured interviews to investigate management control among corporate partners in accounting firms. While other use a combination of interviews, questionnaires and observation. For example, Chow et al. [42] used questionnaires, interviews, field study and multivariate analysis of variance (MANOVA) and studied the relationship between cultural environment and management control. Widener et al. [43] used questionnaire survey and structural equation to study management control.

4.4.2.3 Experiment and Related Topics

Experimental study is a carefully designed and highly controlled one (often need to set up the experimental group and the control group), which set up certain factors to study the relation among variables. Because of the difficulty and high cost of setting up an experiment, experimental study is not common in management control research. Experimental studies are mostly used in studying the impact of culture on management control of different countries. Such as Chow et al. [44, 45] and some other researchers conducted a few experiments to compare the influence between Singapore and US or Japanese and US. Furthermore, Coletti et al. [46] used sophomores and juniors to simulate enterprises and studied the effect of different enterprises Management Control on building trust.

4.4.2.4 Normative Analysis and Related Subjects

We defined that the normative analysis, including logically theoretical analysis and a new framework construction, was a method of using classic theories, logical arguments and deduction to develop a new theory or to analyze a problem. According to Table 4.8, Normative Analysis is the most frequently used on different Management Control (here after referred to as MC) schools and control pattern research, which means it is very suitable for MC framework and pattern research, for example, the study of performance based management control of Otely [16], and New control pattern discussion of Ramanathan [47].

4.5 Conclusions and Implications

Any research should borrow its experiences from its history to carry on. We reviewed and summarized the overseas MC research with their research subjects and research methods. And we raised some suggestions for future theoretical research on MC in China.

4.5.1 Conclusions

Firstly, from the perspective of the foundation and schools of MC research, there are various MC academic disciplines and schools, such as Accounting based MC, Management based MC, Organizational Behavior based MC and others.

Secondly, from the perspective of the evolution of MC research themes, the themes of MC develop with the time and environment. In early research, owing to little reference, scholars mostly focused on the studies of MC thoughts and MC frameworks; In the late 1980s, because of the dramatic changes in the external environment, scholars turned to study the relationship between MC and Strategy and Environment; In the late 1990s, with the globalization of organizations and the booming of Value Chain theories, scholars started to study the MC of different organizations. Moreover, the recent hot topics of MC are the MCS designing for inter-firms, the information systems to support organization MC, and the MC to support R&D and etc.

Thirdly, from the perspective of research methods statistics, normative analysis and empirical research change alternately. In earlier research, the former is more popular; but at a later age, researchers utilized more case studies and investigations, as organizations and environments become more complicated.

Lastly, from the perspective of the relationship between research methods and themes, research themes determine the corresponding method. Normative analysis is used more often in MC school or pattern research, while for strategy, environment, process or different organizations MC research, case study and investigation are more popular.

4.5.2 *Implications*

Firstly, to enrich the theoretical foundation of management control research, and to encourage different MC schools to boom at the same time. In the west, scholars are good at borrowing ideas from other subjects to develop MC. While in our country, the perspective is relatively simple, for instance, it is mainly based on both internal control and accounting research. In the future, we should pay more attention to cross-discipline research and apply the latest achievements to MC research.

Secondly, to pay more attention to the timeliness and activeness of MC, it is useful for MC to play a role in promoting the development of organizations. On the one hand, the scholars should understand some of the problems, such as how close our MC studies do, what MC is required in real economic environment, the shortcomings in existing MC and etc. Using the MC experience from abroad, we should know how to choose a research topic based on the current condition and demands in recent years. For example, we could study the suitable MC modes in our countries, the MC for R&D strategy in the condition of constructing a creative country, and MC and environment under globalization. On the other hand, pay close attention to informal MC in the west, and try to turn passive control into active. Discover the key bottle-neck factors for organization development; furthermore, study the relationship between MC and behaviors and try to make MC active and beneficial in the organization operation.

Thirdly, booms the ways and broadens the caliber of MC data collection, and do more empirical research. Use case studies and survey studies to help overcome the bottleneck problem of database in management accounting and get more detailed data to solve problems directly and efficiently. We should try to do archive research by indirectly using the data in financial reports, such as econometrics methods, which involve tool variables (i.e. proxy variables or instrumental variables). We should also reduce experimental study costs by making full use of government aids or some outside trainings and meetings. Additionally, under a certain condition, we'd better achieve the goals by means of analyzing topics deeply, changing perspectives and methods.

References

1. Ferreira A, Otley D (2009) The design and use of performance management systems: an extended framework for analysis [J]. Manage Account Res 20(4):263–282
2. Flamholtz EG, Randle Y (2000) Growing pains: transitioning from an entrepreneurs to a professionally managed firm [M]. Jossey-Bass, San Francisco
3. Harrison GL, McKinnon JL (1999) Cross-cultural research in management control systems design: a review of the current state [J]. Account Org Soc 24(5–6):483–506
4. Poston RS, Grabski SV (2000) Accounting information systems research: is it another QWERTY? [J]. Int J Account Inform Syst 1(1):9–53
5. Hesford JW, Lee SHS et al (2006) Management accounting: a bibliographic study [J]. Handbooks Manage Account Res 1:3–26
6. Elbashir MZ, Collier PA et al (2011) The role of organizational absorptive capacity in strategic use of business intelligence to support integrated management control systems [J]. Account Rev 86(1):155–184
7. Chenhall RH (2003) Management control systems design within its organizational context: findings from contingency-based research and directions for the future [J]. Account Org Soc 28(2–3):127–168
8. Anthony RN (1965) Planning and control systems: a framework for analysis [M]. Division of Research, Graduate School of Business Administration, Harvard University, Boston
9. Ouchi WG (1977) The relationship between organizational structure and organizational control [J]. Adm Sci Q 22(1):95–113
10. Ouchi WG (1978) The transmission of control through organizational hierarchy [J]. Acad Manage J 21(2):173–192
11. Ouchi WG (1979) A conceptual framework for the design of organizational control mechanisms [J]. Manage Sci 25(9):833–848
12. Merchant KA (1985) Control in business organizations [M]. Pitman, Boston
13. Merchant KA (1982) The control function of management [J]. Sloan Manage Rev 23(4): 43–55
14. Merchant KA (1998) Modern management control systems: text and cases [M]. Prentice Hall, Upper Saddle River
15. Simons R (1995) Levers of control: how managers use innovative control systems to drive strategic renewal [M]. Harvard Business School Press, Boston
16. Otley D (1999) Performance management: a framework for management control systems research [J]. Manage Account Res 10(4):363–382
17. Dermer J, Lucas R (1986) The illusion of managerial control [J]. Account Org Soc 11(6):471–482
18. Flamholtz EG (1983) Accounting, budgeting and control systems in their organizational context: theoretical and empirical perspectives [J]. Account Org Society 8(2–3):153–169
19. Chenhall RH, Euske KL (2007) The role of management control systems in planned organizational change: an analysis of two organizations [J]. Account Org Soc 32(7–8):601–637
20. Bouillon ML, Ferrier GD et al (2006) The economic benefit of goal congruence and implications for management control systems [J]. J Account Public Policy 25(3):265–298
21. Dambrin C, Lambert C et al (2007) Control and change–analysing the process of institutionalization [J]. Manage Account Res 18(2):172–208
22. Malina MA, Selto FH (2001) Communicating and controlling strategy: an empirical study of the effectiveness of the balanced scorecard [J]. J Manage Account Res 13(1):47–90
23. Vosselman EGJ (2002) Towards horizontal archetypes of management control: a transaction cost economics perspective [J]. Manage Account Res 13(1):131–148
24. Abernethy MA, Lillis AM (1995) The impact of manufacturing flexibility on management control system design [J]. Account Org Soc 20(4):241–258
25. Weaver GR, Treviño LK et al (1999) Corporate ethics programs as control system: influences of executive commitment and environmental factors [J]. Acad Manage J 42(1):41–57

26. Khandwalla PN (1973) Effect of competition on the structure of top management control [J]. Acad Manage J 16(2):285–295
27. Wickramasinghe D, Hopper T (2005) A cultural political economy of management accounting controls: a case study of a textile mill in a traditional Sinhalese village [J]. Crit Perspect Account 16(4):473–503
28. Whitley R (1999) Firms, institutions and management control: the comparative analysis of coordination and control systems [J]. Account Org Soc 24(5–6):507–524
29. Golding D (1991) Some everyday rituals in management control [J]. J Manage Stud 28(6):569–583
30. Caglio A, Ditillo A (2008) A review and discussion of management control in inter-firm relationships: achievements and future directions [J]. Account Org Soc 33(7–8):865–898
31. Langfield-Smith K (2008) The relations between transactional characteristics, trust and risk in the start-up phase of a collaborative alliance [J]. Manage Account Res 19(4):344–364
32. Shields MD (1997) Research in management accounting by North Americans in the 1990s [J]. J Manage Account Res 9:3–61
33. Chenhall RH, Smith D (2011) A review of Australian management accounting research: 1980–2009 [J]. Account Finance 51:173–206
34. Zimmerman JL (2001) Conjectures regarding empirical managerial accounting research [J]. J Account Econ 32(1–3):411–427
35. Yin RK (1989) Case study research [M]. Sage, Newbury Park
36. Berry A, Loughton E et al (1991) Control in a financial services company (RIF): a case study [J]. Manage Account Res 2(2):109–139
37. Marginson DEW (1999) Beyond the budgetary control system: towards a two-tiered process of management control [J]. Manage Account Res 10(3):203–230
38. Van der Meer-Kooistra J, Scapens RW (2008) The governance of lateral relations between and within organisations [J]. Manage Account Res 19(4):365–384
39. Efferin S, Hopper T (2007) Management control, culture and ethnicity in a Chinese Indonesian company [J]. Account Org Soc 32(3):223–262
40. Mahama H (2006) Management control systems, cooperation and performance in strategic supply relationships: a survey in the mines [J]. Manage Account Res 17(3):315–339
41. Chapman CS, Kihn L-A (2009) Information system integration, enabling control and performance [J]. Account Org Soc 34(2):151–169
42. Chow C, Shields M et al (1999) The importance of national culture in the design of and preference for management controls for multi-national operations [J]. Account Org Soc 24:441–461
43. Widener SK (2007) An empirical analysis of the levers of control framework [J]. Account Org Soc 32(7–8):757–788
44. Chow C, Shields M et al (1991) The effects of management controls and national culture on manufacturing performance: an experimental investigation [J]. Account Org Soc 16(3):209–226
45. Chow CW, Kato Y et al (1994) National culture and the preference for management controls: an exploratory study of the firm–labor market interface [J]. Account Org Soc 19(4–5):381–400
46. Coletti AL, Sedatole KL et al (2005) The effect of control systems on trust and cooperation in collaborative environments [J]. Account Rev 80(2):477–500
47. Ramanathan KV (1985) A proposed framework for designing management control systems in not-for-profit organizations [J]. Financ Account Manage 1(1):75–92

Chapter 5
Evolution of Western Internal Control Theory

5.1 Internal Check (Before the 1940s)

Internal control developed from internal check, which was born in ancient Egyptian national treasury management. Before the 1940s, scholars were familiar with internal check though internal control had already been mentioned or defined.[1] According to *the Kohler's Dictionary for Accountant*, Internal check system refers to a business process designation which is to provide effective organization and operation and to prevent errors and illegal transactions from occurring. Its main characteristic is duties separation, which requires that any personnel or department should not have full authority to get access to any certain part of business processes. People or departments need cross-checking or cross-controlling. Designing the effective internal check system is to make sure that each individual business process passes through the necessary procedures, and among these procedures, internal check system is always an indispensable part.

Internal check has two basic advantages: first, there is little chance for two or more personnel or departments to unconsciously make one same mistake; second, it significantly lower the possibility of two or more personnel or departments to consciously make accounting frauds by collusion.

According to the functions and contents of internal check, it can be divided into four: physical assets check, physical restrain, authority check and book check. From the perspective of accounting, internal check ideas are mainly about a cross-checking in accounts and an implementation of post separation which was earlier considered an ideal control for avoiding mistakes.

---

[1] The earliest literature of Internal Control Occupation was *Verification of financial statements* revised by American Institute of Certified Public Accountants (AICPA) and Federal Reserve (Fed) in 1929. The earliest definition of Internal Control was *Examination of financial statements by independent public accountants*, a revision based on the former, and was announced in 1936.—According to *The Internal Control Framework of Enterprises: Construction and Operation*, by Yang Youhong, Zhejiang People's Publishing House, 2001 (the 1st Edition): pp 2–3.

X. Zhang, *Enterprise Management Control Systems in China*, Understanding China, DOI 10.1007/978-3-642-54715-7_5,

Internal check, the basis of organizational control and separation, reduces errors and frauds effectively. Therefore, in modern internal control theories, internal check plays an important role in modern internal control theories and applications as well. However, one thing must be clear that internal check is only one part of the internal control, which cannot meet the need of the requirement of internal control not only by its goals but also with its contents or methods.

5.2 Internal Control System (From the Late 1940s to the 1970s)

At the end of the 1940s, internal control replaced internal check. In 1949, the Audit Committees of American Institute of Certified Public Accountants (AICPA) reported in *Internal Control: Elements of a Coordinated System and its Importance to Management and the Independent Public Accountant, Special Report* (American Institute of Certified Public Accountants. Committee on Auditing Procedure, 1949)[2] This firstly made an official definition of Internal Control as it included organization structure designs and all coordinated methods and measures applied in the organization, which were used for protecting assets, inspecting the accuracy of accounting information, improving operation efficiency, and promoting the implementation of given management policies. The concepts defined its contents, methods and objectives, developed the Internal Check theories and methods and contributed to the emergence and the development of Internal Control which gained an extensive attention.

In Oct. 1958, the Audit Committee of AICPA redefined Internal Control in *The Announcement of Audit Procedures No. 29* and divided Internal Control into Accounting Control and Management Control. Internal Accounting Control includes methods and procedures implemented to ensure asset safety and reliable records. The Accounting Control includes the authorization and approval system, control of duties separation of financial records and checks from operation and property custody, the physical control and the internal auditing.

The Internal Management Control includes all the methods and procedures set by organizations to achieve operational efficiency and management implementation. It includes the statistical analysis, the performance reporting, and the training plan for employees, the quality control and etc.

In the middle of the 1970s, Internal Control most focused on system design and auditing and tried to richen the methods of Internal Control System and improve auditing quality and efficiency. During 1973–1976, the investigation of Watergate drew legislatures' and administrations' attentions to the Internal Control problem. The investigations conducted by the Committee of Watergate scandal investigation and the Securities and Exchange Commission (SEC) showed that a lot of U.S. major companies undertook illegal national donations, suspicious or illegal international payments (including bribing foreign governors). Because of the investigations, the U.S. Congress

[2] http://www.google.co.jp/books?id=xCwUAQAAMAAJ&hl=zh-CN

passed The Foreign Corrupt Practices Act of 1977 (FCPA), which included not only the Anti-bribery ordinances, but also the ordinances of Accounting and Internal Control.

The development of the Internal Control concept not only drives the simple Internal Check into Internal Control and develops the definition, content, objective and method of Internal Control but also separates the records reliability from the operations efficiency of Internal Control and proposed Internal Accounting Control and Internal Management Control. Even though, the academics in the West found Internal Accounting Control and Internal Management Control related and inseparable. Therefore, a new concept of Internal Control Structure appeared in the 1980s.[3]

5.3 Internal Control Structure (From the 1980s to the 1990s)

Enterprises started to set up their internal control after the legislation of the *Foreign Corrupt Practices Act* (FCPA). Many occupational groups and local authorities studied internal control from different perspectives as well, for example, Audit Committee of American Institute of Certified Public Accountants (AICPA) declared *Report, Conclusions and Recommendation* and *Statement on Auditing Standards No. 30* (1980), *No. 43* (1982), and *No. 48* (1984). Financial Education Initiative (FEI) declared *Internal Control in U.S. Corporations: The Statement of the Art*, Securities and Exchange Commission (SEC) declared *Statement of Management on Internal Accounting Control*, and Institute of Internal Auditors declared *Statement on Internal Auditing Standards No. 1- Control: Concepts and Responsibilities* and etc.

In 1985, the National Commission on Fraudulent Financial Reporting-Treadway Commission was sponsored jointly by five major professional associations in the United States: the American Accounting Association (AAA), the American Institute of Certified Public Accountants (AICPA), Financial Executives International (FEI), The Institute of Internal Auditors (IIA), and the National Association of Accountants (now the Institute of Management Accountants [IMA]). One of the topics they discussed was the reason why fraudulent financial reporting existed, which included discussion of the imperfect internal control. After 2 years, Treadway Commission declared its report and proposed a lot of valuable suggestions. However, the report immediately received lots of feedback from numerous organizations. After the 1980s, internal control research in the West shifted their focus from a general concept to a specific and deep content. In 1998, AICPA declared *Statement on Auditing Standards (SAS) No. 55*, which replaced *the SAS No. 1* (1972) since Jan. 1990, which first used internal control structure instead of internal control. Internal control structure was indicated to include all policies and processes of reasonable assurance to achieve specific enterprise goals, and cleared that it consisted of the control environment, the accounting system and the control process.

The control environment reflects the attitudes and behaviors of the board, managers, stockholders and the others to controls. It includes management philosophy and operating style, institutional framework, functions of the board and auditing commission,

[3] Wu Shuipeng et al. [1].

personnel policy and process, method to determine power and responsibility, and control of managers' supervision and inspection such as operating plans, budgets, forecasts, profit plans, responsibility accounting, and internal auditing.

The accounting system set the rules of accounting as recognizing, measuring, recording and reporting. An effective accounting system should involve: identifying and recording all legal transactions, classifying transactions and recording, monetary reporting transactions in financial statements, attributing transactions into proper accounting periods, and describing transactions appropriately.

The control procedures refer to all the policies and procedures set by management to make sure that the organizational goals are achieved. The control procedures include the approval authority of businesses and activities, the clear assignment of personnel, the complete accounting entry, ledger settings and records, the control of assets and records, and the independence of auditing.

The internal control structure is on the basis of internal control rules: first, the control environment is formally integrated into internal control as a part of internal control to ensure the setting and operating of an effective internal control system; second, unifying the internal control with its elements and constructions, instead of differentiating accounting control and management control any more. However, there are still some shortages of recognition and description of internal control elements like risk assessing, and supervising.

5.4 Internal Control Integrated Framework (From the 1990s to the Beginning of the Twenty-First Century)

In 1992, owing to the suggestions from the Treadway commission, the Committee Sponsors organized another Commission (Committee of Sponsoring Organizations of The Tread-way Commission COSO) to specialize in internal control research. The National Commission, which proposed an *Internal Control-Integrated Framework*- the COSO report, consisted of five major professional associations: the American Accounting Association (AAA), the American Institute of Certified Public Accountants (AICPA), Financial Executives International (FEI), The Institute of Internal Auditors (IIA), and the National Association of Accountants (now the Institute of Management Accountants [IMA]). The COSO report proposed that internal control was broadly defined as processes executed by an entity's board of directors, management and other personnel to provide reasonable assurance of effectiveness and efficiency of operations, reliability of financial reporting, and compliance with applicable laws and regulations. Those components, coming from management operation modes, should be combined with management process and are as follows:

- Control Environment: The control environment sets the tone of an organization, influencing the control consciousness of its people. It is the foundation for all other components of internal control, providing discipline and structure. Control

environment factors include the integrity, ethical values and competence of the entity's people; management's philosophy and operating style; the way management assigns authority and responsibility, and organizes and develops its people; and the attention and direction provided by the board of directors.
- Risk Assessment: Every entity faces a variety of risks from external and internal sources that must be assessed. A precondition to risk assessment is the establishment of objectives, linked at different levels and internally consistent. Risk assessment is the identification and analysis of relevant risks to the achievement of the objectives and forming a basis for determining how the risks should be managed. Because economic, industry, regulatory and operating conditions will continue to change, mechanisms are needed to identify and deal with the special risks associated with change.
- Control Activities: Control activities are the policies and procedures that help ensure management directives are carried out. They help ensure that necessary actions are taken to address risks to achievement of the entity's objectives. Control activities occur throughout the organization, at all levels and in all functions. They include a range of activities as diverse as approvals, authorizations, verifications, reconciliations, reviews of operating performance, security of assets and segregation of duties.
- Information and Communication: Pertinent information must be identified, captured and communicated in a form and timeframe that enable people to carry out their responsibilities. Information systems produce reports, containing operational, financial and compliance-related information, which make it possible to run and control the business.
- Monitoring: Internal control systems need to be monitored. It is a process that assesses the quality of the system's performance over time.

The COSO report mentioned that the goal of the enterprise was set to provide the direction where enterprise should go and the elements of internal control provided the necessary conditions to make sure enterprise can achieve them, and they were interactive with each other. These components should be in agreement with all goals' categories and vice versa. Therefore, internal control is essential and important to all enterprises and all departments.

5.5 Enterprise Risk Management-Integrated Framework (After the Twenty-First Century)

In 2001, COSO delegated Price Waterhouse Coopers to develop a framework that would be readily usable to evaluate the management and conduct enterprise risk management. During that period, a series of high-profile business scandals and failures happened and investors, company personnel, and other stakeholders suffered tremendous loss. In the aftermath, calls for enhanced corporate governance and risk management, with new law, regulation and listing standards, boomed. People hoped that an enterprise risk management framework with key principles and concepts, a common language, and clear direction and guidance could be set up. COSO declared *Enterprise Risk Management – Integrated Framework* at the right time to fill this need, and they expected the framework to be widely accepted by companies and other organizations and indeed all stakeholders and interested parties.

The *Enterprise Risk Management-Integrated Framework* expands internal control and provides a more robust and extensive focus on the broader subject of enterprise risk management. Practitioners may not only look to this framework both to satisfy their internal control needs , but also can move toward a fuller risk management process.

This enterprise risk management framework is geared to achieving four objectives[4]:

- Strategic- high-level goals, aligned with and supporting its mission
- Operations- effective and efficient use of its resources
- Reporting- reliability of reporting
- Compliance- compliance with applicable laws and regulations.

Enterprise risk management consists of eight interrelated components. These are derived from the way management runs an enterprise and are integrated with the management process. These components are:

- Internal Environment – The internal environment encompasses the tone of an organization, and sets the basis for how risk is viewed and addressed by an entity's members. It includes risk management philosophy and risk appetite, integrity and ethical values, and the environment in which they operate.
- Objective Setting – Objectives must exist before management can identify potential events which will affect their achievement. Enterprise risk management ensures that management takes appropriate procedures to set objectives and that the chosen objectives support and align with the entity's mission and are consistent with its risk appetite.
- Event Identification – Internal and external events affecting achievement of an entity's objectives must be identified, distinguishing between risks and opportunities. Opportunities are channeled back to management's strategy or objective-setting processes.
- Risk Assessment – Risks are analyzed, considering likelihood and impact, as a basis for determining how they should be managed. Risks are assessed on an inherent and a residual basis.
- Risk Response – Management selects risk responses – avoiding, accepting, reducing, or sharing risk. It also develops a set of actions to align risks with the entity's risk tolerance and risk appetite.
- Control Activities – Policies and procedures are established and implemented to help ensure the risk responses are effectively carried out.

[4]Committee of Sponsoring Organizations of the Treadway Commission (COSO) [2].

- Information and Communication – Relevant information is identified, captured, and communicated in a form and timeframe that enable people to carry out their responsibilities. Effective communication also occurs in a broader sense, flowing down, across, and up the entity.
- Monitoring – The entirety of enterprise risk management is monitored and modifications are made as necessary. Monitoring is accomplished through ongoing management activities, separate evaluations, or both.

References

1. Wu Shuipeng, Chen Hanwen, Shao Xiandi (2000) Development of internal control theories. Acc Res 21(5):2–8
2. Committee of Sponsoring Organizations of the Treadway Commission (COSO) (2004) The enterprise risk and management-integrated framework. The Committee of Sponsoring Organizations of the Treadway Commission (COSO), America

Chapter 6
The Evolution of Western Management Control Theory

6.1 The Birth of Management Control

The idea of management control came along with the early management theories which involved pure control idea and the development of classic management contributed its firm theoretical foundation to management control. Therefore, the early management provided the beneficial condition for the generation of management control.

Charles Babbage pushed forward the development of management control by improving management theory. In the early nineteenth century, Babbage [1] was very concerned about how to improve the manufacturing process and production system. He came up with the improved methods after meticulously analyzing the operation process, skill, and the cost of each program. Later during the industrial revolution, Babbage made his further contribution to management control. He studied the reason why the division of labor helped increase productivity and proposed a salary plus profit sharing system to motivate the employees. He also put forward many constructive suggestions for managers to implement management control.

The Mary Parker Follett's research in management gave birth to the ideological essence of the coming management control. As an excellent classical management theorists focusing on control problems, Follett M.P [2] proposed the enlightening thought of almost modern control theories. Follett argued that it was the complicated interactive relationship of what the manager controls rather than simply the material elements. She insisted that the control was based on "the people", that is, the implementation of the control depends on those self-regulated and self-directed individuals and groups who have common interests and common goals. Follett seemed to be too idealistic in considering the consistency of the organization's goals, as she thought control was the control of events rather than the control of people, the control of the inter-relationships rather than the control among organization levels. She further considered coordination as the interactive relationship of all the factors within a framework, which involved the direct contact of all related personnel.

X. Zhang, *Enterprise Management Control Systems in China*, Understanding China,
DOI 10.1007/978-3-642-54715-7_6, © Springer-Verlag Berlin Heidelberg 2014

The point of the principles she proposed is to ensure the expected performance of the organization, and the application of "basic principles" actually is control itself.

The scientific management is the cornerstone of management control. In the early twentieth century, scientific management was very popular, the representative of it was Taylor and his famous book, *Principles of Scientific Management* [3]. Taylor carried out lots of research to discover how to improve the efficiency of workers, and conducted a series of experiments. He believed that the central issue of scientific management was to improve labor productivity. In order to improve labor productivity, "first class worker" must be hired. Make sure all employees are able to master the standardized operation method and understand the proper use of standardized tools, machines and materials, at the same time, set and use the standardized operating environment. To motivate workers to work hard, piecework system should be used. Employees and employers should realize that it is beneficial for both sides to improve labor productivity, thus collaboration should be achieved. In order to improve labor productivity, planning and executive functions should be separated. The traditional experience based working pattern should be replaced by scientific working method. In order to improve efficiency, function management should be implemented. Meanwhile, he also proposed the "exception principle" in management control. Taylor's viewpoints represent the basis and essence of scientific management. By studying the above ideas, we find that scientific management theory followed the path of control standards, system control and strict control, which laid the foundation of ideological principles of management control.

In 1920, *Industrial control*, the first book ever completely took management control as its theme, written by Francis M, Lawson, totally and officially introduced control principle to scientific management. That book consists of six articles. And its aim is "To bring the basic principles of command and control to those workers…" [4]. The descendants thought this book was to "bring control principle to scientific management, and make sure scientific management is properly applied" [4].

By the mid-twentieth century, Fayol [5] and Max Weber made a significant contribution to management theory and the theory of functions of control. Fayol considered control as one of the five functions of management and thought it suitable for everything within the organization. For him, control meant "inspect the consistency between real execution and the plan, the orders and the principles"; Weber's viewpoints of control were mainly exhibited in his book "*The Theory of Social and Economic Organization*". He advocated the establishment with a highly structured, formalized, impersonalized "ideal organization system", which he considered the most reasonable way to forcibly control over individuals and the most effective measures to achieve the goals and to improve labor productivity. Additionally, it was superior to other organizations in terms of accuracy, stability, discipline and reliability.

In the early stage of management control, most theorists were concerned about real practical problems and had a strong desire to solve those specific problems. These early thoughts of management control laid a good foundation for the future theory development. However, although the thoughts of theorists with practical experience were popular and beneficial to later research, they are too rational and economic, and too anxious to search for "generally applicable" methods for those problems, which basically caused the research stuck in "job control", and could not really go deep into the theoretical level of "management control".

With the help of the development of early management control, Western management control theorists made tremendous progress. To summarize, we can find that the research was mainly focused on the concept of management control, framework of management control system, pattern of management control system and the relationship between management control system and control environment.

6.2 The Discussion About the Concept of Management Control

There has been a debate ever since the concept of management control was initially raised; the early management control appeared as a function of management. Until the mid-twentieth century, with the emergence of cybernetics and systems theory, many scholars began to study management control from the perspective of cybernetics and systems theory. Later, more scholars studied management control from the perspective of accounting and financial management. Nowadays, the latter one is more popular. At the meanwhile, under the increasingly complex environmental condition of modern organizations, management, organizational behavior, psychology and other disciplines are borrowed to help develop management control, and moreover the non-financial criteria and other means of control are gradually accepted into management control system.

The meaning of management control in the early management: Early management treated management control as a function of management, Diemer [6] believed that control meant the adjustment made by power to ensure the consistency with enterprise rules of affairs. After that, he further described "Control requires management to know what should be done and what is being done in all branches and departments. If what is being done deviates from what should be done, control means discovering why this happened and understanding how to overcome the defects, disadvantages or excessive cost and thinking of remedies" (1924). Although Diemer's view of management control was from a general perspective, it was closer to the institution control of modern control systems, it only covered the most basic part of management control and could not fully represent all the meanings of management control.

The impact of Cybernetics and system theory on the concept of management control: In 1948, *Weiner's* "Cybernetics: Or Control and Communication in the Animal and the Machine" [7] published and was widely spread, exerting an important effect on the management control research. The main contribution of Cybernetics to the extremely complicated management control systems is that it tries to apply the relevant and simple feedback mechanism to explain the behaviors of complex systems. Many scholars believe that formal control must be reflected in the nature of the idea of cybernetics [8]. Cybernetics based management control considered management control took finance and accounting as a means, and set up a feedback loop with standards, evaluation and correction. At the same time, system theory was gradually integrated into the management control research. System theory's contribution lies in applying a "systems approach" to management control, and leading people no longer to focus only on a single variable control, but the overall control, namely, the system perspective. With the introduction of systems theory, the definition of the management control system became another debate alongside the concept of management control, which caused people to consider establishing an open system or a closed system.

General view of management control: Machin [9] discussed the terms of "management", "control" and "system" individually in a critical review of management control system, and argued that the study of management control systems should focus on "the formalized, developed, organization-wide data processing system, which are set up to facilitate management control operation". Meanwhile, he borrowed Anthony's definition that management control is the process to ensure the acquisition, effective and efficient use of resources in achieving the organizational goals. The biggest advantage of Machin's definition is that it avoided the debate on the concept of management control and left the space for theorists to accommodate differences, that is, theorists can study one single issue with different ideas. Even though, it is the "tolerance" that leads to the lack of a precise definition and the failure to establish a complete, independent framework of management control system.

Financial and accounting based management control: Anthony [10] defined management control as "the process through which the managers achieve organizational goals and also ensure the effectiveness and efficiency of the use and allocation of resources". He argued that the management control is in the middle of strategic formulation and job control, where strategic planning refers to the entire organization's long-term goal setting, while job control is to ensure that the current task is well executed. Through the link of the two in management control, global objectives are broken down into secondary targets of each component within the organization; the future development target is given more realistic contents and long-term goals are converted to shorter period goals. In the definition, the precondition of the operation of management control is the organization hierarchy system, meaning the management control at various management levels from the specific pressure on the organization's certain level. Anthony's MCS is widely used in the field of management accounting. However, a lot of criticism is received by the descendants because of too much emphasis on the use of financial and accounting methods as means to help management control.

Nevertheless, Anthony made pioneering contributions to management control, he divided management control into three levels, which was beneficial for in-depth and detailed study of the different levels of control. In fact, Anthony in the earlier studies had emphasized the importance of sociology, psychology and behavioral science, but owing to financial and accounting based control was relatively easy to form control technology and methodology, therefore, management control was conducted basically by utilizing basic accounting principles and financial plans. Especially later, Anthony refined the definition of management control as “managers influence other members in the organization to implement organizational strategy” [11], and it became a mainstream in management control after combined with modern control measures.

6.3 The Discussion on Management Control System Framework

At different stages of the development of management control, people structured their control system according to their own definition of management control. Because of that, the research on the management control system framework developed a lot.

6.3.1 *Cybernetics Based Management Control System Framework*

The Management control system under Cybernetics tries to apply the simple and relevant feedback mechanism to explain the behaviors in complex systems. Peter Lorange and Michael S. Scott Morton [12], the representatives of this view, built up the early management control system framework model.

Peter Lorange and Michael S. Scott Morton [12] considered that the fundamental goal of the management control system was to assist management to achieve the organizational goals. They argued that the standardized management control system framework included the following aspects: (a) identifying the related control variables; (b) designing short-term plans; (c) the whole record of the real execution of short-term plan; (d) variance analysis. As shown in Fig. 6.1.

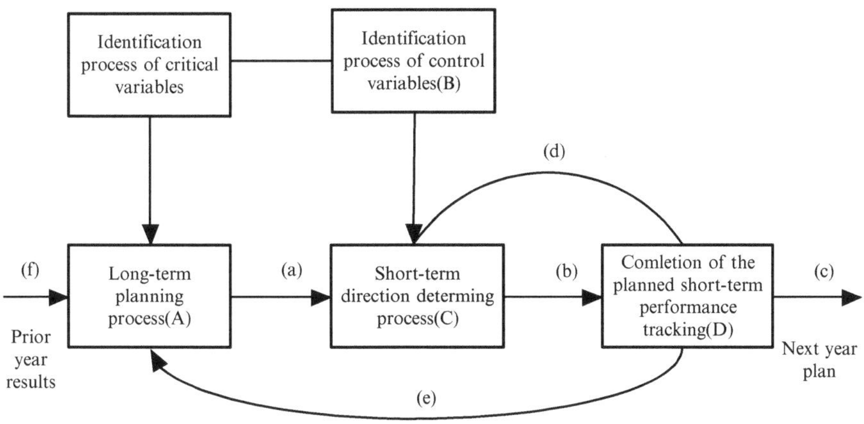

Fig. 6.1 Management control system framework built by Lorange e.g. (Lorange and Scott Morton [12])

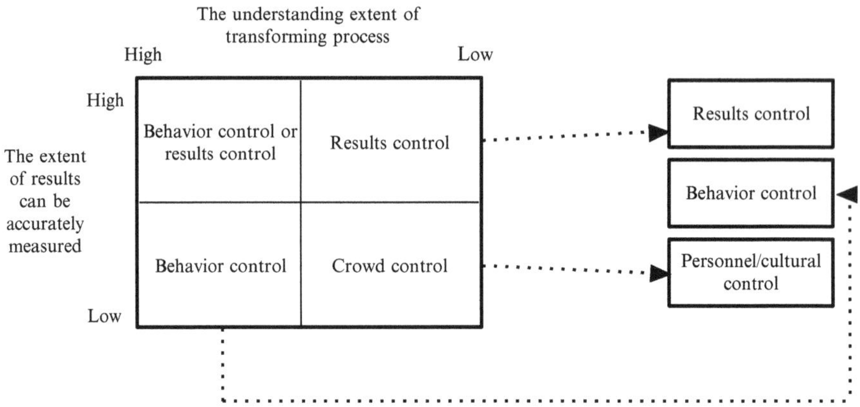

Fig. 6.2 Behavioral control schematics by Ouchi and Merchant

As from the figure above, the management control system framework of Lorange is based on control feedback, a narrow sense of management control, which involves management control process, but could not objectively reflect the overall effects of various factors on management and control system.

6.3.2 Behavior-Based Management Control Systems Framework

Kenneth Merchant, the proposer of this system, pointed out that management control should start from behavior control. He defined management control as "a system including all measures to ensure correct behaviors" [13]. Merchant [14] divided controls into three categories: result control, behavior control and personnel/cultural control. Result control is achieved by the rewards and punishments of the final result. It causes employees to pay attention to the behavioral consequences and encourages them to strive for expected results. Behavior control is used to ensure the consistency between the behavior of the staff and what the organization expects. It reduces the concurrency of unexpected behavior. Personnel control and culture control are used to ensure that employees fully understand organizational goals, to help employees with ability training, to select the competent candidates for organizations, and to train staffs to be self-monitoring, self-restraint and understand corporate values.[1] Merchant's control methods are familiar with result control, behavior control and group control raised by Ouchi, which was earlier. As shown in Fig. 6.2 (on the left of Ouchi, right side of Merchant).

[1] In behavioral control, Merchant "control of management" did not involve cultural control in 1982 in Sloan Management Review, Merchant added cultural control in 1998.

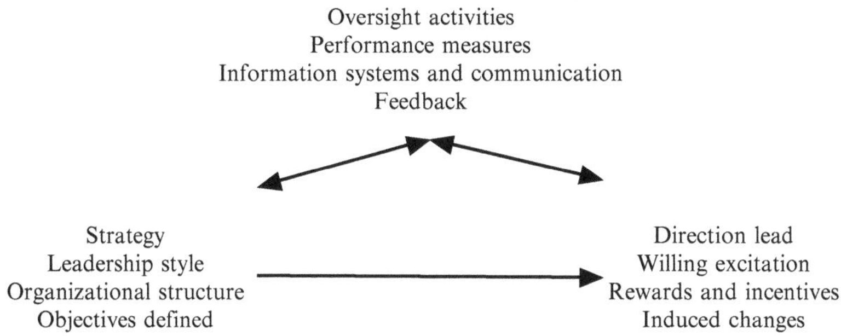

Fig. 6.3 Management control system integrated framework by Rotch (Rotch [15])

6.3.3 Management Based Management Control Systems Framework

The management control system framework raised by William Rotch [15], to a certain extent, overcomes the deficiency of Lorange's. It reflects the environment, the implementation process and the communication and feedback of management control system. Shown in Fig. 6.3.

In this framework, the left column can be regarded as the environment of management control system, the right column can be regarded as the goals of management control, the top can be regarded as the process of management control system. There are two major problems in this framework: First, Rotch took strategy, leadership style, organizational structure and goals as the control environment, but external environment, production technology, human resource management, management philosophy, and other environment variables are also involved in a controlled environment in the west. Therefore, the factors listed in the above figure do not adequately reflect the effects of the entire control environment; Second, the biggest drawback of this framework is that the description of the implementation of management control simply include activities of performance measurement, communication and feedback to post-supervision, which are parts of management control, however, it omits the prior processes such as goal setting and decomposing of strategic plan and the like. Thus, it can only be regarded as an incomplete reflection of management control.

6.3.4 Management Control Systems Framework Relying on Control Means

Perhaps inspired by previous studies, Robert Simons [16] subsequently proposed four management control lever: Boundary Control Lever, Diagnostic Control Lever, Belief Control Lever and Interactive Control Lever.[2] Each lever itself was put into a

[2] Boundary Control Lever, is an organization "brake" which clearly intended to ensure the organization know what not to do, in addition to employees do anything right according to the organization

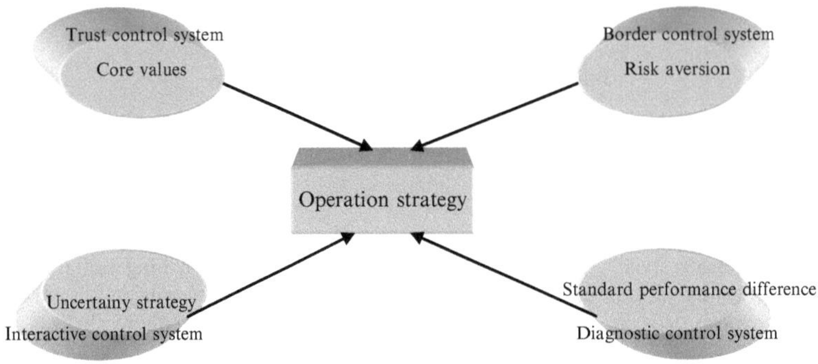

Fig. 6.4 Four kinds of management control leverage (Simons [16])

state where the leverage played a role in policy and methods – management control system, which also produced four systems, boundary control systems, diagnostic control system, belief control system and interactive control system. As shown in Fig. 6.4.

The four control levers have already covered means of management control, such as "direction guidance, willingness excitation, rewards and incentives leads to changes and the like", and at the meanwhile integrate information communication and feedback into the system, making up the biggest drawback of the framework of management control system designed by Rotch.

However, there is also a major problem in this framework, that is, the under consideration of control environment. In an era when "Contingency approach has become the main theme of the study of management control systems" [17], it is difficult to design a scientific and effective management control system simply focusing on management control system itself without considering control environment. A development direction in the future should be to explore this framework on the basis of considering the control environment.

6.3.5 Management Control Systems Framework Relying on Financial and Accounting Control Means

A typical representative of this concept is Anthony. Management control system framework built by Anthony is reflected in his book "management control system", the frame structure is divided into three parts [11]. Chapter 1 is the substance of the

strategic objectives; Diagnostic Control Lever, is an "instrument dials" in performance measurement, comparison criteria and correcting deviations, to monitor the realization of organizational goals; Belief Control Lever, is an "engine" to motivate employees to create new opportunities, which is to stimulate and guide the organization to explore and discover and pursue organization's core values; Interactive Control Lever, is the catalyst about potential information, assumptions and action plans, which aimed concern constantly changing information to enable senior managers to consider potential strategic.

management control system, introducing the concept of the book. The first part is the management control environment, including understanding of strategy, organizational behavior, responsibility center – revenue and cost centers, profit centers, transfer prices, the use of capital measurement and control of six chapters, and it describes the management control environment. The second part is the management control process, including strategic planning, budgeting, analysis of financial and performance reports, performance evaluation and executive compensation of five chapters, it describes the typical management control process steps, such as strategic planning, budgeting, control the run and run the program. The third part is the change of management control, including different strategic controls, modern control methods, service organizations, financial services organizations, multinational organization and project management control of six chapters, it describes the management control system variables, such as: how to change strategy, service organizations, multi-organization or project control.

Management control system designed by Anthony has two main characteristics: One is that the environment of management control system is taken into consideration and fully discussed. The other is that management control method is based on financial, accounting as basic means of control, such as transfer pricing, budgeting, executive compensation.

The limitation of the Anthony management control system is that too much attention is put on accounting perspective, thus making the management control system relatively narrow. In fact, as reflected in the mode of management control systems built by Simons, management control is not confined to financial and accounting control only. With the development of behavioral sciences, psychology and other related disciplines, management control means more focus on the behavioral perspective. The Anthony management control system framework provides a relatively complete theoretical system on the nature of the management control system, management control environment and management control procedures, and a good, borrowable application mode to practitioners as well.

6.3.6 Management Control Systems Framework Based on the Balance of the Formal Means of Control and Non-formal Means of Control

Management control system defined by Joseph A. Maciariello and Calvin J. Kirby [18] is committed to seeking a balance between the formal and non-formal control systems. They thought that the management control system is a set of interrelated information communication framework, benefit for information processing which aims to help managers to coordinate various parts of the continuing organization in order to achieve organizational goals. The management control system framework they built is reflected in their book "management control system: using an adaptive system to attain control". The book is divided into three parts; the first part is the management control system and management control; the second part is the control system design from the mutual support system model; the third part is the control system for special applications. Among them, the first part is the basic definition of management control systems; Part III is a special type of organization management control system applications, such as the management and control of multinational companies, non-profit organization management control; the second part is the main part of system framework of the management control including the style and culture and control system design, organizational structure, self-governing body, the responsibility center and performance measurement, remuneration system, communication and integration, strategic planning and programming, capital budgeting methods, business plan, the traditional system of management costs, operating costs, and continuous improvement methods.

Management control system in the framework of Maciariello makes full use of the theory of management accounting, managerial economics, organizational behavior and other related disciplines. Its most important feature is the establishment of a mutually supported formal and non-formal control system. Both formal and non-formal control systems are composed of the organization's management style and culture, the part of the remuneration system, coordination and integration and control procedures. An overall framework of management control system is formed through the two systems. In particular, it emphasizes the role of shared values in management control systems and the function of supporting organization's values that subsystems should have. In addition, a notable feature is that it also stresses that the design of control systems should be in accordance with an easy-to change way, in order to adapt to environmental changes in that constant adjustment is very important for today's organizations and innovation and continuous improvement are the fundamentals of the adjustment.

A significant contribution of Maciariello is the initial introduction of non-formal control to the establishment of management control system, which better meets the demands of increasingly complicated organizations nowadays and in the future. At the same time, contemporary organizations, both within the organizational boundaries and across organizational boundaries, have shown the characteristics of flexibility, adaptability and continuous learning, but previous research management control systems seldom support these features. The view of Maciariello to design a management control system based on the adaptation to environmental changes is a positively beneficial exploration for the constant adjustment and maximizing the effect of management control system, which is in line with the main direction of the future development of management control theory.

6.3.7 The Overall Management Control Systems Framework Based on Performance Management Style

David Otley is an advocator of the system, he advocated that "strategic planning, management control and task control should not be fragmented, strategic planning and implementation of the strategy should be integrated" [19]. He hoped to establish

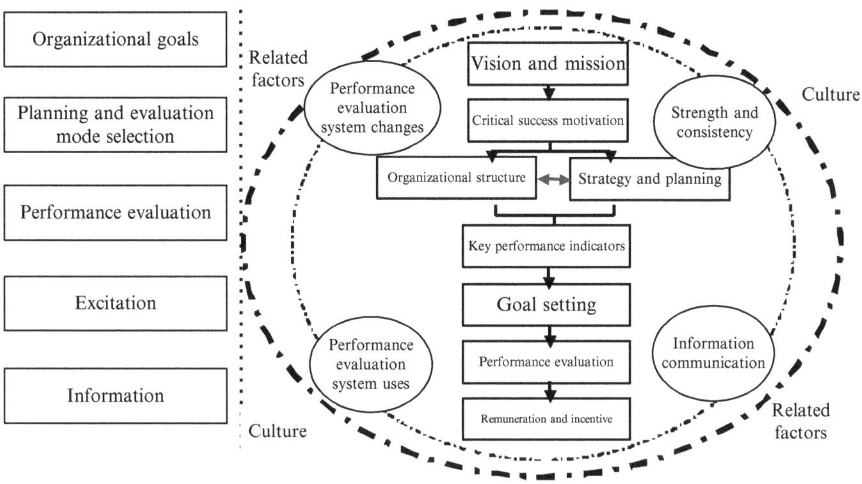

Fig. 6.5 Performance management style management control schematics by Otley in 1999 and 2009

a comprehensive framework of management control by means of a performance management system and the idea of full control. Otley's [20] management control system consists of five parts (embodied by five question): The first part is to emphasize the organizational goals and assessment of these objectives and methods; the second part is about the planning and implementation of strategies and plans, performance metrics, and assessment of the implementation process; the third part is to set the level of performance targets and setting process; the fourth part is the incentive system; the fifth part is concerned about providing adequate information on performance monitoring and support learning. Ferreira and Otley [21] refined and expanded the prior framework by the fusion of Simon's idea of the control levers, extending 5–12 (Fig. 6.5 shows a block and elliptical).

6.4 The Discussion on the Development of Management Control Mode

Otley et al. [22] defined four development model of the management control system by means of Scott's (1981) definition of organizational model development: closed rational mode, closed natural patterns, open rational mode and open natural mode. Closed rational mode of management control literature assumes that the most important processes and events that occur within the organization, and potentially assumes a closed system model of the organization by its very nature is generally coherent. A rational solution has been stressed, which even can be seen in a lot of contemporary literature; management control literature of the closed natural mode emphasizes the importance of spontaneous behavior under unplanned closed system, and the informal structure of the organic arrangements to supplement the use of rational design of the control system. Management control literature of open rational mode is aware of the high dependence of the organization on the environment, emphasizing the link between the management control system and the external environment, but its idea has returned to the stage of rational pursuit of a clear goal. It is also aware that the environment should not be seen merely as a factor to obey; it may also be manipulated and managed. Meanwhile, the theory of this mode is also very concerned about the value or the impact of culture on the conduct of members of the organization.

Table 6.1 gives the general classification of research on management control systems since 1965.

The rise of the four modes indicated the framework for the development of management control studies, but it should be noted that the management control of these four modes are not completely separate, in the same period, these different ideas often cross the coexistence and mutual influence. Furthermore, it can't be said that one pattern is superior to another, among systems varying from close to open and rational to natural. Which mode will function to a greater extent depends on the historical conditions, the reality of the organization and the external environment. In contemporary society, on the one hand, with the absorption of theories in other relevant disciplines and increasing environmental uncertainties faced by the organization, open natural mode will be of more significance to enterprise's practice activities.

6.5 The Discussion on the Control Environment and Management Control Systems

During the development of the concept of management control and management control system, large numbers of explorations and research were done, on issues of whether control environment should be considered and which management control system is needed under a specific condition, to make management control system better improve efficiency and effectiveness. These theories show three researching tendencies: one is not to consider the relationship between the management control system and control environment, believing that there is an optimal control design method to design a control system mode, which is generally applicable for any organization regardless of any environment, we will summarize it as management control system optimal theory. Another is to consider the relationship between the management control system and control environment, believing that the factors that affect every organization control system is unique, and therefore cannot be applied to study the management control system of general principles and patterns. It emphasizes that an effective management control system could not be established until the analysis of the specific environment of enterprises is done. This view is concluded as situation-specific mode theory; the last one is a compromise between these two views. When considering the relationship between the management control system and control environment, it combines the concept of scientific management,

Table 6.1 Representative of four modes and perspectives[a]

Development model	Closed system mode		Open system mode	
	Rational mode	Natural mode	Rational mode	Natural mode
Research base	Classical management theory	Behavioral approach	Systems and contingency approach	Radical view
Representative	Classical theorists£° Woodward (1958, 1965, 1970); Burns and Stalker (1961); Drucker (1946); Simon (1954)	Argyris (1952); Hopwood (1972, 1974a, 1974b); Vickers (1965, 1967); Otely and Berry (1980)	Ouchi (1979); Bill(1972); Lowe and Machin (1983); Lowe and Mckinsey (1971); Otely (1980)	Ai Zhu (1989); Ansari and Bell (1991); Laughlin and Broadbent (1993)
Mainstream	Assumed that the most important processes and events are occurring within the organization, and emphasize rational solutions	Paying attention to the importance of unplanned, spontaneous behavior within the organization emphasize the organic structure of informal arrangement emphasize	Stressed the organization's high dependence on the environment, control thought is still rational, ask for a clear goal	Environmental factors may also be operated and managed, while being obedient, began to focus on values or culture impact on the organizational members' behavior

[a]This form progress and modify based on "On Behalf of Four Modes Perspective" chart created by Otley e.g.

and believes that the control system classified by primary segment of the business model would make certain versatility. This view is the contingency theory in the management and control system, and is called contingency theory of control.

6.5.1 Management Control System Optimal Theory

The point of Optimal management control system theory comes from the theory of scientific management. There is a potential assumption under the principle of scientific management, that is, there is a better way to design the operational process in order to achieve the optimization of efficiency and effectiveness of the management. After Copley and Taylor [23] pointed out that the control was the core idea of scientific management, this concept naturally extended to the theory of management control systems, forming the theoretical basis for the optimal management control system theory. It implied that there must exist one but only one control system which could maximize the management effect. Since the formation of this concept, people have been being committed to exploring one universally applicable management control mode in the absence of control environment.

The Western theorist's community has done a lot of work to try to determine "a best way" in order to operate the control system. Hofstede [24] was a typical representative of this method , and he applied it to the budget control. Americans extended the budget in the performance evaluation and control, but it caused resentment of many managers and organizational dysfunction. Hofstede sought to make the coordination of invention in the United States and budget experience in the Europe which appeared to be positive but rarely useful. He applied system theory, control theory and other theories in his article, listing a few pages of recommendations on how to make effective use of budget without bad effects, and hinted that it would be absolutely universally applicable.

"The combination of many strategic planning models and applications are built on the generally applicable view", Hambrick and Lei [25]. The view which emphasizes a rational solution to problems is the same in organization and system theory, and the concept of how the simple rational research to do better can even be seen in a lot of popular contemporary literature. However, as it is deemed that a set of optimal management control system can be applied in any control environment, completely ignoring the difference of the internal and external environment of the type of tissue. Therefore, when people gave the experienced data of the relationship between the contingency controls, this universally applicable view can no longer be regarded as effectively describing the control system [26].

6.5.2 Situation-Specific Mode Theories

Situation-specific mode is another extreme way exactly contrary to the optimal management control system. Situational specific mode theory confirms that the factors affecting each organization control system are unique; therefore, we cannot apply the general principles and models to study the management control system. Under the support of this view, researchers had to study separately the control environment of each business; they tend to use case study method to build enterprise management control system.

Case study analyzes each organization's internal and external environment, use different management control system in full accordance with different environment. Highly targeted, it may be more meaningful for individual enterprises. But it is impossible for energy limited theorists to do research simply based on single enterprises, if so, the theoretical study of the management control system will lose value and the meaning of existence.

In "the rational management control", Lisl Klein [27] mainly carried out a detailed survey on issues of a particular product planning and production control, budget and cost control, and production methods to identify and improve analysis, and designed an effective management control system. Although for product, you can greatly improve the efficiency and effectiveness, but for other management control systems, only the research method and ideas can be learned, a relatively common mode could not.

Sverre Hogheim et al. [28] analyzed the relationship between the different elements of management control within the system based on an actual case in the Norwegian city. Although still against the background of case study, they obtained relevancy of two levels, namely, management control system with decision and conduction, and have gradually gone beyond the narrow research on designing the system simply through case study.

6.5.3 Contingency Control Theory

Contingency control theory is the appliance of the organization theory in the study of management control systems. Contingency theory is that the organization is constituted of a number of sub-systems, among which there is a relationship of interdependence and at the meanwhile maintains an interactive relationship with its external environment. In particular, it stresses the variability of the organization, while also tries to understand how organizations operate under specific environment and different conditions. The ultimate purpose of the contingency theory is the design and application of the most suitable organization system and management methods in certain circumstances.

In the ideology of contingency theory, contingency control theory is a pattern situated between two extreme theories, the optimal management control system theory and situation-specific theory. Contingency control theory feels that the suitability of different control systems depends on its business model. However, compared with the "situation-specific" mode, contingency control theory combines the concept of scientific management, believing that control system may be of certain versatility by the main classification of business model. Its basic assumption is that organizational performance will be improved provided that the variables in environment and control system could better adapt to each other. At present,

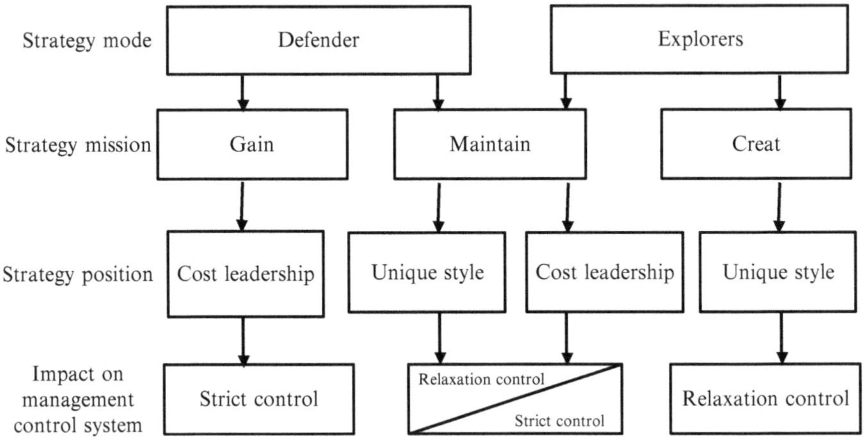

Fig. 6.6 Strategy and management control diagram

the view of contingency control theory has been generally accepted and becomes the basic starting point of the management control system. People began working on certain organizations with some common environmental characteristics, analyzing organizational environment factors influencing the effectiveness of the operation of different mode of management control systems and building corresponding modes under different environment.

Early research on contingency control can be classified by complexity of the analysis. They can be divided into three levels of analysis according to contingency variables, control variables and outcome variables included in the early literature of control. With the increase in the level of analysis, the study design becomes more complex, but it does not mean that the higher level of analysis is superior to the lower level because each level has its own advantages and disadvantages.

6.5.3.1 Level 1 Analysis

Level 1 analysis: This level of analysis is basically to explore the relationship between a contingency factor and a control mechanism. The analysis potentially assumes that it increases the possibility for the enterprise to adopt a specific control mechanism on condition of a contingency factor.

There are two typical examples of this study, one is that Kald et al. [29] re-classified and reinterpreted the correlation between the previous strategy and management control systems, and then re-divided the different types of strategy to conclude that different strategic types have different effects on the management control system, as shown in Fig. 6.6.

Another typical example is Macintosh and Daft [30]. Thompson [31] divided the interdependence of different departments into three types, the collection of dependence, sequence dependence and interdependence framework. On the basis of that, they tested the interdependence among departments and the correlation among operating budget, period statistical report and operating standards in management control. They concluded that, as for the collection of interdependence, a standard operating procedure is given more emphasis; while for sequence interdependence, it stresses budget and statistic report. When a department is interdependent, subjective control is more important, rather than the formal control. And finally they concluded that the role of control system reflected the adaptability between information needs generated by interdependence and the supply of information provided by the control system.

Although most contingency control analysis follows this kind of research design approach, however, studies in this level haven't ever considered if the association between contingency factors and control mechanism will exert any influence on enterprise's performance, nor do they exam the correlation of this mechanism designed on the basis of a contingency variable with other control mechanisms.

6.5.3.2 Level 2 Analysis

In the analysis of this level, people seek for the coupled effect based on the connection of contingency factors and multidimensional control mechanisms. This type of analysis assumes that the multidimensional control mechanism is contained in this analysis, but it fails to reveal the supplementary or alternative relationship that may exist between control variables in various control mechanisms. Substitution of control system refers to the application of different control mechanisms may obtain the same expected results. Complementation of control system means the application of some certain control mechanism in a complementary manner, so that these control mechanisms jointly play a role in achieving the efficiency and effectiveness of the management control.

Many researchers have illustrated the need for analysis of this level, but few have proved the conclusion. Waterhouse and Tiessenn [32] are good researchers of this level; they illustrate two contingency variables relevant to organizational environment, namely, technology and the environment. They assume that these two variables will affect the design of management control system as well as that the impact of the two variables on management control systems is distinct and separated from each other. Their study on technique is based on Paro's definition, believing that the measurement of technique ranges from routine procedures to unconventional production and the research on environmental uncertainty covers a consecutive process from high uncertainty to the highly predictable external environment. Waterhouse and Tiessen assume that the organization is always trying to focus on power as much as possible, explicitly present control procedures and utilize mechanical control. If the technique is unsurpassed and the environment is highly predictable, then centralized control is the optimum choice, standard cost control center is seen as a typical example of the machine control system. However, under the condition of environmental uncertainty, it's difficult to conduct direct control by means of explicitly displaying the procedures and evaluating performance in accordance with established criteria. As the uncertainty of the environment variables is getting higher and higher, the organization will tend to use subjective, organic control system. The typical control system includes a high degree of freedom right of managers, the supervision of result output by the efforts of managers, cautious selection of group members and the process of their socialization. The mechanical control system and organic control system may be alternative or complementary in two respective circumstances, excellent technique together with highly predictable environment and highly uncertain environment.

The difficulty is that there are no clear answers as to whether different control mechanisms are alternative or complementary, to what extent they are alternative or complementary, the position they occupy in their own management control systems, etc.

6.5.3.3 Level 3 Analysis

In this level, the analysis involves multidimensional contingency factors which influence the design of an optimal control system. Gresov [33] pointed out that when making a simultaneous analysis of several contingency factors, the requirements of control system may be conflicting. The design of the control system needs to express its contingency as well, then it may involve a balanced relationship which can avoid being suitable for all contingency variables [33, 34]. If all contingency factors require the same type of control mechanism in order to achieve the optimization of the control system, the design of control system will be very direct and simple, but conflicting contingency factors tend to lead to inconsistency with the requirements of the control system. The presence of these conflicts implies that the design will differentiate from at least one contingency, thus it is uneasy to create the optimal control mechanism, nor direct to overcome these conflicts.

One way to resolve these conflicts is to design the control system of a hybrid, and to include all control components designed for the contingency factors. Unfortunately, this control system cannot be internally consistent, because it is the contingency factors what it aims to present. Child [35] pointed out that the internal consistency of the control system design improved performance and inadaptability on this design will result in lower performance. There is also an option; an enterprise could design a control system to make it consistent with major contingency factors, while ignoring other contingency factors. However, Gresov [33] have demonstrated the fact that it could lead to a decline in the performance of the business when ignoring a contingency factor. In summary, conflicting contingency variables will result in a certain loss in efficiency of the control system.

As an example of a conflicting contingency, Fisher and Govindarajan [34] described the potential conflict between the control needs and the competitive strategy during the product life cycle of strategic business unit. They also tested the mission of creating and harvesting along with low cost strategy and differentiation strategy. The authors believed that control design mechanism needed by creation and differentiation strategy is similar, that is also true for harvest and low cost strategy. That is, if the product life cycle of strategic business unit and competitive strategy is about creating/differentiation, or harvest/low cost control mechanism, design requirements are consistent. However, when the low cost strategy and creating mission is applied simultaneously, or the differentiation strategy and the harvesting mission likewise, the conflict between the contingency variables will be intensified, this conflict has increased the possibility for control system to deviate from a contingency demand to reverse the impact of the results of the strategic business unit.

This level makes people recognize the conflicting contingency variables are able to identify the non-adaptive control system or the deviation between the control system design and demand. What is more, it also shows that there are defects in certain research ideas of the two previous levels of analysis.

In order to solve the problem of conflict on this third level institute, a development direction for future research should be the devotion to the relationship among the contingency variables. At present, research on the relationship among the contingency variables is too little. Research on the impact of single contingency variable on management control system has been dominating contingency theory for a long time. The discussion of the multi-contingency variables basically remained at isolated levels. On the one hand, we should make it clear when exploring the relationship among contingency variables, that many contingent factors actually do not matter, which increases the conflicts of contingency, however making people devoted to the solution of coordination or change the control environment to cater to the relatively efficient management control system. On the other hand, clearing the affiliation, causality or side-by-side relationship among contingency variables will help to seize the mainstream of control environment and design an effective system accordingly.

From the discussion above, it can be seen that, in the three major schools of theory, control system optimization theory and context-specific mode theory cannot obtain long-term viability because of the drawbacks on theoretical starting point of their own; management control system will eventually be in accordance with contingency direction cybernetics. Meanwhile, since the current contingency cybernetics research is still in the process of exploration and discussion, studies on the design of management control system will be a long developing process.

References

1. Babbage C (1832) On the economics of machines and manufactures [M]. Charles Knight, London
2. Follett MP (1896) The speaker of the house of representative [M]. Longmans Green, New York
3. Taylor FW (1911) The principles of scientific management [M]. Harper Bros, New York
4. Francis ML (1920) Industrial control: the application to industry of direction, control and light [M]. Sir I Pitman, London/New York
5. Fayol H (1949) General and industrial management [M]. Sir Isaac Pitman and Sons Ltd., London

6. Diemer H (1915) Industrial organization and management [M]. La Salle Extension University, Chicago
7. Weiner N (1948) Cybernetics: or control and communication in the animal and the machine [M]. MIT Press, New York
8. Green SG, Welsh MA (1988) Cybernetics and dependence: reframing the control concept [J]. Acad Manage Rev 13(2):287–301
9. Machin JLJ (1983) Management control systems: whence and whither [M]. Macmillan, London
10. Anthony RN (1965) Planning and control systems: a framework for analysis [M]. Harvard University, Boston
11. Anthony RN, Govindarajan V (1998) Management control systems. McGraw-Hill Companies Inc., Burr Ridge
12. Lorange P, Scott Morton MS (1974) A framework for management control systems. Sloan Management Review (Fall)
13. Merchant KA (1982) The control function of management. Sloan Manage Rev 23(4):43–55
14. Merchant KA (1998) Modern management control systems: text and cases [M]. Prentice Hall, Upper Saddle River
15. Rotch W (1993) Management control systems: one view of components and their interdependence. Br J Manage 4(3):191–203
16. Simons R (1995) Control in an age of empowerment [J]. Harv Bus Rev 73(2):80–88
17. Dent JF (1990) Strategy, organization and control: some possibilities for accounting research [J]. Account Org Soc 15(1–2):3–24
18. Maciariello JA, Kirby CJ (1994) Management control systems: using adaptive systems to attain control [M]. Prentice Hall, Englewood Cliffs
19. Otley DT, Berry AJ (1980) Control, organisation and accounting. Account Org Soc 5(2):231–234
20. Otley DT (1999) Performance management: a framework for management control systems research [J]. Manage Account Res 10(4):363–382
21. Ferreira A, Otley D (2009) The design and use of performance management systems: an extended framework for analysis [J]. Manage Account Res 20(4):263–282
22. Otley DT, Broadbent J, Berry A (1995) Research in management control: an overview of its development [J]. Br J Manage 6(1):31–44
23. Copley FB, Taylor FW (1923) Father of scientific management (two volumes) [M]. Harper and Brothers
24. Hofstede GH (1968) The game of budget control [M]. Tavistock, London
25. Hambrick DC, Lei D (1985) Toward an empirical prioritization of contingency variables for business strategy [J]. Acad Manage J 28(4):763–788
26. Fisher J (1998) Contingency theory, management control systems and firm outcomes: past results and future directions [J]. Behav Res Account 10(Supplement):47–64
27. Klein L (1965) Rationality in management control [J]. J Manage Stud 2(3):351–361
28. Høgheim S, Monsen N, Olsen RH, Olson O (1989) The two worlds of management control [J]. Financ Account Manage 5(3):163–178
29. Magnus K, Nilsson F, Rapp B (2000) On strategy and management control: the importance of classifying the strategy of the business [J]. Br J Manage 11(3):197–212
30. Macintosh NB, Daft RL (1987) Management control systems and departmental interdependencies: an empirical study [J]. Account Org Soc 12(1):49–61
31. Thompson JD (1967) Organizations in action [M]. McGraw-Hill, New York
32. Waterhouse JH, Tiessen P (1978) A contingency framework for management accounting systems research [J]. Account Org Soc 3(1):65–76
33. Gresov C (1989) Exploring fit and misfit with multiple contingencies [J]. Adm Sci Q 34:431–453
34. Fisher L, Govindarajan V (1993) Incentive compensation design, strategic business unit mission, and competitive strategy [J]. J Manage Account Res 8:129–144
35. Child J (1975) Managerial and organizational factors associated with company performance-Part II [J]. J Manage Stud 12:12–27

Part III
Study on Theoretical Framework of Management Control System

Chapter 7
Theoretical Basis of Management Control System

7.1 Economics and Management Control

Management control is the total of control processes which are conducted by the internal controllers in order to ensure the effectiveness of operating activities. The objective of management control is the effectiveness of operating activities. What is the effectiveness of operating activities? How can it be achieved? The answers to these questions might construct the base and the core of conducting management control, and they also must be resolved firstly. Economics can exactly answer these questions and establish a theoretical basis.

Economics is a branch of social science that researches how to allocate the limited resources to obtain the maximum satisfaction with the infinite human needs. It addresses three basic economic issues such as: (1) what and how much to produce; (2) how to produce, namely what kind of techniques could be used to assemble resources and to produce the required products; (3) for whom to produce and how to distribute. The three essential elements in economic activities are human needs, resources and the production technology.

The direct goal of economic activities is to meet human needs which include material needs and cultural needs. Human needs are characterized by the diversity and the insatiability in the long term. The extent of human needs being met is not only associated with their historical period and geographical position, but also is influenced by two factors from the perspective of efficiency. One factor is all of the useful products or labor services for consumption or further production under the permission restriction of resources and technology. The other factor is the reasonable allocation of these products or services among different organizations. The former reflects the level of outputs, the latter reflects the level of utility of allocation and consumption.

Resources are the means or wealth used to produce the required products. Those can be divided into labor resources, capital resources and nature resources. Modern economics regards entrepreneurs as the fourth resource. Resources can also be divided into two categories: human resources and material resources if labor

X. Zhang, *Enterprise Management Control Systems in China*, Understanding China,
DOI 10.1007/978-3-642-54715-7_7,

resources merge with entrepreneur resources, capital resources merge with nature resources. Resources have three features: (1) most of them are limited in quantity; (2) they have multiple usages; (3) They can be allocated in different ways to produce certain products. The input in economics mainly refers to these resources.

Production technology means the joint name of the knowledge that is used to transform the resources into products or services to meet the human needs. The quantity and quality of technology and resources limit the satisfaction level of human needs.

Production function refers to the relation between the fixed resource input and the maximum output under certain technological condition. It can reflect the relationship between resource input, output and production technology.

Welfare function shows the relation between maximum utility and relevant output or resources input under certain technical condition, and it is similar to the production function.

Efficiency is the ratio of the output to input. Economic efficiency refers to the ratio of the output to input which are measured by money value. Precisely speaking, in western economics efficiency is Pareto Efficiency or Pareto Optimal, and it refers to a status of economic resources allocation which could not make one individual be better off without making at least any one worse off. In micro production theory, efficiency is the ratio of the available output to the resource input. In welfare economics, efficiency is the ratio of the utility to the output. Therefore, with certain resources input, the improvement of production efficiency will lead to the increase of total available output; under certain output condition, improving the efficiency in consumption will increase the total utility. In brief, with the certain resources, improvement of economic efficiency can make human needs to be better satisfied. This is why efficiency is the core of economic.

As above, the economic basic concepts and theories scientifically analyze the efficiency and effectiveness of the resources input and allocation, and it set a solid theoretical foundation for the establishment of management control system.

7.2 Management and Management Control

Management is a branch of social science that studies the theory and approaches of management. As a part of management science system, the theories and methods of management control are necessarily influenced by those of management.

7.2.1 Connotation of Management and Management Control

The connotation of management is to explain what is management as well as its what are contents and approach. Management is a kind of activities, which execute some functions to acquire, allocate and utilize human efforts and material resources efficiently to accomplish desired goals. This definition generally unifies the characteristics, functions and goals which are associated with the management control.

Management is the kind of activity to efficiently accomplish objective, while management control is the process to ensure the accomplishment of objectives as is driven by those activities

Management activities contribute to the functions of management which includes planning, organizing, commanding, coordinating and controlling. Each of them has different effect. In general, management control refers to the controlling function of management, which is involved in all the fields of management. In macroscopic terms, management control is a system consisted of standard setting; performance evaluation and correcting. This kind of system mainly emphasize quantitative control.

The objective of management is to achieve organization's objectives by acquiring, allocating and utilizing the available resources effectively. The objectives of management control is to ensure the operation effectiveness, so that strategy can be implemented, ultimately the organization's objectives are accomplished.

7.2.2 Contents of Management and Management Control

The content of management is determined by management activities. Henri Fayol, the father of modern management, divided the enterprise activities into six categories as followings[1]:

- Technical activities, which involve producing and making products.
- Commercial activities, which involve purchasing, marketing, trading.
- Financial activities, financing and investing properly.
- Security activities, which involve personnel and property protection.
- Accounting activities, which involve inventory auditing, balance sheet preparation, costing, and statistics analysis.
- Management activities, which involve planning, organizing, leading, coordinating and controlling.

In the above activities, the content of management exists among the other five activities.

In the process of ensuring the accomplishment of organization's strategy and goals, it is the adoption of management control which entails the means and methods that control all the content of management mentioned above. Therefore, the content of the management control and management are consistent.

7.2.3 Approaches of Management and Management Control

The approaches of management include both the research methods and application methods. There are 11 categories of studying management science and theory: empirical (or case)approach, interpersonal behavior approach, group behavior

[1] Henri Fayol and Cao Yongxiang [1].

approach, cooperative social systems approach, sociotechnical system approach, decision theory approach, systems approach, mathematical approach, contingency approach, managerial task approach and operational approach. These approaches play the similar important guidance role in studying management control theories and methods, especially the interpersonal behavior approach, systems approach and case approach.

The applied management methods are mainly reflected by methods to exert the management functions, including the planning method, organizing method, commanding method, coordinating and controlling method. In narrow sense, it is obvious that although all the methods are important to build the management control system in general, the effect of controlling method on management control is much greater./Many controlling methods are widely used in management control, among which the traditional approaches include budget control, statistical control, reporting control, analysis control, auditing control whilst the modern approaches contain procedure control, profit and loss control, ROI control and so on.

7.3 Accounting and Management Control

Management control involves many issues of measurement and report. So it serves accounting and also needs support from accounting, especially from management accounting.

Accounting is an independent discipline built up with the development of commodity economy and the improvement of modern accounting procedures and methods. Accounting formulates its theoretical system, taking the accounting functions, objects, procedures and methods as its study objects and adopting certain study methods, in order to reveal the process of reflection and supervision of economic activities by accounting, and promote accounting to serve the economic life better.[2] Accounting is a kind of economic management work which adopts a serial of procedures and methods by monetary measurement standard to continuously records business transactions, and reflects and supervises the process of value movement in business transactions. The basic procedures and methods of accounting are recognition, measurement, record and report. Figure 7.1 reflects the status of four accounting steps.

These four steps of accounting procedure and method are closely connected with management control and they form the foundation of management control elements, procedure and method. Among these four parts, measurement and reporting are the key points, while recognition is the basis of measurement and record is the basis of report. Accordingly, we demonstrate the relationship between accounting and management control from two aspects, that is, measurement and report.

[2] Feng Shuping [2].

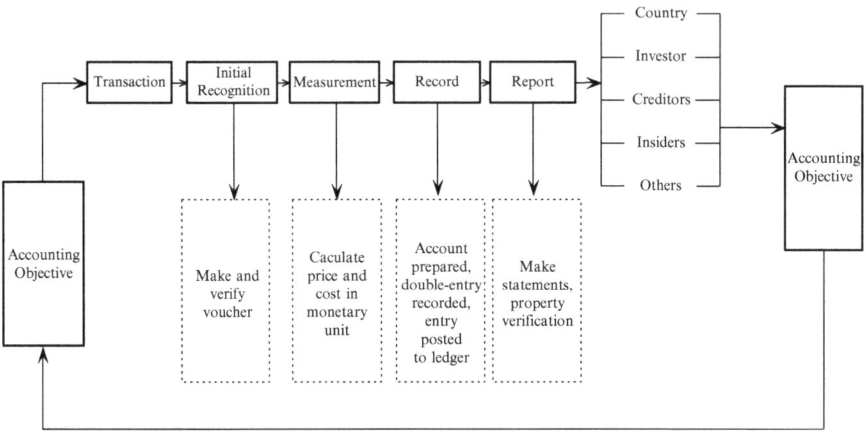

Fig. 7.1 Accounting recognition, measurement, record and report (Wu Shuipeng [3])

7.3.1 Accounting Measurement and Management Control

Accounting is a process of measurement. Measurement is the core function of accounting which mainly resolves the problems of accounting measurement unit and measurement attribution. The unit of accounting measurement has gone through two stages. First, a kind of symbol was changed into material objects; second, material objects transformed into currency. Accounting could continuously, systematically, comprehensively and integrally reflect organization's business activities which are measured by currency, which is incomparable by other disciplines or measurement units. Accounting measurement attribution includes five categories: historical cost, current cost, current market price, net realizable value and present value of future cash flows, among which historical cost is always dominant no matter in traditional accounting or in modern accounting. The foundation of accounting measurement is accounting recognition that determines what should be measured, which account should be recorded in and when to recognize.

Accounting measurement is one of the most important tools and means of management control. To ensure an organization's effectiveness of management control over its operating activities, accounting measurement should be utilized, such as for financing activities measurement, investing activities measurement, operating activities measurement, outputting measurement and allocating activities measurement. The importance of accounting measurement derives from the organizational goals as well as its comprehensiveness and integrity reflected by business activities. However, physical measurement could not achieve this purpose. Certainly, management control could use non-accounting measurement means to control activities as the complement of accounting measurement.

The accounting measurement of management control is embodied in the elements, procedures and methods of management control. It is this inseparability that drives the generation of modern management accounting. And meanwhile, the innovation of modern management accounting promotes the development of management control.

The expansion of management control scope promotes the development of management accounting. The modern management control has experienced the transformation from operating management control to strategy management control and activity management control, which expands the development space of management accounting. On the basis of traditional production and operation management accounting, the creation and development of strategy management accounting and activity management accounting are both related to management control development.

The improvement of procedure of management control promotes the development of management accounting. Enterprise management control cannot work without management accounting reports during the process of strategic target decomposition, control standards setting, internal control reporting, operating performance evaluation and manager motivation. In order to satisfy all the information needed by the five steps of enterprise management control, management accounting must create and perfect the category and contents of managerial reports, expand the contents and quantity of decision-making and controlling information provided by management accounting, and develop management accounting theory.

The innovation of management control method motivates the management accounting development. With the evolution of modern management science, the approaches of enterprise management control have been innovated and perfected continuously, and the emergence of these approaches provided supports and guarantees to the improvement of management accounting techniques and methods, and also promoted the development of management accounting method system.[3]

7.3.2 Accounting Reports and Management Control

Accounting reports are the final products of the entire accounting system, and also the written files to reflect the enterprise financial conditions and operating fruits in the condensed, comprehensive, systematic and classified form. Accounting reports contain external financial statements, notes to financial statements and explanations to financial conditions.

Accounting statements consist of balance sheet, income statement and the statement of cash flows. All the financial activities are directly or indirectly reflected by accounting statements, as Fig. 7.2 shows.

[3]Zhang Xianzhi [4].

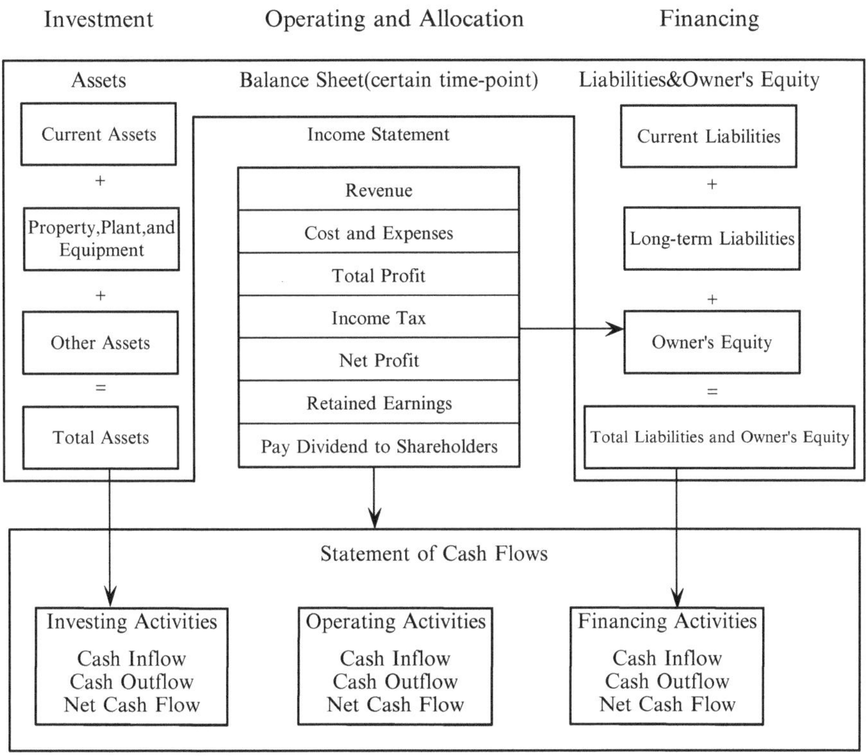

Fig. 7.2 Financial activities and accounting statements

As showed above, accounting statements reflect the financing activities, investing activities, operating activities and distribution activities of enterprise financial activities comprehensively and systematically, which is reflected from static to dynamic and from accruals basis to cash basis. It is the accounting reports and relevant information that are used to reflect the operating condition and performance and find out the key variables in operating activities, identify the deviation comparing to control standards, evaluating the operating performance to conduct the rewards or punishment.

It should be mentioned that the so-called accounting reports generally refer to the financial accounting reports. From the aspect of management control, both financial accounting reports and management accounting reports are significant. Management accounting reports are the documents which reflect the status of enterprise management process and operating performance. Management accounting reports mainly include all kinds of accounting statements and notes which are used for internal uses, such as decision-making, controlling, evaluation and communication. Management accounting reports and financial accounting reports complement each other and comprise the modern accounting report system.

7.4 Cybernetics and Management Control

7.4.1 Connotation of Cybernetics

The word "cybernetics" is originated from the Greek language, which means "steering or navigating techniques" and contains the connotation of regulating, manipulating, management, commanding and supervising. Cybernetics is the theoretical study of communication and process control. This theory indicates that almost all the systems could be regarded as an automatic control system, such as automated machine, nervous system, biosystem, even the economic system and social systems in spite of their respective features. In the automatic control system, there is a special adjustment device to control the operation of system and maintain itself stability and orientation function.

The basic points of cybernetics theory is that the common fundamental characteristics shared by all the control systems are the process of information exchanges and feedbacks which could be used to obtain the cognition, analysis and controlling of the system. The purpose of cybernetics theory applied in management activities is to make the manage objects operate properly according to the plan or target and to keep in a certain status. After building the integral target, any system must adjust its operating mechanism by controlling; correct the deviation in order to ensure the optimum adaptive condition to realize the desired objective.

Comparing the control in cybernetics to that in management, there is commonness in their basic control procedure, that is, information feedbacks and systematicness. But there are still several differences.

Firstly, the control in cybernetics is a simple information feedback. Its correcting actions are always able to put into effect immediately or to correct automatically in a certain program. Comparatively, control is relatively more complex. It is difficult to implement timely and automatically, no matter feedback system or correcting system.

Secondly, the information feedback in cybernetics is definite and simple; while the management control information is always uncertain and complex as it's an information system to summarize various information. Management information system plays a decisive role in management control.

Thirdly, the control objective of cybernetics is to correct bias promptly to maintain it in the reasonable and allowed range. The objective of management control is not only to correct and meet determined goals but also to achieve higher target by continuously innovation. From the perspective of management, the real control is not limited to measure deviation, but try to pull the unexpected activities back into the right way. It means that control should not only identify problems, but also resolve them to achieve the current goals and long-term targets.

Therefore, we should understand, grasp and use control techniques form the viewpoint of management under the direction of basic theories and methods of cybernetics. These techniques are classified into real-time control, feedback control and feed-forward control by the controlling node; or indirect control and direct control by the control mode.

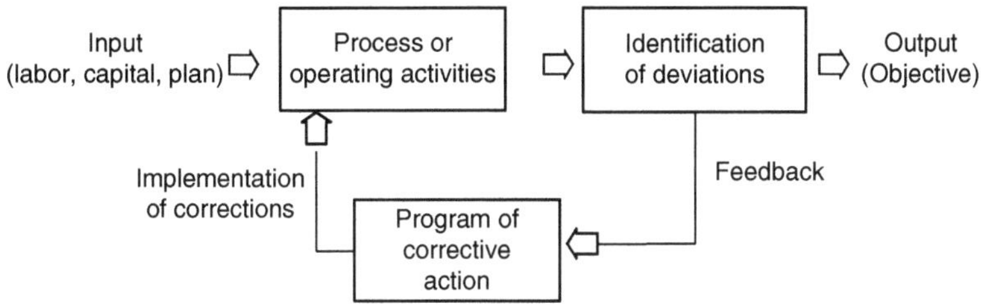

Fig. 7.3 Feedback control

7.4.2 *Feedback Control, Real-Time Control and Feed-Forward Control*

7.4.2.1 Feedback Control

People always consider control as a feedback control which compare the actual performance to the standards, then analyze the bias and implement the corrections to achieve the desired performance. A simple feedback system is shown in Fig. 7.3.[4]

Feedback control could control the final result and the intermediary output of the system. The former is called end feedback; the latter is called local feedback. Local feedback plays an important role in enhancing the functions of management control system.

Feedback control system has some effect in management, but it can hardly execute real-time control, because it spends much time to gather information, compare and analyze deviation, develop and implement the correcting program.

7.4.2.2 Real-Time Control

Real-time control is also called spot control, which is usually used by the line manager to control the actual process. Personally managers could supervise the subordinate staffs in the commanding chain process. The content of real-time control includes: instructing the right ways and procedures of works to subordinates; supervising subordinates to achieve the planned goals; identifying deviations and take corrective actions immediately.

As a real-time, spot and process control, it requires good quality of the control environment. Firstly, real-time control needs real-time information. It does not make sense without real-tame data. Secondly, real-time control requires proper

[4] Partly based on and adapted from Weihrich et al. [5].

authorization. The spot manager or process manager cannot implement real-time control without the authority to correct deviations and make some rewards or punishments. Thirdly, real-time control asks the controller to acquire higher qualification and the ability of response to the changing circumstance under the unified command.

Although real-time control is beneficial to management activities control, but its requirement to control environment and situation, as well as its costs are higher than feedback control.

7.4.2.3 Feedforward Control

Feed-forward control means the manager could perceive the coming deviations and take actions immediately to avoid them in order to accomplish the desired objectives. It is a control concept and method ideology towards future.

The major differences between feed-forward control and feedback control are showed as follows:

Firstly, feedback control put the outcomes of a system into deviation analysis to prevent the bias that have occurred from keeping on or happening again. Feed-forward control monitor the changing information and disturbance variables that system output as the inputs, to prevent the deviation between quality and quantity of resources from occurring and correct them before the final output getting influenced.

Secondly, feed-forward control is more complex than feedback control, because it is very complicated and difficult to determine the disturbance variables which could influence the inputs. While the outputs, inputs and the process information of feedback control are always known or definite.

As a control to the resource input, the contents of feed-forward control includes: human resource input control, capital resource input control and material resource input control.

The characteristics of feed-forward control determine that it needs to have certain conditions and some higher requirements:

- Make a thorough and careful analysis of the control system, and define the important input variables.
- Establish a model of the feed-forward system.
- Update the input variables and disturbance factors timely.
- Ensure the accuracy and timeliness of inputs.
- Assess the differences between the actual inputs and preplanned inputs timely.
- Take actions to solve problems.

The relationships of feed-forward control, feedback control and real-time control are depicted in Fig. 7.4.

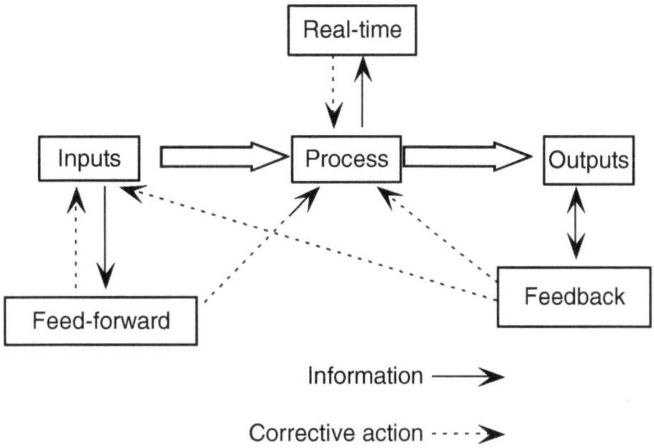

Fig. 7.4 Feed-forward control, feedback control and real-time control

7.4.3 *Indirect Control and Direct Control*

7.4.3.1 Indirect Control

Indirect control is to find out the causes of negative effects, and trace the accountability and correct mistakes in practice. It is actually a kind of afterwards adjustment. People might not notice the forthcoming problems and fail to take actions in advance to prevent them, but to identify the deviation between actual performance and the standards and then correct them.

The reasons for this bias mainly exist in three aspects: (1) unreasonable or inaccurate standard; (2) varied or uncertain environment; (3) ability of manager, like knowledge and capability of judgment. Indirect control could primarily solve the deviations attributing to manager's ability. On one hand, it can correct the adverse deviation by the manager's poor ability. On the other hand, it can improve the qualification and ability of managers.

The weakness of indirect control is mainly in afterwards correction, that is, measures are taken only after the unfavorable variances or losses have occurred. The cost of this control process may be not so high, but the loss caused could be very serious.

7.4.3.2 Direct Control

Instead of directly governing the relative organization and personnel by administrative means, direct control is to train better managers to use management concepts, techniques and theories, and to think over management issues and tasks with the viewpoint of system, so that the bad consequences from poor management could be eliminated.

Contrasted to indirect control, direct control is a kind of preventive-control by improving the qualification of managers. A qualified manager could perceive the impending problems and take actions to correct them timely. The so-called qualified manager refers to the person who can conduct management systematically by applying the management concept, rules and methods expertly. The higher the manager's quality is, the less the quantity of indirect control.

Direct control could avoid risks by overcoming the shortcomings brought by afterwards correction of indirect control; Meanwhile, direct control is also helpful to improve the manager's quality.

Traditional control approaches are often belonging to indirect control. Basically speaking, direct control should be emphasized to make control effectively. But quite high qualities of senior managers and subordinates are required in direct control without which direct control would not only miss the desired effect but even make greater losses.

7.5 Systems Theory and Management Control

System theory is the methodology of modern science comprehensive results. The so-called "system" is an organic entity with definite traits and functions, constituted by a number of interrelated essential elements. "System" is the established way or method to perform a type of activities or series of activities and these activities often emerge repeatedly as a cycle.

System theory study the general mode, structure and the law of system, and its core idea is the integration concept of a system. Its basic thought method is to regard the research and process object as a system, analyze the structure and function of system, and study the mutual relations among systems, elements and environment and the regularity of its alteration, and optimize the systematic point of view to scrutiny the problem.

To correctly understand the meaning and characteristic of the system theory, the following should be grasped:

- The system is an entity whose contents are greater than the total of each part of the contents that the system contains. Each system has its own subsystems and belongs to a larger system at the same time.
- The system can be regarded both as "closed" and "open" which is determined primarily by the influences of the environment on system.
- The closed system has a trend of recession without the consideration of environment, or absorption of "energy" from the change of environment. The open system improves continuously with the change of environment.
- A system must have a feedback system to reach balance. This feedback system could provide the necessary information for the conversion of input, producing, output mode and to the balance of the system.

- The open system can use different methods to obtain the expected results. In operation management, there are different inputs and different processes to achieve the same output or target, and there is no unique optimal way.

The important contribution of system theory to management control is that its "systemic approach" makes people focus on the overall control of organization, that is, the construction of management control system, rather than the simple control of a certain variables alienate from its environment.

To build a sound management control system, we must analyze the environment of the management control system, define its elements, and establish its program on the basis of the general pattern, structure and laws of system theory. They are the organic components of the integral management control system and the independent subsystem of management control system as well.

References

1. Henri Fayol, Cao Yongxiang (Translation) (1999) Administration industrielle et générale. Unity Press, Beijing, p 3 (Chinese)
2. Feng Shuping (2002) Concise dictionary of accounting. China Financial and Economic Publishing House, Beijing
3. Wu Shuipeng (2002) China's account theory research. China Financial and Economic Publishing House, Beijing, p 72
4. Zhang Xianzhi (2012) The application fields of modern enterprise management control. Finance Acc 7(6):15–17
5. Weihrich H, Cannice MV, Koontz H (2010) Management: a global and entrepreneurial perspective. Tata McGraw Hill Education Private Limited, New Delhi, p 429

Chapter 8
Management Control Elements and Management Control System

8.1 Some Perspectives on the Elements of Management Control System

Management control, as a system, should perform one or several activities regularly or repeatedly. What are the basic elements of one typical internal management control system? In terms of perspectives on control elements of management control systems, there are three-element control systems, four-element control systems and five-element control systems at present. Even the systems are all called three-element control system, or four-element control systems, or five-element control systems, the connotation of their specific control element is different.

8.1.1 The Viewpoint of Three-Element Management Control System

There are many viewpoints or statements about three-element management control, among which two mainly thoughts are concluded as followings.

(A) From the perspective of the function of management, management control elements could be defined according to the management procedures, which are (1) Control standards; (2) Performance evaluation; (3) Correction of deviations.

   Most scholars support this standpoint despite of the minor differences among their statements. For example, Robinson [1] put forward three elements of control: predicting, recording results as well as identifying variances and responsibilities. Newman [2, 3] defined three key phases or elements of control process: setting control standards according to strategies; evaluating and reporting performance; taking corrective actions.

(B) From the perspective of internal control structure, internal control elements are divided into three elements according to the institutional structure, that is, control environment, accounting system, and control procedure.

X. Zhang, *Enterprise Management Control Systems in China*, Understanding China,
DOI 10.1007/978-3-642-54715-7_8, © Springer-Verlag Berlin Heidelberg 2014

8.1.2 The Viewpoint of Four-Element Management Control System

(A) The paper "*A Framework for Management Control Systems*" by Lorange and Morton [4] thought that the fundamental role of management control systems was to help management departments to accomplish the organization's objectives, and the following key points (elements) supply a normal framework for management control to attain the organization's goals:

(1) Identifying related control variables;
(2) Designing good short-term plans;
(3) Recording the completion extent of short-term plans about all control variables;
(4) Analyzing deviations.

(B) The manuscript "Management Control Systems" by Robert N Anthony [5] suggested that internal management control systems contained four elements: measurement, evaluation, execution and communication.

(1) Measurement is to identify the events occurring in the control process, that is, to reflect the realities;
(2) Evaluation is to compare the deviations of the reality to the standards, that is, to compare the reality to the standards;
(3) Execution is to correct the differences between the realities and the standards, that is, to correct the deviations;
(4) Communication is to deliver and exchange information timely through measurement, evaluation and execution

8.1.3 The Viewpoint of Five-Element Management Control System

(A) Gutenberg [6] supplied five elements about a management control system:

(1) Standard. The control standards must be available before implementing the control otherwise there will be an absence of basis when judging.
(2) Information system. The management control system supplies all kinds of information about the realities that happens in the process of management control.
(3) Capability of assessment. The management control system should be able to identity and analyze whatever situations according to standards.
(4) Capability of rectifications. The management control system should be able to correct the deviations according to the results of judges so as to meet the standard.
(5) Capability of connection. The management control system should be able to link up the standards, information system, the capability of assessment and rectifications timely so that they could become an organic entity.

(B) (COSO) [7, 8] also supplied five elements of internal control in both Internal Control-Integrated Framework and Enterprise Risk Management-Integrated Framework:

(1) Control environment
Control environment sets the tone of an organization, influencing the control consciousness of its people. It is the foundation for all other components of internal control, providing discipline and structure.

(2) Risk assessment
Risk assessment is the identification and analysis of relevant risks to achievement of the objectives, forming a basis for determining how the risks should be managed.

(3) Control activities
Control activities are the policies and procedures that help ensure management directives could be carried out. They help to ensure that necessary actions are taken to address risks for achievement of the entity's objectives. They include a range of activities as diverse as approvals, authorizations, verifications, reconciliations, etc.

(4) Information and communication
Pertinent information must be identified, captured and communicated in a form and timeframe that enable people to carry out their responsibilities.

(5) Monitoring
It is a process that assesses the quality of the system's performance over time. This is accomplished through ongoing monitoring activities, separate evaluations or a combination of the two.

The above six perspectives about management control elements have both similarities and differences. The similarities are mainly manifested in that they all regard measurement, evaluation and correction as the basic elements of management control. The differences are mainly presented as follows: Perspective I and III neglects the communication among measurement, evaluation and correction while Perspective IV and VI both underlines the role of communication; Perspective II and IV emphasizes the element of control environment while Perspective I, III and V ignores it; Perspective III and VI highlight control variables and risk elements while the others overlook them; only Perspective VI considers the element of monitoring.

The similarities of the above viewpoints arise from the understanding about control essence and control procedure, which are measurement, evaluation and correction, are basically the same. The differences or individualities mainly result from the following reasons.

Firstly, the cognitions about the connotation of element are different. What are elements? What are the contents of elements?

Secondly, the demarcations about the scope of each element are different. For example, some people regard standard, report and evaluation as the elements of evaluation, while some other people think that standard, report and evaluation are three independent elements; some people think that control standards contain control variables and control standards establishment, while some other people regard them as two independent elements.

Lastly, their comprehensions about the connotation of management control systems are different. For example, some people think they are closed systems while some other people think they are open systems.

8.2 The Construction of Management Control Systems Based on Management Control Elements

8.2.1 Theoretical Basis that Determines the Elements of Management Control System

The premise of establishing the framework of management control systems is to conceptualize management control elements. To construct a framework of management control element system, the above problems originated from different perspectives on management control elements should be solved first.

8.2.1.1 Connotation of Element and the Elements of Management Control System

Essential factor (or key point) is the essence, nature or composition of an object. In other words, defining the elements is the most important and factor that constructs an object and the essence will be changed if one of them is omitted. The elements of management control systems are the elements that reflect the essence of management and the component of management control systems. The elements of management control reflect the purpose, nature and procedure, while the elements of management control systems reflect the systematic characteristics of management control. From this perspective, the elements of management control and the elements of management control system are different.

8.2.1.2 Characteristics of Element and Those of Management Control Systems

As discussed previously, people's demarcations about the scope of each element are different. Some people divide one element into several elements, while some other people combine several elements into one. Therefore, how to define the scope of element is a complex question. To explore the demarcation about the scope of the element, at least two basic characteristics of element are defined firstly.

One is indispensability. That is, if one element is omitted, the essence of an object will be changed. For example, as control standard is an element of control, it will not be a kind of control on the absence of control standard.

The other is impartibility. That is, the element should reflect the most fundamental element of an object with independent and explicit range. For example, if control standards can be divided into control variables and control standards, it is better regard control variables and control standards as two elements.

8.2.1.3 Connotation of Management Control System and Scope of Elements

The scope of management control system elements is closely related to the common sense of the connotation of management control system. If management control system is regarded as an open system, controlling environment and monitoring will both be the elements of management control system. If management control system is regarded as a closed system, controlling environment and monitoring will not be the elements of management control system.

8.2.2 Ten Elements of Management Control Systems

According to the theoretical basis and connotation of management control system, we conclude management control elements into ten basic units.

8.2.2.1 Control Environment

Control environment is the circumstance that an organization faces when implementing management control, which includes external environment and internal environment. External environment consists of the national politics, economy, social development environment, industry environment, regional environment, etc. Internal environment contains integrity and ethical values an organization embraces, organizational strategy, organizational structure, division of functions and powers, responsibility centers, human resource policies and practices, etc. From the perspective of internal control, internal management control environment has great impact on the control methods and means of different organizations, and internal management control will be ineffective without considering the control environment.

8.2.2.2 Control Variables

Control variables are the key elements and risk elements that influence the strategic objectives of an organization. Whether the organization objectives can be achieved or not depends on the control of risk elements and value drivers that affect most organizational objectives. Therefore, to perfect internal management control, finding out critical control especially variables about risk elements is fatal. For example, an enterprise can regard asset-liability ratio as a control variable of financing, regard the ratio of intangible asset to total asset as a control variable of investment, regard ROA as a control variable of capital management centers, regard the rate of cost reduction as a control variable of cost centers, and so on.

8.2.2.3 Control Standards

Control standards are the bases and criterions of an organizational control and they are the quantification of control variables. Control standards plan what an organization should do and the degree of its action. Control standards are the decomposition of strategic control objectives of an organization. According to control objects, control standards can be divided into input control standards, process control standards and result control standards. According to control bases, control standards can be divided into budget control standards, industry control standards, historical control standards, etc. According to the forms of control standards, they can also be divided into ration control standards and total amount control standards. In a word, the validity of control standards directly affects the effectiveness of management control.

8.2.2.4 Information Reports

Information reports are the process of measurement, record and report all kinds of information about the organization's activities, and they reflect what the organization is doing. Relevance and reliability are the two most basic quality requirements to information reports of management control. The relevance of management control information reports are reflected in control variables and control standards, while the reliability are reflected in the reality of the organization's activities. Information reports mainly consist of accounting reports, statistical reports and business reports.

8.2.2.5 Execution of Evaluation

Execution of evaluation is the process of assessment and appraisal on an organization's activities. Execution of evaluation is actually the process of comparing information reports with control standards and analyzing them. Therefore, the result of evaluation depends on the quality of control standards and information reports and then determines the effectiveness of correction. To ensure the evaluation precise and timely, distinguishing the reasons that result to the differences between the realities and standards is critical, which include both subjective and objective elements, both controllable and uncontrollable elements.

8.2.2.6 Correction

Correction is the process of adjusting or correcting the unfavorable variance between the realities and control standards after evaluation. The essence of control is correction, so to speak, and it is the key point to ensure the realization of control standards and objectives. Correction can be divided into "loose control" and "tight control" according to the requirement of control degree. Loose control is the kind of control that allows relatively large deviations (such as 5 %) between the real reports and control standards. Tight control is the kind of control that allows smaller deviations (such as 2 %) between the real reports and control standards.

8.2.2.7 Performance Evaluation

Performance evaluation is the process of evaluating management control results or performance. The performance of an organization may be different from that of managers. The operating performance evaluation of management control attaches great importance to the performance of managers or controllers. The main principles of performance evaluation are: firstly, combining the indicators of operating results with the indicators of drivers; secondly, combining internal evaluation with external evaluation; lastly, combining financial evaluation indicators with non-financial evaluation indicators.

8.2.2.8 Incentive Mechanism

Incentive mechanism is the process of reward or punishment to managers according to the result of performance evaluation. To ensure management control run effectively in the long term, the result of management control should be linked with managers' compensation. Management compensation mainly consists of wages, benefits and incentives. Incentive plans are often set on the basis of the contribution of the management. Incentives reflect the contributed value of the management and the level of management control should be united with managerial incentives. From the perspective of control, incentive mechanism is critical for management compensation.

8.2.2.9 Communication

Communication is the process of delivering information timely among the above management control elements, and it is the basis and assurance of management control. The control standards will not be established scientifically while there is the absence of the specification of control environment and control variables; without the communication of control standards and information reports, evaluation and correction will not be implemented effectively. Hence, without timely and accurate communication among each management control elements, there will be no effective management control systems. It is necessary to communicate in the process of management control to establish an effective management control system.

8.2.2.10 Monitoring

Monitoring is to monitor the quality of management control implementation. The management controllers themselves should be controlled or monitored, and this is an element of a perfect control system. If there is no monitoring or evaluation, the efficiency and effectiveness will decline. Internal auditing, for example, has great function in the system of internal control, and its role is to monitor management controllers.

The ten elements above all together constitute a perfect management control system. Each element has an important function in the process of management control, and the quality of management control will be affected without any element.

References

1. Dauten PM Jr, Gammill HL, Robinson SC (1958) Our concept of controlling need re-thinking. J Acad Manage 1(3):41–55
2. Newman WH (1984) Managerial control. Science Research Associates, Chicago
3. Newman WH (1951) Administrative action. Prentice-Hall, New York
4. Lorange P, Scott Morton MS (1974) A framework for management control systems. Sloan Manage Rev 16(1):41–56
5. Anthony RN, Govindarajan V (1998) Management control systems. McGraw-Hill Companies Inc., Burr Ridge
6. Gutenberg E (1951) Grundlagen der Betriebswirtschaftslehre, vol 1, Die Produktion. Springer, Berlin
7. Committee of Sponsoring Organizations of the Treadway Commission (COSO) (1992) Internal control-integrated framework, America, September
8. Committee of Sponsoring Organizations of the Treadway Commission (COSO) (2004) Enterprise risk management-integrated framework, America, September

Chapter 9
Management Control Environment and Management Control System

9.1 Connation and Categories of Control Environment

The internal management system elements define the general framework of management control element system. This framework indicates that management control system is an open system. As the first element of management control system, control environment has an important influence on the management control mode and plays a significant role in the establishment and application of management control system. This chapter mainly studies the connation of control environment and its influences on management control system formulation.

9.1.1 The General Environment and Environment of Management Control System

Environment means the surrounding circumstances such as natural environment and social environment.[1] Environment is regional and relative, such as enterprise environment, industry environment, national environment, international environment and etc. Industry environment is the determinant of enterprise environment, and national environment is the decisive factor of industry environment. From the aspect of system theory, the so-called environment is the sum of all systems which affects the studied system except the studied system itself.[2]

The environment of management control system refers to the sum of all systems that influence management control system. It should be pointed out that the management control system discussed here is a closed system; control environment is the sum of total factors outside this closed system. Actually, a closed system could

---

[1] Cihai, Shanghai [1].

[2] Zhou Shouhua et al. [2].

X. Zhang, *Enterprise Management Control Systems in China*, Understanding China, DOI 10.1007/978-3-642-54715-7_9, © Springer-Verlag Berlin Heidelberg 2014

turn into an open system when it changes with the environment factors or takes environment factors into account. Management control system in essence is an open system, which is the basic premise of our study.

9.1.2 Categories of Management Control Environment

Because a certain system environment often regards other systems as its environment, there are many ways to categorize enterprise control environment.

According to American COSO reports, the internal control environment factors mainly include the integrity, ethical values and competence of the entity's people; management's philosophy and operating style; the way management assigns authority and responsibility, and organizes and develops its people; and the attention and direction provided by the board of directors.

In the book '*Management Control System*', Robert Anthony describes management control environment as understanding strategies; organizational structure; responsibility center; enterprise culture; and human resource.[3]

Some Chinese scholars have discussed this issue, but mainly took the COSO reports as the basic framework.

It should be noticed that the above two kinds of internal control environment categorization grasp the key factors of internal control. But from the point of regional and relative perspective, these two methods seem to be lack of systematic and comprehensiveness. So it would be more reasonable to divide the management control environment into organizational external environment and internal environment.

9.2 External Environment and Management Control System

As an important system to carry out enterprise strategy to ensure the organizational strategic target implementation, the exertion of management control system function is related to the understanding of external environment which determines the organization strategic target. Taking enterprises as example, the external environment includes social environment; political environment; technical environment; business environment; industry competitive environment; suppliers and customers environment and etc. It is shown in Fig. 9.1.

The enterprise external environments shown in Fig. 9.1 are also the external environment of enterprise management control, because to some extent they have some impact on the choice and operation of enterprise management control system. Every environment category actually contains many factors. Social and political climate includes ethic, culture, religion, ecology and etc.; government activities include systems, laws, rules and regulations; international business conditions

[3] Anthony [3].

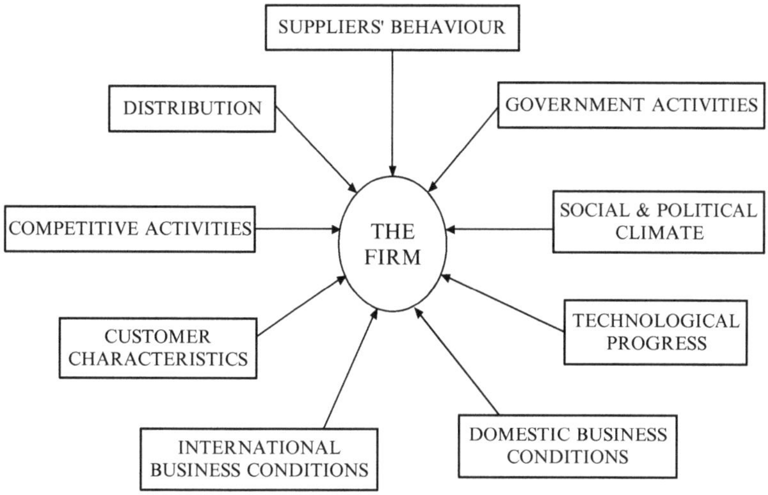

Fig. 9.1 External environment of management control (Wilson and Su Tong [4])

contain international capital market, exchange rate, inflation and etc. This chapter mainly discusses the relation between external environment and management control system from the aspects of ethical environment and economic system with Chinese features.

9.2.1 Ethical Environment and Management Control System

For a long time, people have always been focusing on the most direct factors influencing the enterprise goals such as the variations of corporate stakeholders, national price policy, interest rate policy, tax policy, while ethical environment is usually neglected. As the establishment of China's socialist market economy system and its enhanced influence on enterprises, the public began to attach importance to moral environment and call upon the moral integrity after Enron event in USA and Yinguangxia event in China. Public expectations have turned into less toleration, stronger moral consciousness and higher corporate behavior. The lack of social credit has led to increasing regulation and control over the corporate governance and management practices.

Moral environment has various influences on enterprise management control system, and among them, enterprise management control objective has the most crucial and dominant impact.

Enterprise management control objective and the enterprise goals are usually consistent. While the enterprise goal is in accordance with business owners, such as production output value maximum, sales revenue maximum, profit maximization, shareholders value maximization, enterprise value maximization, stakeholders interest maximization, social benefit maximization and etc. Business owners' goals are often affected by moral environment.

Changes in ethical environment and public expectation might drive the revolution of corporate goal or mission: The concept of unrestrained freedom and supremacy of profits has given a way to the concept of benefiting the society. Enterprises and society are sharing a kind of interdependent relationship. In this relationship, a healthy running corporate will lead the society to a long-term healthy movement, and vice versa.

There are three questions about the relationship between enterprise profits and social benefits:

Firstly, a ridiculous argument existing considers that enterprises cannot assume the moral responsibility because it could make them abandon many opportunities to gain profit or transfer the attention on profit to cause the profit declination. Actually, the research shows that when managers consider social goals, short-term profit may rise or fall. However, two long-term observations also fortify the organically merging of social goals and enterprise profit goals.

Secondly, It is might not be proper that the profit could lead to right resources allocation for social optimum usage. In 1970, when Friedman began to explicitly describe the relationship of profit and resources, there was neither cost related with water and air which were used for production, nor the vital cost of waste disposal. But from 1980s, these so-called externality cost increased sharply, these costs in the polluters were not included in the calculation of profit under GAAP. Generally, the pollution discharge cost was paid by other company's profits or borne by the towns and the government. So the relation of the original corporate profits and social resources was not that directly as what Friedman found. As the increase of these externally related costs, the relation of profit and resource usage would be more inapplicable unless the traditional profit calculation framework was revised or made-up. Perhaps environment accounting or corporate's plan of buying Sewage Discharge Permission would solve the embarrassing problem.

Finally, profit must be restrained in the scope of social laws and ethical code. This view was not accepted by those people who regard profit and freedom as the supreme. Obviously, enterprises will inevitably move into a chaotic operation in an unrestricted environment. Framework with a minimum necessary rule should be effective to our market with low-cost operation and should protect all participating members. To strengthen control is a response to the reducing shameful behavior and the increasing social moral need. Most profits supremacy supporters were not aware of that to strengthen self-concerns to achieve better moral governance and behavior is just the way to avoid government regulation enhancement.

Because of these reasons above, the profit supremacy target has evolved into determining the interdependency of enterprises and society. Future success would depend on the extent that the enterprise weighing the profit and the social goal. Enterprises will not succeed without the emergence of a new style of governance and report. If moral and social goals could not be combined successfully together or balanced organically, shareholders' interests will always be superior to other stakeholders' interests, the tension between enterprise and society will continue to rise.

9.2.2 Economic System and Management Control System

China's economic system has gone through two important transformations since the reform and opening-up, that is, (1) The planned economy changed into the planned commodity economy, (2) the planned commodity economy developed into the socialist market economy. Both these transformations steadily lead to the change of the enterprise operation. The simple production model transferred into the manufacturing operation model, and the manufacturing operation model changed into capital operation model. The changes of the operating ways finally caused the transformation of internal control as well.

9.2.2.1 Enterprise Management Control in Planned Economy System

From the founding of P. R. China in 1949 to 1978 before the reform and opening-up, China was under a planned economy or administrative commanding economy. All decisions involving production, distribution and even consumption, were made by government planning agencies, such as what, how much and how to produce, from where to acquire resources, whom to sell. Hence, enterprises only played the role of a production unit. Under this circumstance, enterprises' management control purely ensured the completion of the production task. Its functions were mainly production control, material management, productivity and technology efficiency monitoring rather than value management control. The method of corporate management control was regulation control, which meant that the enterprises could operate only by abiding by the regulatory rules and therefore weakening the power of managers and staff.

9.2.2.2 Enterprise Management Control in Planned Commodity Economy System

From 1978 to the end of 1991, the objective of Chinese economic reform was to establish a planned commodity economy and to solve many problems left behind by the planned economy through the combination of planned economy and commodity economy . This period can be separated into two stages:

The first Stage was from the end of 1978 to September of 1984, the basic idea of this reform was to expand private right, render the benefits to them and change the highly centralized planned economy system. Enterprises began to emphasize on managing their business according to economic law, especially the value law. And the enterprise operation transferred from pure production-oriented to production management. Meanwhile, the objective of enterprise management control is not only focusing on the production quantity, but also focus on the value and the linkage of production, supply and sales, aiming at the revenue and profit target. The content of enterprise management control is not only the production procedure control, but also the purchasing and selling process control. The method of enterprise management control is no longer simplified; the manager and staff have some control power.

The second stage was from October of 1984 to the end of 1993, and the basic idea is the separation of government and enterprises as well as the separation of ownership and operation rights. During this period, the reform transformed from retained profit and tax for profit into the factory director responsibility system, contracting system, renting system, and joint stock system piloting in few enterprise. Because of the separation mentioned, enterprise operators' management power over assets occupancy, use and dispose is increased, and the responsibility for assets was enhanced. The objective of enterprises' management control afterwards was not only revenues or profits, but also rate of the profits by assets occupancy. Hence, company directors took more responsibilities on return on assets (ROA) and the content of management control extended to investment and asset control. Accordingly, the method of enterprises management control began to diversify. Contracting, piecework rate, activity control and operation control were widely used.

9.2.2.3 Enterprise Management Control in Socialist Market Economy System

From the beginning of 1992, the reform of China has transformed from policy regulating towards a system innovation, stepping into a new stage of establishing socialist market economy. The direction of enterprise reform is to establish a modern enterprise system with clear ownership structures, well defined rights and responsibilities, separation of government and enterprise, scientific management. The corporate operation model has transformed from production operation to asset operation, then further into capital operation model. The target of management control made a progress from the pursuit of simple profits and the maximization of profits under certain assets to the maximization of profits under certain capital, namely the basic target of capital appreciation. The functions of enterprise management control extended further into capital amount control, capital structure control, capital cost control, capital profit control and capital distribution control. Consequently, the control system developed from a closed one into an open one. The control approaches of authorization have been widely adopted; not only the boundary control but also the diagnostic control, trust control and other control methods are promoted in some enterprises.

9.3 Internal Environment and Management Control System

The external environment of management control takes the whole corporate as a management control system. If we take the enterprise MCS as a part of enterprise management system, then the enterprise MCS must involve the enterprise internal factors. Figure 9.2 shows the relationship of enterprise MCS and other systems.

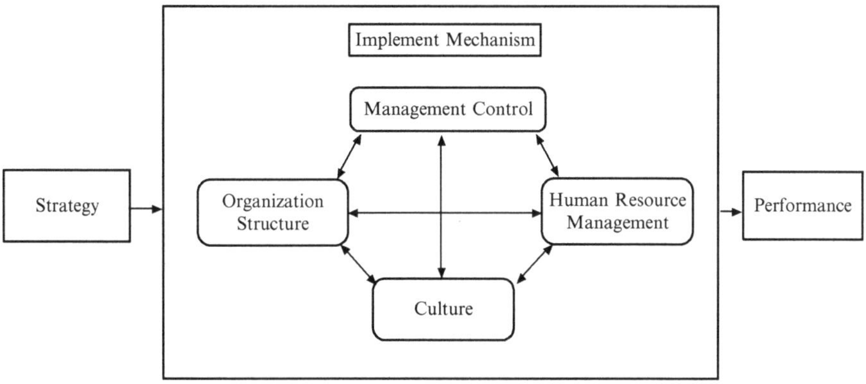

Fig. 9.2 Management control environment (Anthony [3])

It shows that the operation of enterprise MCS must conform to the requirement of enterprise strategic goals and take the conditions of organizational structure, enterprise culture, human resources. These form the important internal environment affecting and determining the operation of enterprise MCS. As the influences of enterprise culture and human resource which are closely related to the external ethical environment have been discussed before, here we only investigate the relationship of enterprise strategic environment, organizational structure and enterprise management control.

9.3.1 Enterprise Strategy and MCS

Strategy has a significant impact on the establishment of MCS which is a process conducted by the manager to influence other members to accomplish corporate strategies. There are two aspects to studying the relationship of corporate strategy and MCS.

9.3.1.1 Relationship of Strategy Formulation and Management Control

Management control is a kind of planning and controlling activity in an organization. There are at least three types of organization planning and controlling activity: strategy formulation; management control; and task control. The relation of strategy formulation and management control is clear: Strategy formulation is the process to decide strategic objectives and to achieve these objectives. Management control is the process to assure the implementation of those strategies. The differences between the strategy formulation and management control includes: firstly, the former decides the new strategy and the latter decides how to implement strategy. From the viewpoint of systems design, the most important distinction between them is that

Table 9.1 Strategy levels

Strategy level	Key strategic issues	Generic strategic options	Primary organizational involved
Corporate level	Are we in the right mix of industries? What industry or subindustry should the enterprise is involved?	Single industry Related diversification Unrelated diversification	Corporate office
Business unit level	What should be the mission of the business unit?	Build Hold Harvest Dives	Corporate office and business unit general manager
	How should the business unit compete to realize its mission?	Low cost Differentiation	Business unit general manager

strategy formulation is essentially unsystematic, while management control is systematic. Besides, analysis of a proposed strategy usually involves relatively few people. By contrast, the management control process involves managers and their staffs at all levels in the organization. Strategy formulation only concerns a part of organization and influences a certain strategy rather than the other strategies; Management control process necessarily concerns the entire organization in order to coordinate each part of management control.

9.3.1.2 Strategy Levels and Management Control

Generally speaking, enterprise strategies include two levels: strategies for the whole organization and strategies for business units within the organization. Figure 9.1 describes the key strategic issues, strategic options and organizational levels involved (Table 9.1).

The key points and methods of management control vary with the different level of strategy. Managers at each level should choose the matching method and key points of management control according to its strategy issues and strategy choices.

9.3.2 Organizational Structure and MCS

An enterprise's organizational structure has a major influence on its management control methods and contents. The organizational structure includes enterprise management system and enterprise responsibility center. From the standpoint of enterprise management system, a firm's organizational structure can be grouped into three categories: functional structure; business unit structure; and shareholding structure. Different structure of management control methods and authorities has its own characteristic.

Management control method of functional organizations belongs to the direct control with centralized power. For example, from the view of financial control, the headquarter financial department as a united powerful department, conducts the highly centralized management of capital gathering, usage and distribution, even the assignment of financial staff, and take the leadership in the subordinate financial department.

Business unit structure of management control combines the direct control and indirect control together. Headquarter has direct control power to each business unit or division, and each business unit or division has autonomy. Taking the financial control for example, the headquarter has the major financial power and only make decision for vital and overall financial events, such as significant financing or investing activities, then delegate the secondary power to business units or divisions. Under this structure, the headquarter splits the financial power with its members so that each enterprise has some autonomy to operate.

Share-holding structure has a kind of indirect management control which delegates the control power. From the standpoint of financial control, the financial decision-making power is conducted by each member of the organization separately. And member enterprises make decisions, operate, manage and record accounts independently. But generally speaking, not all the subsidiaries or departments have the complete financial control power. The headquarter only delegates the power belonging to their directly controlled subsidiaries to them, so that they could decide their own management system model (centralized, decentralized, or delegated) to their subordinates.

From the perspective of responsibility centers, the organization can divide into cost center, revenue center, profit center and investment center. Different center has its respective contents of management control. For example, service sector can be defined as cost center, or profit center. Obviously, these two types of responsibility center have different control contents.

9.3.3 Corporate Governance Structure and MCS

The Corporation Governance Structure Description stated by the USA business round-table conference in 1997 has pointed out the impact of corporate governance on MCS in its definition of corporate governance structure. They argued that corporate governance structure is not an abstract goal, but a series of structure or system aiming to pursue the organizational goal and is conducted by the shareholders, board of directors and management team.[4] The choice of corporate governance structure is to cater for the firm's goals or the effective accomplishment of these goals, while MCS is the specific tool to carry out the strategy as well as the organizational goals. Consequently, corporate governance necessarily affects the MCS.

---

[4] Li Kongyue and Luo Biliang [5].

It has an important impact on the efficiency and effectiveness of MCS that whether there is an independent director among the board of directors or not, and what is the proportion of independent director. Although MCS is for managers to ensure the accomplishment of organizational goal, independent director has responsibility and obligation to assist the managers for the promotion of operating activities, improvement of the firm's fame and increase of the corporate's value. There is an empirical study shows that (1) the optimal board of directors tends to make the independent directors occupy the dominate status; (2) the average annual profit of this kind of company is higher than the others in the same industry. After investigating 154 American big public trading companies in 1998, Millstein and Mac Avoy found that companies with positive independent directors had been going better than those with passive non-independent directors.

It also has significant impact on MCS that whether there is auditing committee in the board of directors, and what is the substantial functions of auditing committee. The supervision to the effectiveness and efficiency of management control and the reliability of financial report is an internal supervision which includes the advanced, real-time and post-supervision control. Contrasted with it, CPA and security committee mainly conduct the post-supervision which is weaker than the advanced, real-time supervision. So, without auditing committee, the impact of post-supervision is less. Meantime, auditing committee has so deep and wide influences on the development of MCS that whether the auditing committee could properly dispose its relationship with the board of directors, senior managers, CFO, internal auditing department, external auditors and relative experts; conduct timely information communication; propose the internal management control regulation scientifically, precisely, objectively and fairly; supervise the reviewing function of internal auditing department, and investigate the compliance of corporate regulation; whether it has enough power and resources to support the fulfillment of each function.

9.3.4 Production Technology and MCS

Technology is the practical application of science to transform inputs (material, information, concepts) into organizational outputs (products and services), and the relative hardware (machines and tools), raw material, human resources, software and knowledge. According to the characteristic of manufacturing, the technology can be divided into small-batch, large-batch, process production and standardized mass production.[5][6]

Different type of technology has different level of complexity. The so-called complexity is the degree of mechanization in the manufacturing process. From the small-batch and single-piece production to mass production, the degree of mechanization improves continually as well as the complexity level. The impact on the management control system is varied with the level of complexity.

---

[5] Woodward [6].

For standard, undifferentiated products manufacturers, they always adopt mass production technology, namely, with a higher degree of mechanization as well as a higher level of complexity. But it is easy to obtain information in production process, so that the participators can use objective and standard procedure to solve problems and measure outputs easily. Under this condition, MCS is usually a traditional, formal, and financial mode system.

For the organizations which produce highly specialized, nonstandard and different products, its degree of mechanization is low as well as the levels of complexity; But it is hard to gather the information of production process. Once problems occur, it is difficult to precisely analyze the reasons and render solutions through the existing technology and procedure. It only depends on the participators' work experience, intuition and analysis judgment ability because problems have many exceptions. It is difficult to measure outputs. Under this condition, flexible reaction control and an open communication with high level are recommended.

9.3.5 Human Resources and MCS

From the basic goal of management control, "to improve the efficiency and effectiveness of management activities", it could be known that the object of management control is to manage activities. As the affected person or actor of each operating management activity, human resources must influence the MCS.

The impact of human resources on MCS can be summarized into two aspects: human resource management and human resource quality.

From the standpoint of human resource management, the connotation of modern human resource management is the process to acquire, integrate, maintain, motivate, control adjustments, to develop human resources."[6][7]. During this process, its management mode could be divided into two types, event-centered and human-centered. The event-centered management mode regards the staff as a cost burden and treats them as a tool that focus on the input, usage and control, emphasizing the single static control and management of event. And it stresses more on controlling by administrative orders, rules and regulations, severe budget constraint and other regular formal control means. The human-centered management mode regards employees as valuable resource, pays attention to meet the needs of the employee's personal development, stresses on people motivation and development. This management way emphasizes more on the organizational culture or customs and other informal control mode.

From the point of the human resource quality, moral quality and professional quality is the main aspects of human resource measurement. The moral quality can ensure the staff "do the right things", and it determines the consistency level of employees' behaviors and managers' expectations. For a good moral quality staff, the organization will more easily adopt flexible control methods and informal

[6] Lin Zeyan [7].

control means, instead of hard constraints. Professional quality can ensure that the staff "do things properly", and determine the consistency level of employees' outputs and manager' expectations. It also takes flexible control method and informal control means to the highly professional employees.

9.3.6 Management Philosophy, Leadership Style and MCS

Management philosophy is the basic policy or values for the organization to implement management. By according to Chinese traditional cultures, the management philosophy is classified into three basic categories, Confucian managerial school, Legalist managerial school; and Taoist managerial school. Going through the eastern and western cultures, the connotation of management has universal applicability. Confucian and Legalist are two different managerial schools on the contrary, while the saying that "complying with the objective law" and "governing by non-interference" of Taoist is a higher level to discuss. So we only discuss the impacts on MCS from both Confucian managerial school and Legalist managerial school.

Deriving from "innate purity human nature", Confucian managerial philosophy emphasizes moral control. By taking moral infection and education as main approaches and adopting human management based on the principles of humanity and human nature, it sets examples by one's own action, convinces people by moral and team spirit. Legalist managerial philosophy derives from "the evil of human nature", emphasize legal control, takes rules and regulations as control means, conduct rewards and punishments, implement the policy that "there must be laws for people to follow; the laws should be strictly observed; the enforcement of laws must be strict; law-breakers must be prosecuted." The emphases of both these two schools are different, but they are not mutually exclusive. In corporate governance, there are different ways to treat people at different hierarchy and positions.

In terms of leadership style, scholars [8] have proposed an effective Fiedler Contingency model on the basis of extensive research.[7] It holds the point that any leadership style may be effective, and their effectiveness entirely depends on their ability to adapt to environment. There are two types of leadership style, task-based and relational. A leader is considered to be a tolerant and considerate leader if he or she could speak highly of the even most unfavorite colleague, promoting friendly relations between people, namely a relational style leader; If he gives low evaluation to the most unfavorite colleague, he is a kind of task-based leader, who only cares about the order and control rather than people. Task-based leadership style tends to adopt regular control system which has clear reporting relation and responsibilities relation, the information feedback prefers a bottom-up communicating level by level, rather than the proactive communication from top to bottom. Relational leadership

[7] Xu Guohua and Zhang De [8].

style tends to be an informal control system, the leaders conduct controls depending on the prestige of the individual and genial personality, information feedback and communication are more smoothly.

9.4 Implications of Management Control Environment and MCS

According to the researches on management control environment and MCS, there are several conclusions and implications just as follows:

(A) The evolution of management control system mode is not separated from the changes of management control environment. The variation of control environment leads to the change of management control system mode.
(B) Management control system mode is closely related with external economic environment of the enterprises. Management control system mode is developing with the improvement of the economic system and economic environment.
(C) In the identical external environment, although the basic target of management control is consistent, management control system modes might vary with corporate internal environment. The establishment of enterprise internal MCS should conduct a comprehensive control from different perspectives by different ways.
(D) For different type and different management basis of enterprise or organization, although there are many methods to conduct management control, the focus of each management control method is different. The establishment of enterprise internal MCS must choose the emphasis according to the environment.
(E) MCS external environment of China is different from that of foreign countries. There is only a part of the enterprises are staying in the authorized operating stage; the mode of open and natural controls is not suitable for the majority of enterprises in China.
(F) Because the internal MCS environment of Chinese enterprises differ considerably, a unified management control system mode is not applicable. The coexistence of various management controls is the fundamental characteristic of Chinese MCS mode for the future in the long run.

References

1. Cihai (1980) Shanghai Lexicographical Publishing House, Shanghai, p 1205 (Chinese)
2. Zhou Shouhua, Lu Zhengfei, Tang Guliang (2000) Issues of modern corporate finance. Donbei University of Finance and Economics Press, Dalian
3. Anthony RN (1998) Management control Systems, 9th edn. McGraw-Hill, Burr Ridge
4. Wilson R, Su Tong (Translation) (1988) Cost control handbook. Peking University Press, Beijing, p 116 (Chinese)

5. Li Kongyue, Luo Biliang (2002) The theory of corporate governance structure: an overview. Contemp Finance Econ 23(8):61–64
6. Woodward J (1980) Organization theory and practice, 2nd edn. Oxford University Press, Oxford, p 50
7. Lin Zeyan (2001) Position-performance-payment. China CITIC Press, Beijing, p 109
8. Xu Guohua, Zhang De (1998) Management. Tsinghua University Press, Beijing, p 218

Chapter 10
Management Control Procedures and Management Control System

10.1 Management Control Procedures [1]

The investigation of management control system from the perspective of management control elements can meet the general needs of describing the MCS. Management control is the process by which managers influence other members of the organization to implement organization's strategies. Researching management control system from the perspective of control procedures can interpret the fundamental purpose of MCS better. As to management control procedures, researching them from different categories, levels or perspectives, the result may be different. If management control is regarded as a closed system, that is, the control environment is certain, the procedures of management control system are called formal control process. At present, three-step control procedures, four-step control procedures and five-step control procedures exist and are all belonging to formal process. If management control is regarded as an open system, namely, given uncertain and continuously changeable control environment, the procedures of management control system are called informal control process. Formal control process and informal control process are different. From the systematic and a long-term point of view, informal control process is inevitable, but formal control process is more scientific and operable from a specific and short-term point of view. In addition, the premise of our research about management control system is that the control environment is certain (a systematical research on control environment has been made in Chap. 9). Therefore, the focus of this chapter is on the formal control process.

10.1.1 Three-Step Control Procedures

Three-Step control procedures divide the control process into three procedures according to the control function of management. In some fields, such as *Management* and *Cybernetics*, control process is divided into three steps: setting standards, performance evaluation and correcting deviations.

X. Zhang, *Enterprise Management Control Systems in China*, Understanding China,
DOI 10.1007/978-3-642-54715-7_10, © Springer-Verlag Berlin Heidelberg 2014

10.1.2 Four-Step Control Procedures

The thought of Four-Step Control Procedure is common with Three-Step Control Procedure, and the minor difference is that Four-Step Control Procedure subdivides some steps further. For example, control process is divided into the following four steps in the manuscript "*Management Control and Managerial Economics*"[1]: (1) Setting control standards; (2) Evaluating the effectiveness of activities; (3) Preparing control reports; (4) Correcting errors.

10.1.3 Five-Step Control Procedures

Properly speaking, the Five-Step Control Procedure is the procedure of management control systems. Robert Anthony divided management control procedure into five steps in his notable manuscript *"Management Control Systems"*[2]:

1. Strategic planning;
2. Budget preparation;
3. Analyzing financial performance reports;
4. Performance measurement;
5. Management compensation.

Strictly speaking, management control procedure and the procedure of management control system are different. Here the procedures of management control system (shown in Fig. 10.1) are going to be dealt with.

As shown in Fig. 10.1, Five-Step Control Procedure is more suitable to theory and practice of management control than the other two kinds. However, the procedure of Anthony's management control system is actually a budget control systems. Management control model is not the only one kind of budget control model because budget standard is not the only one kind of control standards (management control models will be discussed in detail in Part 4 of this book). Therefore, we define management control procedures into the following five steps:

1. Decomposing strategic objectives;
2. Setting control standards;
3. Management control reports;
4. Operating performance evaluation;
5. Management compensation.

Each step to implement these management control procedures can be divided into many substeps, which all together constitute a systematic matrix graph of management control procedures as shown in Fig. 10.2.

[1] Luo Ruiren and Zeng Fanzheng [2].

[2] Anthony [3].

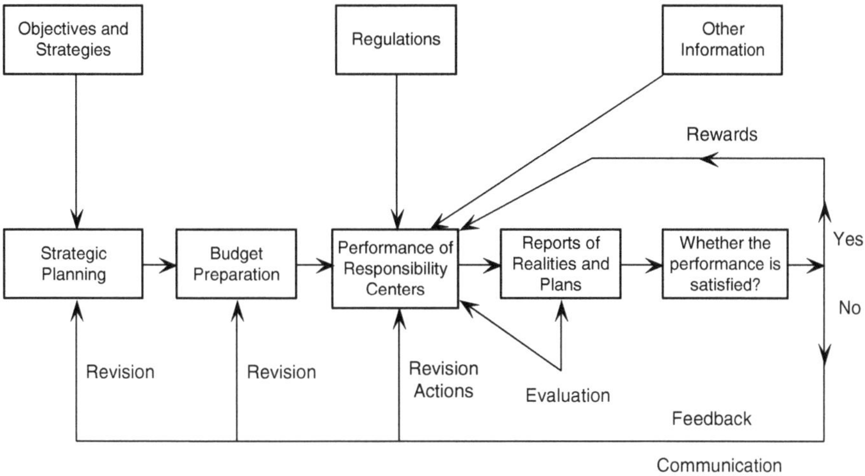

Fig. 10.1 The procedures of management control systems

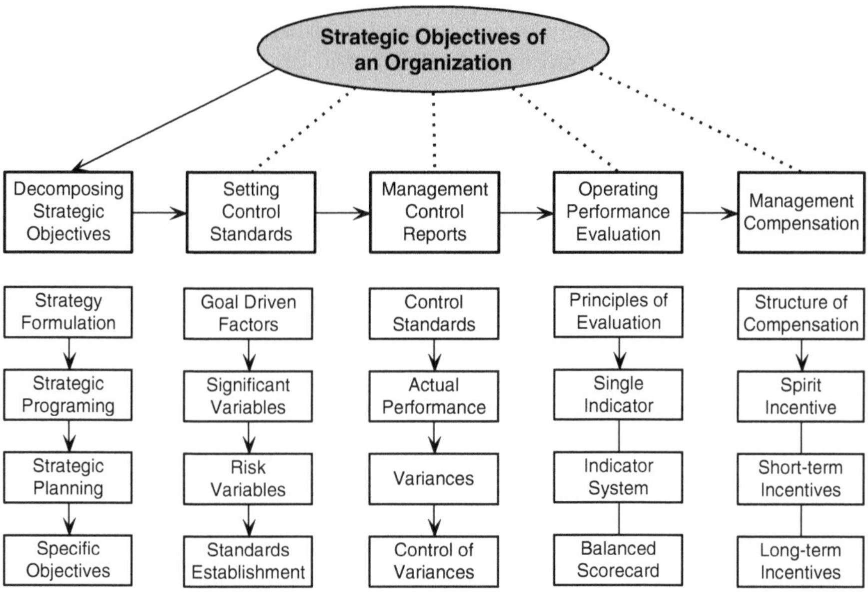

Fig. 10.2 Procedures and systems of management control

10.2 Decomposition of Strategic Objectives

Strategy demarcates the general direction of an organization to achieve its objectives. Strategy formulation is the strategic process of determining and achieving the objectives of an organization. The objectives of an organization contain both financial objectives and non-financial objectives. Non-profit organizations also have their own objectives. In the process of strategy formulation, organization objectives are often assumed as known, but sometimes strategy formulation also pays some attention to objectives. An organization can choose one approach from many alternatives to realize its objectives, which is called strategic selection. The process of strategy formulation is also the process of strategic selection. After the strategy of an organization has been determined, the basic task of management control is how to realize the objectives and strategies of an organization.

There are some differences between strategy formulation and management control. Strategy formulation is the process of determining new strategies; management control is the process of deciding how to implement strategies. From the standpoint of system design, the most important distinction between them is that strategy formulation is essentially unsystematic. Analysis of a proposed strategy usually involves relatively few people-the sponsor of the idea, headquarters staff, and senior management. By contrast, the management control process involves managers and their staffs at all levels in the organization. In addition, strategy formulation almost always involves only part of the organization; it may result in changes in one or a few existing strategies, but many other strategies are unaffected by it. The management control process necessarily involves the whole organization; an important aspect of the process is to ensure that various parts could be coordinated with one another.

Strategic objectives decomposition is the first step of management control. As is shown in Fig. 10.2, the process of strategic objectives decomposition starts from organizational objectives to control standards. As the relationship between organizational objectives and strategy formulation has been illustrated previously, the following relationships should also be explained to understand the process of strategy decomposition: the relationship between strategy formulation and strategic programming, the relationship between strategic programming and strategic planning, the relationship between strategic planning and control standards.

Intuitively, strategy is a kind of great and significant planning. Strategic planning is to prepare a kind of long-term strategic planning, and it determines the projects accepted by the organization in the next year and the quantity of resources that the projects need. Strategy formulation reflects the direction of an organization made by the management, while strategic planning pays attention to the long-term plan of resource allocation and the usage on the condition that the direction of the organization has been determined.

Strategic programming determines the rational scheme (typically 1 year) of resource allocation to realize the long-term strategic planning of an organization. Therefore, strategic planning decomposes strategic programming, which is the practice of strategic programming. In the process of management control, strategic programming is pivotal. On one hand, it materializes, institutionalizes, and systematizes the objectives and programming; on the other hand, it is the basis of setting control variables and standards.

10.3 Control Standards Establishment

Management control should be carried out according to the intention of the managers which is related to organizational objectives and control variables. Therefore, setting control standards on the basis of strategic planning is an important step for implementing effective controls.

10.3.1 Procedures of Setting Control Standards

To be specific, the procedure of setting control standards contains the following four steps:

- Specifying the elements that affect the organization objectives, or goal drivers;
- Identifying significant variables that affect the implementation of strategic objectives;
- Defining critical risk variables as the focal of control;
- Setting advanced and feasible management control standards.

10.3.2 Formats and Contents of Control Standards

The formats of control standards are: quantitative standards versus qualitative standards; efficiency (ratios or relative number) standards versus performance (total amount or absolute number) criteria.

The contents of control standards include financial standards and non-financial standards. The most widely used financial standards are mainly budgeted standards, such as financial budget, operational budget, capital expenditure budget, etc. The Balanced Scorecard approach is a typical kind of non-financial standards which is mainly concerned with customers, suppliers, employees, etc.

10.3.3 Categories and Levels of Control Standards

The levels of control standards include empirical standards, historical standard, industry standards, budgeted standards, etc.

10.3.3.1 Empirical Standards

Empirical standards are formed on the basis of large amounts of practical experience. As is known widely, the empirical standard of current ratio is about 2:1 and that of quick ratio is 1:1. Most people have the intuition that the ratio of current liabilities to tangible assets cannot be more 80 %, otherwise the organization will be set in operational distress; the ratio of inventory to net working capital cannot be more than 80 % either. All above intuitions are called the voice of experience or empirical standards. Some people also call this kind of standards absolute standards, and they think these standards are generally accepted which can be applied to whatever corporation or industry, whenever, and whatever kinds of environment. However, empirical standards couldn't be a kind of absolute standards suitable to all fields or conditions, and it is just suitable to the general case. For example, although the current ratio of a corporation is more than 2:1, its credit policy is worse and there are a lot of accounts receivables and overstocked inventories. Nevertheless, another corporation's current ratio is less than 2:1, but it is successful in managing its receivables, inventories and cash. In this case, we couldn't say that the former corporation's liquidity or solvency is better than the later. Therefore, while using empirical standards, we must be cautious and shouldn't apply them mechanically.

10.3.3.2 Historical Standards

Historical standards are formed on the basis of organization's actual performance at certain point of time. This kind of standards is helpful to evaluate the operating results and financial position of an enterprise. Historical standard may be the best level in history of an enterprise, and it can also be the level of performance under an enterprise's normal operating conditions. The advantages of historical standards are: (a) reliability, it is the level the enterprise has reached; (b) comparability, the enterprise could compare the stands from different time. The disadvantages of historical standards: (a) conservatism, the real condition at present may be different from that of history; (b) practical limitations, it just reflects the changes of the enterprise itself and can't evaluate the industry level and position totally. Especially for external analysis, just using historical standards is far from enough.

10.3.3.3 Industry Standards

Industry standards are formulated on the base of industry and they reflect the basic level of financial position and operating results in certain industry. Industry standards also include the level of advanced enterprise's performance in a certain industry. By using industry standards in the process of management control, an enterprise could improve its position and level in that industry. For example, assuming the ROA of an industry is 10 %, if an enterprise's ROA is just 8 %, investors will not accept it. Industry standards can also be used to judge the variation trend of an enterprise. In the period of economic depression, if one enterprise's profit ratio declines from 12 % to 9 % while the industry's profit ratio declines from 12 % to 6 %, then we can get the conclusion that the profitability of this enterprise is very good.

It should be pointed out that there are three limitations to apply industry standards. Firstly, sometimes two companies from the same industry cannot be compared. For example, even if the two companies are both from petroleum industry, one may buy crude oil from market to produce petroleum products while the other may produce crude oil itself, then these two companies cannot be compared. Secondly, because some big companies are often cross-industry operation, the level of profit and risk may be different from an enterprise in a different business, then it is obviously not suitable to use the common industry standards in this condition. The way to solve this problem is segmental reporting which includes revenue, profit, assets and expenses from different operating business. Thirdly, industry standards are also restrained by the enterprise's accounting policies. If enterprises in the same industry adopt different accounting policies, the accuracy of evaluation may be seriously influenced. For example, because of different valuation methods when sending out inventories, both their value and cost will be affected directly. Therefore, when using industry standards, the above limitations should be taken into account.

10.3.3.4 Budgeted Standards

Budgeted standards are target standards that formulated on the basis of the enterprise's operating condition and position. Budgeted standards are popular in some new industries, newly established enterprises and monopolistic enterprises. For other industries and enterprises, using budgeted standards is also helpful, because budgeted standards could reflect the position of one enterprise totally by combining industry standards with historical standards. Especially for internal control, budgeted standards have more advantages, and they can be used to evaluate the management's performance of different departments, which will affect the realization of one enterprise's total target. However, budgeted standards are often affected by human factors and correspondingly lack of objectivity.

10.4 Management Control Reports

The key to management control is to control the practical economy operation by virtue of utilizing control standards. Therefore, on the basis of setting control standards, it is a very important step of management control to measure and reflect the conditions of practical economy operation. The key point of this step is to prepare management control reports.

10.4.1 The System and Contents of Management Control Reports

The theoretical basis of management control reports system should be the demand of information decision-making by internal stakeholders. From different perspectives, related decisions could be divided differently. For example, from the perspective of business process, they can be divided into purchase decision, production

Table 10.1 Management control reports system

Operation responsibility center	Management control reports system	Core responsibility objectives	Concrete reports
Capital operation centers	Capital operation reports	ROE	
Asset operation centers	Asset operation reports	ROA	
Merchandising operation centers	Merchandising operation reports	Return on sales/sales margins	
Production operation centers	Production operation reports	Ratio of cost to output value	

decision, sales decision, pricing decision, R&D on new product decision, etc. From the perspective of responsibility objectives, they can be divided into investment decision, profit decision, cost decision, etc. Each classification has its management control reports system. In our opinion, in the condition of market economy system and modern enterprise system, an enterprise's operating decisions should be divided into capital operation decisions, asset operation decisions, merchandising operation decisions and production operation decisions, which totally formed four levels of responsibility center. Every responsibility center has its own report system according to its core responsibility objectives or sub-objectives. Therefore, the management control reports system can be established which includes capital operation reports, asset operation reports, merchandising operation reports and production operation reports, as shown in Table 10.1.

10.4.1.1 Capital Operation Report System

Capital operation is tightly connected with the business pattern of capital-operating enterprise. The target of capital operation is capital increment and the core of management is capital gains. That is, the management objective of capital-operating enterprise is to realize capital increment or profit maximization. Therefore, the connotation of capital operation is that it is a kind of operating activities aiming to improve the economic returns by optimizing the resource allocation based on capital. Its activities include capital flowing, acquisition, reconstruction, participation in investment, holding investment and so on, which are aimed to realize the increment of capital, in other words, to get as much as capital gains with certain inputs.

The core indicator that reflects the core objectives of capital operation is ROE. There are many factors that influence ROE, such as ROA, capital structure, interest, etc. To achieve the objectives of capital operation, that is, to improve ROE, two main aspects should be emphasized. On one hand, ROA should be improved first which means doing a good job in asset operation. On the other hand, capital policy should be emphasized which means to decrease the cost of capital, especially the cost of debt capital, to utilize capital structure and reasonably evade tax through taxation policies.

In conclusion, the system of capital operation reports should include asset operation report (which will be described in the next part); capital cost report, capital structure report, income tax report, EVA report, etc. Capital cost report mainly supplies information about different kinds of capital and their changes, especially the specific contents of debt cost. At the same time, it supplies the comparative information of ROA with indebted interest. Capital structure report mainly supplies the kind of information about enterprise's capital structure, financial structure, debt structure, owner's equity structure and so on. It also contains some information about changes in capital structure, optimizing criterion and the effectiveness of capital structure optimization. Income tax report mainly provides information about the payment and return of income tax, the changes of income tax caused by income tax policy changes. EVA report mainly provides information about enterprise's capital increment, especially the EVA information about different investment centers, which will play a pivotal role in investment decision and capital operation performance evaluation.

10.4.1.2 Asset Operation Report System

Asset operation is closely connected with business pattern of asset-operating enterprise. The basic character of asset operation is that it regards asset as the input of the enterprise resource and asset management through asset allocation, reconstruction, utilization, etc. In the condition of asset operation, merchandising operation or production operation should be based on asset operation, that is, asset operation determines merchandising operation and production operation. The objective of asset-operating enterprise is to pursue asset increment or profit maximization. Therefore, the connotation of asset operation is the reasonable allocation and asset application in order to maximize profit with a fixed asset input.

The indicator that reflects the core objective of asset operation is ROA. There are two main factors that influence ROA, total assets turnover and return on sales. To do well in asset operation and improve ROA, two main aspects should also be stressed. On one hand, merchandising operation should be emphasized first to improve sales margin or the profitability of an enterprise's merchandises. On the other hand, asset allocation and reconstruction should also be stressed to improve the efficiency of asset utilization and increase the turnover of total asset. To accelerate the operation of total asset, the key point is to optimize asset structure, making the best use of all kinds of asset, and avoiding the waste and loss due to assets idleness.

Therefore, asset operation report system mainly includes merchandising operation report (which will be described in the next part), asset structure report, the degree of asset utilization report, external investment report, asset loss and non-performing asset report, the effectiveness of asset utilization report, asset reconstruction report, etc. Asset structure report mainly provides information about all kind of detailed asset structure, such as production structure, material structure, aging accounts receivable, fixed asset detailed structure, intangible assets structure, etc. The degree of asset utilization report mainly provides information about the degree of utilization of all kinds of assets. External investment report provides information about external investment structure and investment income. Asset loss and non-performing asset report mainly provides information about the condition and position of asset loss and idleness. The effectiveness of asset utilization report provides information about the impact of asset turnover and the efficiency of asset utilization on the improvement of revenues and capital. Asset reconstruction report mainly provides information about asset reconstruction and its impact on asset structure and the effectiveness of asset utilization.

10.4.1.3 Merchandising Operation Report System

Merchandising operation is closely connected with the business pattern of merchandise-operating enterprise. The basic character of merchandising operation is that it regards commodity as the core content of management, which includes the management of supply, produce, sales and related financing and investment management. The objective of merchandising-operating enterprise is to pursue the perfect connection among supply, produce, sales and the profitability of commodity. Therefore, the basic connotation of merchandising operation is organizing the activities of supply, produce, sales which is oriented by market, producing and selling as more as commodity the society needs with a fixed amount of labor and material consumption, and making as more profit as possible.

The indicator that reflects the core objectives of merchandising operation is operating profit margin which is influenced by the factor of quantity, the selling price, and expenses and so on. To do well in merchandising operation and realize the objective of profit maximum, two main direct goals are essential: one is to increase the operating profit margin; the other is to enlarge the scale and level of sales. The relationship between operating profit margin and its affecting factors shows that to achieve the objective of operating profit maximum, the increasing of production quantity and the decreasing of production cost are the prerequisites. At the same time, the balance between supply and demand, the rise of selling price, the decrease of purchase cost and related expenses should all be emphasized.

Therefore, merchandising operation report system mainly includes production operating report (which will be described in the next part), operating revenue report, sales price report, market share report, purchase price report, administrative expenses report, operating expenses report, financial expenses report, non-operating income and expenses report, etc. Operating revenue report provides the information about sales volume, distribution channels and sales revenue, etc. Sales price report provides information about the sales price and its changes of all kinds of commodities and customers. Market share report provides information about the market share and its changes of different kinds of commodities. Purchase price report provides information about the purchase price and its changes of all kinds of commodities and suppliers. Period expenses report provides information about the structure and sum of different kinds of expenses. For some important expenses, a single report is also necessary, like service charge after sales and business entertainment expenses. Non-operating income and expenses report provides the detailed information about extraordinary items of income and expenses.

10.4.1.4 Production Operation Report System

Production operation is tightly connected with business pattern of production-operating enterprise. The basic character of simple production operation is that it just pays attention on manufacture and ignores the activities of supply, selling, financing and investing. The objective of production-operating enterprise is to fulfill the task and decrease production consumption. Therefore, the basic connotation of production operation is the organizing the manufacturing of product according to enterprise strategic planning and the timely producing of a certain amount of qualified products with a fixed amount of labor and material consumption.

The indicator that reflects the core objective of production operation is the ratio of cost to output value (or revenue) which is influenced by the elements of output, price, cost and expenses. To reduce the ratio of cost to output value (or revenue), on one hand, the output, quality and price of the product should be improved; on the other hand, production cost should be reduced which includes material cost, labor cost and manufacturing overhead.

Therefore, production operation report system mainly includes product cost report, unit cost report, labor cost report, manufacturing overhead report, the ratio of cost to output value report of all kinds of product, the report of the impact of technical-economic indicator on the cost, waste products report, etc. Among these reports, the preparation of product cost report, unit cost report and the report of all kinds of cost items are almost the same as current enterprise cost reports. The ratio of cost to output value report of all kinds of product provides information about ratio of cost to output value of all products and different kinds of products. Waste products report provides information about the quantity of waste products and their causes. The report of the impact of technical-economic indicator on the cost provides information about the influence of different kinds of labor efficiency, technology efficiency, management efficiency and resources use efficiency on product cost.

The typical four systems of management control reports are shown in Fig. 10.3.

10.4.2 The Format of Management Control Reports

Management control report is actually the performance report of the entire organization and every department. The general format is shown in Table 10.2. The category and contents of management control report should be designed according to management control standards. For example, the numbers of budget control reports should be consistent with the numbers of internal budgets; the contents of control report should be consistent with the budget.

The preparation procedure of management control reports. As is shown in Table 10.2, the preparation of management control report should follow the steps of control standard, actual performance, variance measurement, degree of variance and variance analysis, among which the most critical steps are actual performance measurement and variance analysis. Actual performance measurement includes

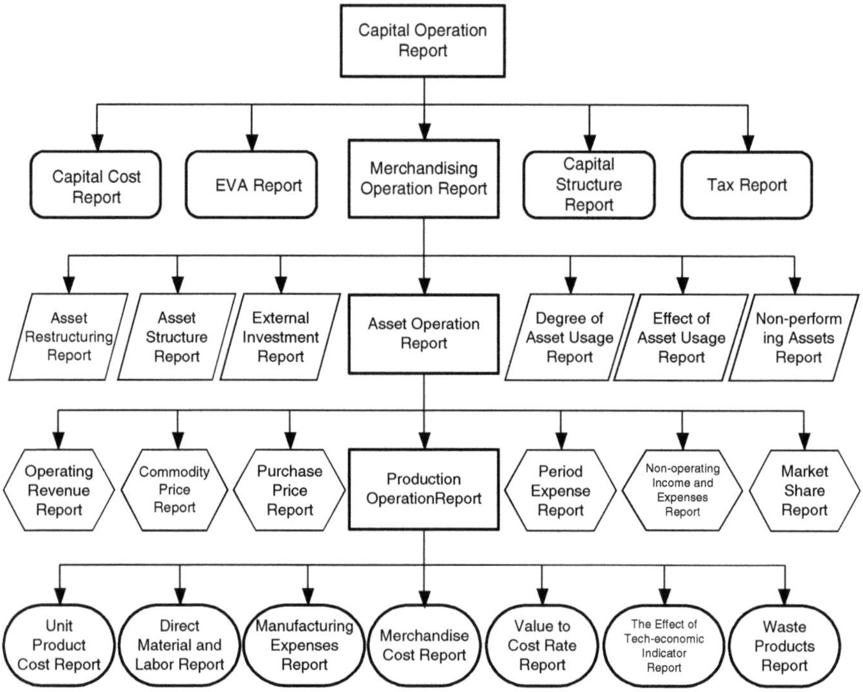

Fig. 10.3 The system diagram of management control reports

Table 10.2 Management control report

	Control standard	Actual performance	Variance measurement	Degree of variance	Variance analysis	Note
Department 1						
Item 1						
Item 2						
…						
Department 2						
Item 1						
Item 2						
…						
Department 3						
Item 1						
Item 2						
…						

financial accounting, statistical accounting and administrative accounting, etc. In the process of management control, these accounting should be consistent with control standard and meet the requirement of control at first, then, these accounting should be timely and correct the variance just in time. And this is the basic requirement for an organization's management control; otherwise the process of control will lose its way.

The key point of variance analysis is to analyze the reasons of variance; especially the controllable variance and uncontrollable variance should be distinguished clearly so as to identify the key points. In addition, determining the degree of control on the basis of the degree of variance is an important step of management control. Control procedures can be subdivided into tight control and loose control according to the degree of importance and variance, and some should be corrected when the variance is more than 1 %, while some should be corrected only when the variance is more than 5 %.

10.5 Operating Performance Evaluation

Operating performance evaluation is actually also the evaluation of control performance. If there is no evaluation about the effectiveness of control, the enthusiasm of the controllers will be weakened. Especially, attentions should be paid on that the performance of an organization which is not the same as the performance evaluation of the management or controllers. The operating performance evaluation of management control pays more attention on the performance evaluation of the management or controllers.

The principles of operating performance evaluation include: (a) the principle of the unity of organization performance evaluation and the management performance evaluation; (b) the principle of the unity of operating result evaluation indicators and goal driven evaluation indicators; (c) the principle of the unity of organization internal evaluation and external evaluation; (d) the principle of the unity of financial evaluation indicators and non-financial evaluation indicators.

There are primarily three popular methods to evaluate operating performance at present in both theoretical and practical fields, that is, single-indicator evaluation; indicator-system evaluation; Balanced Scorecard evaluation.

1. Single-indicator evaluation is to take the most comprehensive operating performance evaluation index so as to control the strategic objectives of the organization. EVA (Economic Value Added, or Economic Profit) is a widely accepted indicator of this kind. The formula of EVA is as follows:

$$\text{EVA} = \text{Operating Profit after Tax} - \text{Capital Cost}$$
$$(\text{Operating Profit after Tax} = \text{Operating Profit} - \text{Income Tax};$$
$$\text{Capital Cost} = \text{Investment Cost} \times \text{Weighted Average Cost of Capital})$$

The steps of calculating EVA are as follows:

Step 1: Choosing the starting point of calculating EVA. For example, we can regard operating profit as the starting point, and then adjust it with interest expenses and operating investment income.

Step 2: Adjusting the initially adjusted operating profit further to eliminate accounting distortion.

Step 3: Calculating investing cost. We should calculate adjusted investing cost on the basis of formula and then adjust it further to eliminate accounting distortion.

Step 4: Calculating the equity capital cost, weighed average capital cost and the enterprise's capital cost as well.

Step 5: Deducting the income tax and capital cost calculated in step 4 with adjusted operating profit calculated in step 2, then EVA can be arrived.

A positive EVA indicates that the operation creates value for the enterprise, while a negative EVA indicates that the operation erodes the value of the enterprise. A higher EVA, a better operating performance.

Among the single indicator evaluation, there is also a method of MVA (Market Value Added). MVA shows the way of shareholders' wealth increase, which is realized by maximizing the difference between total market value of an enterprise and the total capital supplied by the investors. The formula of MVA is as follows:

$$MVA = \text{Market Value of the Enterprise} - \text{Book Value of the Enterprise's Total Capital}$$

Total market value is the sum of the book value of liability and the market value of equity, while total capital is the sum of the book value of liability and equity.

MVA evaluates the impact of an organization's behavior on shareholders' wealth since its beginning, while EVA evaluates the impact of management in one specific year.

2. Indicator system evaluation evaluates operating performance from different perspectives or aspects with a series of indicators. According to the characteristics of different methods, indicator system evaluation can be subdivided into indicator decomposition evaluation system and indicator synthesis evaluation system. Indicator decomposition evaluation system starts with the most comprehensive indicator and it is decomposed into different levels of indicator system that reflects different processes and aspects of operating performance. The Du Pont System of financial analysis is a typical evaluation system of this kind.

Indicator synthesis evaluation system evaluates operating performance with a comprehensive index which is based on different processes or aspects of operating activities. The method of comprehensive index of operating performance evaluation and current efficiency coefficient method of enterprise performance evaluation are both belonging to indicator synthesis evaluation system.

3. Balanced Scorecard is actually a kind of evaluation system of indicator system, but it is different from traditional indicator evaluation system in that it has innovations in indicator classification, evaluation characteristics and evaluation procedures.

The characteristics of Balanced Scorecard are reflected as follows: (a) the balance between financial evaluation and non-financial evaluation; (b) the balance between internal evaluation and external evaluation; (c) the balance between result evaluation and driver (process) evaluation; (d) the balance between quantitative evaluation and qualitative evaluation; (e) the balance between short-term evaluation and long-term evaluation.

The contents of Balanced Scorecard consist of four types of indicators. The first is financial indicator which is used to evaluate the financial result of an organization, that is, what has been done for the shareholders; the second is customer indicator which is used to evaluate the vision of an organization, that is, what it dose for the customers; the third is internal operating indicator which is used to assess the condition of business process designed by the management; the fourth is learning and growth indicator which is used to evaluate the condition of organizational innovation and improvement to realize corporate vision and strategy.

The procedure of Balanced Scorecard is as follows: (1) establishing corporate vision and strategy; (2) specifying the objectives from the four perspectives of Balanced Scorecard; (3) selecting the best indicator according to the objectives; (4) communicating and educating within the enterprise; (5) determining the standard and the weight of different types of indicators; (6) combining the compensation with Balanced Scorecard evaluation; (7) adjusting the indicators and the standard of Balanced Scorecard continuously.

10.6 Executive Compensation

Managers are the subject of management control. The control motivation of manager is inevitably related to his or her self-interest. Therefore, the effectiveness of management control should be linked to executive compensation to ensure that the process of management control could run effectively in a long-term. From this viewpoint, executive compensation is not only the end of management control, but also the start of management control.

Executive compensation mainly consists of three parts, salary, benefits and incentives. Salary is usually determined according to the education background, experience, previous performance and job position of the manager. Benefits are usually determined according to the total performance of the enterprise and the job position of the managers. Incentives are usually determined according to the contribution of the managers to the organization. Wages and benefits reflect the basic value of the managers while incentives mean the contribution value of the manager. The level or effectiveness of management control should be mainly connected to the incentives given to the managers. From the standpoint of control, managerial incentive is the key to executive compensation.

Managerial incentive can be subdivided into spirit incentive and material incentive. Spirit incentive includes perquisite consumption, promotion incentive, granted incentive (authorization or honorary title) and so on. Material incentive includes short-term incentive (such as reward and annual salary system) and long-term incentive (such as stock option). Spirit incentive and material incentive are both essential in the process of management control and neither can be neglected.

Of cause, on the condition that the social physical wealth is not so abundant, the function of material incentive may be more outstanding. In terms of material incentive, the long-term incentive may be more important.

At present, the way of long-term incentive in practice mainly includes stock option, stock appreciation right, phantom stock, performance shares, etc. Among them, stock option is the most popular long-term incentive. Stock option is an option whose underlying assets or goods are the stock [4]. There are two kinds of stock options in incentives: (1) Incentive Stock Option. Its exercise price equals to the market price, and the value of this stock option comes from the distribution of after-tax profits. Using this kind of stock option, there are no issues about compensation cost recognition and expense allocation. (2) Remuneration Stock Option. Its exercise priced doesn't equal to the market price, and the value of this stock option is determined by the difference between the market price at the grant date and the exercise price. The value of remuneration stock option is a component of employee wage income and labor cost of the enterprise.

References

1. Zhang Xianzhi (2003) Management control systems based on management procedures [J]. Finance Acc 25(11):65–79
2. Luo Ruiren, Zeng Fanzheng (1997) Management control and managerial economics. Hongqi Press, Beijing
3. Anthony RN (1998) Management control systems, 9th edn. McGraw-Hill, Burr Ridge
4. Zhang Xianzhi (2002) Research on theory of stock option and its application in company incentives. Accout Res 23(7):16–24

Part IV
Study on the Framework of Management Control System Mode

Chapter 11
The Framework of Management Control Mode

11.1 Evolution and Implications of Internal Management Control Mode

11.1.1 Classification and Evolution of the Internal Management Control Mode

Management control system model reflects the mechanisms, modalities and methods of the operation of the management control system. The classification methods of management control system mode are various, which is exactly the cause of the emergence of different management control system modes. From the perspective of the evolution of the management control system mode, the division of the management control system mode should be based on two main points: first is the change of management control period or phase; second is the change of management control environment. Among the studies of the evolution of the management control system mode, representative figures and perspectives can be summarized as follows:

11.1.1.1 Richard Wilson Summarized the Development of Control Modes as Follows in His Book "Cost Control Handbook"[1]

(A) The typical bureaucratic control. Superiors order subordinates, and subordinates must obey.
(B) The establishment of specific management and procedures (such as rules and regulations), and decision-making and management control has the form of a plan.
(C) Incentive system provides a further control mechanism, such as piece wages

[1] Wilson [1].

X. Zhang, *Enterprise Management Control Systems in China*, Understanding China,
DOI 10.1007/978-3-642-54715-7_11, © Springer-Verlag Berlin Heidelberg 2014

(D) Technology provides control system in two ways: first, compulsion of techniques of production made manager can control operation; second, the development of management techniques made managers who owned this technique can finish complex tasks, keeping operation controlling.
(E) Authorized managers with expertise in a certain constraints can effectively control.

11.1.1.2 Robert Simons Presented Four Management Control System Modes in the "Control in an Age of Empowerment"[2]

(A) Boundary Control Systems. The purpose of Boundary Control Systems is providing the organization the range of acceptable activities, which should be limited in the trusted system that determines the opportunity, but not outside of this range. The boundary control is to define what things the personnel in the organization could not do.
(B) Diagnostic Control Systems. Diagnostic control systems are used to monitor the results and to correct the deviation of the control system. "Diagnostic control systems work like the dials on the control panel of an airplane cockpit, enabling the pilot to scan for signs of abnormal functioning and to keep critical performance variables within preset limits." The use of diagnostic control system in enterprise management is to help managers track whether individual, department or production line away from the corporate strategic goals. Managers use diagnostic control systems for measurement, comparison and adjustment, to monitor the realization of the goal.
(C) Belief Control Systems. Belief control systems are corresponding to boundary control systems. The belief control system can be viewed as Yang and boundary control as Yin in the Chinese philosophy of yin and yang. The purpose of the belief control systems is to stimulate and guide the enterprise or organization to explore and discover, to pursue the core values of the enterprise or organization. The belief control systems should attract all the participants to take care of the company's value creation.
(D) Interactive Control Systems. Interactive control systems are systems that put emphasis on futures and changes. Interactive control systems track the uncertainty, so that the senior manager could stay awake at night; interactive control systems focus on constantly changing information, making senior managers consider potential strategy.

[2] Simons [2].

11.1.1.3 Scott Divided the Management Control System into Four Stages (Scott, W. Richard 1981)

(A) Closed rational system stage. This stage of the control mode tends not to consider internal and external control environment of an enterprise, and makes internal management control objectives explicit, quantitative, and determine the operational status of the managers in the control system.
(B) Closed natural systems stage. This stage of the control model, while doesn't take the changes of the internal and external corporate control environment into account, but its internal management control objectives is uncertain, so that managers can determine and adjust the target.
(C) Open and rational system stage. This stage of the control mode tends to consider the changes of the internal and external corporate control environment, but its internal management control objectives are clear, quantitative, and managers cannot freely adjust the control objectives.
(D) Open and natural systems stage. This stage of the control mode tends to consider internal and external control environment of an enterprise, while its internal management control objectives are adjusted by managers according to changes in the control environment.

Scott concluded the four stages and considered that the evolution of the management control system is transiting from a closed system to an open system; from a rational system to the natural system.

11.1.2 The Implications of the Evolution of Management Control System Mode

The evolution of the management control system gives us the following implications:

Firstly, internal management control system mode is closely related to the external economic environment. Management control system develops with the development and changes of the economic system and the economic environment.

Secondly, in the same external environment, due to different internal environment, management control system mode may also be different though the fundamental goal of management control is the same. The establishment of internal management control system should be in different angles, in different ways to conduct a comprehensive control.

Thirdly, the focus of management control lever of the business or organization with different types and management bases should be different, so various management methods or leverages may be used. To establish internal management control system the organization should select management control which is based on the characteristics of enterprises.

11.2 Four Mode Frameworks of the Management Control System

According to the theory and the evolution of mode of enterprise management control systems, and combining with our current economic system and economic environment, framework of our internal management control system mode consists of rule-based control system, budgetary control system, evaluation control system and incentive control system.

11.2.1 Rule-Based Control System

11.2.1.1 Connotation of Rule-Based Control System

From a macroeconomic viewpoint, the rule can also refer to rules of politics, economy, culture and other aspects under certain historical conditions. From an economic sense, the rule refers to a "Institutions are the rules of the game in a society or, more formally, are the humanly devised constraints that shape human interaction…using economic terms, that means rules define and limit the collection of personal decision-making." [3].[3] These constraints can be informal (such as social norms, practices and ethical standards), they can also be a conscious design or regulated formal constraints (such as political rules, economic rules and contracts, etc.). In brief, the rule should be regarded as regulations of the game, or the rule is regulation or guideline that requires members to comply with.

Rule-based control refers to regulating and limiting people's behavior through the form of regulations, guidelines and other norms to achieve a certain goal. Rule-based control in the internal management control refers to regulating and limiting managers and employees at all levels through the form of regulations, guidelines and other norms to achieve a organizational goals, and to ensure that management activities are not contrary to or conducive to the realization of the organization's strategic goals.

As a model for the management control system, the rule-based control system should have the basic elements and basic procedures of the management control system. From the perspective of control program or control link, it includes rule establishment, rule implementation, rule evaluation and reward. The basic characteristic of the rule-based control system is controlling by means of rules or regulations.

11.2.1.2 Classification of Rule-Based Control System

From the hierarchy point of view, rule-based control system includes strategic control system, management control system, and operation control system. Strategic control system includes: the articles of association, the company's strategic

[3] North [3].

planning, corporate structure, and corporate governance system. Management control system includes: rules of financial control, rules of human resources, and rules of marketing control, rules of purchase control, rules of production and technology, rules of cost control. Operation control system includes: production processes, purchase processes, storage processes.

11.2.1.3 The Purpose and Effect of the Rule-Based Control System

Generally, the objective of the rule-based control system is consistent with management control objectives, which is the pursuit of operational efficiency and effectiveness. The specific objective is to work according to the rules and regulations, and to do the right thing which does not violate corporate target. Therefore, the objective of rule-based control system is to make managers and employees clear about what they can do and what they cannot do.

11.2.1.4 The Merits and Demerits of the Rule-Based Control System

The merits of rule-based control system manifest in: clear codes of conduct; simple to operate, easy to full implementation; environment and conditions of the rule-based control system establishment are less restricted. The demerits of rule-based control system manifest in: limiting the initiative of the managers and staff; insufficient quantitative control, lack of direct convergence with business objectives.

11.2.1.5 Applicable Conditions and Scope of the Rule-Based Control System

Rule-based control system is applicable to all organizations or enterprises. Enterprises that lack of management bases should reinforce the construction of the rule-based control system.

11.2.2 Budgetary Control System

11.2.2.1 The Connotation of Budgetary Control System

Budget refers to the scheme which configures the resources in a certain period to achieve a certain purpose.[4] The budget is a plan of a certain period prepared in digital or currency.[5] Visibly the budget is a form of plan, the plan can be divided into

---

[4] *American Heritage Dictionary (solution)*, see "King soft".

[5] Western and China differ on the meaning of the budget: In China, the "budget" generally refers to the expected income and expenses through legal procedures approved by the government departments, institutions and enterprises in a certain period. The budget in Western concept refers to the

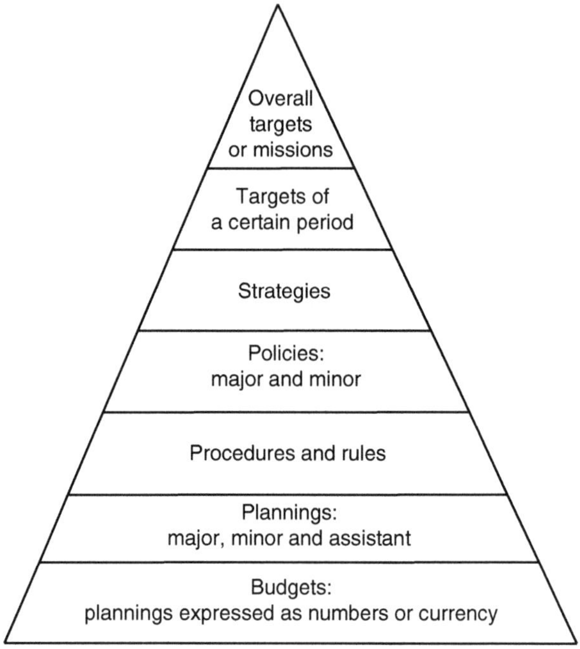

Fig. 11.1 Plan of hierarchical levels (Harold Koontz and Huang Dishi [5])

the overall goal or mission, a certain period goals, strategies, policies, procedures, planning and budget categories and levels, as shown in Fig. 11.1.

The figure above illustrates that the budget is an organic part and the foundation and foothold of the program. The planning function of budget reflects the nature of budget, so budget was also called budget plan by someone. The connotation of budget plan can be summarized in three aspects: first is to reflect "how much", such as the inputs and outputs for the realization of operation objectives; second is to illustrate "why", that is why the inputs and outputs are these; third is to reflect "when", that is when the inputs and outputs happen.

The budget is a forecast which expects the allocation and usage of future resource and effects, therefore, the available methods for determining budget figures are statistical methods, experience methods and engineering methods.

The function of budget is the budgetary control. Budgetary control refers to the process of regulating the organization's objectives and economic behavior through the form of budget plan, adjusting and modifying management behavior and target deviation to ensure achievement of objectives, strategies, policies and planning of all levels. From the perspective of control link, budgetary control includes the formulation of budget or budget planning, enforcement of budget, variance analysis of budget and correcting deviations.

---

number of program instructions, not just a reflection of the amount. See Luo Ruiren and Zeng Fanzheng [4], p. 47.

As a mode of the management control system, budgetary control system should include links of budget planning, budgetary control, evaluation of budget and incentives of budget. The basic characteristics of the rule-based control system emphasize the process control and focus on timely correction.

11.2.2.2 Classification of the Budgetary Control System

From the perspective of budget hierarchy, the budgetary control system includes the company's budget (enterprise group budget, subsidiary or business unit budget), department budget and project budget; from the perspective of budget content, it includes the operating budget, financial budget, capital expenditure budget; from the perspective of budget procedures, it includes budget content, budget control point, budget control standards, and so on; from the perspective of budget methods, it includes fixed budget, flexible budget, zero-based budget, incremental budget, regular budget and rolling budget.

11.2.2.3 The Purpose and Effect of the Budgetary Control System

The objective of the budgetary control system is consistent with management control objective, which is the pursuit of operational efficiency and effectiveness. The specific objective is to finish the quantitative targets independently during the operation process based on budgetary control standards. Therefore, the effect of the budgetary control system is to enable managers and employees to clear their own quantitative targets, and to discover the impact of behavioral deviations on the target in the course of operation, correcting deviations at any time sequentially, and to ensure the completion of the objectives and tasks.

11.2.2.4 The Merits and Demerits of the Budgetary Control System

The merits of budgetary control system manifest in: clear quantitative criteria of corporate behavior; close links of overall business and individual goals; outstanding control process; discovering problems and correcting deviations timely. The demerits of budgetary control system manifest in: complex formulation of budgetary control system; limiting the initiative of managers and staff to some extent; the budget standards rigidity making control cannot change with the environmental changes.

11.2.2.5 The Applicable Conditions and Scope of the Budgetary Control System

Like the rule-based control system, budgetary control system is applicable to all organizations or enterprises. However, it is difficult to establish and implement budgetary control system for the enterprises with poor business environment and infrastructure; budget control is relatively easy for the enterprises with superb environment and bases, but too much emphasis on budget control can bind the initiative.

11.2.3 Evaluation Control System

11.2.3.1 The Connotation of Evaluation Control System

Evaluation refers to that the subject of evaluation makes an objective, fair and accurate judgment on the activities and results of the object of evaluation within a certain period using certain procedures and methods. This judgment is a professional judgment. Evaluation of management control refers to that stakeholders make an objective, fair and accurate judgment on the operations and results in the organization within a certain period using certain procedures and methods in order to achieve a certain purpose.

Evaluation control refers to regulating the economic objectives and economic behaviors of the managers and staff at all levels in the organization through the way of evaluation. The evaluation control emphasizes the control objectives rather than control processes, as long as the management objectives at all levels are achieved, the organizational strategic objectives will be achieved.

As a mode of management control system, evaluation control system should include strategic planning, evaluation criteria (selection of criteria, standard of criteria and criteria calculation), evaluation procedures and methods, evaluation reports, reward and punishment links. The basic characteristics of evaluation control system are target control or result control, emphasizing on results rather than processes.

11.2.3.2 Classification of the Evaluation Control System

From the perspective of control hierarchy, the evaluation control system includes the evaluation control of board for senior manager, evaluation control of senior manager for department manager, evaluation control of department manager for project manager and evaluation control of project manager for staff. From the perspective of control content, the evaluation control system includes financial performance evaluation, management performance evaluation, quality and technique performance evaluation, and task performance evaluation.

11.2.3.3 The Purpose and Effect of the Evaluation Control System

The objective of the evaluation control system is consistent with management control objective, which is the pursuit of operational efficiency and effectiveness. The effect of evaluation control system is to make managers and staff at all levels clear the relationships among their own work efficiency (purpose), benefits and the targets of superior and the same level, so that it can mobilize their initiative, explore the potential, regulate their behavior, and struggle to achieve individual goals and enterprise's objectives.

11.2.3.4 The Merits and Demerits of the Evaluation Control System

The merits of evaluation control system: there are clear control objectives, but also the flexibility, it is helpful for managers and employees to bring our subjective initiative into play during the process of achieving goals. The demerits of evaluation control system: Lack of program or process control, and it is not conducive to discover and correct the deviation timely. Compared with budgetary control system and rule-based control system, evaluation control system is a higher level of control.

11.2.3.5 The Applicable Conditions and Scope of the Evaluation Control System

It needs high quality of managers and employees, firm establishment of corporate culture and philosophy, the workers' contribution and pride when enterprises select and apply the evaluation control system.

11.2.4 Incentive Control System

11.2.4.1 The Connotation of Incentive Control System

Incentive refers to inspiring, guiding, maintaining and regulating the behaviors of organizations' members to achieve the goals of the organization and its members effectively through designing appropriate forms of reward and working environment. Management experts think that incentive refers to making objects exciting and tense psychologically, and making members act positively and pay more time and efforts through the use of some means or manners by subjects in order to achieve the desired goal of the main incentive.

As can be viewed from the meaning of the term "incentive", incentive not only has positive aspects, emphasizing the interests guided but also includes the meaning of constraints and control. Both sides of the incentive meaning are the unity of opposites, positive incentive stimulus leads to the occurrence of an act, and the control is to regulate the behavior of occurrence, to meet certain direction, and limit certain spatial and temporal scales. Incentive without control will be stress-free and control without incentive will lose power. Accordingly, the incentive itself may also be referred to the incentive control. As a management control, incentive control refers to controlling the behavior of managers and coordinating the behavior of managers and business goals (or business owners' target) by way of incentive.

As a mode of management control system, incentive control system should include strategic planning, selection of incentive ways, incentive constraints (contracts) and performance evaluation links. The basic characteristics of the incentive control system are the interest-oriented control and the coordination of the objectives of the stakeholders.

11.2.4.2 Classification of the Incentive Control System

From the perspective of control hierarchy, the incentive control system includes incentives of owners to top managers and incentives of top managers to lower level managers. From the perspective of control ways, the incentive control system includes stock option (or regarding stocks) incentive, annual salary incentive, performance-linked incentive, bonuses incentive, and so on.

11.2.4.3 The Purpose and Effect of the Incentive Control System

The objective of the incentive control system is consistent with management control objective, which is the pursuit of operational efficiency and effectiveness. The specific objective is to create the greatest value for the organization or enterprise through coordination of managers and owners' interests and objectives. The effect of incentive control system is to make managers, especially senior managers to coordinate the goals of managers and owners, and adjust these goals with constantly changing social economy and technical environment, so as to create greater value or wealth.

11.2.4.4 The Merits and Demerits of the Incentive Control System

The merits of incentive control system: associating the interests of the managers with the interests of the owner; regulating the behavior of managers through the interests' constraint mechanism; adjusting the goals with constantly changing social economy and technical environment to ensure the achievement of maximum corporate value. The merits of incentive control system: the specific objectives are not clear; require a higher quality of corporate culture and managers. The incentive control system is a high level and more flexible control system.

11.2.4.5 The Applicable Conditions and Scope of the Incentive Control System

The application of incentive control system requires companies to have a higher level of management and good environment for economic operation.

11.3 Comparison of the Four Modes of the Management Control System

Rule-based control system, budgetary control system, evaluation control system and incentive control system, these four control system constitute the overall framework of enterprise management control system mode. This management control system model framework has the following characteristics and innovations:

Firstly, the four management control system have distinctions and different features, in the aspects of control mode, control objectives and control advantages and control disorder as shown in Table 11.1.

Comparative descriptions of the four management control systems illustrate that various management control systems have their own control target and control characteristic; different control objectives and control modes have their own advantages and disadvantages; the control environment is essential in choosing control system, only selecting the management control which adapts to their environment can carry out effective control.

Secondly, the four management control system modes are layered and applicable. The so-called layered characteristic refers to that the four management control systems are not in the same grade from the perspective of the control of environmental requirements and control authorization: the authorization of incentive control and requirement of control environment are the highest, and followed by evaluation control; and then budgetary control; the authorization of rule-based control and requirement of control environment are minimum. The layered characteristic is shown in Fig. 11.2.

Figure 11.2 also reflects the applicable conditions of currently four kinds of management control system modes in China. According to China current circumstances of control environment, most enterprises still need to adopt a

Table 11.1 Comparison of four management control system

Control system	Control feature	Control objective	Control advantage	Control disorder	Control environment
Rule-based control system	Rules	Do right thing	Clear rules and easy to operate	Lack of quantitative and initiative	Poor management foundation and environment
Budgetary control system	Processes	Complete task	Quantitative targets and regulate timely	Lack of change and the initiative	Better management foundation and environment
Evaluation control system	Objectives	Excavate potential	Outstand results and encourage enterprise	Lack of process control and the environment	Well management foundation and environment
Incentive control system	Profits	Create wealth	Related profits and change flexibly	Lack of corresponding environment and conditions	Excellent management foundation and environment

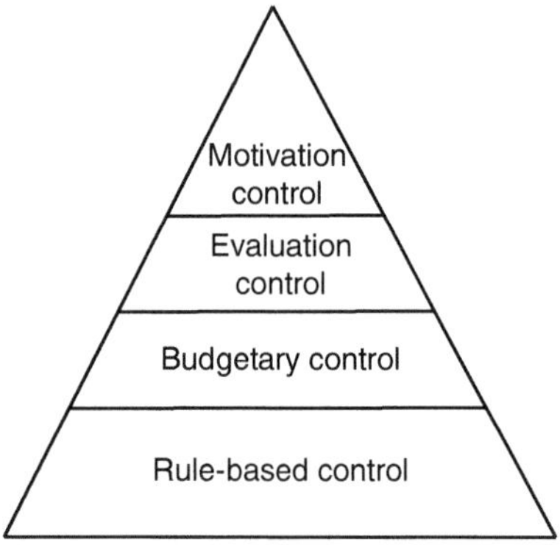

Fig. 11.2 Level of management control systems

rule-based control system; followed by the budgetary control system; less enterprises can adopt evaluation control system mode; fewer enterprises can directly adopt incentive control system mode.

Thirdly, the four kinds of management control system modes are both independent and uniform. The so-called independence refers to that each can operate as a stand-alone control system, for instance, some enterprises can adopt rule-based control system and some enterprises can adopt budgetary control system. The so-called uniformity refers to that the same enterprise can use two or more control systems simultaneously, and control enterprises from the perspective of the rules, procedures, objectives and interests respectively. For instance, an enterprise group can mainly adopt budgetary management control system and supplemented by other control mode, the characteristic of this mode is that the group company adopt budget-control system mode and the subsidiary can adopt rule-based control system, evaluation control system or incentive control system according to their environmental characteristics.

Fourthly, the four kinds of management control systems have integrity, and flexibility. Because various management control systems enable management control to regulate effectively to achieve common goals from different angles and at different levels, in different ways, so as to form a complete system of management control. But enterprises, departments or projects can use different control methods flexibly according to their own environment and requirements.

References

1. Wilson R (1975) Cost control handbook. Gower Press, Epping
2. Robert Simons (1995) Control in an age of empowerment. Harvard Business Review (March–April)
3. North DC (1990) Institutions, institutional change and economic performance. Cambridge University Press, Cambridge
4. Luo Ruiren, Zeng Fanzheng (1997) Management control and management economics. Red Flag Press, Beijing
5. Harold Koontz, Huang Dishi (1987) (Translated) Management, 1st edn. China Social Sciences Press, Beijing, p 187

Chapter 12
The Mode of Rule-Based Control System

12.1 Definition of Rule-Based Control System

Rule-based control systems mean that enterprises regulate and restrict the behaviors of the management at all levels and the staffs in the form of regulations and provisions, to ensure that management activities do not violate or are disadvantageous to the realization of strategic objectives. The role of rule-based control systems is to make managers and employees understand what things should be done and what things should not be done. Everything should go according to the rules and regulations, and do the right things without going against corporate objectives.

As a mode of management control systems, rule-based control systems should be consistent with the management control systems on overall objectives. From the hierarchical standpoint, rule-based control systems include strategic control regulations, management control regulations, and activity control regulations. From the view of control elements, rule-based control systems include regulation control environment, regulation control standards, regulation control evaluation and correction etc. From the perspective of control procedures or control links, rule-based control systems contain regulation formulation, regulation implementing, regulation examining, rewards and punishment. As a model of management control systems, rule-based control systems must have clear objectives before establishing the control system. Rule-based control should serve for the realization of organization's overall objectives, and the fundamental objective is to regulate and restrict the behaviors of the management at all levels and the staffs in business activities, to ensure the realization of strategic objectives smoothly. The following describes the connotation of rule-based control systems from the perspective of control procedures.

X. Zhang, *Enterprise Management Control Systems in China*, Understanding China,
DOI 10.1007/978-3-642-54715-7_12, © Springer-Verlag Berlin Heidelberg 2014

12.1.1 *Formulation of Rules*

To adapt to the new economic era, the key of management control systems is "establishing institutions or standards" based on the actual situation of the strategy of enterprises. In an economic organization, from a team to individual employees, from higher authorities to subordinate departments, from the manager to the general staff, everyone should act in accordance with normalized ideas and standardized procedures. If the management control regulations are not been made, the management of a company would be left in chaos and liberalism, resulting in the situation with no legal basis and no chapters to follow.

The formulation of management control regulations should be compatible with the whole organization's strategic objectives, organizational structure and corporate governance structure. Therefore, when designing the management control regulation systems, the operating strategic objectives, organizational structure and corporate governance structure of enterprises must be analyzed deeply, in order to be grasped accurately and implemented and practiced effectively in the design of the system of management control regulation.

12.1.1.1 Principles of Formulation of Rules

In fact, most companies have their own management regulations; however, the key issue is that the regulations are often not so standardized but random. It is common to see that Chinese enterprises value human relations more than the rules. In the enterprise which is sustained by human relations, the prevalence is the loyalty to individual rather than to the organization's objectives. This loyalty is conducive to maintain harmonious interpersonal relationships, but also makes enterprises' various management systems become a mere formality because of lacking rational, objective and fair management control systems. For getting a variety of certifications, some other companies make a wide range of rules and regulations, but shelve these regulations aside in practical work. Therefore, when making management control regulations, enterprises should comply with the following principles:

(A) Consistent with national laws, regulations and financial discipline, to ensure the seriousness, rationality, scientism and completeness of the regulations;
(B) From the overall view, enterprises should make the regulations with the premise of improving operating efficiency and reducing costs;
(C) Consistent with the actual condition, enterprises should make sure that management control objectives are clear, and communicate fully with the relevant functional departments, so that the regulations can be operable and convergent;
(D) According to the thought of the management control systems, make sure that the management control regulations of enterprises should be normalized and standardized;

(E) The procedures of management regulation making should be clear and explicitly authorized. Regulating the behaviors of managers and staff by strict management control regulations can ensure the development of enterprises in the predetermined direction;
(F) When making the management control regulations, enterprises should take into account the cultural background of the company and give full consideration to the staff's willingness to accept the regulations, because the staff also plays a crucial role in the successes and failures of the management control regulations.

12.1.1.2 Basic Procedures of Formulation of Rules

The general steps of Formulation of Rules contain preparation phase, formulation phase and correction phase.

(A) Preparation phase

Whether the regulations made can achieve the expected objectives depends largely on the preparation work to be done fully, in detail and comprehensively. During the preparation phase, enterprises should do well in the following tasks: (1) be clear with the contents and objectives of the regulations; (2) determine the timing of the regulations and prepare the work schedule; (3) implement the responsibility of regulation makers; (4) execute depth research and investigation in order to formulate the regulations in accord with actual requirements.

(B) Formulation phase

According to the research findings, analyze and program the project of regulation making, preliminarily with defining the scope, content and other aspects. The project should be demonstrated by relevant experts in order to obtain a consensus to facilitate the progress of formulating work. Once the project is confirmed, enterprises should make division of labor based on the regulation and implement the personnel and time schedules.

(C) Correction phase

The design of any regulation requires a gradual process, including the formulation of management control regulation, because it could not maintain the status quo. With the changing internal and external environment, it is an inevitable part to revise the regulations in regulation making, and it requires a continuous revision and improvement process. Enterprises should establish the appropriate regulatory agencies to correct the management control regulations at any time, ensuring that the regulations continue to improve for a long time and promote enterprises to achieve their strategic objectives successfully.

12.1.2 Enforcement of Rules

Whether management control regulations are successful depends on the effect of the enforcement. Effective enforcement will bring huge economic benefits for the enterprises, however, executing blindly or lacking supervision over the enforcement will be counter-productive or even fail to achieve the expected effect. Accordingly, the prospects of Enforcement of Rules are bleak, and the management control regulations exist in name only. This will lead to a violation of the predetermined strategic objectives. Therefore, Enforcement of Rules has become a priority, increasingly prominent and important. The enforcement of rules must rely on the strong support of the executives and the guidance and propulsion of middle management. The managers must keep track of the implementation of the regulations.

During the implementation of the regulations, there may exist the phenomenon that some of the responsible units take short-term behavior at times to accomplish the regulation objectives, which makes that it is an optimal result to the department but not to the whole enterprise. Therefore, it is necessary to monitor each other between the responsible units and the functional departments, so that they can contain each other inherently to ensure the effective operation of the regulation implementing mechanisms.

12.1.3 Evaluation of Rules

As an important part of regulation control systems, Evaluation of Rules has its own working procedure, which mainly includes five basic steps:

Firstly, determine the subjects of regulation examining. The subjects of regulation examining mainly aim at the management at all levels and the staffs. That is the specific conditions they implement the control regulations.

Secondly, analyze and measure various factors to determine the basis for setting examination indexes. Find and analyze the key factors in enterprises' success, continuously measure the processing situations of the regulations and compare with the expected indicators to find the differences and analyze the causes.

Thirdly, design examination indexes and determine appraisal standards. Examination indexes are the basis for management control in regulation control systems. After setting the basis of the examination indexes, enterprises need to design a variety of qualitative and quantitative examination indexes. After that, it is necessary to determine the appraisal standards, which should be a wide range of both quantitative evaluation and qualitative analysis, involving financial indicators, and non-financial indicators.

Fourthly, analyze the examination results and draw conclusions. Examiners need to analyze, evaluate comprehensively and draw conclusions by comparing the actual implementation to the appraisal standards with a range of assessment methods.

Fifthly, prepare regulation examining report. The regulation examining report is not only the output but also the conclusive document of the regulation control systems. Examiners obtain the information related to the examining subjects through accounting information systems and other information systems and then get the examination index data or implementation of the examining subjects after processing and sorting. Compare the data or implementation with the appraisal standards, analyze the differences, find out the causes, responsibilities and effects of the differences, draw the conclusion about the strengths and weaknesses of examining subjects' performance and then prepare the final examining report.

12.1.4 Rewards and Punishment

The vitality of enterprises stems from the enthusiasm and creativity of the managers and the staff. Due to the diversity and gradations of human's requirement and the complexity of the incentive, there are a variety of methods to arouse the enthusiasm of people. Rewards and punishments are two of the most important tools in the management control systems. They play an important role in stimulating the enthusiasm and creativity of all managers and employees, implementing regulation control objectives, and implement for the organization's strategic objectives at every level.

12.2 Contents of the Rule-Based Control System

The Rule-based control systems include strategic control regulations, management control regulations, and activity control regulations.

12.2.1 Strategic Control Regulations

Strategic control regulations are a series of regulations which aim at formulating and controlling organizational goals and strategy, to ensure that enterprises have made the right choice about the organizational goals and strategy. The strategy is the direction and key of the operation of an organization or company and is the embodiment of the interests of stakeholders. Therefore, strategic control is based on all related aspects of corporate governance. From this perspective, the contents of strategic control regulations include Articles of Association, company's strategic planning, corporate structure, and corporate governance regulations.

12.2.1.1 Articles of Association

Articles of Association are the specifications which can control and constrain the company's management and staff and can adjust the company's internal relations and economic behaviors. As the company's basic code of conduct, Articles of Association are the basic regulation specifications of corporate governance or strategic control. The Articles of Association is the self-governance rules of the company's strategic control, and is the backbone of the company's management control regulations. All staff must serve and obey the Articles of Association. It has the following functions:

(A) Articles of Association are the most important conditions and documents when establish a company. The Articles of Association of the Company are required to be reviewed by the examination and approval authorities and registration authorities, to decide whether to grant approval or registration.
(B) Articles of Association are the key legal documents to settle the relationship between rights and duties of the company. Once approved by the relevant authorities and ratified by the company registration authority, it produces legal effects externally. Companies are entitled to the rights and assume all the obligations in accordance with the Articles of Association.
(C) Articles of Association are the basic legal basis for companies to operate with others. The Articles of Association regulate the principles and rules of the organization and activities, which provide the condition and credit basis for investors, creditors and the third party to carry out economic ties with the company.

12.2.1.2 Strategic Planning

Strategic planning of the company is the global plan of the enterprise, which set the overall goal for the organization to seek the status of the organization in the environment. It mainly includes the program to be taken and the quantity of resources required to be allocated in the next year of the program. Among Strategic control, management control and operational control, strategic planning is the least systematic control. The final result is the organization's objectives, strategies and related policies. Strategic planning is difficult to be described as a standardized system, because it is more abstract and cannot be absolutely accurate. Therefore, enterprises must have a global or overall thought in formulating the strategic planning of the company. At the same time, a company's strategic planning cannot be separated from the company's environment, which requires both considering the interactions within internal environment and between the external environment, but also ensuring the relative stability of strategic planning at one stage, because maintaining the relative stability means saving the variable cost. Therefore, the creators of the strategic planning must have a higher risk awareness, which can help in selecting the enterprises' operation target and business direction in the uncertain future. And it is necessary to fully consider the impact of the environment, but also to maintain the relative stability. In addition, when formulating the corporate strategic planning, enterprises should be forward-looking and have a clear direction. A good strategic planning is just like a lighthouse, which can predict the future, provide the way for employees, and point out the direction and goal of development.

Formulation of corporate strategic planning, on the one hand, can make the organization's strategic objectives more specific, institutionalized and systematic; on the other hand, is the basis of clearing control variables and establishing the control standards. Its specific roles are mainly reflected in the following points: firstly, it provides the guarantee for implementing and coordinating the activities of the organization; Secondly, it can define the direction and manner of organization members' action; thirdly, it provide the basis for raising and integrating organizational resources; lastly, it lay the foundation for inspecting and controlling the activities of the organization.

Strategic planning mainly includes the following three parts: foundation of planning, the main body of planning as well as implementation and review of planning. All these are some kinds of target management which put strategic planning as the core and built on the basis of adapting to the environment both inside and outside the enterprise. It covers all the business activities of the enterprise. No matter what type and size the organization is all should be based on it.

12.2.1.3 Organizational Structure

The company's organizational structure is the basic form or framework of division of labor and collaboration within the organization. In an enterprise, the means of division of labor and collaboration is varied, of which the organizational structure is just one of them. Operators and managers can determine the way of division of labor between staff at any time through issuing instructions and commands, and then adjust the way to the operating. A group may also implement effective division of labor through tacit understanding with each other. For a small organization, this is sufficient to maintain their working relationship. However, with the expansion of the size of the organization, depending only on individual instruction and tacit understanding is not enough, so it needs organizational structure to provide a framework. Regulate the management object, the scope of work, the route for communicating and other matters in advance.

The purpose of the organizational structure is to establish and perfect an appropriate function structure, that is everyone has a clear understanding about what should be done and Who should take the consequences of responsibility through designing and maintaining the function structure and the relationship between duties and authority. With organizational structure, enterprises can overcome the difficulties caused by the confusion and unclear responsibility, and establish a harmonious working environment. The organizational structure is the core of rule-based control and the means to achieve the goal, and plays an important role in implementing the corporate strategy smoothly. Designing organizational structure scientifically is just as to create an optimized management control system, which is a necessary condition to achieve management control objectives and improve the economic efficiency of enterprises. In other words, designing organizational structure is a hardware design and the central task of management control, and has a significant effect in binding the organization's performance.

Establishing the company's organizational structure should adhere to the following principles: (1) all sectors of the organizational structure are required to cooperate with each other actively and communicate the information effectively; (2) organizational structure can coordinate the production and operational activities in all the various functional departments; (3) organizational structure must maximize to stimulate the enthusiasm of the staff. As far as organizational structure design, it should be characterized with concise, optimization, and high efficiency. Among them, concise and optimization are the preconditions for high efficiency. Concise and optimization require the creators to follow comprehensive and integrity principles, so the functions cannot be divided too elaborately, or each department would act on its own and value its own goal most, which would do harm to the interests of the overall objectives. The high operation efficiency of organizational structure is considered as one of the main measures in some excellent contemporary Western companies. This requires each department, each link, and even each person in the organizational structure, for the sake of a unified goal, to combine into the most appropriate structure, so that they can achieve the most effective internal coordination, have so many things done quickly and accurately, reduce duplication of work and possess flexible response capabilities. When facing the complex and volatile environment, the high efficiency of this organization help enterprises to make rapid reaction and decision, so as to maintain a strong competitive advantage. In short, a management control system composed of an organization structure with concise, optimization, and high efficiency, plays an important role in reducing the distortion of accounting information, mitigating the conflicts of goals, and improving the quality of decision-making and implementation.

12.2.1.4 Corporate Governance Mechanism

Corporate governance is essentially a kind of management control regulations in modern enterprises, and also a scientific management mode. It is the general way of management conducted by the companies all over the world. As an important part of management control regulations, Corporate Governance Mechanism mainly refers to a set of institutional arrangements of control, coordination, supervision, rewards and punishment of the entity owners' operating management and performance. Through formulating a set of rules with formal or informal, internal or external all included, enterprises can coordinate the interests between the company and its all stakeholders and reduce agency costs and risks, so that the company's board and the management should take its responsibility to effectively use the funds they are entrusted with, ensure the decision-making scientific, and prevent the manager from deviating from the owner's interests, ultimately safeguard the interests of all parties of the company. Because there is some divergence of interests in company between operators and owners, it is very necessary of the corporate governance mechanism based on the allocation of power to maintain of the rights and interests of each party.

Establishing Corporate Governance Mechanism should adhere to the following principles:

(A) The establishment of the corporate governance mechanism must ensure the long-term strategic plan and institutional objectives are achieved;
(B) The corporate governance mechanism must be established on condition that the rights and interests of all the stakeholders should be protected, in particular to ensure that minority shareholders enjoy equal status;
(C) The corporate government mechanism must be practical and workable.

The basic contents of the corporate governance mechanism contain the following aspects: (1) regulating the rights of shareholders and the shareholders' Meetings; (2) regulating the procedure of selecting and appointing directors, the obligations of the directors, the composition and duties of the Board of Directors, the Rules of Procedure of the Board of Directors, the rules of independent director and the key responsibilities of the Special Committee of the Board of Directors; (3) regulating the duties, composition, and Rules of Procedure of the Board of Supervisors; (4) regulating the performance evaluation of directors, supervisors and managers, and the appointment of managers; (5) regulating the information disclosure and transparency, the company's ongoing information disclosure, the disclosure of the information on corporate government, and the disclosure of shareholders' equity.

12.2.2 Rules of Management Control

Rules of management control refer to all the rules and regulations which help to ensure organizational strategy and the goals achieved on the basis of choosing organizational goals and strategies. Rules of management control mainly include: Rules of Financial control, Rules of Human Resources, Rules of Purchase control, Rules of Marketing control, Rules of Production and Technology Control and Rules of Cost control.

12.2.2.1 Rules of Financial Control

Rules of Financial control mainly include the Basic Rules of Financial Management, Rules of Cash Management, Rules of Assets Management, as well as Rules of Financial and Accounting Institutions and Personnel Management.

(A) Basic Rules of Financial Management include:
The first is the rules of internal tied-up. The rules collectively refer to the regulations, organizations, methods and procedures which maintain the integrity of the company's assets, ensure the accuracy and reliability of the accounting records, as well as plan, control and evaluate the economic activities comprehensively.

The second is the rules of internal audit. The internal audit means that the enterprise should designate a person inside the accounting institution to examine and check the related accounting documents. The key areas to audit are accounting credence, accounting bookkeeping, accounting reports, financial planning and the consistence of property supplies and accounts, etc.

The third is the rules of approving financial revenue and expenditure, which are about preparing the plans of financial income and expenditure and regulating the authority, process and responsibility of approval. Establishing a sound financial approval system is a key component to Financial Accounting.

The fourth is the rules of original records management. The original records are the basic link of accounting calculation, including the original records about the supplies, the production, the finished products, personnel, payroll and financial accounting. The unit should regulate the format and the method to fill in various original records depending on the specific circumstances.

The fifth is the rules of quota management. Quota is the standard that enterprises should be up to in the use of human, material and financial resources in the production process. Quota management refers to developing a scientific and reasonable quota of labor, cost of various materials, expenses, quality, fixed assets using and material reserve, etc.

The sixth is the rules of measurement and acceptance. The rules mainly aim at regulating a variety of means in detecting the quality and quantity of the property or material used by the staff.

The seventh is the rules of property checking. Enterprises should check up the property at regular intervals to ensure that the accounting records conform to the physical assets and cash holdings. Enterprises should formulate different checking methods based on various checking objects, such as cash, bank deposits, inventory, and fixed assets, and provide for the corresponding processing methods.

The eighth is the rules of financial reporting and financial analysis. Financial reports are the written documents which reflect the financial condition, operating results and cash flows of the enterprise over a certain period, including balance sheet, income statement, cash flow statement, other additional charts and financial situation statement. Financial analysis is based on the financial reports, using factor analysis, comparative analysis and other methods to analyze the liquidity, operating capacity, profitability and solvency of the enterprise, and submitting the analysis reports to evaluate the past, measure the present and predict the future

The ninth is the rules of accounting files management. The accounting files are important historical materials and evidence to record and reflect the business practices. Companies must develop the explicit rules about filing, consulting, confidentiality, destruction and other sectors of accounting files.

The tenth is the rules of computerization management. Computerized accounting is the direction of development of accounting. Enterprises should develop the suitable rules for the enterprise about setting computerized accounting jobs, managing computer hardware and software, as well as managing operating procedures and computerized accounting files.

(B) Basic Rules of Cash Management include:
The first is the rules of capital budget and final accounts. In order to urge enterprises to coordinate and flexibly use the funds and thereby improving the economic efficiency of enterprises, the financial department should implement the yearly (monthly, quarterly) capital budget and final accounts for enterprises in conjunction with the relevant business departments.

The second is the rules of financial settlement center management. Financial settlement center is the financial services organization within the financial system, and it is an interior functional department which adjusts the capital surplus and deficiency of individual department of enterprises, takes the advantage of centralized capital, and improves the effectiveness of funds utilization. The rules should clearly define the roles and responsibilities of the financial center, the structure and duties of the management organization, the method of capital settlement management and internal loan management.

The third is the rules of loan guarantee management. In order to reduce the risk of guarantees and ensure the safety and added value of the assets, enterprises should formulate this rule In accordance with the object and scope of the guarantee, warranty conditions, guarantee approval and processing, guarantee management and the responsibility for violation.

The fourth is the rules of financing management. In order to meet the need of normal production and operation in each department, enterprises must raise the funds in demand. Owner's equity financing and debt financing are the major sources of funding, so it is necessary to strengthen the management of the owner's equity and liabilities. The owner's equity can be managed from the perspective of input, maintenance, appreciation and changes of the capital funds, as well as the capital reserve, and surplus reserve; the liability management is mainly to strengthen the management of long-term liabilities and current liabilities.

The fifth is the rules of investment management. The rules principally regulate the investment policy of enterprises from the perspectives of investment feasibility study, internal investment management and external investment management.

The sixth is the rules of profit and its distribution management. The rules mainly consist of target profit management rules, profit forming management rules and profit distribution management rules.

(C) Basic Rules of Assets Management include:
The first is the rules of monetary assets management. It includes the rules of cash management, the rules of bank deposit management, and the rules of foreign currency transaction management. The rules of cash management include the scope of cash using, the verification of cash limits, the provisions of cash receipts and payments as well as cash calculating and checking. The rules of bank deposit management include the scope and manner of bank settlement, the checking and calculating of bank account and the method of check

management. Foreign currency transaction management mainly includes the management of foreign currency assets and liabilities as well as the calculation of exchange gains and losses.

The second is the rules of inventory management. Based on the principles of reducing capital occupying and ensuring the safety and integrity of the inventory assets, inventory management should establish and improve a series of rules about pricing, acceptance, deliver, keeping and checking.

The third is the rules of fixed-assets management, which cover the valuation and depreciation of fixed assets, the roles and responsibilities of fixed-asset management, the day-to-day management of fixed assets and the change management of fixed asset.

The fourth is the rules of construction in progress management, which consist of the feasibility analysis of the construction in progress, the rules of project approval, the procurement and custody rules of supplies and equipment, the management of the construction in progress, the completion acceptance and settlement of the project and the accounting of construction in progress, etc.

The fifth is the rules of intangible assets management, which consist of the valuation of intangible assets, the management of acquiring the assets, day-to-day management and the management of transferring the assets.

(D) The contents of Rules of Assets Management include:

The first is setting the financial and accounting institutions. Financial and accounting institutions generally include the chief accountant, the Minister of Finance, Accounting department and Finance department. Accounting department and Finance department should properly divide the respective functions, and establish the relevant post.

The second is defining the responsibilities of accounting leadership, which include the powers and responsibilities of the chief executive officers, the chief accountants and the chief financial officers of enterprises.

The third is the system of accounting job responsibility, which mainly makes specific provisions about the responsibilities of the chief accountant, the cashier, as well as the accountants in charge of material accounting, current accounting, payroll accounting, cost accounting, accounting files management and general ledger statements, etc.

The fourth is the system of financial job responsibility, which mainly makes specific provisions about the responsibilities of the chief financial officer, as well as the employees in charge of comprehensive financial management, cost management, financial audit management, financing, foreign investment, liquidity accounting and management, fixed asset accounting and management and profit accounting and management, etc.

12.2.2.2 Rules of Human Resource Control

The contents of Rules of Human Resource control include:

(A) The Rules of Human Resource Planning

Human resources planning applies the basic principles of management for planning the demand of labor, namely the enterprises come up with the planning of staff requirements according to the changes in the environment and based on the predict of the development of future career. The rules mainly provide the role of human resource planning, the procedures of developing human resources planning, the prediction methods of human resource requirements and the forecasting methods of human resource supply.

(B) The Rules of Job Analysis

Job analysis is a process to determine the tasks, activities and responsibilities of the jobs, and which in China, is also known as position analysis. The rules should provide the role, the procedures and the methods of job analysis as well as the contents of job description.

(C) The Rules of Staff Recruitment

The rules mainly provide the procedures of staff recruitment, the methods of recruitment and other things.

(D) Incentive System

Incentive usually refers to the process to mobilize the enthusiasm of staff, inspire and encourage employees to achieve organizational goals. The main provisions of the Incentive System are the role of incentive, the basic requirements of incentive and various methods of incentive.

(E) The Rules of Education and Training

The rules mainly provide the objectives and levels of education and training, and the methods and principles of training.

(F) The Rules of Staff Salaries and Remuneration

There are the basic wage system, the bonuses and incentive system and employee benefits system in the salary and remuneration system. The rules provide the elements, principles and methods of these three sections.

(G) The rules of Performance Evaluation

The rules mainly provide the purposes, principles, procedures and the methods of performance evaluation.

(H) The Rules of Team Building

The rules provide the kinds of teams, the goal of team building, the procedures of team building and the evaluation of team building.

(I) The Rules of Career Management

Career management means that through the design of the staff's work and career development program, enterprises can coordinate the individual needs of staff and the needs of the whole business organization in order to achieve the common growth and development of individuals and businesses. The rules mainly consist of career self-management rules, career planning management rules, career approach management rules and career cycle management rules.

12.2.2.3 Rules of Purchase Control

The contents of Rules of Purchase Control include:

(A) The Rules of Purchasing Plan Management

The compilation principles of materials purchasing plan should both ensure the continuity of production and operation, and occupy the funds as little as possible in order to prevent the backlog of goods and materials. Material procurement plan must include the name, size, model, unit, quantity, price range and other information of the material, and should be reported to the competent authorities or the leader for approval.

(B) The Rules of Purchasing Decision Management

Enterprises can set up a purchasing management team to perform the functions of determining and supervising the price and quality of the materials to be purchased. Enterprises also could manage the purchasing materials in the form of hierarchical decentralized based on the categories and price.

(C) The Rules of Bidding and Purchasing Management

The rules make provisions about the materials, principles, objects, and procedures of bidding and purchasing.

(D) The Rules of Price Supervision

The purchasing management team supervises the price through the forms of auditing the purchasing plans, the purchasing price and the purchasing bills.

(E) The Rules of Quality Inspection and Supervision

The quality control personnel should inspect the quantity and quality of the purchasing materials, with the untested or substandard not be formally put in storage and handled settlement.

(F) The Rules of Payment and Acceptance

The rules mainly provide the procedures of acceptance and payment.

12.2.2.4 Rules of Marketing Control

The contents of Rules of Marketing Control include:

(A) The Rules of Sales Management

The rules mainly include sales forecasting, sales planning, sales contract signing, the management of approval and cancellation, as well as the management of sales returns.

(B) The Rules of Accounts Receivable Management

The rules include the responsibility of personnel who handle accounts receivable, the management of accounts receivable, the collection and cleaning of accounts receivable, the management of wiping account and the settlement of the loss on bad debt.

12.2.2.5 Rules of Production and Technology Control

The contents of Rules of Production and Technology Control include:

(A) The Rules of Production Planning Management

The rules mainly refer to the various indicators and preparation procedures which should be clearly defined when enterprises prepare the production planning, as well as the principles which should be followed in the preparation process. The rules usually include long-term production planning management rules and short-term production planning management rules.

(B) The Rules of Production Technology Management

The rules mainly include the tasks, contents and plans of production technology management. The rules mainly make provision for the improvement, introduction, transfer and other matters of production technology.

(C) The Rules of Production Factors Management

The rules principally consist of staff organization management rules and production equipment management rules. Staff organization management mainly provides the tasks and content of staff management, the division and collaboration of staff, and the specific responsibilities of each production position. The rules of production equipment management mainly make provisions for the tasks and contents of equipment management, as well as the selection, evaluation, usage, maintenance and renovation of equipment.

(D) The rules of logistics management

The rules principally provide the basic tasks and the main contents of logistics management, and scientifically and reasonably determine the consumption quota and reserves of each supply.

(E) The Rules of Product Management

The rules mainly consist of the rules of finished products (semi-product) management and the rules of product development management. The main contents include managing the circulation and statistics of the work-in-process in workshop and the work-in-process inventory; determining the reasonable reserves of semi-product and work-in-process and examining the rates of whole sets; enhancing storage management and playing the control role as the middle warehouse; developing the new types of products and the development direction, as well as determining the development strategy of product and the development methods and processes of the new product.

(F) The Rules of Quality Management

The rules should make provisions for the quality indicators of product, quality standards of product, quality management in the design and trial process, quality management in the manufacturing processes, quality management in the using process, as well as the concept, role, content and operation mechanism of quality assurance system.

12.2.2.6 Rules of Cost Control [1]

The contents of the Rules of Cost control:

1. Basic rules of cost management . The content of the rules: Dividing costs and expenses correctly, determining the scope of costs and expenses, establishing a strict rule of requisitioning materials and establishing management rules of vouchers and books.
2. Rules of cost planning and responsibility. On the basis of determining the target profit, enterprises determine the target cost, divide the target cost by according to the kinds of products and cost items, formulate each consumption quota and formulate the planned cost of each product. Accordingly, enterprises can make each workshop, team and person enforce the rules of target cost and make each responsibility center calculate, control, analysis and evaluate costs.
3. Rules of cost calculating and control. Calculating costs refers to collecting and distributing costs in use of category costing method and process costing method. Cost control refers to enterprises calculate and examine actual production costs exactly according to the standard of costs and expenses on the basis of rules of target cost and responsibility. Cost control includes hierarchical concentrative control, comprehensive and overall control, beforehand control, intermediate control and afterwards control.
4. Rules of cost analysis and evaluation. Cost analysis refers to assessing and summarizing the cost formation, identifying the factors that affect costs, revealing the cause of conservation and waste and seeking further ways to reduce costs. Cost evaluation refers to assessing the achievement of each responsible unit according to cost planning and complete and reliable cost information and combines it with rules of rewards and penalties.

5. Containment rules of each business department. The containment rules refers to that the financial department and each business department supervise and inspect each other on the management and control of costs and expenses, aiming to reduce the probability of fraud and error.

12.2.3 Rules of Operating Control

Rules of operating control refer to the rule in use of which the managers of responsibility centers regulate operating behavior. It includes rules of production procedure control, rules of procurement procedure control, and rules of storage procedure control and so on.

12.2.3.1 Rules of Production Procedure Control

The content of rules of production procedure control includes: (1) Operating rules of process plan. (2) Operating rules of production plan. (3) Operating rules of production supervision. (4) Operating rules of consigned process. (5) Operating rules of product quality supervision. (6) Operating rules of manufacturing supervision. (7) Operating rules of maintenance. (8) Operating rules safety production. (9) Operating rules of production cost.

12.2.3.2 Rules of Purchase Procedure Control

The content of rules of purchase procedure control includes: (1) Operating rules of purchase requisition. (2) Operating rules of procurement. (3) Operating rules of acceptance check. (4) Operating rules of payment. (5) Operating rules of insurance.

12.2.3.3 Rules of Storage Procedure Control

The content of rules of storage procedure control includes: (1) Operating rules of warehousing of storage materials. (2) Operating rules of stockpile of storage materials. (3) Operating rules of picking materials, returning materials and waste disposal. (4) Operating rules of stores inventory.

12.3 Standard and Report of Rule-Based Control

The standard of rule-based control is the criterion for managers to enforce control and the necessary means of enforcement of effective rule-based control. The appropriateness of the standards will affect the effect of the enforcement of rule-based control directly. In order to formulate rational standard of rule-based control, enterprises should analyze the status of the enforcement of related rules in each historical period and study related rules that similar enterprises or enterprises in the same industry enforce.

The principles of the standard of rule-based control:

The standard of rule-based control should help enterprises to achieve organizational objectives;

The standard of rule-based control should make it convenient for enterprises to evaluate the work performance of the staff and internal managers of organizations;

Enterprises should make the standard of rule-based control timely and elastic and combine it with their future developments.

The standard of rule-based control should be stable as far as possible.

The standard of rule-based control includes quantitative standard, qualitative standard, financial standard and non-financial standard.

The report of rule-based control is the output information and the conclusive file of rule-based control system. The subjects of rule-based control system emphasize the key points of rule-based control through observing the rule-based control environment; they evaluate, compare and analyze the status of the enforcement of related rule-based control in the whole organization and each department according to the standard of rule-based control; thereby, they find out the reasons, responsibilities and effects of differences, draw conclusions and finally produce the report of rule-based control.. The report of rule-based control is a key step to true measurement and reflection of economic operational status in the process of management control.

12.4 The Evaluation and Rectification of Rule-Based Control System[1]

12.4.1 The Evaluation of Rule-Based Control System

The evaluation of rule-based control system can be divided into two parts involving the integrity evaluation and the effectiveness evaluation. The evaluation of integrity consists of three layers of meaning. Firstly, the rule-based control system should run through the entire managerial activities, which means there should be appropriate rules being applied to each activity. Secondly, the employees are required to master the rules. Thirdly, the control system should be systematic, which means every managerial department can function coordinative to realize the overall objective of the system. The evaluation of effectiveness involves two layers of meaning.

[1]Refer to Zhang Xianzhi [2].

Firstly, the control system must comply with the laws and reflect the national laws, regulations and policies. Secondly, the control system should be implemented effectively. All departments and all employees must endeavor to maintain the solemnity of the management control system. Any person should not have special powers beyond the system.

12.4.2 The Rectification of Rule-Based Control System

The rectification aims to check and verify the errors in the process. The actual condition of implementation should be compared to the standards of control system to discover the deviations. Then appropriate measures should be taken to minimize the effect of these errors so that the management control system within an organization can be relatively stable [3].

There are two different treatments to the deviations. Firstly, can the deviation be accepted? If the answer is yes, the subject of control does not have to intervene and the executor will be allowed to continue his work. Secondly, are the regulations of management control system in line with the real conditions? If the answer is yes, the deviations are caused by the executor. Further analysis of the cause and corresponding measures should be taken to correct the process of executors. If the answer is no, it is the management control system itself that should be responsible for the deviations. The controller should rectify or supplement the current management control system.

There are two methods which can be used by the subject of control to rectify the deviations. One is to intervene directly, which means the subject of control commands the executors to replace their previous means of action with the standard ones directly and compulsorily. The other is to intervene directly, which means the subject of control sets up an effective incentive system and then correct the behaviors of executors automatically.

12.5 Practice of Rule-Based Control System in Chinese Enterprise

Previously, this book described the difference among strategy control, management control and operation control and also introduced the common requirements of rule-based control system. As is known to all, Chinese enterprises pay a lot of attention to the rules. Here comes the question, what particular rules should be set up within Chinese enterprises? On 26th April 2010, a joint conference was held in Beijing by Ministry of Finance along with Securities Regulatory Commission, Audit Commission, the SASAC, China Banking Regulatory Commission and China Insurance Regulatory Commission. During the conference, the *Enterprise Internal*

Control guidelines were released grandly [4]. These guidelines along with *Enterprise Internal Control Basic Standards*, which was released in May 2008, built the internal control system in Chinese enterprises together.[2] While the *Enterprise Internal Control guideline* is the core of the entire internal control norm system, it presents the detailed requirements for the basic management system. In terms of its contents, the concept of internal control put forward in the guidelines is generalized management control. It nearly covers the principal activities of an enterprise, such as the development of strategy, organizational structure, the stream of capital and preparation of financial report.

The guidelines can be divided into three categories, namely the control environment guidelines, the control activity guidelines and the control methods guidelines, which basically cover the transactions and events related to the cash flow, material flow, human flow and information flow within an organization.

12.5.1 The Guidelines for Control Environment

The control environment is the basis of the enterprises to implement internal control. It dominates the awareness of internal control among entire staff and also affects the attitude and behavior of the staff when they implement control activities and assume their responsibilities. There are five parts involving organizational structure, development strategy, human resources, corporate culture and social responsibility.

12.5.1.1 Organizational Structure

The development strategy in an enterprise is based on the scientific organizational structure, which consists of governance structure and internal structure. If the governance structure exists in name only or else the management lacks the ability to make decisions scientifically or to operate benignly, the company may finally fail. Meanwhile, without an appropriate allocation of responsibilities, internal departments may be overlapping or missing, which will certainly leads to inefficiency. In order to prevent and resolve such risks, there must be detailed requirements in the guidelines for organizational structure. For example, the guidelines should emphasize the importance of obeying national laws and regulations. It should also clarify the responsibilities and procedures of each department to make sure the process of

[2]Ministry of Finance, the Commission, the Audit Commission, the SASAC, China Banking Regulatory Commission, China Insurance Regulatory Commission and other departments jointly issued a notice that these standards must be implemented first in the companies which are both listed on domestic and foreign market from 1st January, 2011. Then the scope will expand to all the companies listed on the Shanghai Stock Exchange and Shenzhen Stock Exchange main board since 1st January, 2012. The time when it will be implemented in the SME and GEM board listed companies is not official decided. Meanwhile, non-listed medium-sized or large enterprises are encouraged to implement these standards in advance.

decision-making, implementation and supervision is separated. Meanwhile, when it comes to an important event such as decision-making, transactions and appointments and dismissals or large sums of payments (commonly known as "three important events and one large sum"), the corresponding department should examine and approve the event together. Especially when a company owns subsidiaries, it should set up a matching system to manage its subsidiaries.

12.5.1.2 Development Strategy

Enterprise is the main body of the market economy. In order to develop sustainably, the key point for an enterprise is to set up suitable and flexible development strategy. During the survey, it is discovered that the lack of clear and proper development or the inadequate implementation will result in negative consequences. For example, an enterprise may develop blindly without comparative advantages and sufficient impetus. Or else, some enterprises may develop in an aggressive way that ignores the real condition of them, which finally leads to excessive expansion or even fail. It is also discovered that some enterprises change their development strategies too often that results in the huge waste of resources and finally fail to survive. Therefore, the guidelines for development strategy put forward corresponding solutions to these potential problems such as clarifying the standards to develop, implement and evaluate a strategy.

12.5.1.3 Human Resources

Snapping up talents has become the linchpin for an enterprise to succeed in today's intense competition. It's undeniable that human resources are the intelligence treasuries in an enterprise. The core competitiveness can be greatly enhanced if the human resources are properly allocated. However, if an enterprise lacks enough talents or just the opposite, has redundant staff, it is hard to realize its strategy. If the incentive system is imperfect and the key staff is under improper surveillance, it may lead to inefficiency or the loss of talents. Moreover, without reasonable talents withdrawal mechanism, it may bring lawsuits to an enterprise that will damage its reputation. In order to prevent and mitigate these crucial risks, the guidelines for human resources clarify the corresponding requirements such as to establish and improve talents withdrawal mechanism (involving resignation, dissolution of the labor contract, retirement and so on), to set up a remuneration system linked with the performance.

12.5.1.4 Social Responsibilities

To grow with society and environment sustainably, an enterprise has to take its social responsibilities. The guidelines for social responsibilities focus on the weak points including four parts. Firstly, it requires the enterprise to set up strict safe production management system, practices and contingency plans as well as responsibility tracing system. Secondly, the enterprise has to establish standards for production procedure in order to control and examine the quality of productions. Thirdly, the enterprise should attach importance to protecting environment and conserving resources in order to improve resources utilization efficiency. At last, the enterprise should safeguard the lawful rights and interests of staff.

12.5.1.5 Corporate Culture

Corporate culture is a general term for values, business philosophy and spirit of an enterprise that are accepted and respected by the whole staff, which is formed gradually during the course of production and operation. It is the spirit of an enterprise and it runs throughout the whole process. Moreover, it is the impetus for an enterprise to grow sustainably. In reality, some enterprises fail because of the serious problems in corporate culture. There should be corresponding requirements in the guidelines for corporate culture.

12.5.2 The Guidelines for Control Activities

The enterprise should not only improve the internal control environment, but also set up appropriate standards to control specific activities. The guidelines for control activities consist of nine detailed guidelines. They are guidelines for capital activities, procurement activities, asset management, sales, research and development, projects, guarantee business, outsourcing and financial reporting.

12.5.2.1 Capital Activities

Capital activities refer to corporate financing, investment and fund operation activities. Capital is the blood for production and operation cycle in an enterprise. It is the backbone of an enterprise, which determines the competitiveness and sustainable development of an enterprise. Each potential risk may lead to great loss if dealt with carelessly. Therefore, the guidelines for capital activities should put forward detailed control requirements concerning the financing, investment and fund operation activities.

12.5.2.2 Procurement Activities

Procurement activities refer to the purchases of supplies (or accept services) and related payments. In some Chinese enterprises, when dealing with the procurement activities, there are some problems that should be paid great attention to. For example, the purchase plan is unreasonable, the choice of suppliers is inappropriate, the pricing process is unscientific. In addition, the authorization process and the examination of goods purchased should also be overviewed strictly. Therefore, the guidelines for procurement activities should strengthen the surveillance of above problems to make sure that enough and proper goods are prepared for the production and operation of an enterprise.

12.5.2.3 Asset Management

To strengthen the asset management, to ensure the safety and integrity of the assets, to improve the efficiency of property, it is helpful to maintain normal production and operation, which is also conducive to the furtherance of the enterprise development strategy. In order to prevent and mitigate the crucial risks, the guidelines for asset management clarify the following requirements. Firstly, an enterprise should standardize the inventory management process which involves the acquisition process, acceptance of storage, raw material processing, warehousing, requisitioned issued and inventory disposal. Secondly, an enterprise should strengthen the maintenance and management of buildings, machinery and equipment and other types of fixed assets. In addition, staff should get proper pre-training for the operation of fixed assets. The enterprise should make insurance policies for the assets and control the mortgage of fixed assets. Thirdly, an enterprise has to make specific provisions concerning the intangible assets such as brands, trademarks, patents, proprietary technology and land use rights.

12.5.2.4 Sales

The enterprise should strengthen the management of sales, deliveries and payments. Under proper management, the enterprise can standardize the sales behavior, expand market share and finally realize the objective. The guidelines for sales put up corresponding measures such as pricing credit regulations, the examination and approval regulations for the sales contract, the sales delivery regulations, customer service and receivables management regulations.

12.5.2.5 Research and Development

Research and development activities usually imply significant risks. For example, there are not enough proofs and demonstrations for the research projects which may result in huge waste of resources. If there are not sufficient talents for the research or the process is not overviewed properly, the cost may be too high or even worse the research will fail. Finally, if the research only stays at the theoretical level, the enterprise may not benefit well from it. Therefore, the guidelines for research and development points out corresponding measures to prevent these risks involving setting up feasibility study system, authorization system, post responsibility system and achievements examination system.

12.5.2.6 Projects

Projects are usually closely associated with the enterprise development strategy accompanying with the transfer of large sums of money and supplies, which commonly involve great uncertainty and risks. As a consequence, the guidelines for projects clearly points out that the enterprise should strengthen the surveillance over the construction of projects and set up detailed management system. To ensure the quality and progress of the projects, the enterprise should standardize the process such as bidding, cost, construction, inspection and other aspects.

12.5.2.7 Guarantee Business

Under normal circumstances, the enterprises should limit the guarantee business activities strictly. If a guarantee business is unavoidable, the enterprise has to establish policies and management system for the guarantee business. In these policies, the guarantee object, the limitations of guarantee and the forbidden guarantee objects should be pointed out clearly. Meanwhile, the process of investigation and assessment, examination and approval and the implementation of guarantee business should be standardized.

12.5.2.8 Outsourcing

As is known to all, outsourcing activities have been widely used in telecommunications, mobile phones, financial and other industries, which provide the energy for the enterprises to optimize the allocation of resources, accelerates business restructuring and improve operational efficiency. However, when an enterprise chooses to outsource its operations, it may face significant risks. Thus the guidelines for outsourcing must state clearly that the enterprises engaged in outsourcing business should establish and improve the outsourcing management system, which points out the conditions and procedures of outsourcing. Moreover, the responsibilities of corresponding department should be allocated properly. To fully benefit from outsourcing, the enterprise must have a strict oversight system.

12.5.2.9 Financial Statements

Financial statement is one of the most important forms for the enterprise to disclose its financial information. To the listed companies, financial statements are the important basis for investors to make decisions. From the perspective of state-owned enterprises, they may become an important information source for the government to make economic decisions. In order to prevent and mitigate the risks, the guidelines for financial statements require the enterprise to set up appropriate accounting system in accordance with the national unified accounting standards. The financial statement disclosed must be integrated and accurate in calculation. In addition, prompt submission is also required. Meanwhile, the enterprise should also establish a financial analysis system which aims to obtain a comprehensive analysis of the business management status and problems. The enterprise should hold financial analysis meeting on a regular basis in order to take full advantage of the entire financial information presented by financial statements.

12.5.3 The Guidelines for Control Methods

This kind of guidelines emphasizes on the nature of tools which is related to the overall business or management. There are four parts involving overall budget, contract management, and internal information transmission and information systems.

12.5.3.1 Overall Budget

The guidelines for overall budget require the enterprise to strengthen the leadership of corresponding budget work. Firstly, the responsibilities of each department should be allocated appropriately and the procedures of authorization should be stated clearly. Secondly, the entire process of budget preparation can be established and improved accordingly. In order to make sure the budget is based on reasonable proofs, the procedures and methods should be clearly defined. At last, the system should be established that aims to analyze the implementation and performance of budget and conduct internal audits on the implementation of the budget.

12.5.3.2 Contract Management

Contract management is often ignored by most enterprises, which is definitely the weakest part in the internal control. The guidelines for contract management focus on evaluations of the implementation of contracts. The enterprise should at least make an analytical assessment of the overall conditions of contracts as well as the conditions of major contracts each year in order to improve the system.

12.5.3.3 Internal Information Transmission

Internal information transmission is the process of production and management information passed between the internal management levels through internal reporting format. Therefore, the application guidelines require enterprises to establish a scientific internal information transmission system. The contents of information, confidentiality requirements, transfer mode, as well as the duties and powers of the management level should be stated explicitly. In this way, the internal reports can be taken full advantage of.

12.5.3.4 Information Systems

Information systems can be used to strengthen internal control, which helps reduce the human factor and improve the efficiency and effectiveness of control. However, there are risks inside information system, which need to be controlled. Thus according to the application guidelines for information systems, the plan of establishing the information system should be in accordance with the organizational structure, business scope, geographic distribution and technical capacity. In addition, the enterprise should increase investment on the development and maintenance of the information system in order to optimize the management process and prevent operational risks.

12.6 Strength and Weakness of Rule-Based Control System

12.6.1 Advantages of Rule-Based Control System

12.6.1.1 It Makes the Operating Regulation of Enterprises Clearer

Rule-based control system has clear direction and responsibility and specification, so that it can make sure that the idea of management control will be achieved and then avoid the problems of unclear responsibilities, prevarication and unclear issues of power.

12.6.1.2 It Is Easy for All Staff to Enforce Rule-Based Control

The effect of rule-based control system is that enterprises can regulate the behaviors of managers and staff, ask them to work by rules and regulations and conform to the enterprises' objectives, make it clear for managers and staff what is should or should not be done, let managers and staff know organizations' requirements, operate easily, so that it will conducive to the enforcement of the rules.

12.6.1.3 There Is Less Limitation to the Environment and Conditions

Rule-based control system has a quite low requirement on the environment and it is not subject to harsh conditions. Any organization needs rule-based control that is suitable for any organization or enterprise to regulate behaviors of managers and staff.

12.6.2 Disadvantages of Rule-Based Control System

12.6.2.1 It Imposes Restrictions on the Initiative of Managers and Staff

The rigidity of the rule-based control system sometimes makes it difficult for organizations to be as flexible as other management systems. High degree of institutionalization may cause managers and employees lose their subjective initiative. That is because that the cognitive system will quietly decide our behaviors. Everyone will feel unalterable and justified that they should work under these rules and never make other choices. Thus, to some extent the system rule-based control system may limit people's thinking space and creativity and foresight.

12.6.2.2 It Does Not Have Enough Quantitative Control or Be Lack of Convergence with Business Objectives Directly

Rule-based control systems mainly focus on the qualitative control, but not on the quantitative control. The lack of quantitative control makes people feel too abstract about control requirement and lack direct contact with the overall objective of the enterprise, which will lead to deviating from the direction of control system and the effects of control cannot be accurately reflected.

12.7 Suitable Environment of Rule-Based Control System

Rule-based control is the basis of other control systems. Compared to Budgetary Control, Evaluation Control and Incentive Control, the operation of rule-based control system does not have a high requirement on the organization's management infrastructure and the environment. Whether new or mature enterprises, sunset or sunrise industry enterprises, small or large organizations, all of them have a rule-based control system in operation. In other words, any kind of organization has a rule-based control system and a rule-based control system is applicable to or applied to all of the organization. Thus, rule-based control system requires quite low standard on the management environment. However, low demands on management infrastructure and the environment do not mean that the rule-based control system is not crucial to organizations. On the contrary, it is commonly used by the majority of organizations and becomes an important part of management control because of low requirement on management infrastructure and the environment. The lower an organization management infrastructure is, the more to increase the enforcement of rule-based control.

A key factor that the rule-based control system can play a role in organization controls is that rule-based control must be suitable for the organization's environment, which means external and internal environment of enterprises. The starting point of the rule-based control system should be the organization's external environment because the rule-based control system is determined by the external environment firstly and then determines the contents of the rule-based control system based on the organization's internal environment. That is the only way to ensure that the rule- based control system can be applicable to organization's internal and external environment and to guarantee that the rule-based control system can play an effective role in the organization.

References

1. Wilson R (1975) Cost control handbook. Gower Press, Epping
2. Zhang Xianzhi (2004) On the construction of the internal management control practices research (the internal research topic of Dongbei University of Finance and Economics Accounting Research Center)
3. Simons R (1995) Control in an age of empowerment. Harvard Business Review, March–April
4. The Ministry of Finance, the CSRC, the National Audit Office and the CIRC (2010) The basic internal control norms for enterprises. China Financial Science Press, Beijing

Chapter 13
The Mode of Budgetary Control System

13.1 Definition of Budgetary Control System

Budgetary control is defined as regulating organizational objectives and the process of economic behavior by establishing budgets, making adjustments and corrections of deviation between managerial behavior and objective, and guaranteeing the realization of all levels of objectives, strategies, policies and programming. In view of control elements, budgetary control includes formulating and implementing budgets, variance analysis and correction of deviations.

In essence, budgetary control systems are part of comprehensive budgetary management system, in other words the systems belong to integrated management control system that is based on the budgets including multi dimensional processes and staff. These systems also possess comprehensive control and binding force of an enterprise's overall business activities and departments. The following three aspects may help to form a better understanding of the "comprehensive" nature of budgetary control systems.

13.1.1 Comprehensive Coverage

Budgetary control should cover the entire company, which includes the headquarters, divisions and related functional departments and the associates, as well as associates' non-business units and functional departments. In practice, many enterprises mainly focus on expense budget and capital budget, which are only temporary solutions. But the comprehensive budget is a consolidated summary of various functional budgets, such as sales budget, procurement budget, capital budget, and financial budget, etc.; usually, the financial department is the key to budgetary management, but in fact, all business activities are involved in comprehensive budget, which includes marketing, production, procurement, research and development and financial activities, etc. In order to conduct business activities effectively, enterprises need to prepare financial budget along with operating budget and capital budget.

X. Zhang, *Enterprise Management Control Systems in China*, Understanding China,
DOI 10.1007/978-3-642-54715-7_13,

13.1.2 Whole Course Control

On the basis of budget, control activities run through the whole course of business activities, and can be classified as beforehand control, intermediate control and afterwards control. Beforehand control consists of setting budgetary objective and budgetary planning; Intermediate control involves the enforcement of budget; and afterwards control depends on evaluation of budget. The control activities mentioned above, form a complete budgetary control cycle and are part and parcel of budgetary control system. A number of enterprises attach great importance to budgetary planning, but take little notice of intermediate control. They neither implement the planning positively, nor monitor it effectively, let along perform systematic analysis. Some other enterprises completely ignore afterwards control. Their appraisal mechanism which reveals a poor combination of budget implementation and evaluation is not budget-related.

13.1.3 Full Participation

The design and operation of budgetary control system is a complicated and systematic project, which must be highly valued by top management, meanwhile, the whole staff should be involved. When implementing budgetary control, the overall budgetary objective has to be decomposed and distributed to respective departments. And this the staffs who work in those departments to form a clear understanding of their targets and tasks. In order to achieve the objective, joint efforts should be made by all members from top to bottom, however, if everyone acts in his own way without cooperation, then the objective is hard to achieve, and consequently, enterprise value will be undermined.

13.2 Procedures of Budgetary Control System

As a pattern of management control system, budgetary control system should include setting of budgetary objective, budgetary planning (including budgetary planning, budgetary approval and budgetary notification), enforcement of budget (including control of budgetary implementation, budgetary analysis and budgetary adjustment) and evaluation of budget (including budget evaluation and budget motivation), etc. As shown in Fig. 13.1.

13.2.1 Setting of Budgetary Objective

Strategic planning is the starting point of management control system, while budgetary objective is the starting point of the budgetary control. Thus, the setting of budgetary objective is the starting point of budgetary control system as well as the

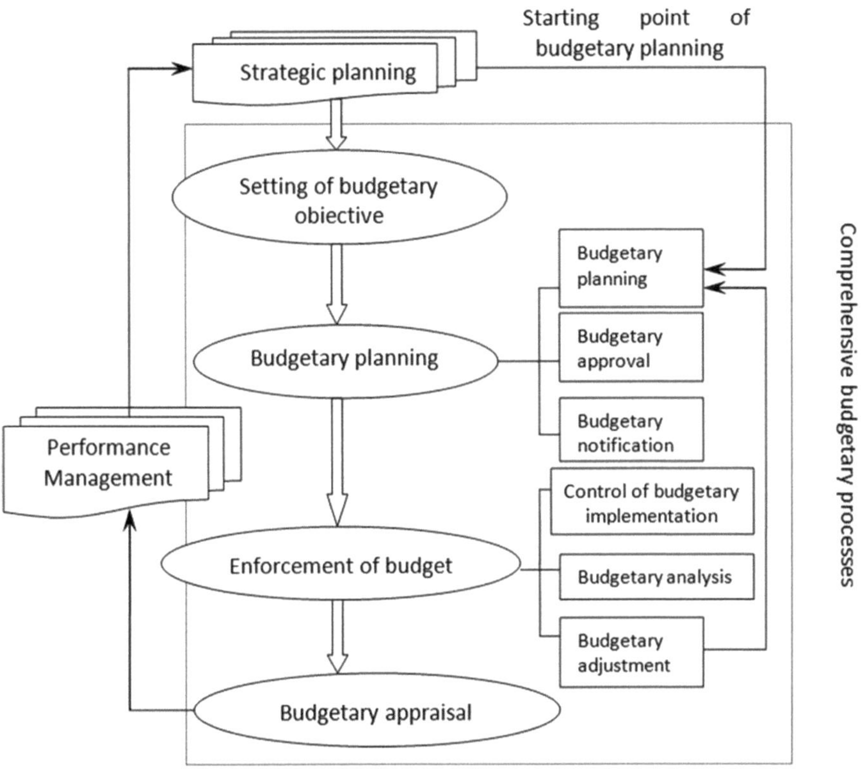

Fig. 13.1 Budgetary control system

fundamental basis of budgetary planning. The setting of strategic planning is based on strategic objective and strategic programming, meanwhile, the setting of budgetary objective is in accordance with strategic planning.

In light of organization hierarchy, budgetary objectives can be divided into general objective and hierarchical objective. On the basis of strategic objective, general objective is a concrete reflection of strategic planning and dominates the budgetary system. Strategic planning varies according to different strategic orientations, which in turn leads to distinct budgetary objectives.

Meanwhile, the setting of general budgetary objective is based on both sides, that is, external environment and internal resources. On one hand, the objective is restrained by competitors. On the other hand, it is limited by resources. In light of function, general budgetary objective can be viewed as the connection between enterprise and its external environment, which defines development directions and level of competitiveness. At the same time, it regulates the structure of resource allocation. Moreover, it provides a yardstick for clarifying hierarchical objective. As the refinement and foundation of general budgetary objective, hierarchical objective imposes direct incentive and restraint on related departments and principals, which in turn largely depends upon the feasibility of general budgetary objective and the effectiveness of mechanism of incentive and constraint. What's more, it decides whether the enterprise will survive or not. Consequently, when carrying out budgetary control, the complexity of budgetary objective should be carefully monitored by management. Western empirical study indicated that, as a rule of thumb, 'rigid and realizable budget' will bring about the best outcome, and only in this way could motivation and control be performed effectively.

13.2.2 Budgetary Planning

Budgetary planning refers to the process of setting general budgetary objective and decomposing it into hierarchical objectives for implementation. In other words, it is the process of ascertaining budgetary control standards. As an essential part of budgetary control system, the quality of budgetary planning has a direct impact on the outcome of budgetary implementation as well as the performance evaluation of implementers.

Budgetary planning is a course of participation and coordination. Participation allows implementers to comment on the planning rather than merely forced to do so. On one side, it largely reduces the degree of information asymmetry between management and implementers. On the other side, it arouses participants' sense of responsibility and creativity. In this way, organizational goals are acknowledged by implementers and greater goal congruence may be achieved. Coordination, in terms of budgetary planning refers to the process of negotiation and consultation before submitting the budget to superior for approval. The preparation of budgetary planning has to experience dozens of iterations, both top-down and bottom-up. By this means, the final budget will not only satisfy overall interests but also enhance departmental coordination, as well as conform to reality. Thereby, the risk of unrealistic decisions made by top management's may be mitigated. Budgetary planning involves each department and individual, which in turn needs full participation and support.

13.2.3 Enforcement of Budget

Enforcement of budget includes implementing the budget, monitoring the process of implementation and analyzing the outcome.

Enforcement of budget is the key to budgetary objective. It is at the heart of budgetary control system. Above all, the effective enforcement of budget relies on budget constraint mechanism. On one hand, the concrete responsibility performance standards play key role in the enforcement of responsibility budgets. When setting standards, the enterprise should not only abide by the principle of controllability, but also consider the limitation of striving for competitive advantages. On the other hand, determinants of the ultimate outcome of budgetary control are whether all kinds of economic resources are given full play, especially employees' initiative, creativity and sense of responsibility. In addition, budget coordination, budget analysis, budget adjustment, budget supervision and arbitration are essential procedures and pledge to the effective enforcement of budget. In the process of budget implementation, a kind of indispensable means of control mode is called internal report. The control to the above procedures is dynamic, which focuses on regularly monitoring and adjusting implementation effect and its formation, that is, after getting information by means of operation accounting and field observations, it compares output variables of controlled object with control standards in a timely manner, puts forward measures to correct deviations, and constantly eliminates deviations between implementation effect and the established standards. All those activities need a feedback carrier, an internal report, which is also an indispensable control method.

Internal report is the feedback carrier of budgetary control and the reverse process of budgetary control implementation. It presents the process and result of budgetary control to management of all levels. Consequently, it is beneficial to perform intermediate and afterwards control as well as conduct responsibility analysis and performance appraisal. At the meantime, internal report contributes to maintain and control enterprise's assets and profits, and also helps to achieve optimal utilization of resources and management synergy.

During the process of budgetary control implementation, the actual process and effectiveness ranging from different levels of individuals and units to the whole enterprise, are clearly reflected in respective internal responsibility reports by means of bottom-up summary. As mentioned above, the report facilitates the control process by comparing actual performance with relevant budget and taking corrective actions. It directs and coordinates business activities and units to achieve stated targets.

13.2.4 Evaluation of Budget

Evaluation of budget consists of two parts, which are budget assessment and budget motivation.

Budget assessment is to evaluate the performance of each class of department or business unit. It is an effective means of incentive and constraint conducted by management. The assessment has two implications. First of all, it focuses on overall budgetary control system, that is, the evaluation of operating performance. Moreover, it provides a valid way of perfecting and optimizing the system. Secondly, the assessment is an essential measure to budgetary incentive and constraint in that, it appraises the performance of individuals who carry out the budget. It runs through the process of budget implementation. As a consequence, the assessment is not only dynamic and comprehensive but also providing a connecting link within the system, and it has the following benefits: (1) in reference to budgetary responsibility objective, forming a full understanding of the actual performance and providing ideas for coordination of contradictions and correction of errors and deviations; (2) determining the responsibility objective and related indicators as well as contribution discrepancies of each class of unit and individual for rewards and penalties; (3) offering valuable experience to the next budgetary objective and a fundamental basis and pledge to improve the effectiveness of following budgetary control.

Budgetary control system should be combined with performance management, in that incentive mechanism is crucial to the effective running of budgetary control system. Setting of budgetary standards, enforcement of budget as well as timely and accurate feedback, not to mention evaluation of budget, all those activities largely depend upon incentive mechanism. As a consequence, incentive mechanism runs through the whole course of budgetary control system and incentive is an integral part of the system. The purpose of incentive is to engender initiative and a sense of achievement. At the same time, it should observe the rules of material benefits, fairness, differences and diversity. There are generally two types of incentive measures, namely financial incentives (such as bonus) and non-financial incentives (such as promotion and delegation). The establishments of incentive standards may be on the basis of either internal system of rewards and penalties (predictable and fixed) or senior management's subjective judgment (rely on incentive provider's subjective judgment and may reflect environmental change). Incentives can be performed on both individual and group.

13.3 Contents of Budgetary Control System

13.3.1 Contents of Budgetary Planning

The complexity and hierarchy of enterprise's business activities determine that the budgetary control system is not only a comprehensive budgetary system but a comprehensive budgetary management system as well. From the perspective of content, comprehensive budgetary system can be classified into different categories according to various standards, as mentioned below:

13.3.1.1 The Budgetary Hierarchy View

In view of budgetary hierarchy, the system includes enterprise group budget, subsidiary or business unit budget, department budget and project budget, etc. Budgetary hierarchy is corresponding to the organization hierarchy. In an enterprise group, the strategic objective is frequently decomposed top-down along the organization hierarchy, including enterprise group objective, subsidiary or business unit objective, department objective and project objective. Whereas, the order of preparing budget is often bottom-up, first project and department budget then subsidiary or business unit budget and finally enterprise group budget.

13.3.1.2 The Content of Budget View

From the perspective of budgetary content, the comprehensive budgetary system includes operating budget, capital budget and financial budget, etc. Operating budget also called business budget, and reflects the basic production and operating activities which are directly related to day-to-day business, namely sales budget, procurement budget, production budget and administration cost budget. While, capital budget or special decision-making budget applies to the occasional and one-time business in the fields of investment and finance, such as fixed assets purchasing, expanding, reconstructing and updating and relevant fund raising. In terms of value, financial budget mirrors the overall outcome of decision-making and business. It refers to all kinds of budgets concerning financial position, operating achievements and cash flows. Hence, financial budget is also called general budget, for instance, budgetary balance sheet, budgetary income statement and budgetary cash flow statement, etc.

13.3.1.3 The Budget Responsibility View

From the viewpoint of traditional budget responsibility, the budget can be sorted into four budget centers, namely investment center, profit center, cost center and expense center. Each center has its own responsibility scope and business activities and thus leading to distinct budget responsibility and budgetary objective as well as content of budgetary planning. Cost center and expense center are only responsible for cost and expense and hence, their main purpose is to reduce cost and expense, for example, apart from preparing production budget, the production department has to prepare cost budget as well. Profit center is in charge of both revenue and profit targets, as a result, it needs to prepare both operating budget and profit budget. Similarly, investment center has to take into account of profit targets along with return on investment, which consequently should prepare operating budget, capital budget and financial budget as well.

13.3.1.4 The Budget Time View

Based on the time period, the budget may be classified as period budget and project budget. Period budget is used to direct and coordinate production and operation activities. In light of length of time, it falls into three spectrums, namely long-term, interim and short-term budget. As a rule of thumb, longer term budget helps to indicate directions and draw up long range plans of strategic significance with estimation. Operating and financial budgets generally cover a period of 1 year. And the short-term budgets are prepared for periods less than a year, which are more concrete and precise, such as quarterly budget and monthly budget. Whereas, project budget deals with future action towards special events, which is unconstrained by hierarchy and time, such as merger budget and new product developing budget.

Table 13.1 Budgetary planning procedures

Pattern of organization	Single-product and centralized enterprise group	Capital holding and decentralized enterprise group	Production management and combination of centralized and decentralized enterprise group
Mode of management control	Strategic planning	Financial control	Strategic control
Budgetary pattern	Centralized	Decentralized	Combination of centralized and decentralized
Budgetary planning procedures	Top-down	Bottom-up	Negotiated style of budgeting
Advantages	Avoid selfish departmentalism and achieve overall objectives	Stimulate initiative and sense of participation	Avoid selfish departmentalism and stimulate initiative
Disadvantages	Hinder employees to full play their subjective initiatives	Bring about severe self-departmentalism, which in turn hamper the realization of enterprise's overall objectives	Over bargaining may impair the seriousness and effectiveness of budgetary planning

13.3.2 Procedure of Budget

Based on diverse condition and budgetary mode, procedure of budget can be divided into three types, they are top-down, bottom-up and negotiated style of budgeting. It is correlated with organization pattern and budgetary mode. Each organization has its own budgetary mode as well as procedure of budget. As shown in Table 13.1.

13.3.2.1 Top-Down Budget Procedure

The top-down budget procedure is the most traditional budgetary management procedure. Its budget is prepared according to the strategic management requirement of headquarters (group company or company) combined with internal and external conditions, and then put into effect to lower echelons, such as divisions and subsidiaries. During the process stated above, headquarters are the power center of budgets, who take full control over ascertaining budgetary objectives and budgetary planning, while the divisions and subsidiaries only have the right to implement the budget. The top-down is corresponding to parent-subsidiary control mode of strategic planning and belongs to centralized budgetary mode. It is helpful to avoid selfish departmentalism and achieve overall objectives, whereas, the limitation is that its divisions and subsidiaries have a low level of involvement, which hinders them to full play their subjective initiatives.

13.3.2.2 Bottom-Up Budget Procedure

The bottom-up budget procedure stresses that budget is derived from the forecast of each division and subsidiary, as a consequence, they are the principal of budgetary planning, and headquarters are just the authority for final approval. Headquarters' duty is to formulate budgetary objective, such as budgetary return on capital, and the subsidiary is in charge of realizing the objective, for this reason, each division and subsidiary has to prepare and present their budget proposal as action commitment to authorities higher than the budgetee for approval, who then check the reliability of the commitment. Contrary to the top-down, the bottom-up's salient feature is that it stimulates initiative and sense of participation, which leads to a greater acceptance of budgetary objective. However, unless carefully controlled, it may result in setting of targets that are too easy to achieve, or even bring about severe self-departmentalism, which in turn hamper the realization of enterprise's overall objectives. The bottom-up is more common in capitalization-type holdings group, which is the financial control-type of parent-subsidiary management relationship, and belongs to decentralized budgetary mode.

13.3.2.3 Negotiated Budgeting Procedure

Actually, the negotiated budgeting procedure blends the above two approaches, which is an effective budget preparation process. With this approach, budgeting people prepare the first draft of the budget for their area of responsibility, which is 'bottom-up'; but they do so within guidelines established at higher levels, which is 'top-down'. Senior managers review and critique these proposed budgets. A hard-headed approval process helps to ensure that budgeters budgeting people do not 'play games' with the budgeting system. Nevertheless, the review process should be perceived as being fair. The advantage of the process is to avoid "arbitrary" of top-down, and can avoid "cheat" of bottom-up; the disadvantage is that excessive bargaining could undermine strategic budget planning and seriousness, and reduce the efficiency of the budget planning. The negotiated budgeting procedure is corresponding to strategic control-type of parent-subsidiary management relationship and is the most rational and popular approach both in theory and in practice.

13.3.3 Budgetary Control Objective

Budgetary control should be performed in accordance with the purpose of management (controller). Speaking from broad view, the purpose is perceived as organizational objective or control objective and from narrow view, it is treated as budgetary control indicators or standards. Therefore, it is key to implement effective budgetary control when ascertaining budgetary control indicators and standards on the basis of strategic planning.

13.3.3.1 Decomposition of Budgetary Objective

In view of content, key success factors (KSFs) of realizing strategy should be refined and practiced by strategic planning, which therefore has a close relationship with enterprise's overall strategic objective and strategic programming. Those KSFs comprise the control objective of enterprise's business activities which contain both financial and non-financial factors. On the one side, financial performance is a kind of comprehensive afterwards reflection which has lagging and short-term effect. On the other side, more often than not non-financial activities are key factors for improving financial performance, which has been proved in practice. By means of analyzing the basic requirements of business activities regarding strategic objective and strategic programming, strategic planning and KSFs are clarified, which in turn produces more detailed control objectives.

KSFs should be further decomposed into control indicators and control standards which are easy to manipulate and monitor, that is because, KSFs are the determinants of strategic programming and strategic objective. On one hand, qualitative control indicators should be selected to mirror KSFs. On the other hand, control standards should be set up to measure the effectiveness of KSFs. As a major component of strategic planning on financial ground, by way of KSFs, budget can also be quantified as budgetary control indicators and budgetary control standards, and thus provides a basis and benchmarking control activities and strategic objective. This point of view coincides with the concept raised by Schiemann and Lingle, in which they stated that: should be clearly defined corporate strategy, quantify strategic objective and a culture of quantitative management will be established finally.[1]

The formation of the budgetary control indicators and standards mentioned above can be expounded by a concrete example of mature enterprises, as shown in Fig. 13.2. Most of the mature enterprises seek value maximization by setting steady operating and sustainable strategy. Under the guidance of this, the key to obtain strategic success is to achieve profit maximization and avoid risks. While, profit maximization can be achieved by way of boosting revenue and reducing cost as well as increasing and optimizing investment. When considering risk avoidance, three elements should be paid close attention to, namely quality of working capital, improvement of management level and control of financial risks. After setting KSFs and operating strategies, key performance indicators (KPI) can be determined, which include both financial and non-financial indicators. On financial grounds, KPI serves as budgetary control indicators. At the meantime, in line with strategic objectives and market predictions as well as historical and industrial standards, predicting level of budgetary control indicators can be set, that is, setting budgetary control standards. With the help of budgetary control indicators and standards, various layers of budgeting people may start to prepare their corresponding budgets.

In other words, on financial grounds, KPI and its predicting level may become control indicators and standards of the comprehensive budgetary form, which means that they both can be presented on the comprehensive budgetary form. The roles of

[1] Schiemann and Lingle [1].

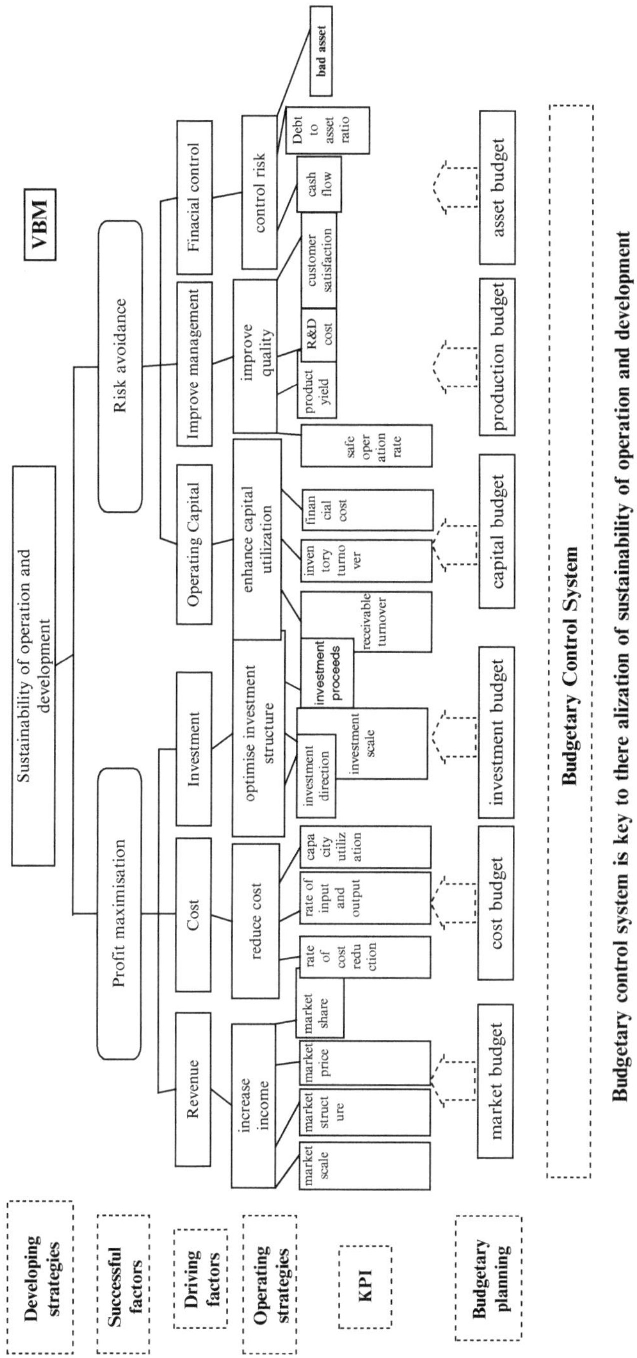

Fig. 13.2 The formation of budgetary control indicator and standards

control indicators and standards are that they provide the foundation of budgetary planning. For instance, when preparing budgetary income statement, enterprise may choose return on equity (ROE) as the control ratio of net profit and set related control standards. Net profit can be figured out according to the articulation between the items presented on the budgetary income statement, whereas, if the ratio of net profit and budgeted net asset can not reach the control standard of ROE, then the budgetary management department will require the budgetary preparation department to adjust other items on the budgetary income statement by means of raising revenue or cutting down cost or even adjusting them both. Accordingly, a series of relevant budgets need to be adjusted as well, for example, when increasing prime operating revenue, the budgeted prime operating revenue should be adjusted at the same time. As a result, enterprise's strategic objectives can be decomposed and implemented layer-by-layer along with establishing corresponding relationship with budgetary planning.

It is worth noting that budgetary control indicators and standards are not only the foundation of budgetary planning and balancing but also the basis of budgetary control and budgetary evaluation as well.

The content mentioned above elaborates the formation of strategic development and planning as well as budgetary control indicators and standards. While, generally speaking, how does the enterprise establish its indicator system of budgetary control and in what way does it set its budgetary control standards?

13.3.3.2 Setting Indicator System of Budgetary Control

Financial objective is the ultimate goal of the enterprise, which is closely related to organizational objective, thus it should mirror shareholders' increased value. In essence, all capital has its relevant cost and shareholders' value can only be improved by obtaining revenue which is higher than its cost of capital. With the help of Economic Value Added (EVA), enterprise is able to properly measure the increase of shareholder wealth. As a consequence, EVA should be the key indicator for evaluating value creation as well as in the indicator system of budgetary control. Thus, the budgetary control indicators can be distinguished into five aspects, which are value creation ability, profitability, growth ability, operation ability and debt-paying ability respectively. By regarding EVA as the core indicator, the indicator system may be decomposed layer-by-layer accordingly, and connections should be made between the system and the above five ability indicators. With reference to performance evaluation system of the owned-country capital, the fundamental choice of setting indicator system of budgetary control is shown in Fig. 13.3. The so-called fundamental choice only provides the scope which is the basis of forming indicator system of budgetary control. Actually, based on diverse background, enterprise may choose distinct fundamental choice indicators in its own way. Moreover, it may also design some special indicators to reflect the characteristics of its organization background. However, the amount of budgetary control indicators can not be too many or too few in that, too many may bring about 'information redundancy' and do not

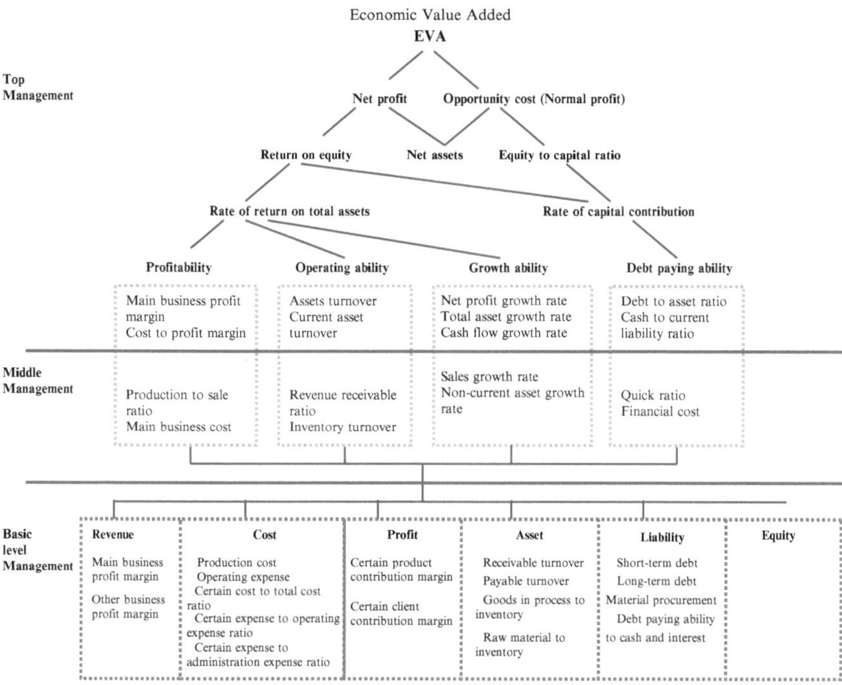

Fig. 13.3 Basic choices of budgetary control indicator system

conform to cost-effective principle, which may even result in ambiguous control objectives; too few makes it unable to completely reflect the content needed to be controlled and attend to one thing and lose another.

13.3.3.3 Setting of Budgetary Control Standards

During the process of setting budgetary control standards, the following four facets are noteworthy:

First of all, historical data should be combined with enterprise's status quo when making vertical analysis. The so-called historical data is the actual result of each performance evaluation indicator based on respective periods, which fully reflects the characteristics of organization background. A case in point is that a cement plant which is the subsidiary company of China Resources carries out balanced score card (BSC). In order to reduce operating cost, they set up a performance evaluation indicator – electricity consumption per ton. However, when they setting respective evaluating standards, they found that this indicator fluctuated with output ranging from 33.14 to 40 kwh, and how to handle the matter on earth? According to statistical analysis, they discovered that the year before last, the month maintaining optimum operating effect was when it reached the groove under current technology (during which period, the output of cement was the highest). As a consequence, the groove was scored 100 points, and according to the fluctuation scope over the years, the score was deducted 10 points each time when electricity consumption went up 10 %. It follows that accumulating, sorting and analyzing enterprise's historical data are key to the setting of performance evaluation standards.

Secondly, by means of horizontal comparison, benchmarking should be made with enterprises of the same industry or stereotype. Serving as the industry standards of evaluating performance, the value of specific indicator mirrors the external environment and technical features of enterprise. On the basis of industry standards, enterprises take into account of key organization background variables, such as external environment and technical features, when formulating prediction standards. But the problem is how to get access to historical data of industry. Gleaned from years of management consultancy, the following approaches can be applied to obtain the data: manual of performance evaluation standards of the owned-country capital (which is revised by the ministry of finance yearly and published accordingly); the data publicly disclosed by quoted company (such as the operating performance ranking list of quoted company announced by the media or management consulting firms); the statistic data of industry associations (a variety of industry associations frequently carry out statistic analysis to enterprises' operating performance); and the official statistical data (including statistic yearbook).

Thirdly, in order to perform strategic planning, KSFs and its logical relationship with strategic objectives should be clarified. Strategic planning and organization background are the premise and basis of the setting of budgetary control standards. During the process of strategic planning, the enterprise should take into account of not only its external environment but also the resources and abilities that can be employed.

Fourthly, other organization background variables, especially the influence of external environment and organizational structure, also need to be considered, thereby, the factors regarding controllable and non-controllable can be distinguished. The time of setting strategic planning may be not the same as that of setting budgetary control standards, while the organizational background is changing rapidly. As a consequence, when setting budgetary control standards in light of specific year, in addition to strategic planning, the changing of organizational background should also be regarded, such as conducting market predictions.

As mentioned above, the process of setting budgetary control standards should be shown as follows in Fig. 13.4.

13.3.4 Budgetary Control Methods

The concept of budgetary control methods falls on to a spectrum, with more inclusive, 'broad' views at one end and 'narrow' views placed at the other. The 'broad' view perceives budgetary control methods as the approaches applied in the budgetary

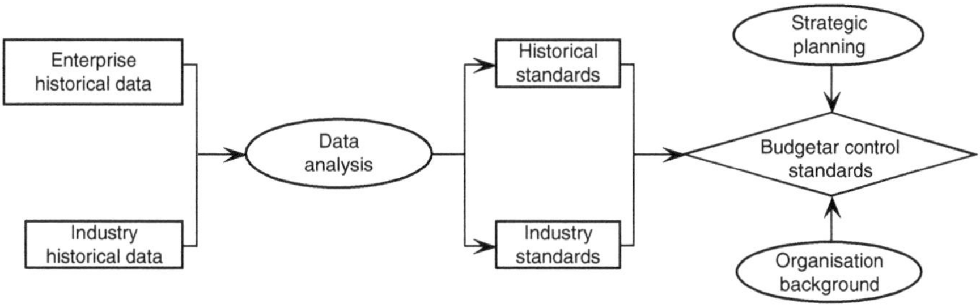

Fig. 13.4 Setting of budgetary control standards

control system, including four approaches, they are budgetary objective setting methods, budgetary planning methods, budgetary implementing methods and budgetary evaluating methods respectively. The budgetary objective setting methods have been discussed in previous section. Budgetary planning methods, i.e. the methods used during the process of budgetary planning. Similarly, budgetary implementing methods are used in the process of budgetary implementation, including budgetary implementation control methods, budgetary analysis control methods and budgetary adjustment control methods, which is the 'narrow' view of budgetary control methods as well as the main part of this Section.

13.3.4.1 Budgetary Planning Methods

A variety of methods can be adopted during the process of budgetary planning, such as fixed budgets and flexible budgets which are based on quantitative features of business; incremental budgets and zero-based budgets (ZBB) which are based on different starting point of budgetary planning; and regular budgets and rolling budgets which are based on different time period. Each type of budgetary planning has its own pros and cons; accordingly, when choosing budgetary planning methods, enterprise should attach great importance to application conditions and scope of the methods. As shown in Table 13.2.

13.3.4.2 Budgetary Implementing Methods

The control of budgetary implementation can be divided into four parts; they are budgetary authorization control, budgetary approval control, budgetary adjustment control and budgetary analysis control respectively.

Budgetary authorization control means that before implementing budgets, the related departments and staff must be authorized by certain approval procedures. By means of authorization control which belongs to beforehand control, the incorrect, improper and illegal economic behavior may be effectively eliminated before happening. As an important internal control approach, it is necessary for budgetary

Table 13.2 Classification and comparison of budgetary planning methods

	Planning method	Definition	Advantage	Disadvantage
Based on capacity	Fixed budget	It is a budget designed to remain unchanged irrespective of the level of activity actually attained	Easy to operate and the level of work is small	First, it is inflexible and rigid Second, it is uneasy to make comparison
	Flexible budget	It is a budget, which by recognizing the difference between fixed, semi-variable and variable costs is designed to change in relation to level of activity attained	First, a wider scope of budget Second, easy to make comparison	First, it is difficult to tell apart variable cost and fixed cost Second, if prepared manually, the amount of work is huge
Based on different starting point	Incremental budget	In light of base period, combined the amount of work and the measures to reduce cost, prepare the budget by way of adjusting related expenses	Easy to understand and implement	First, restricted by expenditure budget, which may in turn lead to protecting the lagging behind Second, result in egalitarianism and simplicity Third, hinder the future development of enterprise
	Zero-based budget	All budgets are based on zero that is starting from the reality	(1) Unrestricted by present expenditure budget (2) Encourage the initiative of reducing cost of all levels (3) Contribute to the future development of enterprise	It brings about vast amount of work and a long time to prepare which may lead to neglecting key point
Based on time period	Regular budget	Setting a constant budgetary period, usually same as accounting period	Coordination with accounting period makes it easy to evaluate the outcome of budgetary implementation	First, blindness Second, hysteresis Third, discontinuity
	Rolling budget	Method in which a budget established at the beginning of an accounting period is continually amended to reflect variances that arise due to changing circumstances	(1) Transparency (2) Timeliness; (3) Continuity, completeness and stability	The amount of work is large

control to set authorization items, permissions and amounts in advance. Budgetary authorization can be further split into budgets distribution, authorization within budgets and off-budget authorization. Budgets distribution refers to defining the decision-making power within the hierarchy during the process of budgetary management. In accordance with governance principles of separation of powers, decision making power of budgetary management should be split into three parts, they are decision-making, implementation and supervision. The board of directors and its affiliated budgetary management committee are the budgetary decision-making body. Management level including subsidiaries and divisions are the budgetary implementation body. Board of supervisors, office of budgetary management committee, financial department and internal audit department are the budgetary supervision body. Before carrying out budgetary management, the power of budgetary decision-making, budgetary implementation and budgetary supervision should be set and clarified in advance. Authorization within budgets means that the budgetary implementing departments and principals authorize normal business activities within scope of authority according to budgetary control standards. It stresses that matters within scope of budgets are decided by chief principal of the budgetary responsible division without asking superior for approval. Off-budgets authorization refers to giving the authorization to uncommon economic behaviors, which emphases those business activities or items beyond range of budgets must be managed by way of budget adjustment or budget super addition and be approved by an authorized person.

After the business activities have taken place, budgetary approval control performs intermediate control to business related reimbursement and appropriation by means of accounting information system. In order to achieve this, first of all, budgets should be combined with accounting and direct correspondence should be established between them. Thus the budgetary control system should be software-based and informationalized (centralized). By setting structural and systematic definitions, the correspondence between budgetary control items and accounting subjects can be clear and precise. During the process of budgetary implementation, when entering and saving accounting documents, instead of the accounting system we should first log-in budgetary control system which will automatically check whether expense budgets and capital budgets exceed relevant yearly and monthly budgetary control standards, and at the meantime, record expense and capital expenditure respectively, and in turn conduct control alert and balance control. As shown in Fig. 13.5, if the item is within budgets and does not exceed the alarm line, then it will enter into the accounting system; If it is within budgets but exceeds the alarm line, it can still enter into accounting system, meanwhile, the system will alarm related business department to control current expense and capital expenditure; If the items are within budgets but the amount exceeds budgets or belongs to off-budget item, they all need to enter into budgetary adjustment procedures. Consequently, it follows that budgetary approval control performs sound real-time and process control to business activities, reimbursement and capital appropriation.

Budget adjustment control means that when the enterprise experiences changes both internally and externally, a large deviation has emerged between budget and reality and thus the original budget will not apply to budgetary revision. Based on

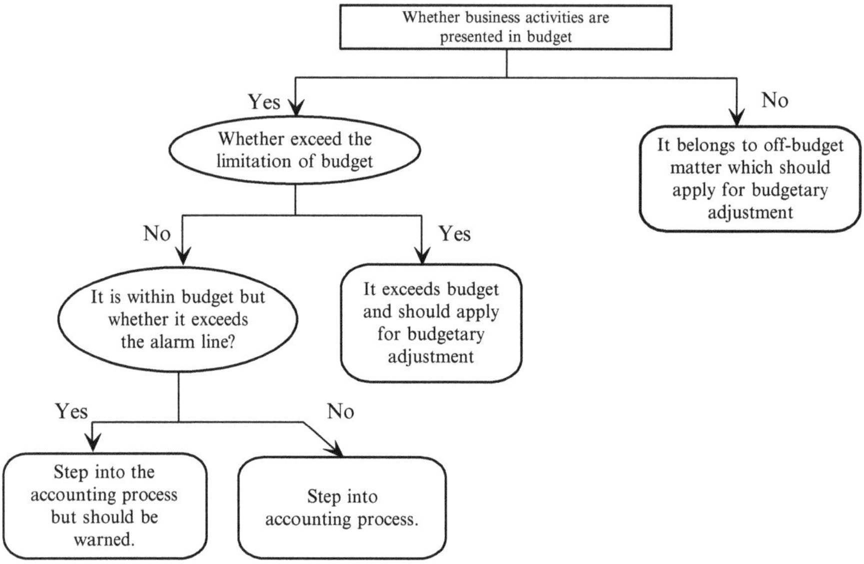

Fig. 13.5 Basic theory of control of budgetary approval

theory, in order to maintain the seriousness of budget, when implemented, it should not be changed easily. However, budget is not rigid or invariable. If significant changes have taken place after budgetary implementation, then budgetary adjustment should be taken into consideration, which embodies the flexibility of budget. The key point is that adjusting budgets should satisfy certain preconditions and follow approval procedures. In line with whether the adjustment has impact on overall budgetary control objectives, it can be divided into budgetary adjustment within objective and off-objective budgetary adjustment. Each type of budgetary adjustment has its own preconditions and approval procedures, thus enterprise should choose a suitable type as required. As a rule of thumb, when the premise of budgetary control objective has changed greatly, such as marketing environment and internal resources, off-objective budgetary adjustment should be performed. Generally, budgetary adjustment experiences three major procedures, namely application, examination and approval. As an unusual matter, budgetary adjustment involves the all aspect, consequently, its authority of examination and approval should be highly centralized. Off-objective budgetary adjustment has to be approved by budgetary management committee, while budgetary adjustment within objective should be approved by person or department that has relevant privileges.

13.3.5 Evaluation of Budgets Methods

In practice, more often than not, enterprises set budgets in a hurry, but the budget did not work well when implementing. In addition, the outcome of budgetary implementation has not been seriously analyzed or evaluated. At present, the analysis and evaluation of budget is the bottleneck of enterprise comprehensive budgetary control system in our country. Major causes of the phenomenon are as follows: (1) Unequal rights and obligations among budgetary departments makes it hard to perform analysis and evaluation. For instance, in some enterprises, service department is in charge of preparing procurement budgets, while the quantity and price of materials are determined by production department. (2) Budgetary analysis mainly focuses on horizontal and structural analysis, which takes little account of ratio and factor analysis. (3) The analysis and evaluation of budgets are not performed with systematism, standardization or tabulated. The budgetary analysis indicator system does not meet the objective of improving capital utilization, moreover, it neither establishes a full set of scientific budgetary analysis procedures, approaches or forms, nor performs post responsibility system of budgetary analysis. (4) Ambiguous incentives bring negative effects to enforcement of budgets. (5) It does not combine with advanced accounting measures.

The key to effective budgetary control is to enforce budgets strictly and enhance the analysis and evaluation of budgets. In order to achieve budgetary control objectives, the occurrence of each transaction should be connected with related budgetary items. In light of budgetary analysis, following measures may be taken:

First of all, set up scientific budgetary analysis procedures and approaches. Serving capital utilization as the analyzing objective, make full use of the Du Pont System to analyze budgetary implementation. Besides using horizontal and vertical analysis to find the deviation between actual result and budgets, factor and trend analysis should also be performed in relation to the deviation of significant matters.

Secondly, set up post responsibility system of budgetary analysis and formulate systematism, standardization and tabulated budgetary analyzing systems. Above all, the specifically formulated budgetary analyzing system defines the responsibility of each department, section and individual, meanwhile, it appoints specialized staff to perform analysis. Next, budgetary analysis should be performed periodically. While analysis and evaluation are efficient ways to see how the budget is performing, and accordingly, the adjustment of next budgetary figures and incentives can be set. Finally, in order to maintain high operability, a full set of budgetary analysis forms should be designed.

Thirdly, set up budgetary control software system. With the help of this, budgetary planning and analysis can be hardened into software program, which in turn improves efficiency of budgetary analysis and avoid the failures lead by human factors as well as strengthen the rigidity of budgetary control.

Fourthly, build budgetary system of rewards and penalties. This is for the purpose of avoiding budgetary implementation to become a mere formality, strengthening the sense of responsibility of related budgetary departments and individuals and insuring the realization of budgetary objectives.

13.4 Functions and Characteristics of Budgetary Control System

13.4.1 Functions of Budgetary Control

Budgetary control system is the small copy of management control system and rules of the game under corporate governance structure. It is a strategic supporting system that coordinates with enterprise's developing strategies as well as a management indicator system that is in line with business flow, capital flow, information flow and human resources flow of the whole enterprise. Moreover, it is a system of behavioral norms integrated into daily operation management. At the meantime, it is also a performance evaluation and incentive system which is connected with the year-end summary. All mentioned above are the reinterpretation of the significance of budgetary control systems which not only ties up budgetary control with overall operating flow, but also reveals the key role that budgetary control has played in the survival and development of enterprise in a deeper way. The functions of budgetary control system are set forth in four facets as follows:

13.4.1.1 Setting Objectives

As the decomposition and refinement of strategic objectives, budget is the implementation of enterprise's budgetary responsibility layer-by-layer, which is also the concrete action plan and measure of realizing budgetary objective of each department. When the profit target has been set, cost reduction target can be determined and so does the target of material cost reduction. For instance, based on performance of last year, the material cost needs to be cut down by 10 %, then the target may be discussed through a round table meeting and put into effect to related production department, technique department and procurement department, as shown in Fig. 13.6:

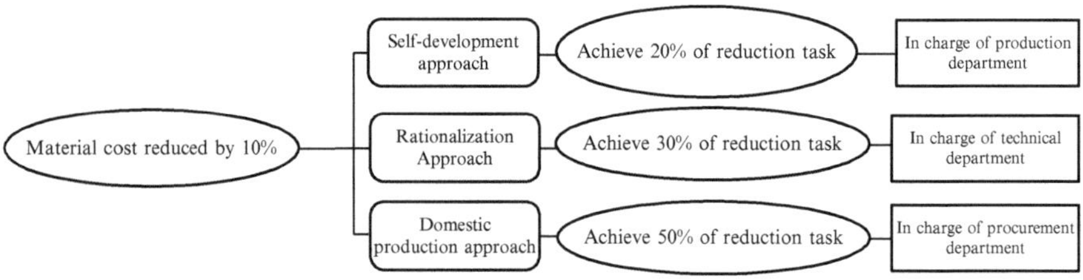

Fig. 13.6 Decomposition and implementation of realizing material cost reduction

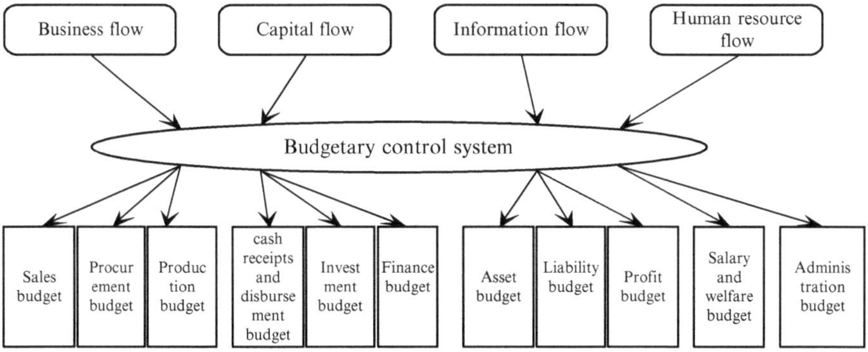

Fig. 13.7 The framework of budgetary control system on the basis of resources integration

13.4.1.2 Resource Integration

Resource is limited, consequently, during the process of realizing strategic objectives, conflicts among different units or individuals are unavoidable, such as long-term and short-term target, overall target and divisional target as well as targets within different departments. All that require enterprise to stand at the height of the overall strategy and based on set targets, make use of a kind of tool to effectively integrate various resources such as capital, technique, material and marketing channel, etc. It has been found that budgetary control system is such a tool as shown in Fig. 13.7.

13.4.1.3 Control Business

Control is a basic function in the budgetary control system, it runs through the process of operating activities. Budgetary planning is a type of beforehand control, and enforcement of budget is intermediate control, while, evaluation of budget is afterwards control. Especially, by making variance analysis between enforcement of budget and budgetary objective, problems can be discovered and solved in a timely manner, during the process of operation and management. Budgetary objective is the foundation of all kinds of business activities including expense reimbursement, capital appropriation and financial accounting, etc. If the item is within budget and conforms to budgetary objective, then it can be performed, contrarily, if the item is not included in the budget or the amount exceeds budget limits, then it needs to be approved. In this way, business activities can be effectively controlled, which in turn helps to realize strategic objectives.

13.4.1.4 Performance Evaluation

Budgetary control system has the function of 'pressing the evil and supporting the good', which means pressing the 'evil' of deviation of strategic objective, while supporting the 'good' of striving for strategic objective realization. The indicators and standards of budgetary control provide objective foundation for evaluating the performance of related departments and staff. Regularly or random check and evaluate the performance of each department, and make comparisons with budgetary objective to guarantee the realization of overall objective, and those are the key to effective management. While, it is noteworthy that the performance evaluation of staff who implements the budget should be incentive related, otherwise, without motivation and pressure, the budget will become a mere formality.

13.4.2 Characteristics of Budgetary Control System

In order to better design and implement budgetary control system, not only its strengths and weaknesses but also its application range and conditions should be taken into consideration.

In general, the advantages of budgetary control system are indicated as follows: defined quantitative criteria for organization behavior, tightly aligning overall objective with individual objective, and highlighting process control which helps to discover problems and correct deviations in a timely manner. To be specific, its merits mainly include:

1. Budgets adopt unified quantitative criteria which is convenient for measurement, integration and comparison.
2. Budgetary control system should coordinate with financial accounting system. The data and standards of budgets are based on the information of financial accounting system, and in turn the financial accounting system performs control in accordance with budgetary standards. Budgetary control system facilitates the development and perfection of financial accounting system.
3. Budgetary control tightly aligns the whole objective with individual objective. Its success has a direct impact on the realization of organization objective.
4. Budgetary control is a part of process control or real-time control. It helps to discover problems and correct deviations in a timely manner, meanwhile, it guards against financial and operating activities stepping into wrong directions.
5. Budget is the foundation of motivation whose premise is evaluation, while, evaluation should be based on budget. This kind of motivation or budgetary motivation fully arouses the enthusiasm of the whole staff to perform budgetary control.

In general, the disadvantages of budgetary control system are indicated as follows: the setting of budgetary control system is complicated. To some extent, it confines the subjective initiatives of managers and staff. The inflexibility of budgetary standards makes it uneasy to adapt to environmental changes. Specifically, its weaknesses are as follows:

1. Budgetary control restrains the initiative of both the person being controlled and the controller. During the process of budgetary control, both sides are performing their management or business activities in line with the budgetary standards.

When control environment changes, it is obvious that following original budgetary standards will lead to problems. However, under rigid budgets, both the controller and the controlled can only follow the budget and are reluctant or have no power to adjust it. If things continue like this, the initiative of both sides will be suppressed.

2. More often than not, budgetary control objective is inconsistent with enterprise (organization) objective. Speaking from the qualitative aspect, enterprise objective may be constant, that is, seeking capital appreciation. While, from the quantitative aspect, it is variable that is, pursuing more value. In view of static, budgetary objective is consistent with enterprise objective, while from the perspective of dynamic, the discrepancy is obvious, which is against the realization of enterprise objective.
3. In light of content, process and approaches, budgetary control is excessively complicated. As a kind of comprehensive control and process control, budgetary control involves people, business and departments of all levels. At the meantime, prepared by figures and currency, its systematicness and accuracy are expected much. These two points determine that budgetary control is a type of complicated control.
4. Budgetary control is adverse to improve efficiency and effectiveness. Perceived as the norms or targets, the setting of budgetary standards has its limitations, which in turn gives rise to the opposition and gambling between controller and the controlled. Neither incremental budget nor zero-based budget can avoid this weak point.

13.5 Application Conditions and Scope of Budgetary Control System

13.5.1 Environment of Budgetary Control System

Control environment involves various aspects, namely corporate strategy, organization structure, responsibility center, human resource and corporate culture, etc. Environment of budgetary control system should include a defined strategy (including strategic objectives, strategic programming and strategic planning), certain human resource quality and a sound corporate culture. Specially, proper organization structure and responsibility center are indispensable. The organization structure is crucial to budgetary control system.

13.5.1.1 Mechanism and Organization of Budgetary Control

The design of budgetary control system involves a series of stages, ranging from enterprise objective and strategy to budgetary objective, planning, implementation and analysis, etc. The realization of targets in each link is rest upon budgetary control mechanism, which in turn forms the basis of budgetary control system.

The organizational system of budgetary control lies at the heart of budgetary control mechanism. Whether the budgetary control organization is scientifically designed or not, will have a great impact on the functions of budgetary control. In China, the organizational system is usually divided into three levels, that is, budgetary committee – the standing body of budgetary committee (financial department) – each competent department of budget. In theory, this kind of organizational structure is beneficial to the realization of budgetary control system. But in practice, the following points are noteworthy:

First of all, strengthen the functions of budgetary committee and highlight its importance to budgetary control system. In practice, the budgetary committee in some enterprises performs practically no function and does not play its due role. In order to avoid this, the functions of budgetary committee must be definite and complete, for example, major issues including the design of budgetary objective, standard and evaluation should be decided by the budgetary committee. Moreover, the committee should hold meetings on regular basis and form institutionalized and standardized management. Meanwhile, budgetary committee has to maintain a standing body to carry out resolutions.

Committee of budgetary management lies at the heart of organization system. Acting as the agent of board of directors, it handles and decides matters of significant importance. Principal of the committee is the chairman or chief executive director, and other members are consisted of people in charge of relevant departments, such as the vice manager of sales department, production department and financial department, etc. As with budgetary management, committee of budgetary management is the top governing body and its main duties are as follows:

1. Drafting relevant documents regarding policies, regulations and systems of budgetary management;
2. Putting forward overall objectives, general principles and preparation basis of annual budget and submitting them to board of directors for approval;
3. Examining capital investment and project budgets of the enterprise;
4. Checking the draft budgets prepared by each department and the overall budgetary bill, commenting and amending them as appropriate, and submitting them to board of directors for approval;
5. Coordinating the conflicts between and among departments during the process of budgetary planning and enforcement of budget;
6. Coming up with improvement suggestions to budgetary organization, planning and control;
7. Presenting examined budget to the board of directors, and issuing formal budget when approved by the board;
8. Attentively analyzing and studying the periodic budgetary report which compares budget with reality, and comment on it;
9. As needed, examining and determining the adjustment of budget;
10. Reconciling and arbitrating the conflicts during the process of budgetary management;
11. Considering the rewards and penalties program that proposed by budget task force, and submit it to the board for approval.

Secondly, improve the status of financial department in budgetary control system, meanwhile, great importance should be attached to it when making budgetary planning, control and analysis. In practice, there are various ways of setting the standing body of budgetary management. While, we hold the view that setting financial department as the standing body is more scientific. Nowadays, owing to the financial-oriented management, the enterprise budget will also be centered in financial budget. Naturally, as the standing body of budgetary committee, the terms of reference of financial department enlarge greatly. At the same time, budgetary committee should make it clear that financial department is its executing agency and in charge of comprehensive budgetary planning, analysis and control.

Thirdly, establish and perfect hierarchical budgetary control system. To some extent, internal control system is also a kind of authorization system. Thus, besides setting primary budgets, to some major departments and projects, more detailed secondary budgets should be established. Set an integrated budgetary control system that consists of a set of procedures, including budgetary planning, implementation, control and analysis, and make each budget-related department to perform its own functions as well as setting the relationship which is equal with responsibility, authority and benefit.

13.5.1.2 Setting of Responsibility Center

Setting of responsibility center is a basic requirement of budgetary control. The responsibility center refers to a unit that can control cost, revenue and capital appropriation within certain limits. It is a combination of responsibility, authority and benefit. In order to better monitor and conduct business activities, enterprise should be split into several progressive responsibility centers, which are closely related to organizational structure. In hierarchical management, according to terms of reference, responsibility centers can be classified as investment center, profit center and cost center. The classification of responsibility centers is essential to budgetary control system in that, the centers are in charge of implementing budgets. During this process, the following points are noteworthy:

First of all, the classification should have clear hierarchy. In order to effectively control business activities, enterprise should be divided into several progressive responsibility centers. Each center programs and controls a part of business activities and accountable to its performance.

Secondly, balance rights and responsibility. Responsibility centers assume their liabilities according to respective operating decision rights, which means that decision rights bring about corresponding economic responsibilities. As a result, when setting responsibility center, economic responsibilities must be in line with decision rights, which will prevent power abuse.

Thirdly, production and operating performances should be clearly defined. In other words, responsibility must be specific, defined and measurable.

Fourthly, the classification of responsibility centers should be combined with business process reengineering.

13.5.2 *Basis of Budgetary Control*

Besides environmental aspect, in order to running budgetary control system effectively, the following aspects should also be taken into consideration:

13.5.2.1 Decentralized Management

Budget is directly linked to organization structure. According to the degree of power concentration, organization can be divided into centralized and decentralized organizations. In a centralized organization, decision rights are centralized on top management whose decisions, orders and instructions must be followed by subordinates. While in a decentralized organization, top management delegates part of authority to lower levels, which enables them to control some of the resources and solve a few problems independently. Organization structure plays a key role in budget participation. In a decentralized organization, if there is a high budget participation, manager will feel that his involvement is the key to the budget, and then a strong sense of achievement arises. On the contrary, the centralized organization stresses less on budget participation. Consequently, the decentralized management that encourages full involvement during the process of budgetary planning, enhances the feasibility and reliability of budgetary indicators, which is beneficial to effective allocation of resources. Moreover, it arouses the self-awareness of employees when implementing budgets, which in turn improves efficiency. Meanwhile, it helps to exchange information among departments and between staff and enterprise. In addition, delegating daily operating authority to relevant responsibility center, enables the centers to act according to actual circumstances in a timely fashion and fully mobilizes employees' initiatives and creativity.

13.5.2.2 Business Process Reengineering (BPR)

BPR involves a fundamental rethinking and redesign of business processes, organization structures and use of technology, to achieve "breakthroughs" in business competitiveness, such as cost, quality, service and speed. During the process of budgetary control, ranging from budgetary planning, enforcement of budget to evaluation of budget, a series of stages should be set up, and among them is BPR. With the development of enterprise, certain problems might emerge, they are: disjunction of organization performance and strategy, strategic programming lacks support of organization; ambiguous positioning of holding groups and parent-subsidiary relationships, the contradictions between centralization and decentralization are gradually highlighted, whilst, standardization and flexibility are difficult to coordinate; a sheer size of organization, arbitrarily setting of departments, unsmooth information channels, loss of information and information distortion, etc. If performed under such circumstances, the outcome is not optimistic. The basic environment of budgetary control system is organizational institution. Thus, when performing the system, organizational structure should be clear and definite. But this does not mean that only when organizational structure is clear and definite, can budgetary control system be performed. In fact, there are interactions between budgetary control and organizational process, they complement each other. In many cases, they are inseparable. In order to implement budgetary control, certain matters must be defined, namely responsibility centers (including investment center, profit center and cost center), management duty (such as business items, time, amount of capital, etc.), information collection and feedback report. All that request enterprises set up specific business process, framework, mainline of management and control points. Business process reengineering should be centered on customer and strategy-oriented. Based on optimizing system process, by performing activity analysis it establishes activity center, whilst by performing process analysis it establishes process center and finally forms a three-tier structure, that is tactical level, managerial level and operating level.

13.5.2.3 Management Information System (MIS)

MIS refers to the system that provides information to all levels of management and staff inside and outside of organization and which is also crucial to management control. Without a favorable MIS, the ideal results of budgetary control cannot be achieved. In a MIS, the information includes budget information, accounting information, statistic information and business information, etc. In view of budgetary control, the information quality of accounting, statistic and business play a key role in performing budgetary control system. As a consequence, MIS must meet the following requirements:

Above all, information should satisfy the need of budgetary control relevance, which means that all kinds of information including financial accounting, statistic accounting and business accounting are serving for budgetary control.

Secondly, the time of information should cater to the timeliness of budgetary control. Budgetary control is process control, as a result, accounting related information and report should be as promptly as possible. In order to achieve this, traditional stereotype of afterwards accounting needs to be changed, moreover, updated information management technique needs to be utilized, such as Enterprise Resource Planning (ERP).

Thirdly, information technology should conform to the reality of budgetary control. The truthfulness of information is the key to control. Many reasons may lead to false information. From the professional angle, misappropriation of accounting technique is a major point. Budgetary control system requires a scientific and reliable information accounting technique, which includes financial accounting technique and other business accounting technique.

13.5.3 Application Conditions of Budgetary Control System

Same as system control, budgetary control system can be applied to all kinds of organizations and enterprises. Whereas, it is difficult to set and implement budgetary control for enterprises whose management and basis are relatively bad. As for the good ones, it is easier, but if they overemphasize budgetary control, then the subjective initiatives might be constrained.

Reference

1. Schiemann WA, Lingle JH (2001) Corporate quantitative management implementation, 1st edn. China Machine Press, Beijing

Chapter 14
The Mode of Evaluation Control System

14.1 Definition of Evaluation Control System

As a mode of management control systems, evaluation control systems have a few subsystems, which include strategic planning, evaluation indexes, evaluation procedures and methods, evaluation reports, rewards and punishment. Especially, the evaluation indexes contain the choices, the standards and the calculation of the indexes.

14.1.1 Strategic Planning

Strategic planning is the start of the management control systems. Similar with budgetary control, evaluation control treats evaluation goals as a start. So both the strategic planning and evaluation goals are the starting point of evaluation control operating of systems, and the evaluation goals are the purpose and guidelines of the operation of the whole system. They decide the choices of evaluation indexes, the set of evaluation criteria and the determination of evaluation methods. The strategic planning should be established on the basis of strategic goals and planning, and the set of the evaluation goals has should be based on the strategic planning. Only these can help to realize the strategic goals and planning. When a corporation going to set and carry out the evaluation control systems, it has to analyze the circumstance, make a strategic plan on the basis of external environment and internal resources of the corporation, and determine the Key Success Factors (KSFs) to set a proper goal. The KSFs are the decisive factors, which affect the corporation and its subordinate organizations to obtain the competitive advantages and to realize the success of strategies. It can be reflected by strategic planning, connecting with the whole corporation strategic goals, and also be represented by the evaluation indexes, affecting and controlling the business activities. Not only financial factors are included in the KSFs, but also the non-financial factors. On the one hand, the financial results

X. Zhang, *Enterprise Management Control Systems in China*, Understanding China,
DOI 10.1007/978-3-642-54715-7_14, © Springer-Verlag Berlin Heidelberg 2014

reflect comprehensive and subsequent event, they have the hysteresis and short-term effect. On the other hand, the non-financial activities are the essential factor to improve the financial results. Many corporation activities proved that non-financial factors eventually affect the financial performance.

14.1.2 Evaluation Index

The establishment of the evaluation indexes is not only the implementation of the evaluation goals, but also the process of dividing KSFs into specific responsibility goals and then giving orders to the practitioners. The reason why the KSFs have to be divided into evaluation indexes is that it is the decisive factor for the corporation and its subordinate organizations. It can only reflect limited aspects. After the governance quantified and divided the comprehensive goals, it becomes manipulative and has clear responsibility.

14.1.3 Evaluation Process and Evaluation Method

Evaluation process is the process to perform evaluation control. The research and establishment of the evaluation control is the foundation and basis of internal evaluation control. It points the direction of the work. Whether the evaluation process is correct or not, it will affect the extent of accuracy of the eventually result. It concludes several steps as follow, establishing the evaluation goals, choosing the evaluation index, setting the evaluation standard, deciding the evaluation method, calculating the evaluation result, putting forward the evaluation conclusion and dealing with the evaluation result.

Evaluation method, which deals with the matter of how to evaluate, is to obtain the evaluation result by using certain methods, evaluation indexes and standards. Evaluation index and standard will lose their functions and become isolated evaluation factor without scientific evaluation methods.[1] There are three methods widely used in practice, they are single evaluation method, comprehensive evaluation method and multi-perspective balanced evaluation method.

14.1.4 Evaluation Report

Evaluation report is the output information and the summarize document of evaluation control systems. The subject of evaluation obtains the related information about the object through the management control systems. Then it come to the conclusion

[1] Rui Zhang [1].

and formulate the evaluation report after processing and calculating the evaluation indexes, comparing the actual and preset standards, analyzing the reason of variances, responsibilities and effects.

No matter what the evaluation report is, it contains evaluation goals, evaluation indexes, evaluation standards, actual performance, variance measurement, variance analysis, evaluation report, suggestions about rewards and punishment, etc. The preparation of the evaluation report should follow several steps, such as calculating evaluation indexes, measuring and analysing variances, reaching the evaluation conclusion, making suggestions about rewards and punishment. Particularly, the essential steps are variance measurement and analysis. The process of designing, preparing, transferring and reporting should obey the following principles. Firstly, adapting to the organization structure and dividing the responsibility center correctly. Secondly, distinguishing the important and unimportant items, and paying attention to the exceptions. Thirdly, dividing the differences which are controlled and uncontrolled, and ensuring the main point of the control. Fourthly, formulating rules and procedures, and regulating the frequency and the useful time of reports.

14.1.5 Rewards and Punishment

Evaluation report is not the final goal of evaluation control systems and the last procedure of evaluation control process. Its essentially purpose is to be an instrument of management, then accelerate managers to improve the operating efficiency by necessary activities. So, the process of evaluation control is not only to prepare the evaluation report, but also to reward or punish the managers by comparing the actual performance with the evaluation standard and then analyzing the reasons. By doing this, on the one hand, it can motivate managers to work harder. On the other hand, it can punish the poor performance managers or sectors after analyzing the objective and subjective reasons. In other words, dealing with the evaluation result correctly and implementing the rewards and punishment can lead to a good circulation of evaluation control.

The long-term effectively running of the evaluation control systems could be guaranteed only if the evaluation control result is linked with the remuneration of managers. However, practically many corporations separate the remuneration plan from performance evaluation. For example, human resources department rather than performance evaluation department design the compensation planning, and it is a widespread phenomenon in China. It will raise the problem that the compensation planning didn't appropriate to the performance evaluation department. The compensation planning contains many factors, which reflect the management choices. It is necessary to distinguish five aspects when designing the compensation planning and implement the rewards and punishment. The first one is financial compensation and substance compensation. The second one is moral incentive and substance incentive. The third one is long-term incentive and short-term incentive. The fourth one is compensation measurement based on formula or subjective judgment. The last one is team reward and individual reward.

14.2 Contents of Evaluation Control System

As one of the internal management control modes, the subjects and objects of evaluation control systems are internal managers. The evaluation goals are reflected by evaluation indexes and the evaluation process contains other elements such as choosing the evaluation index, setting the evaluation standards, deciding the evaluation method, etc. So, the mainly parts of the evaluation control systems are evaluation index, evaluation standard and evaluation methods.

14.2.1 Evaluation Index

Choose the evaluation index is the essential part in setting the evaluation control systems. Whether the choice of evaluation index is correct or not can entirely reflect the performance of the object of evaluation, then directly influence the performance evaluation results.[2] The evaluation indexes should have the character of congruity and precision. Several principles about how to choose the evaluation index are as follows:

14.2.1.1 Connecting the Result Indicators with the Driver Indicators

Result indicators reflect the financial results when corporations achieve the strategic goals, such as the improvement of main business income. While the driver indicators reflect the driving factors to realize the strategic goals. For example, good customer satisfaction may be the important way to improve the prime operation revenue. The result indicators, which similar with lagging index, only tell managers matters already happened and reflect the final results. So managers cannot influence the indicators directly. But managers can influence the operation factors and the driver indicators, which could reflect the reasons why the final result change in a lower operation level. In this way, setting result standards can make managers realize the implication of strategic goal. Setting driver indicators can make managers concentrate on the essential aspect of the corporation and know the way to realize the strategic goals.

It is necessary to mention that although the result indicators have close relationship with the driver indicators, it doesn't mean the driver indicators have the similar

[2]The more accurate definition of the quality characteristics of performance evaluation is the quality requirements, which should be possessed by a performance evaluation index or a set of performance evaluation index system [2]. The so-called congruity means the consistent degree between the impact which the agent behavior affect the performance index and the impact which the agent behavior affect the expected revenue; The precision means the accuracy level which performance index reflect the agent's effort, or the impact level which uncontrolled events (noise) affect the performance index.

questions when the result indicators have. Such as the driver indicator shows the implementation of the strategy is good, but the result indicator shows something wrong. In this situation, it means the choice of result indicators has some problem. It also means maybe we should alter the strategy.

14.2.1.2 Integrating the Financial Index with Non-financial Index

The advantages of financial index are accountable and measurable. But its poor consistency shows in the following aspects. First, it concerns a lot about acquiring and maintaining the short-term financial result, neglects the long-term benefit and the creation of the future value. Second, it is confined to measure financial results about past activities and fails to disclose the key driver indicators, which can improve the operating performance in the strategic level. Third, it cannot be recognized, measure and report the intangible assets and intellectual assets, cannot reflect the whole factors of the corporation performance.

Compared with financial index, non-financial index can improve the consistency and accuracy of the performance evaluation. But the non-financial index also has several problems. First, some indexes cannot be measured. It may lead to subjective randomness and influence the accuracy of the performance evaluation. When it comes to a corporation, however, not all the factors of operating performance can be reflected through the measurement. So, it is necessary for corporation to combine the quantitative index with the qualitative index. Second, the improvement of the non-financial index cannot be reflected by the currency. The ambiguous exist between the relationship of the improvement of non-financial indexes and financial results. In result, it is hard to distinguish the extent that the improvement of non-financial index changes the financial results. The financial results hardly influenced especially in the short-term. Third, some non-financial indexes conflict with each other. Some indexes improved at the cost of other indexes. It may cause the conflict within the department or between the departments. It may also exacerbate the inconsistent problem of performance evaluation and cause managers hard to make right decisions.

14.2.1.3 Integrating the Internal Index with External Index

Internal index is the operating performance index, which is evaluated by the internal stakeholders such as internal operation managers and employees. The goal of performance evaluation is to meet the demand of internal production and operation management, such as inventory turnover ratio. External index is the operating performance index, which is evaluated by the external stakeholders such as shareholders and customers. The goal of performance evaluation is to meet the demand of shareholders and customers, such as return of equity. Corporations have to balance the internal index and external index. Balanced Scorecard is a performance evaluation system, which emphasize the balance between the internal index and external index and take account of interest of different stakeholders.

Some corporations sacrifice its internal improvement to meet the investors' demands by increasing external performance or neglect external performance when they mistakenly consider their internal performance is good. Actually, shareholders, customers, managers and employees are the main participants in the corporations. The corporation strategy will not be achieved without them. Each kind of stakeholders has their own interest goals. Meeting their goals and balance their interests are essential factors to make sure the sustained development of corporations. Strategic goals will be hard to realize if neglecting the interest goal of either side.

14.2.1.4 Integrating Indexes Based on Different Calculation Methods

Financial index can be divided into four types according to different calculation methods: accounting income index, market income index, economic returns index and cash flow index. We always establish the evaluation control systems based on three types except market income index. Because it can only be used for the overall evaluation of listed corporations and cannot be used as performance evaluation for department managers.[3] Different indexes have their own characters. We should select indexes according to evaluation goals when create internal evaluation index system.

The financial income indexes have several drawbacks. The first one is the choice of accounting policy and accounting method, the preparation of financial report is flexible. They lead to a high percent of profit manipulation. The second one is the financial income indexes are hysteresis and have short-term effect. The last one is financial income indexes didn't take all capital costs into account. It can only explain the debt capital cost and neglect the compensation of cost of equity capital. So, it cannot reflect real operating performance.

The economic returns index is difficult to measure. EVA and other indexes, however, make up this weakness. Compared with financial income indexes, EVA has a lot of advantages. First, EVA can reveal the real performance of the corporation by considering the cost of equity capital. Second, to eliminate the inherent effect caused by accounting standards, some adjustments are necessary when calculate the EVA. Third, because of paying attention to the long-term development, EVA can reflect non-financial activities, such as products and human resources development,. Last, EVA is related to enterprise value and favors to safeguard the interests of stakeholders. As a result-based financial performance index, EVA has its limitations too. In contrast, even though financial income indexes have drawbacks, some of them are the basis of economic returns, such as pre-tax profit and return on equity, and some of them can connect with middle managers, such as responsibility centers below the investment center. Because of this, when choosing

[3] Market income index reflects the corporate operating performance based on the share prices in stock market. It includes the market value per share, total market value, market value added (MVA), excess returns and future growth value (FGV), total shareholder return (TSR), etc. These kind of index were affected by many uncontrolled factors.

the internal management performance indexes, the application of economic returns indexes should combine with accounting income indexes.

Except for economic returns index, another type of index used in recent years is the cash flow index. Cash flow can comprehensively reflect the changes of financial position in a given period, and can correctly reflect the quality of corporation profits. Besides, it is hardly influenced by managers. But it cannot reflect the real annual operating performance in the responsibility center, because it has defects in the aspect of recognize and matching. The combination of financial income index with cash flow index can reflect the profits quality better. Except for CVA, Free Cash Flow and Cash Flow Return on Investment are in common use too.

14.2.2 Evaluation Standard

It is necessary to set the evaluation standard after choosing evaluation indexes. How to design the evaluation standard is an essential problem in establishing the performance evaluation index system. There are three pairs of contradictions in the process of forming the evaluation standards.

14.2.2.1 Conflicts Between Relative Basis and Absolute Basis

The standard to divide absolute basis and relative basis is treating actual performance or others as basis. Actual performance is always used as performance evaluation standard in practice,[4] but it is not comfort to the agency theory and also cannot reflect the nature of management control systems. Because of the principal-agent relationship existing between managers and operators, their relationship has non-equilibrium characters, such as different utility functions, information asymmetry and incomplete contract. Therefore, because of the difference of goal function between the consignor and agent and unsymmetrical information between them, many obstacles exist when managers distinguish interferences of absolute basic indexes. Evaluators naturally choose reference under the guidance of comparison.[5] From the perspective of management control, in order to realize the organization goals, the natural of management control is not only to discover deviations between reality and plan, but also to take measures to correct deviations. More important purpose of performance evaluation is to induce agent activities to realize strategic goals. So the performance evaluation only determines the evaluation index, it is not unadvisable to set the target value. To make sure the operating activities in accordance with the strategic goals and plans, managers have to supervise and control the operating in uncertain environment. Therefore, it is necessary to choose standards to guide the operating process.

[4] For example, the profit commission method, which means that executive compensation is calculated by a certain proportion from the realized profit, was used in the process of state-owned enterprises reform in China.

[5] Xiaoqiang Zhi [3].

14.2.2.2 Conflicts Between Different Relative Basis

There are three mainly evaluation standards in the performance evaluation control systems. The first one is the historical standard. This standard regards the average or weighted average performance of one or more historical periods as the criteria. The second one is the industry standard. Industry standard is developed in accordance with industry. It reflects the basic level of financial statement and operating performance in an industry. Both the average level and the advanced level can be used in it. The third one is the budgetary standard. It is a standard set by a company in accordance with its operating conditions and operating statements.

Each standard has its advantages and disadvantages. The advantages of historical standard are higher reliability and comparability. But it can only be applied to vertical comparison but not to horizontal comparison. As a result, it is impossible to obtain an understanding of the strategies and performances of competitors. Neither is it possible to estimate the positions and levels of the entity in the same industry. Because historical standards can only reflect the past, not the present operating environment, the other disadvantage of historical standard is that it lacks the flexible adaptability. Potential irrational factors, such as the effects caused by inflation, calculation diameters and calculation methods, should be removed when considering about the historical performance.

During the process of evaluation, the historical standard will be good to filter the effects caused by systematic uncontrollable factors and will strengthen the relevance between the levels of performance evaluation and hardworking.[6] To evaluate the performance of managers it is necessary to discriminate controllable factors from uncontrollable factors. Two aspects are included in the uncontrollable factors. One is the unsystematic risk, which is caused by the division of rights and responsibilities in the corporate governance structure and is beyond the management's control. Another is the systematic risk. The effects made by this kind of risk can't be avoided by any sector in the corporate governance structure alone.[7] If the industry standard is selected, it will be more conductive to eliminate potential impact made by the systematic risk factors. Though the comparison between the levels of the entity and the industry average or advanced levels, not only can company fairly evaluate the management's performance and ignore the different results between controllable and uncontrollable factors, but also reflect the changes of the competitiveness of the entity. Moreover, the comparison will enhance the concerns of the management on competition [5].

The budgetary standard has its obvious advantages, for it combines the industry standard and the historical standard. It has certain rationality and can describe a rather complete statement of an entity. The differences between fact and budget could show that some aspects or works have defects. That means if one or more sectors cannot reach the goal of the operators, the next step is to analyze the reasons and take measures to make up. It should be noted that the budgetary standard is

[6] Holmstrom [4].

[7] Pingli Li [5], pp. 144–145.

more or less influenced by human and is lack of objective basis. More importantly is that the budgetary standard can only consider the financial strategy and leave non-financial activities alone, which is not complete enough. The only way to solve the former problem is to try the best to choose the correct method. And the key to the latter is to expand the budget so that it accommodates all business activities in the strategy plan.

In the above we discuss the advantages and disadvantages of different standards, which based on different bases. The conclusion is when designing an evaluation standard we should combine the three standards together instead of one. Of course, in the actual operating process we can select a main standard and choose other standards as supplements.

14.2.2.3 Conflicts Between Personal Basis and Group Basis

The character of evaluation objective plays an important role in choosing the evaluation standards. Although it has been clarified previously, it is still possible for evaluation to aim at a manager or a management group. Differences exist between a person and a group. It leads to the third pair of conflictions when choosing the evaluation standards, personal basis and group basis.

If selecting personal basis as performance evaluation standards, it can better reflect the principle of incentive, and clarify responsibilities and rights of different individuals. But for some departments or jobs, it is difficult to separate the performance of individual with others clearly. Even though it can be clearly separated, the opportunity cost is too high. For a department, which needs to rely on teamwork rather than individuals to achieve performance targets, if dividing group performance into individual performance, there is a high possibility to generate a negative incentive effect and then lead to the declination of performance. Zhi Xiaoqiang [3] holds the view that the contradiction between personal basis and group basis is the incentive problem of the group, the choice of personal basis or group basis reflect the preferences of evaluators-cooperation or independent. The information asymmetry is the core problem, because the information about marginal contribution to the overall performance of the managers cannot be obtained or obtained with a high cost, the evaluators should use group basis method. At the same time, the behavior of free rider should be prevented or reduced, which is to clarify all managers' responsibilities in order to achieve the performance evaluation goals.

Correctly handle the relationship between performance evaluation on departments and managers is another issue. Because the uncontrollable factors exist, department performance and managers' performance should be separated when evaluating the performance. Factors, which influence department performance, derive from the external environment and the management means that used by managers.[8] Environmental restrictions are "uncontrollable" variables, management means are

[8] Shengli Du [6].

"controllable" factors, and functions exist between evaluation target and managers. Specially, uncontrollable factors refer to the managers, the generation and variation of these factors are unpredictable and uncontrolled. The external environment factors are uncontrollable factors, which inevitably affect department performance. It is called systematic uncontrollable factors. How to consider these kinds of factors affected managers' performance evaluation has been discussed earlier, we will not discuss it again. Because of the power of managers and division of responsibilities are different, department managers can only be responsible for controlled factors in a part of organizations, such as subsidiary corporations or branch corporations. The factors that are uncontrollable should be excluded when evaluating the performance.[9] Effects from this type of uncontrollable factors to internal management performance can be removed, so it is called non-systematic uncontrollable factors. Removing method is to analyze uncontrollable factors and its influence on the operators' performance. But what should be noted is that the determination of uncontrollable factors and method to determine the effective amount should be specified when determining the evaluation standards. A consensus should also be reached between the assessment and evaluation. Otherwise it will affect the incentive effect of evaluation control and leave risks for the implementation of future performance evaluation and the corresponding compensation plans.[10]

14.2.3 Evaluation Method

When establishing the evaluation index and evaluation standard, evaluation method should be ascertained. There are three kind of methods widely used in practice. They are single evaluation method, comprehensive evaluation method and multi-perspective balanced evaluation method.

14.2.3.1 Single Evaluation Method

Single evaluation method is using single index, calculating the index of actual value, and comparing with evaluation standards, then making evaluation conclusions for operating performance. EVA evaluation system is essentially a single evaluation method. It measures the difference between capital gains and capital cost. The father of American management, Peter Drucker, argues that EVA is a kind of key index, which measures total factor productivity. The advantages of using EVA index lies

[9] In management accounting, for example, evaluating the operating performance of manager in profit center generally separate the fixed cost into controllable and uncontrollable cost. It is because some costs, such as advertising and insurance, are uncontrolled by department managers even it can be traced back to the relevant departments. So the uncontrollable cost should be removed when evaluating the performance of department managers.

[10] Pingli Li [5], p. 145.

in: First, correct some errors and distortions generated by the current accounting standards through accounting adjustment. The application of the accrual basis and prudence principle makes the accounting profit difficult to reflect the actual operating performance and makes accounting profit easily be manipulated. For example, R&D cost, marketing costs, and training costs obviously create value for the company from a long-term perspective, but they are recorded in expenses instead of capital under the current accounting policy. Second, bring the concept of capital cost into the performance evaluation system, not only consider the cost of debt capital, but also consider the cost of equity capital. The calculation of equity capital reflects the minimum returns of risk constraints required by shareholders. Shareholder value can only be created by the premium of the cost of capital profit.

Two essential parts to use EVA evaluation method are the Identification of EVA center and the calculation of EVA index.

The Identification of EVA Center

EVA center means the business units can use EVA as criteria to measure and evaluate the performance of enterprise. This kind of units usually has relatively independent transactions, such as production of goods, sales of certain products, provisions of some products or services. They have relatively independent income statement and balance sheet, or can influence or control the complete items in income statement and the balance sheet. There is a manager (or a group managers) responsible to the operating performance of this unit (EVA value). They have the right to manage this unit performance. Relatively, non-EVA center cannot use EVA to measure and evaluate its internal unit.

Whether to establish EVA center or not depends on the following conditions. (1) Whether the incomes exist or whether the incomes can be measured (whether have the internal transfer prices). (2) Whether engender costs or whether the costs can be identified (whether a reasonable allocation method for public cost exist). (3) Whether should capital be occupied, or whether the occupied capital should be identified (whether a reasonable allocation method of public capital exist). (4) The incomes, costs and capital in this center should be controlled for the person in charge.

Generally, head offices, subsidiary corporations, branch corporations, independent departments and project groups are representatives of EVA center. While the non-EVA centers is mainly concentrated in the finance department, human resources department and R&D department.

The Calculation of EVA

Cited hereby is the example of EVA evaluation method, which carried out by Chinese central enterprises to illustrate the problem. The EVA evaluation method was first officially performed by SASAC of the State Council in central enterprises 2010. The implementation of current EVA in our country is still at initial stage. Complicated calculation rules will reduce the feasibility of EVA, and differences still exist between Chinese accounting standards and international accounting standards. Based on this, the SASAC revised the EVA accounting adjustment items in "temporary method for operating performance evaluation in central enterprises" on December 28, 2009. It mainly concentrated on the adjustment of interest expenses, R&D expenses and extraordinary gains (see Table 14.1). At the same time, it

Table 14.1 Accounting adjustment regulations in computing EVA from SASAC

Adjustment basis	Adjustments		Adjustment method	Adjustment meaning	Adjustment instructions
Net income	Interest expense		Remove the effect of income tax from interest expense, and increase the net income	Avoid duplicated deduction	Some companies directly use "financing expense" replace interest expense. It will underestimate the EVA in companies, which have large interest revenue and financing income
	Extraordinary income	Income from selling high-quality assets	This kind of income usually correspond to "investment income" and "non-operating income and expense" item. Remove the effect of income tax from this income, and decrease the net income	Remove the effect of accidental and abnormal activities. Improve investment standard and quality, encourage enterprise group make the long-term and strategic investment, and encourage member enterprises operating specialized	Include: remove income from substance controlled subsidiary companies (not include income get from secondary market), enterprise group (not include investment enterprise) get incomes by transfer assets, revenue or profits more than 10 % of non-listed companies' overall assets
		Income from selling non-current assets, except the high-quality ones			Include: remove income from substance controlled subsidiary companies (not include income get from secondary market), enterprise group (not include investment enterprise) get incomes by transfer assets, revenue or profits more than 10 % of non-listed companies' overall assets
		Others			Include: income from transfer the assets not related to business development, subsidy income not related to regular activities

	R&D expense	R&D expense from management fees	Remove the effect of income tax from R&D expense, and increase the net income	Capitalize the R&D expense, encourage central enterprises realize upgrading through R&D, and enhance core competitiveness	
		R&D expense recognized in current period from intangible assets			This part can only be removed after form the intangible assets
		Exploration expense	Added back according to a certain proportion no more than 50 %		Enterprise with large exploration expense should be authorized by SASAC
Capital occupancy (average liability + average owner's equity)	Interest-free current liability		Remove the interest-free current liability such as "accounts payable", "notes payable", "accounts received in advance", etc.	Avoid the effect from fluctuated short-term liabilities', without occupied capital expense, encourage managers manage net operating assets properly	Use easy and reversing process to calculate the interest-free current liability, which equals current liability-short term liability-long term liability due within 1 year. Items such as "special accounts payable", "special reserve fund" with large balance caused by undertake the national task, can be removed
			Expense		
	Construction work-in-process		Remove the "construction work-in-process" item from the cost of capital	Support enterprises to expand reproduction in a certain extent, enhance profitability and core competitiveness, guide enterprises deal with the idle and low income assets	

simplifies the adjustment method, such as not considering the amortization temporary, aims to highlight key points, strengthen the operability and promote the implementation of EVA.

EVA = Net Operating Profit After Tax- Capital Cost = Net Operating Profit After Tax- Adjusted Capital × Average Cost of Capital Rate

Net Operating Profit After Tax = Net Income + (Interest Expense + Adjusted Item of R&D-Adjusted Extraordinary Item × 50 %) × (1–25 %)

Adjusted Capital = Average owner's equity + Average liability-Average interest-free current liability - Average construction work-in-process

14.2.3.2 Comprehensive Evaluation Method

Comprehensive evaluation method is based on multiple index system. This method needs to establish a certain function among evaluation index, evaluation standard and evaluation result, and then calculate the actual value of each evaluation index. Comprehensive evaluation conclusions will be made according to the function we have established before. Based on the characteristics of the evaluation method, comprehensive evaluation method can be divided into two systems: the decomposition index evaluation system and the comprehensive index evaluation system. As the decomposition index system lays more emphasis on the analysis, in practice the comprehensive evaluation index system is more preferred, including comprehensive index method and the efficacy coefficient method.

If the comprehensive evaluation index method is chosen, problems like assimilation of indexes, dimensionless of indexes, and the determination of indexes weighting will emerge. The reason why indexes should be assimilated is that the indexes can be divided into three types according to the relationship between the indexes and evaluation standard: the positive index, the inverse index and the appropriate index. Therefore, in choosing the evaluation index, company should try to keep consistency, namely, choose positive or inverse indexes if possible. If we cannot avoid using more indexes, assimilating the indexes is needed.

Why should we realize the dimensionless of indexes? This is because in a comprehensive evaluation index system, different indexes may have different dimensions (unit), which will lead to incomparability or incommensurability. Hence the dimensionless is needed. The basic approach is to convert the evaluation index of different individuals into the same utility unit, in this way could a multiple index evaluation problem be transformed into a single index evaluation problem, and then it could be compared and ranked. Some comprehensive evaluation methods themselves can solve "different dimension" problems in the multiple index system, such as comprehensive index method and efficacy coefficient method.

Why should we determine the index weight? In the comprehensive evaluation index system, the index weight is a symbol of the importance of the evaluation content. Due to imbalanced development, some indexes are more important than others. In order to show the influence of different indexes on the evaluation results, all evaluation indexes need to be weighted so that we can identify the contribution of an index according to its weight. In a certain index system, weight changes will directly affect the evaluation results. Thus it is very important to determine the index weight scientifically in the comprehensive index evaluation system.[11]

According to the comprehensive index method, firstly we need to compare the actual value of an indicator with its standard value and calculate the index of the indicator. To get a sole comprehensive index, we should summary the indexes according to the weight of the indicators. Finally we can make a judgment about the operating performances of an entity according to the comprehensive index. China's Ministry of Finance issued the enterprise economic benefit evaluation index system in 1995 is the application of comprehensive index method. When using this method, what we should pay attention to is the problem whether the comprehensive economic index is higher than 100 %. If the standard value is more advanced, we ought to keep index capped; if the standard value is the mean value, an open-ended index is preferred.

The efficacy coefficient method is based on the principle of multi-objective planning to determine evaluation indexes with a satisfactory value and a not-allowed value, set the satisfaction value as the upper limit and not-allowed value as lower limit, Calculate the satisfactory degree of each index and then transfer it into the corresponding evaluation scores. Evaluate the operating performance after calculating the weighted average of the comprehensive evaluation scores. The calculation formula of the comprehensive score and comprehensive index are same. The only difference lies in the calculation of individual indexes. That is calculation of efficacy coefficient. China's Ministry of Finance and other four ministries announced the state-owned capital performance evaluation system in 1999 is an example of this.

All above is about comprehensive evaluation method for qualitative indexes in the comprehensive evaluation system of operating performance. Analyzing qualitative indexes using comprehensive analysis judgment method, which is also called expert judgment method. It is a method applied by using the knowledge and experience of experts, determining the level of evaluation index in the method of subjective analysis method according to evaluation performance of the object in a specific area and then calculating the score according to the weight parameter and relative indexes. For example, the state-owned capital performance evaluation system is using this method to make comprehensive evaluation for qualitative indicators.

The difficulty to use comprehensive evaluation method is the determination of index weight. Methods to determine the weight of indicators include subjective weighting method and objective weighting method. The subjective weighting method is based on Delphi method, which also known as the method of expert opinion. Performance evaluation systems of state-owned capital in our country use the Delphi method to determine the weights at present. Objective weighting methods include relative weighting method, system effect weighting method (factor analysis method), variation weighting method, proportion weighting method, order weighting method and distance weighting method.

---

[11] Yan Pan and Xiaoke Cheng [7].

Some people think weights are given by people in subjective weighting method. On the one hand, it will lead to overestimation or underestimation of factors. The evaluation results cannot fully reflect the real situation of the object of evaluation. On the other hand, it will induce one-sided pursuit of higher weights of indexes and inevitably affect the objectivity of evaluation.[12] Somebody also thinks, although the evaluation of subjective weighting method is normal and operable, it is difficult to accurately reflect the intrinsic relationship between the index structures, which affects the accuracy of evaluation.[13] However, from the perspective of objective weighting method, someone points out that the objective weighting method determines the weight of each index according to the method of statistics or econometrics and the size of the information provided by observed value of evaluation index sample. So it has strong objectivity with relatively complex calculation.[14] It is also indicates that the importance of objective weighting cannot reflect its own value. The subjective weighting method should also be considered when evaluating the performance. So from the perspective of the method, subjective weighting method and the objective weighting methods have advantages and disadvantages. They should complement their strengths and weaknesses with each other.

According to the agency theory, an important factor in determining the weight distribution is the quality characteristics of evaluation indexes. The quality characteristics of various indicators are different in accordance with different backgrounds. For example, the factors such as different strategies corporation used and different sizes of the corporations will have an impact on the distribution of weight. Based on this, in the process of determining the weight of evaluation indexes, it should analyze according to specific situations, pay attention to differences between corporations and departments in development stages, competitive positions and strategic types, consider the subjective and objective weighting methods together. The determination of the weight of evaluation index doesn't mean it is unchanged. The weights of evaluation indicators should be dynamically and flexibly adjusted when the backgrounds of companies and departments changes.

14.2.3.3 Multi-perspective Balanced Evaluation Method

Multi-perspective balanced evaluation method essentially belongs to the index structure of evaluation systems. However, because of particularity characters in the selection of evaluation index and the establishment of evaluation procedures, it evolved into a separate method of evaluation control. The representatives are balance scorecard and performance prism.

The balanced scorecard is to transmit a series of operating indexes and important tasks into tangible goals and standards in the premise of overall goals and strategies

[12] Zhengming Qian and Weiyan Chen [8].

[13] Jianmin Meng [9].

[14] Guoxiang Xu et al. [10].

were determined. It includes four indexes. The first one is the financial performance indexes, which mainly evaluate what the enterprises have done for shareholders to achieve financial success. The second one is customer performance index, which mainly evaluate what the enterprises have done for customers to achieve the goals. The third one is performance index of internal procedures, which mainly evaluate what procedures' improvements enterprise achieved for shareholders and customers. The last one is the learning and growth performance index, which mainly evaluate the learning, innovation and growth ability of employees to achieve corporation goals. The characters of balanced scorecard system are reflected in five aspects. First, the results indicators and driver indicators are balanced (such as customer satisfaction and sales revenue). Second, the financial indexes and non-financial indexes are balanced (such as product quality and profit). Third, the internal indexes and external indexes are balanced (such as delivery rate and return rate). Fourth, the short-term indexes and long-term indexes are balanced (such as profit and staff training costs). Fifth, balance the quantitative indexes with qualitative indexes (such as employee turnover and employee loyalty).

As a kind of evaluation system, the advantages of balanced scorecard lie in: First, specify the target and strategic, strengthen the internal communication. Second, effectively realize the balance between indexes and emphasize the causal relationship between the indexes. Third, take different interests of stakeholders into account, it is helpful to obtain and maintain competitive advantage. Fourth, consider non-financial performance measures and enhance the connection between process control and results evaluation.

The basic procedures to establish balanced scorecard are as follow. First, establish enterprise vision and strategy. Second, select the appropriate evaluation units. Third, clear the four objectives of the balanced scorecard. Fourth, select the most appropriate indexes according to targets. Fifth, internal communicate and educate. Sixth, determine the standards and weights of all kinds of indexes. Seventh, combine compensation with balanced scorecard. Eighth, implement and revise indexes and standards of balanced scorecard constantly.

While establishing the balance scorecard, it should be noted that: view the balanced scorecard as an implementation of strategic goals; ensure the strategic objectives expressed accurately before applications; acquire support from the non-financial department leaders; apply new balanced scorecard in several places first; discuss with every implementation unit before using balanced scorecard; don't use the Balanced Scorecard to gain additional power control; do not try to standardize it but it should be customized; do not underestimate the necessity and importance of training and communication; no need to be perfect; do not underestimate the cost of implementation.

Of course, the balanced scorecard is not perfect, the defects can be summarized as following: First, although concerned the interests of customers, employees and other stakeholders from different aspects, it failed to recognize the organizational goals and development strategy through analyzing the interests of stakeholders which cannot confirm the key causes to improve the satisfaction of stakeholders accurately. Second, the Balanced Scorecard did not show specific details for the selection of the performance evaluation indexes. Performance evaluation systems not only need the results indicators, but also need process indexes. It needs to combine with strategic planning to reflect how to achieve results. Existing literature hardly concerned guiding principles about how to connect results and methods. Third, existing literature didn't deeply study how to design the performance standards, which is a vital problematic field. Kaplan and Norton did not show how to trade-off in different indexes. Failed to express how to tradeoff among a large number of indicators, the scorecard cannot achieve the "balance ". Fourth, how to link the performance evaluation systems with management compensations is an important problem, Kaplan and Norton hardly give any guidance about it. So the phenomenon often appears in practice is that despite the balanced scorecard is used, the management compensations are still based on the realization of budgetary targets. It is obvious that this behavior will cause destruction impacts to the well-designed Balanced Scorecard. Finally, balance scorecard pays little attention to feedback information. In fact, feedback information provides key information about the degree of the realization of corporation strategy.

From the perspective of experience, the balanced scorecard is mainly suitable for enterprise with following characteristics: high competitive pressures; regarding-oriented or strategic-oriented as guidance; with consultative or democratic leader system; and has high cost management level.[15]

14.3 Strength and Weakness of Evaluation Control System

As a mode of management control systems, evaluation control systems are strategic security systems, which combine with corporation development strategy. It is a control system about the operation, cash, information and human resource flow, target systems, which is code of conduct and goal system that is related to management activities. They play important roles in the modern organizations and appear lots of advantages as corporation strengthen their management. However, as a mode of an artificially created management control, evaluation control system also has defects.

14.3.1 Functions of Evaluation Control System

The functions of evaluation control systems are more and more complete with the development of performance evaluation theories and practices. Evaluation control systems have four functions, namely involving evaluation, control, prediction and incentive.

[15] Dajun Wu and Rongxiang Gao [11].

14.3.1.1 Evaluation Function

Evaluation is the basic function of management control system. Evaluation process is a process of value judgment according to the object's operating results.

14.3.1.2 Control Function

Control is another basic function of evaluation control systems. Whether achieve the strategic goal or not and to what extent can achieve is the essential part to ensure the goal realized. Thus, in order to ensure the tasks to be finished in time, it is necessary to evaluate objective of evaluation in different stages of evaluation. Evaluation can provide controlling information about how to realize strategic goals, find the deviations, analyze objective and subjective reasons and correct deviations which make it possible for operating manager to promote the management methods gradually and guarantee the achievement of ultimate goals.

14.3.1.3 Prediction Function

The purpose of retrospect the past and cognize the recent is to predict future. The important function of evaluation control is to predict the future trends of business activities by using the past and present performance information. It provides supportive information for managers to adjust strategies which enables the managers to better plan the future and grasps the development direction of the company.

14.3.1.4 Incentive Function

Incentive is an important function of evaluation control systems. It is because the evaluation results have deeply effect on the operating activities of corporations and management activities of managers. By calculating the evaluation indexes and comparing with standards, the evaluation results can reflect the advantages and disadvantages of the corporation. At the same time rewards and punishment according to the evaluation results can motivate managers take correct actions and useful measures to change current situations.

14.3.2 Advantages of Evaluation Control System

Evaluation control systems are a kind of mode of management control systems, which treat performance evaluation as core. Similar to objective of management control systems, realizing corporate strategic goals is its ultimate goal. The principles of evaluation control systems, which are as same as target control management of objective, absorb the thoughts of performance management. So, they have similar advantages. It means that not only do they have certain goals to control which is beneficial to the operating manager to reference and rectify themselves but also have flexibility, which is beneficial to exert subjective in evaluating the target process. The advantages of evaluation control are as follows:

14.3.2.1 Specific Objective of Control

In the evaluation control systems, system input is the goal which system has to achieve. The evaluation subject uses the deviation of objective status of controlled system which is relative to the system input to guide or correct future activities. In another word, it means evaluation control systems treat objective of evaluation as a mean of management. They can manage the operating activities by designing, performing, evaluating, and examining the evaluation objectives to realize the strategic goals. Its principle can be described as: regarding goals as the direction of management, controlling the action of every department and every employee according to the objectives, evaluating contributes and allocating compensation based on the degree of realization of objectives, motivating employees by designing, performing and authorizing the objectives to realize overall goals.[16] In order to form a scientific and complete objective system and make sure the realization of the strategic goals, the corporation has to transform the strategic goals into managers' goals and put the management activities, managers and employees into system.

14.3.2.2 Sufficient Flexibility

Evaluation control systems only care about both ends which is how to set up an objective system of evaluation control reasonably on the system input side and how to evaluate the operating performance of controlled systems scientifically on the system output side. However, except providing necessary resource guarantees and counseling, it doesn't care the operating process of controlled systems. That means evaluation control replace the bureaucratic control by self-control. It is conducive to motivate managers and employees' potential and enthusiasm. Even though maximizing the corporation value has been the goals of modern corporations, the agency problem within the enterprise makes managers and employees misunderstand and even deviate from it because of the agency problems. The purpose to perform the evaluation control systems is to coordinate different people's goals, conform personal goals with the overall goals and connect personal performance with organization performance.

[16] Dong Du [12].

14.3.3 Disadvantages of Evaluation Control System

There are no perfect management control system modes neither in practice nor theories. So are the evaluation control systems. Because of its inherent limitations, evaluation control systems also have disadvantages in two aspects as follows.

14.3.3.1 Lack of Process Control

The evaluation control systems are methods to manage and control the objectives. In the operating process, managers' self-control is the main part. Operators should fully accredit and trust the managers and the managers should not supervise or intervene the performance of operational business at different levels. That means evaluation control systems lack procedure control and process control. Obviously, it is not benefit to detect and correct deviations. So it always leads to conditions, which have no chance to changes.

14.3.3.2 High Possibility of Human Arbitrariness

The core of evaluation control systems is the performance evaluation. In order to evaluate the performance objectively, it needs to choose evaluation indexes, determine the evaluation standards and choose evaluation methods reasonably. But, in practice, because of the complexity of transactions, the behaviors of managers are unobservable and high possibility of human arbitrariness when choosing the evaluation indexes, standards and methods, the determination of them may lack of objective. It will lead to resistance from managers, affect the function of evaluation control systems and eventually affect the achievement of strategic goals.

14.4 Application Conditions of Evaluation Control System

14.4.1 Application Conditions of Evaluation Control System

If rule-based control and budgetary control are the basis of management control, evaluation control is the higher level of control. Corporations choose and apply the evaluation control systems not only need good organizational culture, which make workers understand the culture and idea of the business and pride of their own business, but also to have specific strategic goals, high quality of managers and good management foundations. Specifically, to achieve the normally effect of the evaluation control systems, conditions as follows are needed.

14.4.1.1 The Formation of Good Organizational Culture

Organizational culture usually represents the total of a series of interdependent value conceptions and behaviors. These conceptions and behaviors are accumulated for a long time and possessed by all staffs of corporations. It was proved that a corporation, which has a good organizational culture, operators' and managers' behaviors are used to be consistent, they work hard to achieve the strategic goals and operating directions. The harmony, positivity, organization and unified leaders are benefit to improve the operating performance. Certainly, their behaviors have to adapt to external environment changes.[17] The formation of core values is the essential part improving the core competence for the corporations. So, corporations should pay attention to the long-term strategy, future growth and value creation, emphasize the importance of core values, educate and lead the employees and then reach the agreement. Only in this way, can enterprise maximize employees working enthusiasm and realize self-value and corporation goals. For example, the creators of EVA evaluation control systems hold the view that to make EVA working is to create organizational culture, which puts value creation into all the management activities.[18] It needs to set up the interactive internal communication systems. Furthermore, not only the agreement of EVA management of board of directors and governance need them, but also the agreement of value creation by all staffs. The reason is it is difficult to bring profound changes without promises of managers. It is difficult to realize value creations without acceptance of managers and employees.

14.4.1.2 Specific Strategic Goals

Evaluation control system is a kind of target control or target management. That means the nature of evaluation control system is to manage the operating activities by designing, performing, evaluating and examining goals. All the management control activities focus on the target and evaluate the management based on the level of the completion of the target. It is the direction of actions and throughout the entire management activities. So it is not hard to imagine that the evaluation control system will hard to operate without the specific strategic goals. To clarify the goals of evaluation control system, the most important thing is to determine the specific strategic goals. The strategic goals should be based on value and can be implemented and disassembled. Secondly, establish the liability structure, decompose and implement the enterprise strategic target by different layers, so that all levels of managers clear about tasks and responsibilities. Finally, select key performance variables. It means the choice of indicators should be not only affects the likelihood of implementation of the strategy, but also can enhance.

---

[17] Kurt and Heskett [13].

[18] Yang and O'Byrne [14].

14.4.1.3 Managers with High Quality

Whether managers can achieve the strategic goals depend on the implementation of evaluation targets. So operators who want the evaluation control systems work effectively should conform the evaluation targets to strategic goals. In order to reach this point, operators should help managers to realize its evaluation targets as far as possible, fully trust them, motivate them and keep them enthusiastic rather than placing managers on the opposite side or trying to interfere the evaluation process. That means the evaluation control system essentially replace the bureaucratic control by self-control and change “passive enforcement” into “active management”. To maintain the normal operation of the system and evaluate the control effect it not only requires the formation of a cultural atmosphere but also requires managers to have a high quality and profound understanding of the organizational culture and values. Managers should consciously combine personal goals with corporation goals and have a certain degree of team spirit and self-discipline.

14.4.1.4 Good Management Foundation

In order to make the evaluation control systems operate well, enterprises need to have good management foundations. That is to say managers’ talent should be supported by a perfect mechanism and system, namely the structural capital of enterprises. By only relying on these capital structures such as information systems, database, and organizational networks managers and employees can communicate with each other better and create more values and overall operating performance. Organizational capital is the innovation stage for talent of enterprise management. It is the platform that talent people create value for enterprises. If there is no good organizational capital, it will affect the selection of evaluation indexes, the rationality of evaluation standards and timeliness and completeness of the information about calculated results from the perspective of operators. For the object of managers at all levels, they can never conduct production business activities following certain behavior methods and according to the determined economic goals.

14.4.2 Application Scope of Evaluation Control System

Different from rule-based control systems and budgetary control systems, evaluation control systems cannot be applied to all organizations and corporations. Compared with rule-based control systems and budgetary control systems, evaluation control systems belong to a higher level of management control mode. Its characters and application conditions determine the limitation of its applicability. Evaluation control systems need a high level of control environment, not only require enterprises which have good management foundations and clear strategic goals, but also require a high level of management quality and a good corporate culture. Therefore, to enterprises, which have poor control environment and management foundations, establish and evaluate evaluation control systems are difficult, and the effect may not be good. In contrast, to enterprises, which have good control environment and management foundations, establish and apply the evaluation control systems are relatively easy, and more likely to achieve good results.

According to the characteristics of evaluation control systems and commonly used evaluation methods, evaluation control systems are mainly adaptive for enterprises that implement decentralized management, enterprise groups with multiple organizational structures, knowledge-based enterprises that the intellectual capital contributes a lot, enterprises that face competitive pressures, and enterprises with a high cost of management.

References

1. Rui Zhang (2002) The research of corporate strategic operating performance evaluation index systems. China Financial & Economic Publishing House, Beijing
2. Zhiqiang Shang (1998) Multinational corporations performance evaluation system [M]. Shanghai University of Finance and Economics Press, Shanghai
3. Xiaoqiang Zhi (2000) How to choose the performance evaluation standard. Accoun Res 21(11):11–19
4. Holmstrom B (1982) Moral hazard in teams. Bell J Econ 13:324–340
5. Pingli Li (2001) Operator's performance evaluation: mode of stakeholders. Zhe Jiang People's Publishing House, Hangzhou
6. Shengli Du (1999) Corporate operating performance evaluation. Economic Science Press, Beijing, pp 399–400
7. Yan Pan, Xiaoke Cheng (2000) Principal component analysis method in listed corporate operating performance. Account Res 21(1):25–322
8. Zhengming Qian, Weiyan Chen (1999) An empirical investigation of industrial economic benefits evaluation in China and principal component analysis. Stat Res 16(7):51–56
9. Jianmin Meng (2002) Corporate performance evaluation in China. China Financial & Economic Publishing House, Beijing
10. Guoxiang Xu et al (2000) Comprehensive evaluation and empirical investigation of operating performance in listed corporate. Stat Res 21(9):43–50
11. Dajun Wu, Rongxiang Gao (2001) BSC review. Finance Acc 23(11):11–14
12. Dong Du (2002) Management control. Tsinghua University Press, Beijing, pp 141–142
13. Kurt J, Heskett J (2001) translated by Zhong Zeng et al, Corporate culture and operating performance. Huaxia Publishing House, Beijing, pp 176–177
14. Yang SD, O'Byrne SF (2002) translated by Liping Li, EVA & value management. Social Sciences Academic Press, Beijing, pp 60–61

Chapter 15
The Mode of Incentive Control System

15.1 Definition of Incentive Control System

15.1.1 Theoretical Foundation of Incentive System

Since the twentieth century, several incentive problems have been researched which has resulted into the formation of different incentive theories on the basis of various perspectives like management, economy, sociology and psychology. Incentive theories have experienced an evolution from meeting financial needs to meet a variety of needs, from ambiguous incentive conditions to standard incentive conditions and from basic incentive research to incentive process research. This part explains incentive control on the basis of five theories like Agent theory, Human Capital theory, Yardstick Competition Theory, Expectancy theory and Motivation Needs Theory, which are as follows:

15.1.1.1 Agency Theory

From the coordination of the interest relationship between the principal and the agent, agent theory designs a target to motivate the agent to pursue its utility maximization and achieve maximization of the principal's interest. Western economic theory designs a variety of incentive modes to solve the principal-agent problem to strengthen incentive and constraint for the agent. These modes mainly involve to distributing the surplus power to top managers, optimizing compensation combination of wages and funds and stocks, reinforcing competition of managers market and forming market pressure according to managers' past performance to calculate their human capital value in the future, and taking over companies through the capital market.

X. Zhang, *Enterprise Management Control Systems in China*, Understanding China, DOI 10.1007/978-3-642-54715-7_15, © Springer-Verlag Berlin Heidelberg 2014

15.1.1.2 Human Capital Theory

Human capital theory is mainly used to explain the incentive problems of enterprise's top managers. Top managers are a special kind of human capital. Although they are not enterprise owners for material capital, good quality and management ability of top managers are indispensable capital for modern enterprise survival and development. Human capital of top managers is scarce because its generation cycle is longer and training cost is higher. Top managers must pay attention to the cultivation of the inner and outer, which ask them to not only organize and coordinate and rationally allocate enterprise internal various resources of production in order to exert their maximum effectiveness but also undertake various kinds of risks and positively cope with market competition. Obviously, top managers have special and scarce human capital and the incentive and constraint to them should be different from general human capital of employees.

15.1.1.3 Yardstick Competition Theory

Yardstick competition theory compares the agent's performance with other agent's performance under similar conditions to find agent's effort level on some degree. Yardstick competition theory can be applied to many aspects. CEO can judge the degree of managers' effort in his department according to their different performance in similar conditions and reward or punish them. Accordingly, shareholders can decide CEO's remuneration and reward or punish him according to the similar company's performance or the industry average profit.

15.1.1.4 Expectancy Theory

Expectancy theory believes that a person's motivation to do an activity depends on the size of result and the probability generated by the activity. The theory reveals the relationship among individual effort, performance, reward and the personal goals. The theory thinks that a person will be motivated to pay greater efforts if he achieves good performance evaluation for his efforts and then obtains the desired organizational reward. The theory tells people that the reward for the performance is more reasonable than the reward for the qualifications and skills.

15.1.1.5 Motivation Needs Theory

Motivation Needs Theory reflects that individuals in the workplace mainly have three needs: power needs, belonging needs and achievement needs. Entrepreneurs and executives pursue high achievement need and considerable power need and low belonging need. But entrepreneurs have stronger achievement need and lower belonging need than executives have, while entrepreneurs and executives have approximately equal power need.

15.1.2 The Connotation of Incentive Control System

Incentives are those activities that an organization inspires, guides, maintains, and regulates behaviors of members to effectively realize both organizational and individual goals through appropriate motivation mode and efficient working environment. Incentives not only include positive encouragements which focus on common interest but also include constraints and controls, thus incentives themselves can also be treated as incentive controls. Because management controls are also known as "managerial controls", incentive controls are, in this book, those activities that enterprises control managers or executives through incentive methods in order to ensure managers' behaviors in line with enterprises goals. Obviously, the scope of the connotation and denotation of "Incentive Controls" mentioned here are smaller than their original meanings. Besides Regulation Control Systems, Budget Control Systems and Evaluation Control Systems, Incentive Control Systems are a subsystem of management control system and are interest-oriented control. In coordination with the goals of managers and owners, the incentive controls help managers constantly adjust the target and strategy and create greater value for the enterprise according to the changing social economic and technical environment.

As a mode of management control system, Incentive Control Systems should include several parts: strategic planning, incentive option, constraints in motivation and performance evaluation.

15.1.2.1 Strategic Planning and Incentive Target

Strategic planning involves the decisions of markets, products, customers, technology and human resources that must be included in managers' incentive goals. Incentive controls themselves are a part of strategic planning. Strategic planning is the specification and institutionalization of enterprise strategic goals and is the premise and foundation of Incentive Control Systems, Regulation Control Systems, Budget Control Systems and Evaluation Control Systems.

15.1.2.2 Option of Incentive Methods

Incentive methods are those things that can make motivated persons be interested in enterprise goals and contribute their enthusiasm, mental and physical power to the goals. Incentive methods of material or spiritual are the form of incentives or the functional carrier of incentives. Common incentive methods include annual salary system, bonus, gain sharing plan, stock incentive, stock option incentive, management buy-out, etc. [1]. Each kind of incentive methods has different incentive effects, so enterprise should make choices according to size of enterprise, industry, stage of development, enterprise culture and so on.

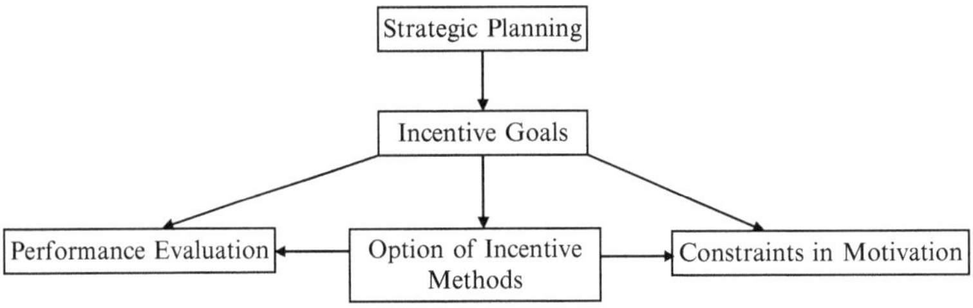

Fig. 15.1 Incentive control system

15.1.2.3 Constraints in Motivation

Constraints in motivation belong to the "controls" of incentive controls and can control the process of management and monitor the results in order to regulate and constraint managers' behaviors. Like other rational risk-averse people, managers will also trade off benefits and risks. To avoid short-term goals and those business strategies which could lead to generating too much risk for the owners, it's necessary to control rationally the risks in incentives. Constraints in motivation include the improvement of corporate governance structure, the consolidation of the roles of the remuneration committee and audit control, the constraints or limitation of financial behaviors in the compensation contracts.

15.1.2.4 Performance Evaluation

Performance evaluation is to use a certain index system and select suitable standards and apply scientific methods to make value judgment for an enterprise's business performance during a certain period. Performance evaluation not only belongs to evaluation control system but also is an important part of Incentive Control System. A reasonable performance evaluation system can prompt incentive control system to play a better role. Performance evaluation in incentive control system includes evaluation index, index standard and index calculation, etc., whose content can refer to the previous chapter.

Incentive Control Systems can be specified by following figure (Fig. 15.1).

15.1.3 The Target of Incentive Control System

In the case of information asymmetry, because the owner can't observe the detailed actions taken by the managers, managers can deviate from what they committed before. Due to the value of asymmetric information, managers don't want to disclose their private information under non-benefit circumstances. However, the motivation

Table 15.1 The target of incentive control systems

Behaviors of managers	Management control system	Goals of incentive controls
Adverse selection	Incentive control system	Real disclosure
Moral hazard		Work hard

and way of managers' behaviors depend on the remuneration provided by the compensation contract. If compensation contract set up incentives controls, managers' behaviors will be induced by compensation contract. At this moment, incentive control system will come up.

In view of the adverse selection problem caused by managers' hidden information, the aim of incentive control systems is to make managers consciously disclosure their true information. In view of moral hazard problem caused by managers' covert action, the aim of incentive control systems is to make managers consciously try their best to work and constantly improve the enterprise's value. Usually the target of incentive control systems can be simply summarized to exert managers' enthusiasm and creativity, guide managers work hard under the established rules in order to meet the overall goals of the organization (Table 15.1).

To be clear, manager's individual goals are not completely excluded from the target of incentive control systems. In fact, the effective operation of incentive control system not only considers managers' individual motivation but also puts emphasis on meeting managers' need because final objective is to attain the owners' goals through managers' individual motives in harmony with the organization's goals.

15.1.4 The Principle of Incentive Control System Design

Incentive control system is not an isolated project but involves all aspects of business management, even can be seen as a system engineering of enterprise management. Incentive control system should follow the following principles:

(A) The principle of Clarity. The principle of clarity is that the incentive target of incentive control system must reflect the enterprise financial target and strategy clearly.
(B) The principle of Participation. Participation principle is that all managers who are supposed to participate activities of incentive mechanism can take part in the formulation process of enterprises' incentive mechanism.
(C) The principle of Stratification. Stratification principle is to design different incentive targets and operation frameworks according to different objects' needs, for example, there should be different incentive modes for the top managers and general managers so as to ensure the directionality of incentive mechanism and utility maximization.
(D) The principle of Appropriateness. Appropriateness principle is that the design of incentive mechanism should avoid the tendency of excessive incentives.

(E) The principle of Controllability. Controllability principle is that the performance evaluation index applied in incentive control system must be controlled by managers, and managers can influence the performance evaluation index related to rewards through normal effort.
(F) The principle of Timeliness. Timeliness principle is that the incentive control systems should provide timely rewards in order to strengthen the managers' understanding of the relationship between business activities and rewards.

15.2 Contents of Incentive Control System

15.2.1 Choice of Incentive Way

There are many kinds of incentive classification. Usually, incentive pattern can be divided into material incentive and mental incentive based on incentive factors. Material incentive includes salary, bonus, stock, stock options, benefits and allowances, etc.; mental incentive includes rights incentive, job incentive, honor and status incentive, etc. Material incentive can be divided into short-term incentive and long-term incentive according to the timeliness of incentive. Short-term incentive includes annual salary system, bonus incentive, performance linked incentive, and income sharing plan, etc., long-term incentive includes stock incentive, stock option incentive, MBO, etc. Here, from the point of view of control levels, incentives are divided into incentives of owners to top managers and incentives of top managers to lower level managers.

15.2.1.1 Incentives of Owners to Top Managers [2]

- **Annual salary system**

Annual salary system is an incentive paying system that defines the management compensation by year. It separate financial interests of managers from employees' interests and directly be linked to business performance in order to realize incentive to managers. It better reflects the labor value of managers and better attracts and retains the talents. Risk-related income represents a significant share in this system in order to connect the interests of the managers with the interests of the enterprise. It can better improve managers' enthusiasm. At present, western developed countries have widely applied this system.

The basic operating procedures of annual salary system:

The first step is to define the compensation structure. Managers' annual salary can be divided into basic salary and risk-related income. Basic salary mainly guarantees managers' daily life needs and is multiplied by a certain adjustment coefficient according to the average wage level. Risk-related income can be further divided into value-added salary and reward salary, the former is paid for target performance and the latter is extra bonus for exceeding the target.

The second step is to define the risk mortgage. The risk mortgage is the main funding sources to punish managers who fail to reach their objectives and prevents managers to overstate profits to some extent. The risk mortgage can be paid once then be extracted from the risk-related income year by year, or can be extracted from the risk-related income every year.

The third step is to define the linking indexes. The indexes should use profit, ROE, maintenance and appreciation of assets value, rate of technique innovation and growth rate of employee average wage, etc. The evaluation standard should base on the average advanced level of industry, taking into consideration of the enterprise actual data in the last few years.

At the end of year, the managers will obtain risk-related income after they complete the targets. If managers fail to fulfill the targets, risk-related income will be deducted. Basic salary and risk mortgage will be also deducted if the risk-related income is not enough.

Besides, an enterprise should pay attention to the following questions when it formulates correctly annual salary system:

Firstly, an enterprise should reasonably determine the basic salary. The basic salary should be determined according to enterprise size and local living standard and is slightly higher than the wages of employees of enterprises. On the one hand lower basic salary cannot safeguard basic life needs, but on the other hand higher basic salary can inhibit the effect of risk-based incentives.

Secondly, an enterprise should accurately formulate the proportion of and amount of salary increase. The main function of salary increase is to improve enterprise economic benefits through motivating top managers by the risk of income. The basis of determining salary increase should be the size of enterprise performance and the degree of risk.

Thirdly, an enterprise should diversify the index system of evaluation. Simple market-value indicators and accounting indicators have advantages and disadvantages. These two kinds of indicators should be combined to use in practice and consider the enterprises' social responsibility.

Fourthly, an enterprise should improve constraint mechanism and restraint on-the-job consumption. Enterprises should reinforce board of directors and board of supervisors to play their supervisory roles through establishing and perfecting corporate government structure.

- **Stock-based incentive**

Stock-based incentive is that modern joint-stock enterprises set their stocks as objects to motivate their directors, supervisors and senior managers and other employees in the long term. With development of the market, China has paid more and more attention to the practice of stock-based incentive, and relevant departments have also made strict rules about stock-based incentive. On January 1, 2006, China Securities Regulatory Commission released "*Listing Corporation Equity Incentive Management Regulation (pilot version)*" [1], on September 30 in the same year, Ministry of Finance and State-owned Assets Supervision and Administration Commission (SASAC) jointly released "*The Pilot Regulation of Equity Incentive*

Implementation in the State-owned Listing Corporation (China)" [3]. Although stock-based incentive in our country has implemented for a short time, since 2010 many listed companies have drafted stock-based incentive plans, and stock-based incentive has achieved a certain effect. In this part, we will introduce Chinese characteristics of stock-based incentive mainly on the basis of the above two regulations.

Rules of incentive objects. The objects of stock-based incentive plans could include the directors, supervisors, senior managers, the core technology (business) personnel, as well as other employees who should be motivated in listed companies, but should not include independent directors.

Rules of sources of stocks. Listed companies that plan to implement stock-based incentive plans can solve sources of stocks through the following ways according to the actual situation of enterprises: (1) shares issuance to incentive objects; (2) repurchase of corporation share; (3) other ways that laws and regulations allowed.

Rules of quantity of granted stocks. Total amount of underlying stocks involved in the effective stock-based incentive plans of a listed company must not exceed the 10 % of the company's total amount of capital stock. Unless approved by special resolution in shareholders meeting, the amount of stocks that is awarded to any incentive object through effective stock-based incentive plans shall not exceed the 1 % of a company's total amount of capital stock.

Rules of forms of stock-based incentive. The ways of stock-based incentive include restricted stock, stock option and other ways allowed by laws and administrative regulations. According to the purpose of stock-based incentive, a listed companies should be guided by option incentive mechanism and determine the stock-based incentive approach combining the characteristics of the industry and the company. Restricted stocks are a certain number of a listed company's shares that incentive objects obtain in accordance with the conditions prescribed by stock-based incentive plan. Stock option are the right of buying a certain number of shares which a listed company give incentive objects at predetermined price within a certain period of time. Incentive objects can buy a certain number of shares of listed companies at predetermined price within a certain period of time with its granted stock options, but they also have right to give up .

Rules of conditions of stock-based incentive. If incentive objects include directors, supervisors and senior managers, listed companies should establish a performance evaluation system and evaluation methods and put performance evaluation indexes as the implementation conditions of stock-based incentive plans.

Regarding the rules of the granted price of stocks and way of determining it: According to the principle of fair market price, listed companies shall ensure the granted price (exercise price) higher than any of the following prices: (1) the closing price of underlying stocks on a trading day before a company announces the abstracts of the stock-based incentive plan draft; (2) the average closing price of underlying stocks within 30 trading days before a company announces the abstracts of stock-based incentive plan draft. In addition, listed companies will make stock-based incentive plan when they make an initial public offering (IPO) of its stocks, and the granted price of stock option is determined according to the above principles after 30 trading days in IPO.

Rules of time limitation of exercise. The validity period of stock-based incentive plan is calculated from the shareholders' meeting day and is usually no more than 10 years. If the validity period of stock-based incentive plan has expired, listed companies shall not confer any equity according to this plan. During the validity period of stock-based incentive plan, listed companies should adapt partial implementation method, the duration between two issues of stocks granted should be more than a full accounting year. During the validity period of stock-based incentive plan, each stock option granted shall set the limitation period and the validity period for stock option, and exercise options according to the schedule set by several times: (1) The limitation period for stock option is calculated from the granted date (authorization) to the effective date (the vesting date) and shall not be less than 2 years. Don't exercise option in limitation period in principle. (2) The validity period for stock option is calculated from the effective date to the failure date and is determined by the listed companies according to the practice but shall not be less than 3 years. During the validity period of stock option the uniform batches exercise approach is applied in principle. Over the validity of exercise, the right becomes void automatically and is none of traceability. Generally, Incentive objects could exercise their options within the period which starts from the second trading day after regular report published and expires in 10 trading days before next report published. However, stock options should not be exercised under the following circumstances: (1) from the progress of discussing significant trading or relevant important events to 2 trading days after the announcement of these trading or events. (2) from the date of occurrence of other major incidents that may affect share price to 2 trading days after the announcement.

Rules of unlock period. Within the validity period of stock-based incentive plan, the lock-up period of each granted restricted stock shall be no less than 2 years. When lock-up period passes, the unlocked (transferred, sold) number of shares is determined according to the stock-based incentive plan and the completion of performance targets. Unlock period shall no less than 3 years. Uniform unlock method is adopted in unlock period in principle.

15.2.1.2 Incentive from Top Managers to Lower Level Managers

- **Post-performance salary mechanism**

Post-performance salary mechanism is the oldest way of incentive and the wage hierarchy decided according to the labor characteristics of position and work value. Post-performance salary mechanism is mainly composed of wage scale, wage standards, position name list and business standards, etc. The content of business standards here include those that should be known and mastered, and responsibility regulations and qualifications, business requirements, etc. Post-performance salary mechanism should ensure a reasonable, system and stable position structure in order to establish a complete set of remuneration system which conforms to the principle of internal fairness according to enterprise business objectives.

Post-performance salary defines the relative value of all kinds of positions according to different positions, to some extent which rules out the subjectivity on determining salary standards. It is more fairer to determine wage level on the basis of the quantitative indexes. At the same time, the salary and position are closely linked, and promotion points out the direction of the career development of managers and is helpful to motivate the enthusiasm and initiative of managers. But this kind of incentives has its own disadvantages and is not conducive for enterprise to change managers' jobs timely when it is necessary, etc.

- **Bonus-based incentive**

Bonus is different from salary. Salary is the basic form of labor compensation, but bonus is a kind of auxiliary form used to supplement the shortage of salary. Bonus and salary are also distinct in nature. Salary is the remuneration for fixed labor, and bonus is the main compensation form for the excess labor, so bonus is the reward of excess labor. In order to make bonus-based incentive work well, we should pay attention to the following questions:

The first question is the scientific goals. Scientific and reasonable task goals should not only consider the history but also consider the development potential; not only be possible to complete but also be higher than existing strengths. Only in this way can lead the potential of managers be stimulated to a greater extent.

The second question is to provide proper incentive power. Providing appropriate incentive force has a realistic significance to motivate managers to complete organizational goals. Determination of the amount of bonuses should not only consider the enterprise industry and regional economic development level, residents' income level, the enterprise affordability, but also take managers' expectations into account.

Thirdly, the principle of fairness is important. Difference is the premise of incentive effectiveness, and non-difference incentive would be useless. Therefore, fair principle is extremely important not only on the absolute income level but also on the relative level. i.e. the individual input–output is equivalent to others.

Fourthly, paying attention to the reward ratio, frequency and time to improve the incentive effect. The managers who make great efforts in the work and achieve remarkable results or make outstanding contributions should be rewarded significantly and it can play as guideline to others. The reward to the "best minority" would not only motivate those excellent employees, and also encourage the "average majority" and even calm down negative effects to those who have poor performance. But the time to reward should be carefully considered. The principle of "timely reward" is adopted for the urgent or temporary assignment.

- **Performance-linked incentives**

Performance-linked incentive is that total wages is positive related to economic output. Economic output here is the proportion of work achievement to the labor consumption in business activities, and it also can be summarized as the proportion of input and output. Under the same labor power, the quality of product or service produced is better, economic output is higher, otherwise, economic output is lower. Performance-linked is a kind of incentive theory based on "team production theory", and it can, in practice, greatly motivate managers and employees of the entire department.

Performance-linked can be roughly divided into two categories: one is that total payroll is linked up with the value of labor. It is suitable for the enterprises in which value is viewed as the main evaluation index. The basic form of performance-linked can be divided into five types: (1) total payroll linked up with profit and tax; (2) total payroll linked up with profit (3) in commercial industry or service industry, total payroll linked up with the proportion of wage to income in a CNY100 operation income; (4) in construction industry, total payroll linked up with the proportion of wage to income in a CNY100 output; (5) for advertisement and IT industry, they can set up a salary increasing fund from added profit and tax, based on a certain proportion. The other is that total wages is determined by productivity. It is suitable for the enterprises in which physical volume is viewed as the main evaluation index. The basic form of performance-linked has two kinds: (1) wages determined by per unit of product, such as wages per ton in mining industry; (2) wages determined by per a thousand of tons and per kilometer in transportation industry.

Enterprises that apply performance-linked incentive should separately define department's reasonable base of total payroll, the basic number of economic indexes and the ratio of total payroll linked to economic. Different enterprises shall develop different economic index system related to total payroll according to their own situation.

- **Gain sharing plan**

Gain sharing plan is based on a pre-selected formula which reflects the productivity and profitability and makes managers and employees share financial benefits. Gain sharing plan is an organizational planning designed to improve productivity and reduce labor costs. Its essence is, that company can improve productivity and share the financial income according to the plan which is devised to reflect performance improvement through the effective use of labor, capital and raw material. Gain sharing plan closely links employees' contribution to the enterprise development and employees' income increase. These contributions include the improvement of product quality, the reduction of cost, the improvement of working methods, increase of production volume, etc. Gain sharing plan has a variety of forms, such as Profit sharing plan, the Scanlon plan, the Rucker plan, the balance plan of risk and return. Among these plans, profit sharing plan, the Scanlon plan and the Rucker plan are closely related to managers.

Gain sharing plan belongs to enterprise team incentive. It motivates employees by giving employees a certain amount of residual claims. Gain sharing plan includes three modes. The first mode is the fixed percentage of profit sharing, i.e. sharing profits with all employees according to the fixed percentage of profit distribution. The second mode is the stepwise ratio profit sharing, i.e. share profits according to the levels of enterprise profit to establish different sharing proportion which can be designed from low to high or can also be designed from high to low. The third mode is the excess profit sharing, i.e. putting a lower profit index as a base and share the extra profits with managers or employees according to the different positions or duties and the performance evaluation results.

Both the Scanlon plan and the Rucker plan belong to cost saving sharing plan. They were named by its designer respectively. They both emphasize participatory management and reduce costs by sharing cost savings. The basic framework is as follows: firstly, determining factors of cost sharing plan, including departments, personnel, time and scope; secondly, determining overall scheme of sharing plan, such as the start-up line of cost sharing, the proportion of sharing, the right to use and use direction after sharing cost, as well as the rate of change in start-up line of the cost sharing in sustainable development, etc.; finally, determining the relationship between the cost sharing plan and the position or department payroll. The Scanlon plan and the Rucker plan have different allocated basis. The Scanlon plan determines bonus incentive according to the staff and management committee in cost reduction progress, but the Rucker plan is based on the historical relationship between the total income of employees and the product value created by employees.

- **Moral incentive**

Moral incentive is comparable to material incentive as mentioned above. Moral incentive is to meet the needs of individual psychology by using a series of non-material ways and change the ideology and inspire work energy. With development of society, improvement of productivity and the progress of science and technology, the content and structure of material needs and spiritual needs are changing, and spirit of entrepreneurs, enterprise culture and employee motivation become more and more important to enterprise development.

Moral incentive was commonly used in Chinese companies in the past, such as ideological and political work to motivate enthusiasm and creativity of workers in the form of praise, comparison, the honorary title awarded. But moral incentive is not limited to these forms, and it also includes career incentive, reputation and status incentive, power incentive, competition incentive, emotional incentive, as well as promotion incentive, dismissal threat, ethics incentive, etc. Aiming at the actual practice of our enterprises, the implementation of moral incentive should be carried out from the following several aspects:

Firstly, Delegation is a good way to meet manager's need for power. As to managers, power and responsibilities are the premise of achievement needs. Managers cannot efficiently work without enough power delegation. Because managers' sense of achievement, on one hand can be achieved during the process of management work, on the other hand can be experienced after reaching a certain level of management result. More delegation of power and responsibilities can not only meet the managers' needs of power, but also meet the needs of their achievement.

Secondly, providing opportunities for personal career development and promotion. Every manager has his own life designing and development goals, so companies will try to give them opportunities of learning, training, and further education. Promotion mechanism should be established to reach a balance of diversity among ages, seniorities, qualifications. Each manager has opportunity to promote or increase salary when they get either a certain seniority or qualification.

Thirdly, strengthening enterprise management to establish a good order. "Fair, just and open" itself for managers is a kind of incentive. Most managers pursue a working environment under which everything can be totally used and everybody can give full play to his talents, so managers could put themselves into enterprise production and business operation activities.

15.2.2 Constraints in Incentives

Constraints in incentives control power and supervise results in order to standardize and restrict behaviors of managers. Many subjects that can play restrictive roles on managers include both external constraints, such as capital market, product market, managers market, and internal constraints, such as board of directors, board of supervisors, union, etc. There are kinds of constraints in incentive, such as constraints of laws and regulations, contract constraints, constraints of internal competition, etc. Among the above constrains compensation contract constraints are the most important ones. Then we will briefly analyze the following constraints for managers: corporate governance structure, committee of compensation, debt contracts, limit of financial behaviors, determination of accounting methods and auditing control constraint to managers.

15.2.2.1 Corporate Government Structure

The separation of ownership and control of modern enterprises will require form a mechanism of checks and balances between owners and managers in order to manage and control enterprises. This mechanism is corporate government structure. Good corporate government structure can not only give managers with enough power of control to manage enterprise freely and leave enough space for managers' innovation, can but also ensure managers to use power of control of enterprise in the interests of owners instead of the interests of the individuals. At present, the biggest risk in incentive control mechanism of state-owned enterprises is the problem of "insider control". Managers actually make enterprise strategic decisions, so managers' power lacks necessary constraints and is prone to incur the behaviors which deviate from the maximization of owners' benefits. Currently, the ways of perfecting corporate government structure and strengthening supervision and control for top managers are to realize multiplication of property rights; improve and perfect principal-agent structure of state-owned assets; strengthen functions and roles of general meeting of shareholders, board of directors and board of supervisors; actively play the role of independent directors; establish information disclosure systems of important matters and financial information forecast system, and so on.

15.2.2.2 Committee of Compensation

Committee of compensation belongs to a part of corporate governance structure, but the constraint effect for incentive control systems is most direct so that it is listed separately. Committee of compensation is established within board of directors and is a specialized agency which aims at evaluating enterprise performance of senior management personnel and making top managers compensation plans. With auditing committee and nominating committee, committee of compensation forms a restriction mechanism which prevents excessive expansion of powers of the managers. Constraint effect of committee of compensation is mainly embodied when committee of compensation can review top managers perform their duties, conduct annual managers' performance evaluation and supervise implementation of compensation plans at the same time. At present, in our country, "*Company Law*" [4] and "*Listed Company Governance Guidelines*" [5] require listed companies to establish a compensation committee which is not necessary requirement for other kinds of companies. Considering special role of committee of compensation in incentive control, we suggest that non-listed companies set up similar agencies according to enterprises' situations and ensure independence, authoritative and professional of their members.

15.2.2.3 Debt Contracts

Most enterprises have debts from commercial banks or company bonds. While managers often have shares of their companies, they are different with lenders and shareholders. Debts can make managers transfer their wealth through asset replacement, cash assets, dividend or reschedule debts and so on, therefore, it is necessary for creditors to sign debt contracts with managers to protect their own interests and to have the effect of constraint for management activities at the same time. Debt contracts usually include commitment contracts and negative contracts. Commitment contracts regulate behaviors of managers that must be complied. Managers must make promises that the use of loan and the purpose of loan are consistent; financial conditions are submitted to creditors who stipulate corresponding accounting standards and regulations; and they'll accept review, etc. Negative contracts directly constraint behaviors of managers which may damage interests of creditors and include the terms of limiting the followings: total liabilities, capital expenditure, leasing, cash dividend payments, share buybacks, acquisition, asset sales, and guarantees, etc.

15.2.2.4 The Limit of Financial Behavior

Some financial behaviors of managers may have a significant impact on incentive effects, such as dividend distribution policy, stock split, stock merger, stock repurchase, determination of stock option value, sources of exercise stocks, etc. Therefore, owners should consider the impact of the above financial behaviors and limit these financial behaviors when they make compensation contracts. Dividend distribution policy is an example of incentive effects. According to signaling theory, dividend is an important index of stock returns. The higher the dividend is, the higher the predicted future stock return is, and hence the higher the stock price is. But after dividend is paid, stock prices will fall. Because stock price determines the size of the benefits from stock-based incentive and stock option incentive, compensation contracts have to limit companies' dividend distribution policy in order to make dividend policy consistent in the validity period of contracts as far as possible.

15.2.2.5 The Determination of Accounting Methods

Under the current situation of compensation contracts based on accounting information, managers have a strong motivation to take opportunistic accounting policy. Due to the status and role of accounting information in incentive mechanism, managers will speculate in accounting choices. Different accounting methods will produce different effects on some incentives, which is especially apparent on accounting treatment of expensing of stock options. Therefore, compensation contracts should determine the methods of accounting recognition, measurement, record and report which may affect incentives exercise and incentives effect. Accounting recognition includes initial recognition, subsequent recognition, derecognition, etc. Accounting measurement includes measurement attributes such as fair value, historical cost and intrinsic value. Accounting disclosure involves such problems as the internal and external financial reports.

15.2.2.6 Audit Control

Audit is a kind of control system which ensures effective implementation of fiduciary responsibility in essence. Audit evaluates and improves effectiveness of risk management, control and governance procedures by providing systematic and standardized methods, so audit is also a kind of special mechanism of managers' behaviors. From the perspective of audit subject, external audit is mainly used as owners' constraints to top managers, and internal audit is applied as top managers' constraints to junior managers. In 1977 International Organization of Supreme Audit Institutions promulgated "*The Lima Declaration of Guidelines on Auditing precepts*" [6], which pointed out in section 1: "Audit is not an end in itself but an indispensable part of a regulatory system whose aim is to reveal deviations from accepted standards and violations of the principles of legality, efficiency, effectiveness and economy of financial management early enough to make it possible to take corrective action in individual cases, to make those accountable accept responsibility, to obtain compensation, or to take steps to prevent – or at least render more difficult – such breaches." As a result, audit's role of restricting for managers can be found.

15.2.3 Performance Evaluation

Performance evaluation is an important foundation of incentive control systems, and managers' rewards and punishments are based on evaluation of its performance. Therefore, a reasonable performance evaluation system must be designed to exert incentive control systems. From the perspective of operation, performance evaluation is a very complex problem. The theoretical circle and practice circle have been exploring constantly how to construct and select evaluation indexes, determine evaluation standards, and invent effective evaluation methods.

About the selection of evaluation indexes, the performance evaluation indexes of managers which can be used independently at present mainly include stock price, net profit, return on equity, and economic value added (EVA) [7]. Among them, stock price that is associated with management remuneration can reflect the future of the enterprise value and shareholders' direct interest requirements, but stock price is affected by a variety of factors in the capital market such capital market efficiency, noise traders and so on. So stock price makes managers take too much risks as an evaluation index. Accounting indexes associating management remuneration such as net profit and return on equity can reflect the results of the production and business operation activities in the past, however, accounting indexes would be often affected by the accounting policy and manipulated by top management, and in many cases, after business activities are finished, current accounting income would be calculated and it would be less timely. Economic value added indexes try to combine the advantages of accounting index and market value index, but EVA's usefulness has yet to be tested in Chinese enterprises. Because each kind of performance evaluation has its advantages and disadvantages, it is necessary to design a set of comprehensive evaluation index system to reflect manager performance.

Evaluation standards are scale plates that make value judgments about manager performance, and value judgments are made according to the evaluation standards, and different standards have different evaluation results. First of all, the standards should be advanced, which is helpful for managers to improve operation and management level; Secondly, the standards should be adaptive, which can reflect the new requirements of enterprise management caused by environmental changes; Thirdly, the standards should be generic to facilitate the comparison between enterprises; Fourthly, the standards should be appropriate. High standards will affect enthusiasm of managers and may lead to demotivation, but too low standards also could affect the motivation and lead to "ratcheting effect".

At present, there are many methods of performance evaluation such as traditional financial evaluation, economic value added, balanced scorecard and so on. Traditional financial evaluation methods are simple and clear, easy to grasp and understand but not conducive to appraise enterprise overall performance. Balanced scorecard methods are the most efficient but are very complex and difficult to apply, and improper use may cause failure. The effect of EVA is in the middle of that of traditional financial evaluation and balanced scorecard, but the application process is more complex and project adjustment is arbitrary. The enterprise performance evaluation methods should be selected according to specific situations instead of generalizations. For the enterprises which have low level of management, traditional financial evaluation methods are still applicable. In addition, these methods are not mutually exclusive. Financial evaluation indexes of balanced scorecard can choose accounting data and financial indicators or can contain the indexes of EVA. EVA can reference traditional methods while avoid the weakness of traditional methods in benchmarking with the help of the idea of the balanced scorecard. Therefore, we could combine a variety of methods when we evaluate managers' performance.

15.3 Strength and Weakness of Incentive Control System

15.3.1 The Role of Incentive Control System

With the rapid development of science and technology, the competition among enterprises intensifies increasingly. The survival and development of the enterprise more and more rely on the creation and reformation of management mode. And the most basic characteristic of the new management mode is "people-oriented", which requires enterprises to value people, rely on people, retain people and make full use of people. Managers' personal behavior motivation, behavior target and way of behavior are induced and controlled by incentive control systems, therefore, the highest level of subsystem in the management control system is Incentive Control System which not only can realize the managers individual development and value, but also can achieve the stated goals, so incentive control system affects the size of the effect of management control system. Now "incentive" has become a global phenomenon and is becoming more and more popular, which is illustrated by the above point in fact.

The role of incentive control systems is mainly manifested in the following three points:

First, managers can be more efficient and reach their potential or talent under a good incentive control system. As Harvard Prof. William James described in his book '*Behavior Management*': hourly wages can trigger 20–30 % working capacity for an individual, while under fully motivation, this figure could reach 80–90 %, which is the three time or four time as much as the former when those who have not fully motivated. Therefore, appropriate incentive control system can significantly increase performance of an organization, and enhance competitiveness of a company.

Secondly, incentive control can attract talented managers who can meet the needs of enterprises to work for the enterprise in the long term. At present, many domestic and abroad enterprises pay high salaries to attract and retain talents. They create good working conditions and provide generous pensions, all kinds of life insurance, better medical treatment and so on. Some companies also provide employee stock, options, free continue education and set up schools and training center for further study.

Thirdly, incentive control can effectively solve the various complex economic relations and contradictions in enterprise operation. In the process of enterprise operation, an enterprise must deal with and coordinate the complex economic relations between owners and managers, among various components, production processes and stakeholders. The ability and effects of dealing with such economic relations and contradictions depend largely on the enterprise system arrangement of profit distribution, and benefit distribution system is the important part of enterprise incentive control system. Therefore, the efficiency of an enterprise incentive control system determines the enterprise's capabilities to deal with and solve all kinds of economic relationships and contradictions, which influences and determines the efficiency of the enterprise operation.

15.3.2 The Advantages and Disadvantages of Incentive Control System

Enterprise incentive control system is a double-edged sword, in one side, it can stimulate employees to work hard and in other side, it can also lead to a higher turnover rate of headcount. Therefore, an enterprise should grasp some advantages and disadvantages when it designs and operates incentive control systems. An enterprise should strive to adopt its good points and avoid its shortcomings.

The advantages of incentive control systems are as follows:

Connecting managers' interests with the interests of the owner and control managers' behaviors through the constraint mechanism of interests;

Adjusting the goals and strategies in time according to the changing environment and ensure the realization of enterprise value maximization goals.

When managers personal pay is based on team performance, incentive control can encourage team work and cooperation among business units.

The disadvantages of incentive control systems include:

Specific objectives are not clear, and the requirements to an enterprise culture and management quality are high. Therefore, an enterprise should be very clear in the motivation objects when it designs incentive control systems, according to different needs to design different incentive targets and operational framework, even different incentive modes. At the same time, incentive control system may have a positive effect when managers have high morale and recognize that they are treated fairly and could be harmonious with each other.

Managers and owners need to have mutual trust and understanding, and this kind of trust and understanding can only be achieved through an open, two-way communication. The design of Incentive Control Systems should emphasize that all managers who are willing to participate in formulating the incentive control rules be included. Generally speaking, as long as managers are willing, they can participate in the enterprise incentive control rules at any time, which is also called "maximize participation constraint principle".

The incentive effect also depends on the control system for examination and assessment. Any shortage of the control system for examination and assessment will damage Incentive Control Systems. The failure of enterprise common incentive generally can be traced back to the choice of performance measure. Enterprise performance evaluation indexes of incentive control should be quantifiable, easy and can show performance improvement clearly. The quantitative indexes should be achieved through managers' normal efforts. If the indexes cannot be attained or the pressure is too large, the incentive control is bound to fail.

15.4 Application Conditions of Incentive Control System

15.4.1 The Environment of Incentive Control System

As an organization an enterprise survives in a certain environment, which requires that the organization structure must be adapted to the external environment. As part of the enterprise organizational structure Incentive Control Systems also must match the external environment. The design of incentive control systems is ignored of the investigation of the running environment so that these incentives in practice often have many difficulties or obstacles. A good environment is more important than "heavily recruitment" and "prize". A good environment not only can avoid a lot of negative effects but also has a more profound lasting incentive effect. The environment related to the enterprise incentive control systems mainly includes:

15.4.1.1 Control System for Examination and Assessment

This system is the basic conditions which guarantee the effectiveness and sustainable development of incentive control systems. Effective incentive control needs the support of effective control system for examination and assessment. Any incentive party who lacks the corresponding control system for examination and assessment will fail.

15.4.1.2 Management Information System

Management information system is the system that provides information for managers, employees at all levels in the organization and organizes external personnel. Management information system is closely related to incentive control systems. It directly affects the efficiency and effect of managers' performance evaluation and is embodied in enterprise management information system and office automation system and so on.

15.4.1.3 Financial Management System

Enterprise incentive control is difficult to operate if it lacks the financial management system. Enterprise managers change remuneration structure and incentive methods and so on, which need to obtain enterprise support and need to change the support into the corresponding financial management system.

15.4.1.4 Strategic Planning

Enterprise incentive control is closely related to performance evaluation and enterprise strategic management. Enterprise strategic goal and model determine regulations control systems, budget control systems, control systems for examination and assessment and incentive control systems. Therefore, the establishment of incentive control systems and control systems for examination and assessment must get the attention of enterprise core leadership and need their direct participation and guidance.

15.4.1.5 Human Resource Management

Human resource management is an important mean of establishing effective incentive control systems. As a core department which is mainly responsible for people, human resources management for enterprise's incentive control plays a role in many aspects. For example, HRM is in charge of formulating reasonable human resource management system and policy, employing and selecting the persons who can meet the needs of enterprise management, and providing knowledge and skills training for employees, etc. Enterprise incentive control is not only to retain the talents and select the talents but also to force unqualified people to leave enterprise. It is one of the basic means of human resource management that the matching analysis of job requirements and the qualities of the talents

15.4.1.6 Enterprise Culture Construction

Enterprise culture is the management concepts and management modes which are suitable for the enterprise characteristics. It is refined and cultivated in the long-term management process. The spirit of enterprise is the core of enterprise culture that melts the enterprise purpose, behavior standards, ethical system, value criterion and rules as a whole and acts the role of guidance, cohesion, constraints, incentives and innovation. Incentive control itself is the external performance of enterprise culture. Enterprise culture changes the direction of the evolution of enterprise incentive control systems. Combining incentive control systems with enterprise culture has the important practical significance to improve the quality of the management team, change the enterprise management style and improve the quality of service.

15.4.1.7 Enterprise Incentive Control Evaluation System

It is one of the important supporting systems to establish and improve evaluation systems for the implementation effects of incentive control system. It's easy to observe the effectiveness of incentive control and the direction of improvement from outside aspects. An enterprise should have the courage to admit the exposed shortcomings or defects in implementation of incentive control systems in order to improve and perfect the systems constantly.

15.4.2 The Application Scope of Incentive Control System

Different enterprises are suitable for various models of incentive control systems according to their economic types and management characteristics, especially in owners' incentive to top managers in the different legal environment, capital market, and product market. In incentive of top managers to junior managers, some incentives' requirements for environmental conditions are low, for example position salary, bonus-based incentive, moral incentive and so on. These incentives can be applied to various types of enterprises and organizations, so we emphatically analyze the application scope of owners' incentives to top managers. From the perspective of enterprises' current situation, the modern enterprise system has not yet been fully established, and the reform of salary system is just starting. The phenomena of insufficient incentive and improper incentive coexists, therefore, we should be cautious about incentives to top managers. In general, the incentives to top managers are suitable for the following types of companies:

15.4.2.1 Listed Companies

Listed companies have a relatively perfect modern enterprise system. Managements in listed companies are in conformity with the market rules. These companies have the indexes which can reflect the market value of companies' performance. Their stocks can circulate but can't be bought back. These companies have dispersed shareholdings, diversification of property rights, non-stated capital, and are supervised by good external supervision systems and are constrained by information disclosure. So the marketization of listed companies is obvious, which is suitable for various incentives. Under the premise that a policy allows, firstly, top managers of listed companies can implement stock options and management buy-back plan; secondly, they can adopt stock-incentives such as virtual stocks, stock appreciation rights, restricted stocks and so on.

15.4.2.2 High-tech Enterprises

High-tech enterprises strongly depend on the talents and technology, technical personnel and management personnel are facing a broad external market. In High-tech enterprises the liquidity of personnel is larger, business risk is higher, growth is better, the effective period of investment project is longer, and it is more difficult to measure performance in the short term, investment in the growing period is larger, and personnel costs is heavier than do in other companies. The above characteristics of high-tech enterprises determine the kind of incentive mode, which must reflect the principles of low cost, high risk and high return. Therefore, under the premise that the policy allows, the stock options and stock incentives are the ideal choices and do not need large investment. Whether managers can obtain the benefits totally depends on the development of the enterprise in the future.

15.4.2.3 Private Enterprises

In private enterprises, equity transfer is easy, and the obstacles in thought and operations are relatively small, and enterprise growth is high. Private enterprises depend on all kinds of talents strongly, and the flow of the talent is market-oriented, hence management is market-oriented. Therefore, for top managers of private enterprises, the incentives should be applied to high-tech enterprises.

In addition to the above three kinds of enterprises, most state-owned enterprises tend to have these characteristics: the property rights are concentrated, the management is often difficult to adapt to market economy, and the appointment and flow of top managers are affected by administrative intervention. Therefore, the state-owned enterprises must take both incentive and constraint into consideration in the incentive plan for senior managers. In an annual salary system, stock incentives and other incentives should be carried out step by step.

References

1. China Securities Regulatory Commission (2006) Listing corporation equity incentive management regulation (pilot version). Website http://www.gov.cn/gzdt/2006-01/04/content_147360.htm
2. Mouritsen J (1998) Driving growth: economic value added versus intellectual capital. Manage Account Res 9:461–482
3. Ministry of Finance and State-owned Assets Supervision and Administration Commission (2006) The Pilot Regulation of Equity Incentive Implementation in the State-owned Listing Corporation (China). website: http://www.sasac.gov.cn/n1180/n20240/n7291323/11898529.html
4. Company law of the people's Republic (2005) Website: http://www.gov.cn/flfg/2005-10/28/content_85478.htm
5. China Securities Regulatory Commission (2002) Code of Corporate Governance for Listed Companies in China (2002). website: http://www.csrc.gov.cn/pub/newsite/ssb/ssflfg/bmgzjwj/ssgszl/200911/t20091110_167722.htm
6. International Organization of Supreme Audit Institutions (1977) "The Lima declaration of guidelines on auditing precepts". website: http://www.intosai.org/issai-executive-summaries/view/article/issai-1-the-lima-declaration.html
7. Xiuli Pan (2002) Criterions of achievement & compensation contract of managers [J]. Accounting Res 23 (7):31–35

Part V
Study on Variation of Management Control System

Chapter 16
Management Control in Special Enterprise

16.1 The Value of Management Control's Research in Special Enterprise

Management control is an organization system, which can ensure the availability of resources and their utilization efficiently so as to achieve organizational strategic objectives. Its theory changes along with the continuous development of the environment of enterprises [1].[1] There are four stages in this process including the Closed Rational Perspective, the Closed Natural Perspective, the Open Rational Perspective and the Open Natural Perspective. There are different mainstream views for each stage.

By reviewing foreign research, we can find that management control is influenced by the background of the enterprise at every stage and it also reflects the characteristics of the background. The existing management control mode at every development stage is influenced by enterprise environment. The gradual change of the enterprise organization further promotes the reform and innovation of enterprise management control mode and then promotes the development of management control research and practical application constantly. The enlightenment learnt from the evolution of the management control theory is several and one of the most important is that the complexity and uncertainty of the enterprise is the basic presumption and logical start of management control research. The design and innovation of the management control mode should be connected to realistic environment; otherwise management control will become a mere form.

Human society is currently transforming from the traditional economy to the new economy, coupled with the accelerating process of global economic integration; enterprise is undergoing unprecedented changes in the internal and external environment. As a complex and open organic system, in order to survive and develop

[1]The environment of enterprises include external environment and internal environment which enterprises face in the process of production and business activities, for example technology, organizational strategy, organizational structure, size, culture, and so on.

X. Zhang, *Enterprise Management Control Systems in China*, Understanding China, DOI 10.1007/978-3-642-54715-7_16, © Springer-Verlag Berlin Heidelberg 2014

in the dramatically changing market, enterprise must be equipped with the ability to detect changes in the internal and external environment, and respond actively. Therefore it is a trend to research management control mode based on different organizational context. With the development of economic globalization, Chinese enterprises' organizational context is changing significantly. We not only have to cope with the strong competition from multinationals, but also face the transformation of economy. All of these have increased the uncertainty of Chinese enterprises organizational context and the potential risks of business operation. On the one hand, enterprises need to delegate more to managers, so as to make rapid response. On the other hand, managers also need to be more strictly controlled to reduce business risks. This is a real problem which needs to be solved urgently. Judging from the practice, different organizational contexts lead to different models of management control. There are a lot of successful models, but also lots of failures, such as the collapse of Barings Bank, the bankruptcy of Enron and the fraud of WorldCom, all demand for design and application of control model based on different organizational context from a reverse side.

This section explains the management control system in Multinational Corporation, business groups and small and medium-sized enterprises based on marketing model, organization type, scale and so on. In practice, the basic programs and methods of management control are applicable to different types of business organization, but unlike other types, the multinational corporation, business groups and small and medium-sized enterprises have their own features, so there are special aspects of management control target, method and contents. Only by correctly distinguishing the commons and differences from various enterprise organization environment, we can choose proper management control mode and make them work effectively to improve the enterprise's management efficiency and eventually achieve their strategic objectives.

16.2 Management Control of Multinational Corporation

16.2.1 Features of Management Control in Multinational Corporation

16.2.1.1 Definition and Characteristics of Multinational Corporation

After World War II, especially after the 1960s, with the rapid development of foreign direct investment, multinational corporation which are the organization carriers of cross-border investment, have developed constantly. They play a more and more important role in international economy, and have developed into an advanced form of a transnational modern business. When people began to study this form of organization, it was preceded by various names and the most commonly used was Multinational Corporation. Multinational Corporation was formally proposed in 1974 by the United Nations Social Economic Council (ECOSOC). Just as multinational corporation have many different names; scholars from different countries provide different interpretations of the definitions of multinational corporation. For example, multinational corporation are defined as international economic organizations which is engaged in international business activities by setting up affiliated agencies (branches or subsidiaries) in several countries with headquarter in one country,[2] which is an international economic organization engaged in international business activities; or hire are two foreign branches or subsidiaries at least, so as to make its own and other foreign branches or subsidiaries' distribution amount and changes of assets, sales, profits, employment exceeds the amount of all companies within a country. In 1986, United Nations Code of Conduct on multinational corporation draft has supplemented and improved the previous definition of multinational corporation, and made a comprehensive specification defined: "multinational corporation are composed of multinational economic entity of two or more countries, which forms contain state-owned, private or mixed ownership, no matter what the legal form and the field of business activities of these entities are, this corporation is operating in a decision-making system and allows the related policies and a common strategy through one or more decision-making center; the economic entity is linked through ownership or other forms, therefore one or more entities can exert effective influence on the activities of other economic entities, in particular, the responsibility of sharing knowledge and resources with other economic entities."[3]

Professor Vernon of multinational research center at Harvard University provides a comprehensive summary about the main features of the multinational corporation.[4] His book "*The economic environment of international business (1972)*", which was published in 1986, lists multinational corporation's three main characteristics: (1) common ownership as a link to connect each other; (2) depending on common combination of resources, such as currency, credit, information, trademarks and patents; (3) controlled by a common strategy. This was regarded as the narrow definition. According to the connotations of the multinational corporation, combined with the practice, we can sum up the characteristics of multinational corporation as follows:

The first one is the difference among national cultures. Multinational corporations engage in production activities in two or more countries or regions at least by setting up branches or subsidiaries. Different countries have different cultural backgrounds, so the same management control mode may have different practical effect in different cultural backgrounds. It is the specific characteristics of culture that guide individuals in different ways and influences management control mode directly. People share different understandings of the meaning of culture, but we can present the cultural connotation by describing a series of independent cultural characteristics.

[2] Zhou Shouhua et al. [2], pp. 207.

[3] UNCTC Current Studies [3].

[4] Vernon [4].

Among these, the most widely used feature is proposed by Hofstede [5].[5] Many studies have examined how different ethnic cultures influence management control mode, and it turns out that the different ethnic cultures do affect the choice of management control mode. For example, in the culture emphasizing individualism, evaluation of the internal performance is generally based on individual, while the performance evaluation based on team is more preferred by the company which emphasizes the collective culture. In low-power-distance culture, managers tend to use the management pattern of decentralized decision-making and participation budgetary. Compared with the high-level ones, companies from cultures with low-level avoidance of uncertainty prefer to use objective criteria to measure performance.[6]

The second is the large scale and complex structure. According to the foreign direct investment database of the United Nations conference on trade and development, the foreign direct investment made by the major developed countries in 2009 are on average 29 % of GDP. And in developed countries, the multinational corporation is the absolutely main force in foreign direct investment. In addition, the majority of the world top 500 companies is multinational corporation; either sales or assets are huge. Large scale is very useful for multinational corporation to reduce production cost, to gain economies of scale, to engage in research and development activities relying on strong financial strength, and to gather information from the world-widely corporation network for decision making. Transnational production and business activities in Multinational corporations are completed by many branches or subsidiaries abroad, which take the equity as a connection, and constitute a multinational network.

The third one is the strategy of globalization. Globalization strategy refers to the multinational corporation focusing on the world market when it is engaged in international operation activities, seeking to build competitive advantages, improving its share of products and services in order to maximize profit. When the multinational corporation formulates strategy, they tend to start from the international situation, considering the overall interests of the company globally instead of the gains and losses of a subsidiary. They consider not only the company's current situation, but also the future development of the entire company. And even the management guideline reflects the characteristics of global strategy. The multinational corporation usually has a central decision-making system to develop the general policies and programs, which reflect the global strategic objectives and are carried out in the daily business activities of the subsidiaries.

[5]According to a questionnaire about nearly 50 countries' IBM employees, Hofstede found four dimension of social values which can distinguish characteristics of each national culture , they are individualism and Collectivism (individualism vs. Collectivism), power distance (great vs. small power distance), uncertainty avoidance (strong vs. weak uncertainty avoidance), masculinity and femininity (masculinity vs. Femininity).

[6]Anthony and Govindarajan [6].

16.2.1.2 Characteristics of Multinational Corporation's Management Control

Although the management control of multinational corporation is similar to the others, the environment of the multinational organizations and characteristics of business characteristics require them to pay special attention to more factors such as national culture, scale and number of subsidiary, internal transfer pricing, exchange rates, taxes etc. These features make the multinational companies' management control have the following characteristics:

First, there is a need to consider the impacts of cultural background difference. Different ethnic and cultural characteristics of countries influence the selection of management control system in multinational corporation. For example, American culture emphasizes on individualism, thus most American companies adopt the decentralized management mode and use the trust management control lever extensively. While in Japanese culture, which emphasizes on collectivism, the idea of family and teamwork is very prominent, so Japanese multinational corporation prefers to choose more centralized management system, and use the diagnostic and marginal control lever extensively. In short, the greater the cultural backgrounds difference between the home and host countries, the more important to decentralize decision-making and grant the subsidiaries enough autonomy, to enhance their abilities to adapt.

Second, there is a need to consider the impact of scale and number of subsidiaries. Practical experience shows that, the larger the subsidiary is, the more difficult to control, in particular the foreign subsidiaries. The reason is that the subsidiary has stronger adaptability and greater autonomy, leading to higher costs of monitoring for parent company. Moreover, it does not conform to the cost-effectiveness principle to design and implement sound management control system in small subsidiaries. Therefore, just running the tightest control in the medium-sized subsidiary is necessary. In addition, with the increasing number of foreign subsidiaries, the higher the degree of information asymmetry between the parent company and subsidiaries is, the more necessary to form more formal and frequent feedback mechanisms as a means of control, which can keep enhancing the control degree to subsidiaries.

Third, there is a need to consider the special problems of transfer pricing methods. Within multinational corporation, transfer price of goods, services and technology reflects a major difference between multinational and general corporations. Although transfer pricing is required for both domestic companies and domestic parts of multinational corporation, there are lots of differences among countries such as taxes, government regulation, tariffs, exchange regulation, capital accumulation, and regulation of joint venture. So transfer pricing in multinational companies' overseas operations is much more complicated. It also needs to consider several other important issues, such as to minimize income tax, to decrease tariffs, to create sound competitive conditions for the subsidiary and to reduce the foreign exchange risk.

Fourth, there is a need to consider the impact of the exchange rate. Multinational corporation operates globally with its subsidiaries and affiliates located in different countries and denominated in different currencies. Exchange rate will affect the business activities and profitability as well as strategy. Multinational Corporation will always encounter foreign exchange risk including transaction risk, exchange risk and economic risk.[7] So the risk of foreign exchange is of great concern in the design of management control systems. For example, from the perspective of performance evaluation, when parent company evaluates subsidiaries there are some exchange rate related issues should be taken into consideration, such as whether should the managers of subsidiaries be responsible for the impact of exchange rate? Which type of exchange rate should be taken as a benchmark? Is it necessary to distinguish different types of exchange risk? And how do different types of exchange risk affect operation results?

Fifth, there is a need to consider the impact of taxation. Taxation is a special distribution based on political power contradictions, and is a manifestation of national sovereignty. Due to development of economy, taxation, as an economic lever, is not the same among countries. This leads to differences among countries, so that multinational corporations need to consider the impact of the tax environment for subsidiaries in case of planning strategies, making budget plans and evaluating performance. Empirical studies show that the investment and income transfer of multinational corporation is closely related to the changes in national tax [8].[8] In addition, when the multinational corporation evaluates the results of strategic business units, they usually use after-tax profitability indicators, and if there are changes of tax rates during the implementation of budget, it is necessary to eliminate the impact.

16.2.1.3 The Specific Goals of Multinational Corporations Management Control

According to the system theory and control theory, the multinational corporation also can be regarded as an organic system which enjoys continuity in movements. There are four aspects of characteristic in this system: collective, correlation, objectivity and adaptability.[9] If such systems of multinational corporation intend to keep operating orderly, effective management and control is necessarily needed, in order to realize the company's global business target. Specific objectives of multinational corporation's management control are mainly embodied in two aspects:

First, promote the consistency of the strategy between subsidiaries or affiliates with the whole multinational corporation. Due to large scale, complex mechanism,

---

[7] Shang Zhiqiang [7], p. 188.

[8] Merchant [8].

[9] Wang Songnian [9], p. 442.

diversified distribution of branches and facing differences of business environment, there are inevitable contradictions and conflicts in the implementation of the business strategy in multinational corporations. For example, in the process of allocating funds and adjusting profit by internal transfer price, improper decision may cause contradictions and conflicts between the headquarters and subsidiaries or affiliated companies. Through the implementation of management control, subsidiaries or branches' deviation from the company's globalization strategy goal and deviation error can be found, thus measures can be taken to correct the deviation so as to the realization of its global strategy goals and plans.

Second, improve the operating efficiency of subsidiaries or affiliates. Multinational corporations have great geographical differences because of scale, complex institutions and branches located in different countries or regions, so the internal agency chains are longer and more complex, which inevitably leads to a large number of internal control problems. To ensure internal operating activities will not be out of control in multinational corporations' subsidiaries or affiliates, it is definitely necessary to establish the budget-based control system and the information feedback mechanisms and evaluation-based control system. Only in this way can the multinational corporation implement its strategic plans. They can get the information and timely feedback, which result in proper evaluation of the subsidiary, which are ultimately beneficial to the realization of the global strategy planning.

16.2.2 The Management Control Mode of Multinational Corporation

As a system, management control uses various control methods for the multifarious management objectives, targets and system statuses.[10] To be more specific, based on the input of control system, management control systems are typically divided into the planning control and objective control.[11] According to conflicts between creativity and domination of managers, some scholars present four types of management control: boundary, diagnostic, beliefs and interactive control systems.[12] There is another classification which divides control systems into three hierarchical levels: bureaucratic, market and clan control.[13] Moreover, some researchers come to the conclusions that the traditional control mechanisms such as rule-based, market and cultural control are included in management control systems.[14] The diversified types of control methods are owing to different perspectives and classified standards.

[10] Du Dong [10], p. 88, Du Dong [11], p. 111.

[11] Du Dong [11], pp. 118–122.

[12] Simons [12].

[13] Zhang Wenkui [13], pp. 23–32.

[14] Lebas and Weigenstein [14], pp. 260–272.

Actually, some methods differ only in names instead of substance For example, boundary control systems delineate the acceptable domain of activity and establish limits which correspond to bureaucratic and rule-based control. Also, the planning control is similar to diagnostic control level. Considering the clan control, some scholars tend to believe that this kind of control is more related to the corporate culture.[15] These methods are not mutually exclusive. On the contrary, to achieve the strategic plan and objectives of an organization, it often requires a mixture use of control method in practice.

Owing to the characteristics and specialties of multinational corporation, there must be a variety of control methods in management control system, such as traditional rule-based controls, typical market controls and so on. Among these methods, the culture control is usually paid the most attention to.

Firstly, for the rule-based controls, subordinates should comply with the superiors' orders. Based on inside regulatory framework, rule-based controls provide enterprises with boundaries where they should search for opportunities not beyond the company' acceptable range. Conventionally, multinational corporations are composed of numerous subsidiaries and affiliates. Due to geographical diversification, there should be a set of systematized regulations in order to monitor and measure these branches' performance against certain management targets. Essentially, budgetary system is a form of rules and regulations of an enterprise. In fact, many global corporations such as Wal-Mart and McDonald's provide a standardized framework of management systems with technical and business specifications. Besides, these companies also require subsidiaries and branches' budgeting, using plans to control their operating activities. It should be mentioned that bureaucratic controls will work more effectively especially by improving corporate governance mechanisms. Indeed, bureaucratic controls appear to be more rigid often than not, thus resulting in a shortage of managers' initiative and activeness. Also, the branches will lack rapid responses and innovation.

Secondly, for the market control, the most significant elements of control systems involve transfer price, horizontal relationship and compensation management. Corporations should depend on the outside market power to control the operation and managerial activities, while within the groups, competition rules and supply-demand relationships are more important. As Adam Smith said, the market control is just like the "invisible hand" which effectively regulates the allocation and competition of resources. For this reason, the market control emphasizes output control which will be a judgment of the decision-making correctness and a signal for managers to keep or modify their administrative behavior. For multinational corporations, there are many subsidiaries inside, thus the horizontal relationship and negotiated price consist of the organizational mechanism. In this case, transfer price becomes the core aspect of management control system. Due to the specific nature of the multinational corporation, besides confirmed standard of general companies, the consideration of internal transfer price involves taxation, government regulation, customs duty, exchange controls, financial accumulation and joint ventures.[16]

[15] Zhang Wenkui [13], pp. 23–32.

[16] Anthony and Govindarajan [6].

Management compensation strengthens the function of market control systems. If manager's compensation is based on the unit performance, it's inevitable to require perfect transfer price. For corporate headquarters, rule-based controls must be expanded to more autonomous rights that boast enthusiasm and creativity for subsidiary managers to exploit new business opportunities. For multinational company headquarters, to achieve its globalization strategy effectively, it also needs to exert managers' initiative effectively in addition to taking the system control. Thus it need to give subsidiary managers greater autonomy, and at the same time management compensation mechanism is needed. Through the subsidiary company managers' performance evaluation, it try to link management compensation to operating performance, in this way subsidiary managers can be encouraged. The accurate evaluation of the managers' performance should not only depend on the transfer price but also rely on the exchange. Performance evaluation systems thus have several guiding principles as follows. In subsidiaries, performance of managers must be distinguished from performance of subsidiaries. In addition, we should take both positive and negative impacts of exchange rate, transaction and economic exposures into account when subsidiaries are measured. While from the perspective of managers, we should eliminate the effects of exchange rate and transaction risks in performance evaluation. Using hedging and centralized coordination to deal with transaction risks are also indispensable. Besides, managers of subsidiaries should be responsible for exchange rates due to economic risks.

Cultural control system is not unique to the other two types of systems. It attempts to stimulate viable patterns of manager behaviors in order to achieve organization objectives. Cultural control mainly embodies internal motivation, goal consistency and uncertainty reduction. Cultural control ensures that all subsidiaries put their faith in global strategy, thus encouraging consistency and efficiency in the pursuit of the objective. Moreover, the group members would build consensus and become able to withstand risks due to the changing competitive environment. While it should be noted that there are different cultures in different countries, consequently, Multinational Corporation's organization culture and subsidiary culture inevitably is different. If we cannot integrate the differences, it may result in greater friction and contradiction which results in an ineffective management control system. Above all, the organizational culture of Multinational Corporation should be designed to take national culture of the host country into consideration.

16.2.3 The Contents of Multinational Corporation's Management Control

Viewed from activities, the contents of management control involve five aspects: production and manufacturing control, purchase and sales control, financial control, human resources control and accounting control, which is also true for multinational companies. However, there are several particularities both in company itself and in their controls. The specifications are mainly reflected in the following aspects.

The first is purchasing and selling control. Control focuses on the commercial activities such as purchasing, sales and trade. Since multinational corporation pay more attention to the implementation and achievement of globalization strategy, establishment and application of transfer price is designed as a flexible tool to meet corporate strategy. In many multinational corporations, transfer price used by managers for control is different from the transfer price for the minimization of taxation and tariff permitted by law. However, laws in many countries have made restrictions of transfer price making. While in practice, multinational corporations still adopt certain method to have lower costs and shift profit. To sum up, multinational headquarter should make clear rules to transfer price making since the price would have significant influence on subsidiaries' profits. The second is financial control. Financial control is the control over a company's financial activities. As for multinational organizations, financial activities are primarily controlled by plan of production, especially the budget. Budget systems are activities to realize organization's established goals and to conduct plans or arrangements for the future. Opposite to other enterprises, they emphasize on globalization strategy without regard for the gains and losses of individual branches. For this reason, budget-making should be based on globalization strategy. Meanwhile, multinational organizations with scale and multiple hierarchies are operating in multicultural environments and facing intensified competition. As a result, budget-making should consider the business environment, including the economy, society, law and policy. All in all, budgeting should include business objects, financial budget, operating budget, production and cost budget, long-term financing budget, R&D budget, acquisitions and so on.[17]

The third is human resource control. Human resource is the most valuable and crucial resource of modern enterprise. To multinational corporation, whether personnel can play their own function will directly influence the realization of strategic targets, thus human resource control becomes very important. Human resource control aims to take control of the acquisition, training, development and promotion of manpower resources. According to the globalization strategy, the basic mission of this control is providing rational allocation of human resources according to the requirements of the company's globalization strategy, and taking various measures to motivate employee' enthusiasm, fully playing their potential to achieve organizational objectives. The control of overseas subsidiary depends on several factors: operating capacity, mutual dependency, history and scale.

The last is accounting control. Accounting control is that the headquarter controls financial position, operating results and cash flows of its subsidiaries. Its crucial form is to audit and analyze financial statements of subsidiaries. In practice, regular reports include monthly, quarterly reports and annual reports of subsidiaries. Each subsidiary should complete and report the financial statements in time. Therefore, they participate in the design of reports' format and the determination of reports' content, and prepare and submit reports in accordance with the relevant provisions. This is an important aspect for multinational corporation to enforce and realize accounting controls. But above all, since the multinational corporation

[17] Wang Songnian [9], p. 433.

operates globally, the actual performance may be measured in different currencies, the exchange rate fluctuations will naturally affect the performance measures of subsidiary. Thus, in reporting business performances, managers must bear in mind different types of exchange-rate risks such as conversion risk, transaction risk and economic risk.

16.3 Management Control of Business Group

16.3.1 Characteristics of Business Group's Management Control

16.3.1.1 Definition and Characteristics of the Business Group

Business Group which was originated in Japan and translated as "Business Group" or "Industrial Group", refers to the group that uses the property right as main connection and coordinates action through shareholding and holding.[18] There are different types of international business groups. Business groups can be roughly divided into two types in theory and practice in China. The first one is that business group is an economic association or composed of core enterprise, fixed layer enterprise, half fixed layer enterprise and loose cooperative enterprise. This traditional understanding is based on transverse joint between enterprises, which does not reflect the true nature and joint motivation of business group. The understanding is that business group is one of the advanced forms of organization which is based on one or several large enterprises as the core, with assets, capital, product, technology as connections. It is a stable and multilevel economic organization jointly organized by a number of enterprises which share common interests and to some extent are influenced by the core enterprise.[19] This concept belongs to the modern sense, which is based on the establishment of poverty relationship to regulate relationships between group members. It is an association of enterprises under uniform economical control and legally independent. Therefore, discussion of this book is also according to this definition.

It should be noted that there is both connection and difference between business group and multinational corporation. On one hand, the business group may belong to multinational corporation. That is, if the business group conducts transnational business, it will become a transnational corporation. If it only operates within a country, it will become a general business group. On the other hand, the difference between the business group and multinational company is the complexity they engaged in. We focus on the study of non-transnational business groups.

---

[18] Wang Bin [15], p. 7.

[19] Zhu Yuanwu [16], p. 4.

Compared to other forms of economic organization, there are some basic characteristics of business group.[20] These characteristics are determined by ownership and organization structure; additionally they influence the groups' production and organization efficiency from different angles and perspective. The first is the monopoly and compatibility of the market structure. The generation of business group and market monopoly is closely linked. The multi-level organizational structure of business group will inevitably become a huge commodity production and sales network in certain economic areas, showing the characteristics of the market structure of monopoly. For example, the sales of top ten largest electronic enterprises in United States and Japan accounted for 65 and 90 % of the industry in 1995 respectively. The compatibility is mainly in the product structure. That is to say, in order to diversify market risk and expand the scale of production, it is not limited to the production of a single product, but developed into an integrated management mode which is multi-product, cross-series and cross-industries.

The second is the chain of property rights and independence of enterprises. Practice and experience shows that property rights are the fundamental link between enterprises within the group. Business group is a collection of legal person enterprise, which is mainly connected by equity, through shareholding, holding, equity participation and other forms to establish a long-term, stable and strong relationship and through its core business—group company implement the management. As every business group is relatively an independent legal person, they can obtain the asset, and autonomous self-financing. Thus, the business group has relative independence in the chain of property rights.

The third is the trend towards interest and collaboration of the members of the enterprise. Members of the business group are individuals with independent legal personality; they have the rights and obligations of independent accounting, independent operating and self-financing. Members of the enterprise pursue the maximization of enterprise value without damaging the overall interest of the group. Business group is not a simple sum of several related companies, but exists as a whole organization; the group pursues a common interest and common strategic objective. In order to achieve a common goal, each enterprise member is required to cooperate objectively in production and business activities, form the advantages and realize the synergistic effect of business group.

The fourth is the openness of the organization and management layer control. Business group is different from the general enterprise; it is a comparatively compact union consists of enterprises with independent legal person status. Relationship between enterprises within group is similar to the relationship in the market; there is an internal market coordination mechanism. So the group's organization management has some degree of openness, but the combination among enterprises' poverty right is mainly realized by shareholding, dominant holding and participation. As a result, its operation is not fully in accordance with the market rules. There is a center of institutions which have an overall grasp of the development and investment of the group, coordinating and controlling member companies. The business group

[20] The contents of this part main reference Zhu Yuanwu's book [16], p. 4.

delivers the management over the members through the hierarchy. So the control of organization and management of business group shows the relative layer.

16.3.1.2 Characteristics of Management Control in Business Group

Determined by the basic features, business group also has some characteristics in management control which are not the same with other enterprises, specifically in the following aspects:

The first is the integrity perspective of management control. Although members of the business group generally possess independent legal personality, common strategic objective and overall strategic planning are needed if the group wants to survive and develop in such drastically changed environment. In order to achieve the strategic goal and strategic planning, the management control for business group members must be from overall perspective, based on the whole and take the whole situation into account. That is to say, it needs to emphasize the integrity and comprehensiveness of management and control system, rather than to be limited to a member-enterprise's interests.

The second is the complexity of management control content. Because of business group's large scale and its unique organization structure, also group members are trans-regional, cross-sectorial and are across different countries, thus two impacts appears. On one hand, it makes contents of management control in business group more various than those in the single enterprise, which presents the complexity. On the other hand, it makes the control span of group management to increase, and the control strength and depth will be reduced, thus increasing the difficulty of the enterprise.

The third is the diversity of management control mode. Because member enterprises in the group are different in many aspects, such as technical level, asset size, equipment status, product structure and geographic location. The management control mode used for member-enterprises reflects the diversified characteristics. Whether the organizational structure of business group is the parent and subsidiary company, division or linear functions of the system, the management control basically belongs to the mixture of system control, market control and group control and due to different mixing proportion, groups' management control turn out to be diverse.

16.3.1.3 Specific Objectives of Management Control in Business Group

For business group, the implementation of management control is by using a set of systems and methods to ensure company's strategic targets and missions realized smoothly in the whole group. Management control occupies the core position in the business group management system and is even more important than the organizational structure.[21] If there is a lack of scientific and rational management control

[21] The contents of this part main reference Zhu Yuanwu's book [16], pp. 4–10.

system, effective operation of organization structure will be impossible. Lacking of incentive mechanism leads to lacking of efficiency and capabilities. Then it may be out of control, units in lower hierarchy act in their own way, such as deviation from enterprise's strategy intent, wastes of company resources, transfers of the interest of the company, and even unnecessary friction. Therefore, the specific objective of management control is to deal with the relationship between centralization and decentralization effectively. In order to make subordinate units give rapid response and independent innovation, enterprises group should find a proper balance of power, responsibility and interests between the business group and the subordinate units. That can meet the strategic goal and does not harm the overall interest of business group.

Specifically, the specific targets that business group should reach during the establishment of internal management control are as follows:

The first is the combination of results management and process management. The management of results is to decompose and refine overall strategic target for each strategic business unit (SBU), thus to determine the responsibility of managers and conduct performance evaluation in order to ensure the realization of the strategic target. The management of process is establishing budget control system as the main method to divide strategic business unit into responsibility center and focus on monitoring daily business activities in order to avoid damaging the interests of the group.

The second is the combination of incentives with constraints. Incentive mechanism is linking distribution of interests to performance evaluation of managers in strategic business unit, in order to ensure the capital value-preserved and value-adding; constraint mechanism is strictly restrict strategic business unit managers and administrators through personnel control and access control, requiring them not to damage enterprise investor's interests in the capital operation, assets operation or commodity operation.

16.3.2 The Mode of Business Group Management Control

The mode of business group management control can also be divided into three types. That is the rule-based control, the market control and the cultural control. Although all divisions or subsidiaries of the business group are members, they differ from each other's in the backgrounds of the organization such as technical level, asset scale, equipment condition, product structure, market environment. So the management controls adopted are basically the combination of the three modes such as the rule-based control, the market control and the cultural control. Therefore according to the business group's strategic objectives and organizational background, we can build the management control system with one kind of control acting as the major control mode with the others as supplements.

Rule-based control is that enterprise establishes a complete set of rules and regulations, including basic system, management system, technique specifications, and business specifications. These rules can coordinate and adjust production and operating activities between the members of enterprise. By the implementation of budget, the enterprise can decompose and transform the strategic goals and planning of business group for the members, in order to organize and control the production and operating activities. The purpose of bureaucratic control mode is to make the production and operating activities of members not exceed the strategic boundaries of the business group as well as in line with the overall interest.

Market control is actually together with the adjustment of the organizational structure. As greater autonomy and independence are introduced into divisions and subsidiaries, each independent divisions and subsidiaries can gain control by market transactions (or mocked market transaction) and internal transfer price financial accounting.[22] In the market control, profit or return on investment is the basis of the control; strategic business unit is regarded as profit or investment center. As long as the profit or return on investment meets the requirements, management from the higher level won't constrain. By internal management performance evaluation system, business group can evaluate the management performance of divisions and subsidiaries and associate the performance evaluation with the manager compensation which is the main means of control.

By culture control, the enterprise management authorities don't want to restrict behaviors among members of the business group simply through instructions, or by pure profit and return on investment. They prefer to form cultural atmosphere and teams with co-operative spirit, through delegating to managers and control by self-discipline culture. As the environment changes more and more profoundly and market competition becomes increasingly fierce, more and more attention is taken to culture control. Of course, it is based on the rule-based control and market control. If there is no rule-based control and market control, culture control may not play its role.

16.3.3 The Contents of Business Group Management Control

With general corporate, the management control in business group also includes the production and manufacturing control, purchasing and sales control, financial control, assets and human resources control, accounting control. But it presents different characteristics, which is embodied in:

The first is the purchasing and selling control. The control of business group's purchasing mainly refers to centralized purchasing of commodities, machinery and equipment. It is usually done by establishing internal bidding committee and establishing price comparison procurement policy, and its aim is to reduce costs of purchasing and operating. The control of business group for sales is mainly manifested in the group's internal trade between various units on transfer pricing. Different from general enterprise, the offering of products or services among members of business group usually occurs at a higher level of responsibility center, such as investment center. So the choice of methods on transfer pricing will affect performance evaluation of member enterprises and their management. Reasonable transfer pricing mechanism should be established in business group.

[22] Zhang Wenkui [13], pp. 23–32.

The second is financial control. The so-called financial control is the control of the financial activities; in short, it is how to raise and use money most effectively. The capital is like the lifeblood of the enterprise, and the enterprise cannot function without capitals. Every enterprise must retain certain amount of cash. Without a certain amount of capital, corporate assets can't be formed, also the normal operation and business activities are difficult. It is especially true for business group. To accomplish its strategic objectives, business group needs to stand in the angle of the group as a whole and make unified managements or reasonable arrangement for internal capital flows in order to raise capital utilization efficiency as much as possible.

The third is human resources control. Human are executors of the system. No matter how perfect the management control system is, if they are not implemented, the system will only become a mere formality and have no effect. So, human resource control is an important part of management control in business group. Among them, the financial personnel accreditation system is the key link of human resource control. To better ensure the group's overall strategic target, to reduce the asymmetry of accounting information, to normalize and constraint enterprise members' financial behavior, and to solve the agency problem effectively, the parent company must implement centralized and unified management for enterprise members' financial personnel.

The fourth is accounting control. The so-called accounting control includes records, statistics, reporting, and analysis of accounting information. The accuracy, timeliness and completeness of the accounting information will affect the rationality of the evaluation on the management performance of subsidiaries or divisions. As the scale of business group increases, the asset size and the operation expands information transmission between business group headquarters and the subsidiary becomes increasingly important, it is urgent to establish the integrated accounting information system to strengthen control within the group.

16.4 Small and Medium Enterprises Management Control

16.4.1 Characteristics of Small and Medium Enterprises Management Control

16.4.1.1 The Definition and Characteristics of Small and Medium Enterprises

The definition of small and medium enterprises varies across countries. United States generally called the enterprise small business which has less than 500 employees.[23] That is what we usually called small and medium enterprises. Small

---

[23] Longenecker [17], p. 1.

business administration in America, which is called SBA, determines the standards of small businesses. Some of the standards are the number of employees and the others are sales, depending on the type of business. In general, 500 employees or the sales of 500 million are widely used.[24] The counterpart of Chinese government has issued standards for SMEs, for example, "SMEs Promotion Law of the People's Republic of China" regulates that, "small and medium enterprises are established legally within the territory of People's Republic of China with various forms of ownership and forms, which are benefit to meet the need of society and to increase employment. They're in line with national industrial policy and the scale of production and operation is small and medium". On June 18, 2011, the Ministry of Industry and Information Technology, the National Bureau of Statistics, the National Development and Reform Commission, the Ministry of Finance jointly formulated and issued the "classification standards provisions of SMEs". In this provision, SMEs are divided into medium, small and micro enterprises. Specific standards are formulated according to the number of employees, operating income, total assets and other indicators, combined with the characteristics of the industry. It adopts triple standards to divide the SMEs. For example, for the field of industrial enterprises, if the number of employees is less than 1,000 or the operating income is less than 400 million RMB, the enterprise is medium, small and micro enterprises. Wherein, the enterprise with more than 300 employees and more than 20 million operating income is medium enterprise; the enterprise with more than 20 employees and more than 3 million operating income in RMB is small enterprise; the enterprise with less than 20 employees and less than 3 million operating income is micro enterprise.

Compared with other types of enterprises, the characteristics of SMEs in their process of establishment and development are mainly reflected in the following aspects:[25]

First, it's easy to create and the organic composition of capital is relatively low. In general, SMEs has the relative scarcity of venture capital and working capital in the beginning. Therefore, the scale of production a capital is relatively smaller. At the same time, due to the lack of funds and personnel, SMEs generally cannot easily get involved in the industry which has relatively high cost of entry or exit.

Second, it is difficult to finance and mainly dependent on self-financing. Compared with large enterprises, SMEs are more difficult in financing in the start-up stage because of its lack of favorable financial data and its low credit level. In this stage, the entrepreneurs are usually self-financing, such as their own personal savings or borrowings from friends. If the investment projects of small and medium enterprises belong to the field of high-tech, venture capitalists will consider investing; venture capitalists will invest a small amount of money, but they will require high returns.

---

[24] Longenecker [17], p. 26.

[25] This part mainly reference to Zhang Yuli and Ren Xuefeng's book [18].

Third, the ownership and operation right are not separated. Although SMEs can obtain venture capital, but it is limited to SMEs in high-tech industry, and very few enterprises can get the support. Therefore, SMEs are largely funded by self-financing, so that both the ownership and the rights of management are concentrated. For most small enterprises, the entrepreneurs are also the owner of the enterprise's assets.

Fourth, management structure is simple. SMEs operators enjoy business decision-making power, so there is no need to create complex organizational structure. In the early stage of SMEs, financial difficulties also forced the enterprise to keep management structure simple in order to reduce expenses. The simplicity of management organization shows in simple organizational structure, concentrated decision-making power and the unification of ownership and management.

Fifth, the enterprise is often with strong familiar characteristics. Most of the SMEs' establishment and governance are built on the basis of some kind of affinity. Although this relationship is not a formal contract, it plays an important role in the internal governance process. But this relationship will cause adverse effects, for example, cronyism; a part of the employees *violated the rules by virtue of their "royalty" status;* decision-making power, command rights and supervision rights are not clearly demarcated; the lack of internal control.

Sixth, growth has significant stages. Although enterprises have a life cycle, the various stages are not entirely different in general corporate. But for SMEs, their growth often has periodical characteristics. Usually successful SMEs go through four stages: the Seed Stage, the Start-up Stage, the Expansion Stage and the Mature Stage. SMEs at different development stages have different characteristics such as the source of value, capital structure, return on investment, business model, risk connotation, level of risk, cash flow. In this regard, this situation results in venture capitalists' phased investment, so that the risk investment has flexible features in order to avoid more losses. On the other hand, this situation determines that management control for SMEs should select a proper way according to the stage features.

Seventh, there are characteristics such as weak competitiveness, difficult operation and high elimination rate. It is heavily affected by the market and external shocks. Due to the small production scale of the SMEs, production technology is usually far worse than that of large enterprise, which causing a huge waste of resources.

The enterprise has low value-added products and technologies, and most of them belong to imitation. The value inherent in the products is mostly human labor, lacking of brand effect. It is difficult for small businesses to compete with large enterprises and foreign-funded enterprises with mature technology and perfect sales network.

16.4.1.2 The Characteristics of Management Control in SMEs

SMEs have different characteristics from non-SMEs in management control because of the basic characteristics abo**ve.** It embodies in the following aspect:

First, SMEs are dependent on entrepreneurs. In the SMEs the ownership and the rights of management are not separated, unlike other enterprises. Even though they have the investment from venture capitalist, the growth of SMEs is mainly dependent on entrepreneurs. Especially the SMEs in high-tech industry, its human capital and intangible assets dominated by human capital can give more contribution to enterprise value than tangible assets do. So that SMEs often presents the characteristics that human capital, growth opportunities and value-driven resources are highly adhesive. Once entrepreneurs die or leave, these SMEs usually cannot operate continually. The internal management control of SMEs usually belongs to the direct control.

Second, SMEs have a flexible variety of management control method. Due to its own characteristics and some limitations of funds, personnel, SMEs adopt different control methods. Each enterprise has its own management control method. Because of the change of managers' thought and growth stage, the enterprise adopts different methods at different stages.

Third, the content of management control is relatively simple. Because of the small scale, less personnel, simple organizational structure, narrow management control span and only one kind of product, the content of management control of SMEs is simple. Also, the level of control difficulty is low, compared to multinational corporation, business group and large enterprise.

16.4.1.3 The Specific Objective of Management Control in SMEs

The objective of management control in SMEs is nothing less than achieving the effectiveness and efficiency of operating activities. The former is a problem that whether the operating activities fit the corporate strategic objectives eventually, that is "what to do"; the latter is a problem that whether the operating activities consider input and output, that is "how to do". In particular, the objective of management control in SMEs is that:

The first is to achieve the goal of profit maximization. As same as other enterprises, the goal of SMEs is also consistent with the owners of capital, which is "Capital Value-preserved and Value-adding". To achieve capital value-preserved and value-adding, the core is to enhance economic benefit and thus maximize profit. Without economic benefit, there is no profit; without profit, there is no capital value-preserved and value-adding. Therefore, maximizing profit is the direct target. There are both theoretical basis and realistic choice to select profit maximization as the SMEs' goal. According to two different sources of survey data, the results show that profit maximization is the preferred goal in SMEs' management. Other objectives are establishing a corporate and brand image to increase the market share and expanding business scale.[26] Therefore, the profit is the first position for the survival and development of SMEs.

The second is to improve the operating efficiency. In order to achieve the goal of profit maximization, it is necessary to improve the efficiency of operating activities. That is, on the one hand, increasing market share and additional economic value of the products through innovation. On the other hand, reducing expenses through management innovation and saving expenditure as much as possible. Due to the lack of funds and personnel, SMEs always seek ways to increase the efficiency of management in the growth process. Simple organizational structure, more concentrated decision-making power and unified ownerships with managers provide conditions for increasing the efficiency of management.

The third is to control intellectual capitals. Traditional enterprises rely on the financial capital or physical capital. For SMEs in high-tech industry, while the financial capital or physical capital is the main source or core of value creating, but they depend on intellectual capital. Therefore, the key of SMEs to achieve the goal of profit maximization is to control the intellectual capital because it can provide the source of value and create value.

16.4.2 The Mode of Management Control in Small and Medium Enterprises

As the same as multinational corporation, business group and large enterprise, the mode of management control of SMEs has three types, that is, rule-based control, marketing control and cultural control. Differently, the degree of attention to the above three types of control methods is not the same in different stages due to the feature of stages.

In the seed stage, there are only innovative ideas and concepts; there are entrepreneurs and technical experts but no managers; without a complete plan, enterprise only carries out some initial development activities, such as market research. In this stage, there is even no enterprise in real sense; the enterprise is virtual and there is no real enterprise organization form based on law; it is just a risk project with lots of instability factors. Therefore, in this stage the mode of management control in SMEs is directly controlled by entrepreneurs.

In the start-up stage, the enterprises have been formally established; the products have been designed and produced, but the risk remains high because the enterprises have no historical record of operating activities and their needs for capitals are relatively large. The enterprises need to produce a small amount of samples to solve technical problems and eliminate technical risks. The enterprises are in the test marketing stage, lacking of visibility and competitiveness; scale of sales has not been formed; market risks are relatively large; the management team has not been perfect; the internal management organization is not fully developed; the enterprises have management risks. So in this stage, in order to monitor and control production

[26] These two documents were separately derived from the following journals: Liu Hong and Wang Xu's [19] and Jin Ming and Zhao Min's [20].

and operation effectively, the SMEs establish a set of rules and regulations, including the basic rules, management system, technical specifications and operational norms, which lay the foundation for future development.

In the growth stage, risk is reduced further and the products are mass-produced; the enterprises maintain the stable development and occupy a certain market share; the enterprises became profitable due to scale of sales. In this stage, the risks faced by SMEs mainly are management of risk. At start-up stage, the managers of enterprise are always entrepreneur himself or his relatives or friends, which make management system a family or workshop style. Various kinds of management issues especially in financial aspect appear when the company begins to have profit. These issues form a "bottleneck" restricting further development.

Therefore in this stage, it is imperative to take further market control on the basis of better rules and regulations. SMEs have simple structure, small production scale and a single business. Also, there doesn't exist problem of internal transfer price generally. But they need to establish internal performance evaluation system to evaluate managers' performance of different departments, at the same time to establish and improve the management compensation mechanism.

In the Mature Stage, the product enters into the industrial production stage; the enterprises have a considerable market share with higher profits. The main risks faced by SMEs are management and policy risks because of the mature technique and instability of market; the enterprises are able to borrow from bank, issue bonds or stocks; enterprises' equity becomes socialized. In this stage, there are chances that managers leave and finance misconduct. To the SMEs, besides funds, the lack and leave of personnel is also an important element of hindering its development. Furthermore, since human capital, growth opportunities and value-driven resource are highly adhesive, winning the talent over becomes a task of top priority of this stage. But improving operators and managers' remuneration constantly will increase the cost of enterprises and reduce the value of the business objectively. Therefore, the cultural control becomes the first choice for owners in this stage. For the owners of SMEs, its main responsibility is to cultivate a sense of trust and interdependence among the internal senior managements and create a win-win environment, forming a strong culture, in order to gather stakeholder groups and establish a senior management team and ensure team' operating in accordance with established mode.

16.4.3 The Contents of Management Control in Small and Medium Enterprises

The key factor restricting the development of SMEs is funds and intellectual capitals including human capital. Therefore, the management control of SMEs should focus on financial and human resources. In particular, the content of management control in SMEs mainly includes the following two aspects:

The first is financial control. It is to supervise and inspect the obtainment, delivery, expenses, revenue and distribution of the funds regularly, and correct deviations.

According to the SMEs' own characteristics and the problems of external environment, the financing channels for SMEs are relatively limited. It is difficult to raise funds by issuing shares or bonds, borrowing from banks and so on. The lack of funds has become the bottlenecks during SMEs' growth. So it becomes a difficult problem that how to obtain the funds and how to effectively use the funds. This problem is accompanied with the growing process of SMEs and SMEs need to solve it. Therefore, for SMEs, the financial control should primarily include, to control the financing and investment, the usage of fixed capital and liquidity, the earnings and the rational allocation of funds. The objective of financial control is to accelerate the turnover of cash flow and achieve capital value-adding.

The second is the control of human resources. In SMEs, especially in high-tech SMEs, the main source of value is intellectual capital rather than financial capital, so the main driving factor of value is human capital, structural capital and social-network capital. Human capital refers to the knowledge, experience and operational capacity to solve customer problems. Among three kinds of intellectual capital, human capital is the key factor. On the one hand, because the knowledge is hidden in persons, the delivery of knowledge must be completed by human behavior. Therefore, enterprise should set up incentive mechanism to reflect the potential of human resources and make tacit knowledge explicit and become the resource of value. On the other hand, since the intellectual capital has the characteristic of running off along with the leave of personnel, managers play important roles in the process of transformation that from intellectual capitals to the permanent capital. Therefore, in order to create value, SMEs should control and use intellectual capitals and human resources' control is the major part of intellectual capital control.

References

1. Otley D, Broadbent J, Berry A (1995) Research in management control: an overview of its development [J]. Br J Manage 6(s1):S31–S44
2. Zhou Shouhua, Lu Zhengfei, Tang Guliang (2000) Issues on modern corporate finance [M]. Dongbei University of Finance & Economics Press, Dalian
3. UNCTC Current Studies (1986) The United Nations code of conduct on transnational corporations, Series A No.4. United Nations Publications, New York
4. Vernon R (1972) The economic environment of international business [M]. Prentice-Hall, Englewood Cliffs
5. Hofstede G (1984) Culture's consequences: international differences in work-related values [M]. Sage, Beverly Hills
6. Anthony RA, Govindarajan V (2010) Management control system. Posts & Telecom Press, Beijing, 12th edition in translation, p. 299
7. Shang Zhiqiang (1998) The multinational corporation's performance evaluation system [M], 1st edn. Shanghai University of Finance & Economics Press, Shanghai
8. Merchant KA, Van der Stede WAD (2003) Management control systems: performance measurement, evaluation and incentives [M]. Prentice-Hall, Harlow

9. Wang Songnian (2001) Frontiers of international accounting [M], 1st edn. Shanghai University of Finance & Economics Press, Shanghai
10. Du Dong (2002) Management control, 1st edn. Tsinghua Press, Beijing
11. Du Dong (2006) Management control [M], 1st edn. Tsinghua Press, Beijing
12. Simons R (1995) Control in an age of empowerment [J]. Harv Bus Rev 73(2):80–88
13. Zhang Wenkui (2003) Large enterprise group management system: organizational structure, management control and corporate governance [J]. J Reform 1:23–32
14. Lebas M, Weigenstein J (1986) Management control: the role of rules, markets and culture [1] [J]. J Manage Stud 23(3):259–272
15. Wang Bin (2002) Finance and accounting research in establishment and operation of the Enterprise Group [M], 1st edn. Economic Science Press, Beijing
16. Zhu Yuanwu (1999) Enterprise group financial theoretical discussion [M], 1st edn. Dongbei University of Finance & Economics Press, Dalian
17. Longenecker JG (2006) Small business management [M], 1st edn. Posts & Telecom press, Beijing
18. Zhang Yuli, Ren Xuefeng (2001) Administrative barriers to small business growth [M], 1st edn. Tianjin University Press, Tianjin
19. Liu Hong, Wang Xu's (2001) The study of management objectives on medium-and-small sized enterprise [J]. J Wuhan Polytech Univ 1:41–43
20. Jin Ming, Zhao Min (2001) SME competitiveness and financing of Zhejiang survey analysis report [M]. Zhejiang Soc Sci 5:54–57

Chapter 17
Management Control in Non-profit Organization

17.1 The Research Value of Non-profit Organization Management Control

As an important part of modern economy, non-profit organization plays a more important role in economic life. Services and goods, provided by non-profit organizations, are essential for the long-term development of profit businesses and affect the good running of the whole society. In many developed countries, non-profit organizations occupy a large proportion in the national economy. Non-profit organizations in China, by contrast, are still in the early stages of development; they occupy a small proportion and have limited influence. Non-profit organizations have a long way to go to meet the requirement of the ongoing political and economic system reforms in China. Hence, to develop the non-profit organizations and to make them the third type power besides the government departments and enterprises or market sectors are of extreme significance in deepening the reform of the political and economic system in China as well as in promoting the development of society.

Management control of China's non-profit organization has been in different stage from that abroad. The domestic research on economy and management has been focusing on profit organizations, neither considering the characteristics nor systematically studying the non-profit organizations. The fact that theory lags behind practice has become one reason for the slow development of non-profit organizations in our country. This section will take non-profit organization management control as the main focus, combining with the characteristics of the non-profit organizations to discuss related issues of management control.

X. Zhang, *Enterprise Management Control Systems in China*, Understanding China,
DOI 10.1007/978-3-642-54715-7_17,

17.2 The Characteristics of Non-profit Organization Management Control

17.2.1 Connotation and Characteristics of Non-profit Organization

17.2.1.1 The Definition and Characteristics of China's Non-profit Organization

The research on non-profit organizations in China has not formed a systematic and mature theory. The definition in civilian non-profit organization accounting system published by China's ministry of finance has long been influencing the existing researches. It defines that non-profit organizations should meet the following three requirements: not for-profit; no unit or individual will possess the ownership of the non-profit organization in spite of their contributions, and thc profits should not be distributed to stakeholders; once a nonprofit organization makes liquidation, the remaining property should still be used for social public welfare in accordance with the provisions.

Though domestic definition considers the development of non-profit organizations in China, the scope is still too limited. According to this definition, non-profit organization includes social organizations, foundations, and private non-enterprise unit, excluding institutional organizations which occupy an important position in China. Institutional organizations refer to social service organizations set up by government or other organizations with state-owned assets involved. They're mainly engaged in activities as education, science and technology, culture, health, in public interest ("Institutional Organization registration management provisional regulations" the state council decree No. 252 and 411) Institutional organizations are generally led by government. The form of an organization or agency is required, as well as legal personality. In current situation, most institutional organizations are founded by the state, and are the subsidiaries of administrative branches. Others are founded by either private or the enterprise group. Compared with enterprises, institutional organizations have the following characteristics: not for-profit and the funds contributed are not for economic interests. From the characteristics above, China's institutional organizations have both the characteristics of government and non-profit organizations. The source of funds, personnel management and functions of institutional organizations are all subject to government control and influence due to current national conditions. At present, the institutional organizations in China have dense administrative background, and close relations with government. Institutional organizations will eventually be transformed to two directions: ones which are closely related to the government functions will be included in the administrative institutions; one with strong independence will eventually be non-profit organizations. Therefore, non-profit organizations should include the institutional organizations in order to ensure that the definition is proactive and able to adapt to changes.

According to the analysis above, we believe that as a kind of organization structure, non-profit organizations should have the following characteristics: (1) not for-profit, the earnings from any activities should not be distributed; (2) the fund invested by stakeholders should neither be withdraw nor be used for economic interest except for the range contracted ex ante; (3) the use of money should be within the limitation of stakeholders. This definition puts non-profit organizations at the same level with enterprises and government, acknowledging its role in social life, and includes most non-profit organizations in China. At the same time, the economic meaning and operational characteristics of non-profit organizations are included in the definition.

17.2.1.2 The Type of Non-profit Organization

The non-profit organizations can be classified differently according to different criteria. At present, the classification system put forward by a study center for non-profit organizations in Johns Hopkins university is used worldwide. This classification system divides non-profit organization into 12 categories and 24 small classes. Recently, there are two kinds of classification methods usually adopted in China.

The first classification is based on funding source. According to the source of funds and the leaders' right of personnel arrangements, China's non-profit organizations can be divided into seven basic types: government funding, government appointed leadership; Private funding, government appointed leadership; Overseas funding, government appointed leadership; government founding, leadership from folk; folk founding, leadership from folk; overseas funding, leadership from folk; overseas funding, leadership from overseas.

The second classification is based on the organization form. Non-profit research institute of Tsinghua University divides non-profit organization into five types in accordance with the organization form: (1) social communities. Membership-style organization which carries out various activities in both social and cultural fields, such as all kinds of societies, school reunions, promotion association, federation, volunteer organizations, and etc. (2) economic groups. Membership-style organization which devoted to economic activities such as industry associations, chambers of commerce, union, and etc. (3) foundations. Non-membership organization engaged in activities ranging from financing to capital operation in a variety of areas, such as project foundation, supported foundation, united organization, and etc. (4) substantive public service institutions, such as various non-governmental hospitals, schools, theaters, nursing homes, research institutes, centers, libraries, museums, and etc. (5) non-profit organizations which are unregistered including unregistered non-profit organizations according to law as well as organizations with commercial registration. The first three kinds of non-profit organizations in our current laws and legal system are referred to as "aggregate corporation", which is the fourth type of legal person defined by general principles of the civil law.

The other three types of legal person are enterprise, official organization, and institutional organization. The fourth type of non-profit organization is referred as "a private-run Non-Enterprise unit".

17.2.2 The Characteristics of the Management Control in Non-profit Organization

17.2.2.1 Lack of Proper Performance Evaluation Indicators

Non-profit organizations cannot use profit as the indicator of performance evaluation. Non-profit organizations are not for profit and most of them must achieve objectives in the absence of profit, so the performance evaluation system which takes profit as indicator should not be applied. As to performance indicators, the main problem for non-profit organizations is diversified targets. Most non-profit organizations are not simply in the pursuit of a single goal. These relatively dispersed goals lack commonality, but are important for the existence and development of organizations. One single goal alone cannot explain the organizations' mission. Secondly, the goal is difficult to be translated into quantitative indicators. Even though non-profit organizations can determine their core goal; it is difficult to measure it. The goals of non-profit organizations are usually qualitative rather than quantitative, which are difficult to measure or compare. In non-profit organizations, therefore, it is difficult to determine the appropriate performance evaluation indicators. "The most serious problem of management control in non-profit organization is the lack of satisfactory, quantitative, and comprehensive performance evaluation indicators."[1]

17.2.2.2 Cultural Differences

In non-profit organizations, there are two distinct groups: one is professionals; and the other is management. Professionals are those who have professional knowledge or skills, are the main providers of organization service, and have the advantage in volume. Management refers to people who have management experience and skills, and are responsible for the daily operation. They implement the mission and execute the strategy. Generally there is little or no overlap between these two groups. Their views on management control are quite different: professionals think the main responsibility of non-profit organization is to provide a wide range of professional services, and fulfill the strategic mission where management control is of no help except as hinder; management believes that in order to achieve goals, it is necessary to manage the limited resources and management control is an effective way to ensure the delivery of organization strategic

[1] Anthony and Govindarajan [1].

planning. Differences of professional knowledge and responsibility lead to different attitudes towards management control, which also increase the difficulties in implementation.

17.2.2.3 The Special Governance Structure

The decisions of non-profit organizations are made by the council, which is mainly composed of professionals, while managers are entitled with all the management functions. Professionals and managers follow the different principles respectively. Professionals are part of decision-making in enterprises but they do not play a dominant role, which is quite different from non-profit organizations. The council composed of professionals plays a decisive role in the decision-making. At the same time, the non-profit purpose of organizations affects the decision model directly. In the non-profit organization's decision-making, the modes of profit organizations are rarely adopted. In non-profit organizations, social purpose and professionals are always dominant. In the decision making process, professionals mainly consider how to maximize social welfare.

Influenced by outside factors, the execution of decision in non-profit organization depends on management. In this regard, non-profit organizations and profit organizations are basically the same. But non-profit organizations never follow the mode of profit organizations and never fully consider the feasibility of decisions and the impact on organizations' survival. Managers in the execution process, therefore, must deal with the negative influence of this decision model to achieve the goals.

17.2.2.4 Strict Institutional Constraints

Compared with enterprises, non-profit organizations are usually under a complex set of laws and regulations, so they have to follow more rules. The impact of these laws or quasi legal requirements mainly concentrates on two aspects: influence from the outside, such as laws, administrative regulations and local rules and regulations; influence from the inside, such as statutes, rules, systems, and agreement and donation contract. These laws or quasi legal requirements restrict activities of non-profit organizations within a certain scope to ensure the non-profit characteristics. At the same time, these demands are also the guidelines for non-profit activities. Only by following these requirements can non-profit organizations achieve the purpose of the sponsors and donors, and ensure the interests of the social public or specific groups. In addition, professional occupies a big proportion in non-profit organizations and some non-profit organizations aim at providing a variety of professional services for themselves. These professionals are usually affiliated to one or a few industries. For professionals, some industry guild regulations or professional ethics have a strong binding force; they must provide services under the written or unwritten rules. So the rules and regulations are special and important for non-profit organizations.

17.2.2.5 Unsound Supervision Mechanism

Because of the special agency relation, there is no sound supervision mechanism inside or outside non-profit organizations.

First, there is vacancy of the internal supervision subject. The main source of funds in non-profit organizations is donation. After donation, the sponsors can no longer withdraw the funds, even if the non-profit organization is terminated. Although the stakeholders can limit the use of funds, stakeholders still do not enjoy the ownership. From this perspective, no one actually really owns the non-profit organization, thus there are no motives to supervise non-profit organizations.

Second, there is no strong external supervision mechanism. Unlike profit organizations or government, the client of non-profit organizations can neither "vote with their feet" by choosing other non-profit organizations, resulting in shifts in resources and cash flows, nor "vote by hand" to fire the inside executives and professionals. Therefore, a rigid supervision mechanism is not formed outside the non-profit organizations.

17.2.2.6 To Provide the Services as the Main Mode of Operation

Most non-profit organizations provide services, which is also the main operation in service organizations.[2] Management control in service organization has two characteristics[3]: first, lack of inventories as a buffer. Main product provided by non-profit organizations is service, which can only generate income in current accounting period rather than be stored as stock. When the environment changes, enterprises can use stock as buffers to decrease the influence from fluctuation of sales, however non-profit organizations have no such choice. Therefore service provided by non-profit organizations must match the demand. Otherwise, the organizational goals cannot be accomplished or resources are wasted. Second, the quality and quantity of the output is difficult to measure. Services do not exist until provided, so we cannot conduct quality inspection in advance. The quality of service is intangible and difficult to make objective and quantitative analysis and comparison. It can only be measured on subjective indicators.

17.2.2.7 Use of Special Accounting System

In either western countries or China, non-profit organizations adopt special accounting system. In western countries, such as the United States, accounting for non-profit organizations consists of two parts: the government accounting and non-profit organization accounting. Similar to western countries, Chinese non-profit

[2]Anthony and Govindarajan [1].

[3]Anthony and Govindarajan [1].

organizations also use two types of accounting systems: non-profit organizations with close ties to the government, such as institutional organizations, which mainly use the budget accounting; non-profit organizations, which exist independently and use specialized non-profit organization accounting.

17.2.2.8 Volunteer Occupies a Large Proportion

Besides full-time employees, there is a large portion of the volunteers without salary in non-profit organizations. These volunteers devote themselves not for financial returns or economic benefits, And the mobility is relatively high. So it is difficult to manage and control these people due to lack of economic incentives.

17.2.3 Target of Non-profit Organization Management Control

The overall target of management control in non-profit organization is to fulfill management fiduciary duty and to serve the public or specific groups. Although this goal sets out direction for management control, it's still not specific enough to guide the management control in practice. So it is necessary to further disseminate the overall target. Management control in non-profit organization should include the following specific objectives:

First, secure the safety of assets. Safety of assets refers to the status which guarantees the normal operation. Because the purpose of non-profit organizations is not for profit, the accounting numbers such as profit is not the focus of management control, and stakeholders who contribute to the non-profit organizations do not seek for value-added. However, assets are still indispensable for any organization's operation. If loss lasts for a long time without effective remedial measures, then the assets would be depleted. Without enough assets, any organization cannot fulfill the target. Likewise, if the safety of assets can't be guaranteed, the aim of "serving the public or specific groups" will be unrealized.

Second, ensure that all management information is provided in detail and in time. Management information mainly refers to information related to management. Non-profit organizations provide services with professional knowledge and professional staff occupies an important position in organization. In contrast to the professionals, management in non-profit organization lacks professional knowledge. But in the implementation of goals, this professional information is crucial for managers. Therefore, we must ensure that this information is accurate to the management. There are two requirements for professional information provided: one is that relevant information should be explained in easily understood ways and should be effectively conveyed to managers; the other is that relevant information should be in a timely manner, to avoid causing any delay for management activities.

Third, reduce all unnecessary costs and expenses. Although non-profit organization is not for profit, the efficiency of assets should still be paid attention in the operating process. We should focus on how to achieve organizational goals during efficient allocation of resources, and how to serve the broader specific groups better with asset available. The decrease of costs and expenses can ensure the safety of organizational assets in the absence of new capital supplement, and then enhance the ability of continuing operation of non-profit organization.

Fourth, comply with the rules of non-profit organization, and accomplish the organization's mission. Rules of non-profit organization reflect the intention of stakeholders, which includes both the purposes of donation and goals of non-profit organization. The rules are the main basis and guide for non-profit organization, especially in the absence of performance evaluation index. The control in accordance with the rules is the guarantee to achieve the fundamental goal of non-profit organization.

Fifth, ensure the adequacy and reliability of accounting information. Because of the agency relation, the investors can only limit the scope of operations after investing, rather than supervise the specific activity. Therefore, only provided with relevant information on the effect and efficiency of the funds, can they really know whether the non-profit organization is operating according to the established organizational goals within the prescribed scope.

17.3 Management Control System of Non-profit Organization

17.3.1 The Participants of Management Control in Non-profit Organizations

Though the investors can formulate articles of association through participating in the decision-making council, they still remain outside the organization and cannot directly be involved in the specific operation and management. And the volunteers may have the advantage in volume, but they are not connected closely to non-profit organizations. Therefore, the managers and professionals are the most powerful within the organization and contribute most to the development. Professionals regard non-profit organizations as a way to achieve the career goal and focus on the effect of serving the public. But they pay little attention to efficiency and even regard the management control as hinder to the organization goal. For managers, both non-profit and profit organizations are designed to allocate resources and achieve specific objectives. The difference is that the goal of non-profit organizations is not in the pursuit of profit, but to serve the public or specific groups. So managers focus on efficiency of the organization and try to optimize the allocation of resources. However, they may ignore the mission.

It would be optimal, if managers and professionals can complement each other. However, the difference in belief, knowledge and goals makes it difficult for them to compromise with each other. Managers are more suitable for management control, because they are committed to efficiency and can make full use of resources compared with the professionals. Though managers' conduct may occasionally deviate from the goal of the organization, it can be corrected through complete articles of association and detailed work process. Professionals can focus on organizational objectives, but may ignore the efficiency of the organization, which will eventually lead to the failure of the organizational goals. Only changing the concept fundamentally, professionals can avoid failure. Compared to the change of attitudes, it is easier to establish complete system and work process. Therefore, the participant of management control in non-profit organizations should be managers.

17.3.2 The Object of Management Control in Non-profit Organization

17.3.2.1 Employees

Many employees in non-profit organizations are professionals, whose skills and services provided are different, while in enterprises most employees provide homogeneous services. At the same time, the professionals usually play an important role in non-profit organizations, and have a great influence on the development of organization.

Besides professionals, there is a special group of employees—volunteers. In foreign non-profit organizations, volunteers occupy a large proportion of employees. Volunteers do not accept payment and have great flexibility and high turnover. Because there lacks economic means to limit volunteers' behavior, managers are very concerned about the control of volunteers to ensure the accordance of their behavior with the goals of organization.

17.3.2.2 Activities

The contact between activities and objects in non-profit organizations is more frequent and relatively direct. Compared with enterprises, non-profit organizations are more likely to get final feedback from the service objects. The objects evaluate the activities of non-profit organizations according to their own experiences. The direct and close contact makes management control difficult and when problems arise, managers have less time to react and must make a quick decision to ensure the achievement of goals.

17.3.2.3 The Decision of Administrative Committee

Decisions mainly focus on non-profit organization goals and professional skills, but lack financial feasibility analysis. In the implementation of these decisions, managers need to make full use of various resources, consider all kinds of contradictions and difficulties that may be faced with, and formulate corresponding solutions. The managers can modify the decision if necessary, under the premise of not changing the goal but to ensure the smooth implementation of the decisions.

17.4 Management Control Procedures and Means in Non-profit Organization

17.4.1 Procedures

17.4.1.1 Organization Goal

The goal is the explanation of the mission and the reason why the investors provide money for non-profit organizations. Specifying organizational goals is to transform the organization mission from an abstract concept into a detailed description. Three factors should be taken into account to confirm the goal: opportunity that the organization can take advantage of, the strengths of organization, and the belief of the members.[4]

17.4.1.2 Strategic Planning

Non-profit organizations must decide how to distribute limited resources to the most valuable activities, so the strategic planning is important for non-profit organizations. In formulating the strategic planning, the main difference between non-profit and profit organizations is that non-profit organizations lack profit evaluation index, which makes project decision more subjective. Managers need to analyze the articles of association, discuss repeatedly with professionals to determine the key factors of goal and allocate resources.

17.4.1.3 The Control Standard

Although non-profit organizations are not for the purpose of profit, they can also adopt financial indicators as control standard. Financial indicators mainly reflect the effect and efficiency of resource utilization as well as the performance.

[4] Drucker [2].

At the same time, the control of non-profit organizations can not completely depend on financial criteria, the professional standard is also important. Non-profit organizations in many cases provide professional services and directly face the client, so the professional standard can be used to improve management control.

17.4.1.4 Performance Assessment

Although the lack of "satisfying, quantitative and comprehensive" performance metrics limits the non-profit organizations' performance assessment, it is still necessary to assess the performance. The assessment includes two aspects: one is the effect of performance, namely whether the activities are consistent with organization's mission, and achieve the purpose of the organization, and are in conformity with the organization's strategic planning; the other is the efficiency of performance, namely whether the activities are consistent with the optimization principle of resources allocation and whether there is inefficiency or waste.

17.4.2 Control Method

17.4.2.1 Budget Control

Budget control is crucial in non-profit organization control. At present, there are two problems with management ideas and methods in budget control.

The first is management ideas. First of all, the non-profit organizations budget control lacks business planning and performance evaluation. Budget is not the core and almost independent of the other management method. Secondly, non-profit organizations lack a common standard of management procedures, and the responsibility of budget is not clear. Finally, the internal attitude towards budget control is not uniform, with considerations that the budget control will hinder the goal of non-profit organizations. The logic of the latter two is consistent: managers are not familiar with the role and principle of management in non-profit organization, making non-profit organizations the opposite of profit organizations. As a result, when making the budget, many managers are simply involved in or provide counseling, rather than function as the leading person.

The second is technical methods. In the budgeting process, how to determine the trend of the budget is the key. Budget tendency is the perquisite of budgeting and budgeting is the basis for the implementation of the budget control. Non-profit organizations cannot tell the trend which will directly affect the implementation of the budget control. At the same time, non-profit organizations often need to deal with emergency, which makes it more complicated to predict the budget trend.

In order to solve these problems, we can start with the following aspects.

The first is to apply the ideas of profit organizations in budget control. Budget control is the mean to transform the goals of the organization to specific actions.

The goal of budget control is to fulfill the organization plan and ensure that the resources are used in key projects, which is the same for any organization. Therefore, in budget control, non-profit organizations should adopt profit organization mode. In the process of formulating and implementing the budget, non-profit organization managers should take a positive attitude. In the whole process of budget control, managers need to clarify non-profit organizational goals, and to conduct budget control respectively based on the strategic planning, according to various professional decisions as well as the connection degree between each project and organizational goals.

The second is to take the cash budget as a major way. In profit organization, budget control includes the cash budget, financial budget, operating budget and capital budget, which can also be applied to non-profit organizations, especially the cash budget. Non-profit organizations cannot seek for profit, but must get enough cash to ensure continuous business activities. Adequacy of cash inflows and the match of cash inflows and outflows in time and the amount should be the core of non-profit organization money budget. A large portion of the money in non-profit organization comes from donations, most of which are limited in specific use and projects. Therefore, when making cash budget, whether the use of cash is limited should be specially considered.

The third is the method of budgeting. Budget in profit organization usually controls revenues and expenses according to different responsibility center. While in non-profit organizations, this usually leads to incorrect choice. If using different responsibility center as the object of the budget, we need profit indicators as standard in budget control, so this method is not suitable for non-profit organizations. In budgeting, non-profit organizations can use project as the subject of budget control. Different projects are the main channel for non-profit organization to achieve its objectives. Using the project as the object of the budget control to analyze the cost and financial situation is a good way to control the operation effect and efficiency of the whole organization.

The fourth is the determination of budget trend. The budget trend forecasts vary among different managers, so when the management changes, the budget should be remade. When budgeting for the first time, managers should rule out the influence of history, and adopt zero-based budget. According to the characteristics of the environment, the new budget should consider specific factors influencing decision-making, such as the usage of funds, whether it is in line with the prescribed direction and the way of donated funds. In the following years, if there are no significant changes in the management team, the budget can be modified based on the zero-based budget. As to budget trend, the factors affecting the quantity of services can be determined by establishing a forecast model. To establish a model considering various factors based on linear regression of past data, and then the quantity changes in the future can be determined. It is important to note that contingency factors should be included in the model, so as to fully predict the future service changes. The quantity change of cash mainly refers to whether the access to funds will be affected. The quality change mainly refers to the change of service quality of the same project. In order to achieve organizational goals, it should determine whether the service changes according to the environmental. The change of the quality of cash mainly refers to whether the use of new money is limited.

Fifth, budget control should maintain flexible. Many non-profit organizations play an important role in some sudden events. Charities, for example, in the event of natural disasters, need to devote into the rescue of the emergency immediately. Reaction towards emergencies has direct influence on achieving the goals of non-profit organizations; therefore incidents should be included in the budget. But the unpredictability of emergencies makes it difficult to have detailed consideration in the budget process, which requires the budget to keep certain elasticity. The flexibility of budget doesn't mean loosening the planning and execution of the budget but establishing the budget and methods for emergencies. When emergencies happen, the non-profit organizations are able to react quickly.

17.4.2.2 The Evaluation of Non-profit Organizations

Some countries where non-profit organizations are highly developed such as America and Britain have a complete assessment system for non-profit organizations.[5] Multi-line of defense ensures the healthy and orderly development of non-profit organizations, including government supervision, independent third-party assessment, peer review, media and public scrutiny, non-profit organizations self-discipline and other factors. The good trend of development of non-profit organizations in these countries illustrates that the organization evaluation system is effective. Similarly, non-profit organizations can also set up corresponding internal organizations to conduct self-discipline assessment for management control.[6] Tsinghua University professor Deng Guosheng puts forward an evaluation framework which is adapted to Chinese institutional background. It is composed of four parts:

First of all, the assessment aims to promote the non-profit organization's responsibility and to improve the social credibility; Second, the mission and strategic planning evaluation aims to clarify the development direction and strategy; Third, the project evaluation aims to promote efficiency and service quality; Fourth, capability assessment aims to promote non-profit organization's ability to complete the mission.

17.4.2.3 Cost Efficiency Analysis

The "proxy indicators" can be used to analyze cost efficiency of a non-profit organization although it is impossible to quantify the performance indicators and organizational goals.[7] This method is based on five kinds of indicators. Namely: "Benefit", "Outcome", "Output", "Input" and "Cost".

[5] Guosheng Deng [3].

[6] Deng Guosheng [3].

[7] Ramanathan [4].

"Benefit" (B) refers to the benefits non-profit organization brings to society and measured by financial indicators. Commonly used indicators are: the indispensable expenses due to the shortage of this service; or the improved efficiency and increased wealth because of this service. "Outcome" (OC) refers to the social benefits non-profit organizations provide and measured by non-financial indicators. "Output" (O) refers to the service provided by non-profit organizations without considering whether the outcome is produced or not. In general, the output is measured using physical form. "Input" (I) refers to all kinds of resources consumed by non-profit organizations and measured by non-financial indicators. "Cost" (C) refers to all resources measured by monetary value that non-profit organizations consume to provide services.

"B and OC" represent what the non-profit organizations contribute to society, the former uses financial measures, and the latter uses non-financial measures. I and C represent what the non-profit organizations consume from society, the former uses non-financial measures and the latter uses financial measures.

Managers can choose the following cost-benefit analysis to conduct management control according to the different needs of non-profit organizations management: B/OC represents the benefits from service provided, illustrating the working effect of non-profit organizations; OC/O represents the success rate of the services offered to illustrate the working effect of non-profit organizations as well as the professional performance; O/I represents the production efficiency to show the efficiency of managers' use of resources; I/C represents the resources consumed by every dollar to illustrate the efficiency of the managers' obtaining of resources.

17.4.2.4 Establish the Internal Promotion System

For numerous non-profit organization volunteers, they don't join the non-profit organizations for economic benefit, but for the challenging work itself. Apart from financial gains, there is no difference between volunteers from non-profit organizations and employees of the profit organizations; they are all in pursuit of a sense of accomplishment and identity. Therefore, a promotion system for volunteers in the non-profit organizations can excite the enthusiasms of volunteers, which plays an important role in promoting the realization of organizational goals.

17.4.2.5 Non-profit Organization Incentive

Compared with profit organizations, the management of a non-profit organization is more difficult, the performance is not easy to measure and the distribution of earnings cannot be used for business. So in order to attract excellent management personnel, and encourage managers to work hard for organizational goals, non-profit organization must provide employees with competitive remuneration. In order to be incentive, compensation in nonprofit organizations should be on the same level with or exceed profit businesses. Considering the above factors, managers' rewards in non-profit organizations should include three parts.

The first part is fixed income. This part occupies the largest portion of rewards; it is the basic payment of managers. Fixed remuneration of managers should be kept on the same level with profit-seeking organizations to attract talented personnel. As long as the goals of organization are realized and the governmental nonprofit organizations are kept as going concern, managers should have this remuneration. In some volunteer-style nonprofit organizations, members are voluntary to provide services. So the fixed income of the management can be slightly lower than profit organizations of the same size.

The second part is related to the size of non-profit organization. The bigger the size of non-profit organization is, the harder for management to control. Larger non-profit organizations face more complex environment, therefore managers need to consider from many aspects; Bigger nonprofits' capital scale is relatively larger, so the responsibility and pressure of management increase; In bigger non-profit organizations, the incentive should be greater to ensure that the management work hard enough. In order to motivate managers, payment should be related to the size of the organization positively except for the fixed part.

The third part is related to the organization's cash flow. For non-profit organization's management, profit targets cannot tell the management's effort and operating results. While the indicators of cash flow play an important role in the survival and development of non-profit organizations. Stable cash inflow illustrates effective management activities. Well-targeted cash outflow reflects the execution of plans by management in order to achieve organizational goals. The match of cash inflows and outflows is an important indicator which reflects the status of non-profit organizations. In nonprofit organization, though the management's payment has nothing to do with profit indicators, it has a positive relationship with the indicators of cash flow.

In addition to using monetary incentives, non-profit organization should also pay attention to reputation incentive to the management personnel. Since the operational surplus in non-profit organizations cannot be used for distribution, the incentive effects of monetary compensation are limited. A lot of outstanding management work for nonprofit organizations, of the pursuit of reputation and social prestige is their main consideration. Certain effect of inciting the management can be achieved through a variety of ways that may improve their social prestige and status.

References

1. Anthony RN, Govindarajan V (2007) Management control systems 12/E [M]. Tata McGraw-Hill Education, India
2. Drucker PF (1989) The nonprofit Drucker, vols I–IV. Leadership Network, Tyler

3. Deng G (2001) The research on evaluation system of non-profit organizations [J]. Chinese Public Admin 17(10):41–43
4. Ramanathan K (1985) A proposed framework for designing management control systems in not-for-profit organizations [J]. Finance Acc Manage 1(1):75–92

Chapter 18
Project Management Control

18.1 Significance of Project Management Control Research

The academic development of project management control is mainly reflected in the research of theories and methodologies of project management control, the United States has paid special attention to the education of management control, and many project management bodies of research have been established successively. A great deal of control project management theory and methodology studies have been carried out by these research institutes, universities, project management professional associations and large enterprises all over the world. The development of project management control makes its theories and methods have made a great progress and formed a professional theory and method system.

In the early twentieth century, project management theories and methods began to be introduced into China. Some foreign experts and scholars have delivered lectures about project management for many times, teaching new ideas, which played an important role in the spread of project management in China.

China has made a great progress in the academic research of project management; however, the attention paid to project management control is not sufficient. Basically speaking, academic articles or books that could be found usually put project management control in its basic theory system. Moreover, the content is scattered and insufficient. Books and articles on management control are also scarce and could not be a system. As for the specialized study of project management control system, it is a blank.

Therefore, there is still a considerable gap in the academic development of management control in our country when compared internationally. The importance of the subject of project management control and its practical significance has not caused sufficient attention in China. In order to eliminate this gap as soon as possible, this chapter will do further research on this respect, aiming at making the academic development of project management control in China to be matured gradually and be in line with developed countries.

X. Zhang, *Enterprise Management Control Systems in China*, Understanding China,
DOI 10.1007/978-3-642-54715-7_18, © Springer-Verlag Berlin Heidelberg 2014

In the practice of project management, project activities are full of risks and difficulties. With the development of economy and science and technology, projects are getting bigger and bigger, and more and more complex. Due to so many organizations participating in the project implementation, so many works of different natures and so many resources to be input, the completion of project goals and plans under the resource constraints will mainly depend on the effective control over the implementation of project management activities. The premise and key to realize the ultimate goals is to carry out effective management control during the process of project management.

In the early 1980s of twentieth century, China began to apply project management in practice. Project management control techniques have been used in some major projects and received a good effect. But we must admit that in regard of the project management practice; there is still a great gap between China and other countries. During the course of implementing project management activities, there are still a lot of loopholes in management control, such as a lack of planning, lack of systematic approach and coordination, etc. Thus, it is extremely significant in paying full attention to the application of project management control system in practice, to overcome the shortcomings of management control, and to constantly promote the comprehensive development of project management control in practice in China.

18.2 The Connotation, Characteristics and Goals of Project Management Control

18.2.1 The Connotation and Characteristics of Project Management

18.2.1.1 The Connotation of Project and Project Management

Project exists in a large number of organizational operation processes. It is a series of management activities to accomplish the ultimate goal of an organization. Although projects differ greatly in their nature, scale, the amount of investment and requirements of techniques applied, they all undergo the whole process of startup, planning, implementation and closeout.

Project management is to plan, organize, coordinate and control project and its resources in project management activities using certain theoretical knowledge and technical methods aggregated with the joint efforts of project managers and employees. Its aim is to realize the special project target and eventually reach the requirements and expectations of stakeholders.

18.2.1.2 The Characteristics of Project Management

1. Project management is the management activity to collect comprehensive knowledge. Project is a relatively complex job, which usually consists of multiple parts and works with multiple organizations involved. There will be many unknown factors in its execution among which each factor is often with uncertainty. It also needs to organize personnel from different places within a temporary organization, to achieve project goals under a condition with relatively strict constraints of technical performance, cost, schedule, etc. All these factors determine that the project management must use knowledge of a variety of disciplines to solve problems.
2. The project management is an exploratory management activity. Its main difference from the general repetitive management is that project is a one-time activity to fulfill specified requirements; it needs to be both risk-bearing and creative. The creativeness of project mainly depends on the development and support of science and technology projects, and creativeness is always exploratory.[1] Based on experiences from repeated failures in exploratory, project management accumulated a large number of experienced technical reserves and strain capacity.
3. Project management is a management activity with special institution. Contrast to repetitive management, project management need to build a management institution for a specific task. The institution is not bound by any organization; it must make corresponding decisions in time and release the instructions, to ensure the achievement of the ultimate project goals.
4. Project management has a life cycle. The essence of project management is the job to plan and control a one-off job and to achieve the desired target within a prescribed period of time. Once the target has been met, project will lose its meaning of existence and collapses. So the related project management also has a predictable life cycle.

18.2.2 The Connotation and Characteristics of Project Management and Control

18.2.2.1 The Connotation of Project Management Control

In the process of the implementation of the project plan, due to the risk and difficulty inherent in the project, the progress of project often deviates from the expected track.

---

[1] Bi Xing and Zhai Li [1].

In order to achieve the ultimate goal, project managers need to make plans according to the project schedule and control the scope, schedule and cost of the project. If deviation appears, the manager should also alter the plan and put forward corrections after analyzing its reasons, and finally make an evaluation on the implementation result of the project. All this kind of management activities is project management control.

18.2.2.2 The Characteristics of Project Management Control

Compared with the organization management control, project management control has the following features:

1. Project management control system is prior to the sustainable operation organization. They must establish a satisfactory relationship to make both of them fit each other in some way.
2. Project management control and sustainable operation organization management control have different emphasis. Among them, project management control mainly focuses on the project, and its purpose at a specific period is to produce the most satisfactory products at the lowest cost. Meanwhile, sustainable operation organization management control focuses on cost instead, and the purpose mainly concentrates on activities and products in a particular period.
3. Project management control usually tends to emphasize more on the trade-off among the implementation scope, the production schedule and cost. Despite a similar case in sustainable operation organization management control, it is not that typical.
4. The project management control over project plan is of greater difficulty. The construction projects, consultation activities, research and development projects are affected frequently by geographic conditions, climate, logistical services and other unforeseen changes in the environmental conditions, and it makes the project often change greatly and bring about unexpected troubles. Whereas, the sustainable operation plan usually does not incur significant regular changes.
5. The performance standard of project management control is more difficult to determine. The performance standard of sustainable operation organization is often formulated according to the evaluation of repetitive project activities, which is much easier to be determined and more reliable than that of project. However, performance standard is usually used only once for different projects. And it's more difficult to be determined for management control in project.

18.2.3 Specific Goals of Project Management Control

The basic goal of project management control is to ensure the conformity of project management activities to the plan. Project management control is concerned with looking for and identifying the deviation from the plan, and taking appropriate actions to achieve the desired results. As is known, for a project, the goal is usually measured by indicators like schedule, cost, technology and quality. The function of project management control is to adjust activities, resource and events to achieve the schedule, cost and technical goals regulated in the project plan.

According to the basic goal of project management control, the specific goals of project management control can be summarized as follows:

18.2.3.1 To Reduce Costs and Improve Performance

The main target of project management control is to save expenses, and to achieve the maximum economic benefits at the lowest consumption. The project management control could realize this target through a variety of special and comprehensive controls. And this requires constantly tracking and inspecting a series of financial and technical indicators, such as cost, labor productivity, sales growth, quality, consumption rate, etc.

18.2.3.2 To Search for Deviations and Restrict the Accumulation

Mistakes, failures and deviations could appear in any job. Then what should be done in project management control is to actively look for deviations and analyze their consequences. Generally speaking, small deviation will not bring serious damage to one organization immediately, but if they keep happening and accumulating, very serious consequences will arise. Thus, the target of project management control is to discover deviations in time restrict their accumulation and take corrective actions as soon as possible.

The final effect pursued by project management control is to make the organization work in order and it is quite necessary to establish effective control systems. These control systems need to conduct a comprehensive control over the organization's resources, working and operating procedures to make the organization run in order and under control, and to drive the management of project to be carried out smoothly.

18.3 Project Management Control System

18.3.1 Subject of Project Management Control

In any project, its investors, manager, management and customers will all monitor its scope, progress, quality and cost just for their own consideration. The responsibility, the power and the interest of all these stakeholders constitute the subject of a project management control system.

18.3.1.1 Project Investors

Investors of the project are the final decision maker. They have the decision-making power over the schedule, the cost, the quality as well as the comprehensive management of the project, and they could exert a decisive impact on the project management control.

18.3.1.2 Project Customers

As for project strategy, customers should set project objectives, identify project background, assist to formulate and approve project plans. Customers play an important role in respect of key milestones and cost and quality controls.

18.3.1.3 Project Management

Project management is expected to (1) determine the project requirements (specific scope, schedule and cost); (2) put forward project constraints and assumptions; (3) to examine, approve and launch the resources input planning and project management control process; (4) to establish specific management control criteria; (5) to control the performance, schedule, quality, cost and risk; (6) to approve in stages and to listen to project reporting and evaluation results.

18.3.1.4 Project Manager

Project manager is in charge of drafting project startup, determining the core team members, formulating project planning, and is responsible for project implementation, project progress reporting, process reviewing and risk control controlling.

The organization or group that tries to fulfill all the requirements above is a project team.

18.3.2 Object of Project Management Control

The project management control is a whole system composed of a series of temporary tasks. The purpose of this system is to realize the goal of project management by using scientific project management control technologies. It is worth noting that the object of project management control cannot be confused with that of enterprise management. Project is only a small part of a large enterprise system. Enterprise management goals are extensive, while the main purpose of project management control is to achieve the intended target of the project.

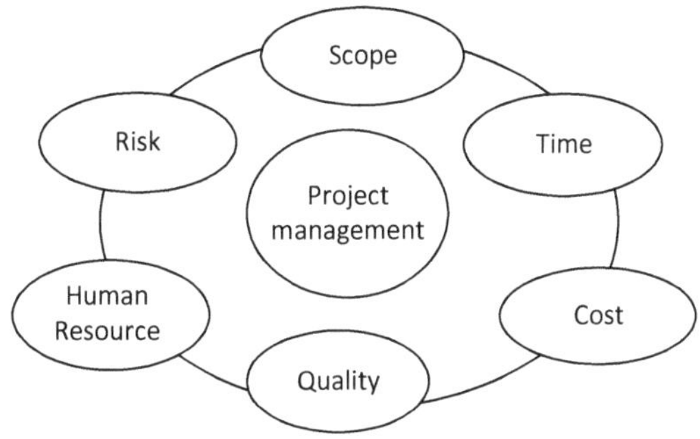

Fig. 18.1 Contents of project management control

18.3.3 Contents of Project Management Control

According to the Project Management Body of Knowledge (PMBOK) launched by Project Management Institute (PMI)[2] in 1987, the main contents of project management control include the following items: scope management control, time management control, cost management control, quality management, human resources management control, and risk management control, etc. The core content of project management control is to achieve a full range of control from aspects of scope, time, cost, quality, human resources, risk and to achieve a higher operating efficiency under the budget (as shown in Fig. 18.1).

18.3.3.1 Scope of Project Management Control

The project scope is the working scope of the project. It refers to all the works of the project team to finish aiming to provide products, services or achievements that conform to requirements. It's also the basis of the project schedule, cost and quality.[3]

Project scope management control mainly refers to the management control over the plan and its change of the project scope.

Management control over project plan mainly refers to demarcate the project scope and inspect the following matters: whether the goals of project scope plan are complete and accurate; whether the plan indicators are reliable and effective; whether the definition of project scope could ensure the realization of goals; whether the benefits of project is greater than the costs; whether there is a need of further supporting research on project scope definition, and so on.

Management control over project scope change mainly refers to implement a good control when scope of project is changed just according to the actual situation, the variation requirements and the scope of the project. After the project begins, the scope will change with the changes in a variety of conditions and environment,

---

[2] PMI [2].

[3] Wang Xiaojin [3].

which may lead to a great change in the project schedule, cost or quality. Thus, enforcing the strict control over project scope variation is the key to ensure project successfully completed.

18.3.3.2 Project Time Management Control

To complete the project on time and with a high quality is the most expected thing on work for every project manager. However, in practice, delay happens occasionally. Correspondingly, how to reasonably arrange project time is a key content of project management control. Project time management control mainly refers to a series of management control process and activities necessary to ensure the project to be completed on time. Its purpose is to ensure the timely completion of projects, the reasonable allocation of resources and the maximum playing of working efficiency. Project time management control includes the definition and confirmation of specific contents of project activities; and the management control over the sorting of project contents, the estimated time limit for a project, the sharing allocation of resources, the project schedule, etc. Among them, the project plan time limit control is the most important work in project time management control. It emphasizes an organic combination of beforehand control, in-process control and afterwards control, including the control over influencing factors of changes in project time limit plan, the performance measurement of the completion of project time limit plan, and the reactions towards the deviation incurred in implementation, etc.

18.3.3.3 Project Cost Management Control

The project cost management control mainly refers to the management control activities concerning project budget, project cost estimation and forecast to ensure the actual cost is less than the project budget.

Project cost estimation is based on the project resource requirements plan and a variety of market price information. It's to estimate and determine the cost of every activity and the whole project and mainly includes three types: (1) rough order of magnitude (ROM), the main accuracy concept of project cost and applied in the early stage; (2) budget magnitude , assign funds into organizations budget; (3) decisive magnitude, providing an accurate project cost estimation. Project cost management control mainly refers to the control aiming to complete the resources cost rough estimation.

Project cost budget is the benchmark of project cost control. It's also an important reference to prepare and implement project schedules. In the process of the project implementation, project cost budget and forecast control try hard to control the actual cost within the budget, and constantly predict the trend of the project cost based on actual cost repeatedly revise the original estimation, and carry out a reasonable management control over the total cost of the project.

18.3.3.4 Project Quality Management Control

Project quality is the sum of all the features and performance of products or service to meet the explicit and implicit demands of stakeholders.[4]

Project quality management control mainly refers to the project management control activities carried out to guarantee the project quality. Its fundamental purpose is to secure the consistency with the quality specification for the final delivery of the project output. It mainly includes a series of activities involved with the measurement of the actual situation of project quality, the comparison of actual project quality and project quality standards, the confirmation of project quality errors and problems, the cause analysis of project quality problem, and the corrective measures to eliminate these gap and problems.

18.3.3.5 Project Human Resource Management Control

The requirement of human resource management control is to integrate human resources and finally achieve organizational goals by means of both incentives to develop human resource potentials and constraint mechanisms formed in these incentives. It includes many management control activities, such as the control of project planning and designs, that of the acquirement equipment of project personnel as well as the control of staff development and team building.

18.3.3.6 Project Risk Management Control

The characteristics of project determine that the implementation of project will encounter various risks. If these risks cannot be well identified and controlled, the entire project will fail. So the most critical part of project management control is to control uncertainty and risky events or problems. By identifying, defining and assessing risk, project risk management control cognizes project risks, and on the basis of which various risk corrections, management methods, techniques are applied to implement an effective control over project risk and ensure the achievement of project goals.

18.4 Project Management Control Procedures

18.4.1 Project Planning

Project management control procedures include three steps, which are project planning, project implementation and project evaluation.

[4]Wang Xiaojin [3].

18.4.1.1 The Connotation of Project Planning

Project planning is the process to predict the future, and put forward effective schemes, policies, measures and means to achieve goals, and solve problem. It is a document used to coordinate all the other plans and to understand and control the implementation of project,[5] and is the foundation of the project management control in implementation. Project plan is involved with traditional tasks, resources, timing and cost, etc. Meanwhile, it needs to make a good preparation for the project to manage its change, communication, quality, risks, procurement and team.[6]

In the project planning stage, firstly, the project planning team needs to make a rough estimation for the project, so that during the project decision–making process, the estimation could be divided into detailed parts as product details, specific schedule and cost budget, providing a benchmark for progress evaluation and project control. Secondly, this team needs to prepare for the plan, by ensuring the person in charge of this implementation will be involved in the plan preparation and by conducting risk analysis and forecasting possible obstacles that may occur.

The quality of project planning will directly affect the quality of project. To prevent problems such as not being rigorous, too much options or poor operability, a detailed plan that through the entire project is expected. The more detailed the project plan, the stronger the control, but with higher project management expenditure, and vice versa.

18.4.1.2 The Composition of Project Plan

The final project plan is made up of three parts: scope, schedule and cost.

First, the scope plan of project is the process to define the project scope and write instruction. Project plan could illustrate the reason to undertake the project, the goals of the plan and the key deliverables. A detailed explanation of each project activity, the person and organization in charge of the project is expected. If the project scope changes, an effective control needs implementing. Related technical documents and project plans should be modified on the basis of the work breakdown structure, the project progress report and the scope plan of project.

Second, the project schedule plan basically has the following subprocedures. First, to confirm the activities of the project; second, to determine the activity sequence, that is, to find out the successive relationship between these activities; third, to specially estimate the time for each activity; Fourth, to prepare schedule plan, namely, to research and analyze the order, timing, and resource requirements of each activity and then formulate the project time schedule plan.

[5] Lai Yifei [4], p. 76.

[6] Horine (author) and Chen Yanxin (translation) [5], p. 34.

Time control should be on the basis of project schedule, progress report and change request. When time change occurs, the modification of information and files related to project schedule management are expected. Sometimes, adjustment of the overall project schedule is required if necessary.

Third, the cost plan of project is usually called budget control. As an important part of the project plan, it mainly includes three sub-processes, that is, resource planning, cost estimating and preparing cost plans.

Cost control should be based on relevant cost benchmark, progress report, change request, and cost plan. The main contents of control are as follows: one is to supervise cost implementation, to find out variances as well as its causes; the other one is to prevent incorrect, unreasonable, or unauthorized changes from being brought into the cost benchmark.

18.4.2 Project Implementation[7]

In the process of project implementation, management of the project generally pays the most attention to issues such as whether the project can be completed on time, and whether the cost has overrun.

18.4.2.1 To Deal with Reports

Project managers shall deal with three different types of report in a timely manner: problem reports, progress reports and financial reports.

Problem reports include problems already happened and those expected to happen. Project managers must respond to them so as to take corrective actions in time. Generally speaking, managers will spend most of their time on processing this type of reports, and they must decide which problem should be solved in person, and which should be authorized to others.

Progress report is to compare the actual time and cost of the fulfilled work to its planed time and cost, and to make a quantitative measurement. Its purpose is to make a better arrangement for the next step. Managers should analyze progress report as carefully as possible, because analysis may reveal potential problems that have not been shown in the report. Managers need to recognize these problems and find solutions.

Financial reports are the accurate project cost reports. However, from the point of management control, these reports do not have the cost information that is as important as that in the progress reports.

[7] Anthony et al. [6], pp. 331–336.

18.4.2.2 Correction and Modification

If a project is very complex, or the planed target is not practical, or the organization's operating environment has greatly changed, the plan will lack objective basis, being highly likely to incur one or more deviation of scope, schedule or cost from the plan. The most common phenomenon is cost overrun, that is, the actual cost exceeds budget cost. This situation will directly lead to modifications of the original plan. To those problems resulting from mistakes in work, the administration and supervision should be strengthened so as to ensure that the work and the target will be close to or agree with each other.

18.4.3 Project Evaluation[8]

Project evaluation has two independent aspects. One is the performance evaluation of the project, and another is the project outcome evaluation. The former is carried out shortly after the project has been completed, the latter can only be carried out after a few years.

18.4.3.1 Performance Evaluation

The performance evaluation implemented by projects has two aspects, project management evaluation and project management process evaluation. The former aims to help make a decision about project managers, including bonuses, promotions, constructive criticism and reappointment and the latter aims to discover the best way to carry out future projects. In most cases, these evaluations are informal. If the project result is not satisfactory, but the project is very important, a formal evaluation will be required. Moreover, the formal evaluation of a very successful project can provide effective methods to improve future projects results.

18.4.3.2 Result Evaluation

If the time isn't long enough, the project's success or failure cannot be judged. It will take several years to measure the actual benefits and costs. For many projects, since the expected returns cannot be represented in an objective and measurable form, and the real benefits cannot be measured, the result evaluation is very difficult. As it's impossible to quantitatively measure the income and cost, only the judgment of people who have a deep understanding of the finished projects could be relied on. It applies to many projects, such as projects engaged by government and

[8] Anthony et al. [6], pp. 337–339.

non-profit organizations, research and development projects engaged by many scientific research units, and projects aimed at promoting peace or eliminating environmental pollution, etc.

The selection of evaluation criteria should include the following:

First, the project must be important enough to ensure that in the formal evaluation, a lot of material resources and manpower could be input.

Second, the results could be expressed quantitatively. Especially, when the project aims to create considerable increased profits, the actual profits could be measured.

Third, the evaluation results should help to take actions. Particularly, the analysis should provide good suggestions and decision-making patterns for future projects.

18.5 Project Management Control Method

Project management control method is a communication system that takes all kinds of documents, reports, charts, etc as the main tool. Its main method is to hold regular or irregular meetings participated by related personnel. It is accompanied by communication with all aspects of information.

The various files required by project management control are those to be prepared after the scope, the scale, the task and the schedule of the project have been confirmed. They mainly include contracts, rules of work scope, rules of responsibility division, rules of progress as well as files of technical scope and plan.

Project reports mainly have three forms, daily reports, exception reports and special analysis report. Because the written report is real and clear, the description of management control system is easily to take it.

But in fact, these reports are usually not as important as information obtained by project managers. They could collect information by talking to people doing actual work, from his staffs, the regular or special meetings, the informal memos, and the secretly observations to the working status as well. From these sources, managers could learn about the potential problems and some conditions that could result in variances. This information can also help managers to understand the significance of informal reports, for formal reports may fail to describe some important events that have an influence in practice.

In many cases, if problems could be found before preparing formal report, appropriate corrective actions will be expected. Formal report does nothing more than confirming the information obtained by managers from informal sources. Nonetheless, the formal report is still indispensable. It keeps a record of the information obtained by managers from informal sources in form of files. Later if there are challenges against the project, especially about its result, these recorded files will be extremely important. In addition, subordinates who read the report may find that it is not the accurate description of actual condition, and hence take steps to correct these misunderstandings.

Project management control meetings mainly refer to the regularly or irregularly held special meetings concerned with the process and problems of related projects during their implementation. The main purpose of these meetings is to check, evaluate, analyze and formulate corrections.

It should be pointed out that, the management methods above can only be applied to small and medium-sized projects. Large and medium-sized enterprises usually input more expensive resources and have more complex contents and harsh constraints. Accordingly, a project information management control system based on computer will be needed to develop.

References

1. Bi Xing, Zhai Li (2000) Project management [M]. Fudan University Press, Shanghai
2. PMI (2008) A guide to the project management body of knowledge, 4th edn. Electronic Industry Press, Beijing
3. Wang Xiaojin (2011) Methodology of project management [M]. People's Publishing House, Beijing, p 115
4. Lai Yifei (2011) Introduction to project management [M]. Tsinghua university press, Beijing, p 76
5. Horine GM (author), Chen Yanxin (translation) (2011) Project management book written for you [M], 2nd edn. People's Posts and Telecommunications Press, Beijing, p 34
6. Anthony RN, Govindarajan V (author), Liu XiaoLun, Zhu Xiaohui (translation) (2010) Management control system [M], 12th edn. People's Posts and Telecommunications Press, Beijing, pp 331–339
7. Horine GM (author), Chen Yanxin (translation) (2011) Absolute beginner's guide to project management [M], 2nd edn. People's Posts and Telecommunications Press, Beijing

MIX
Papier aus verantwortungsvollen Quellen
Paper from responsible sources
FSC® C105338
FSC
www.fsc.org

If you have any concerns about our products,
you can contact us on
ProductSafety@springernature.com

In case Publisher is established outside the EU,
the EU authorized representative is:
Springer Nature Customer Service Center GmbH
Europaplatz 3, 69115 Heidelberg, Germany

Printed by Libri Plureos GmbH
in Hamburg, Germany